Success or Failure
Begins in the Early School Years

Publication Number 844
AMERICAN LECTURE SERIES®

A Monograph in
The BANNERSTONE DIVISION *of*
AMERICAN LECTURES IN SPECIAL EDUCATION

Edited by
MORRIS VAL JONES, Ph.D.
Sacramento State College
Sacramento, California

MARY LU KOST

Success or Failure
Begins in the Early School Years

With a Foreword by

Robert E. Valett, Ed.D.

Professor of Education
Fresno State College
Fresno, California

CHARLES C THOMAS • PUBLISHER
Springfield • Illinois • U.S.A.

Published and Distributed Throughout the World by
CHARLES C THOMAS • PUBLISHER
BANNERSTONE HOUSE
301-327 East Lawrence Avenue, Springfield, Illinois, U.S.A.

© *1972, by* CHARLES C THOMAS • PUBLISHER
ISBN 0-398-02334-4 (cloth)
ISBN 0-398-02486-3 (paper)
Library of Congress Catalog Card Number: 74-184601

With THOMAS BOOKS *careful attention is given to all details of manufacturing and design. It is the Publisher's desire to present books that are satisfactory as to their physical qualities and artistic possibilities and appropriate for their particular use.* THOMAS BOOKS *will be true to those laws of quality that assure a good name and good will.*

Printed in the United States of America
EE-11

In loving memory of my former principal and friend, the late Thelma E. Clark, whose dedication to problem children, whose encouragement and sharp, accurate criticisms, stimulated me to pursue my work.

Foreword

FOR MANY YEARS teachers of exceptional and disadvantaged children have been using special techniques and instructional programs which have been successful in enabling their children to learn. Most of these approaches have gradually evolved out of a long history of attempts by dedicated educators to individualize their teaching. For example, the awareness of developmental levels and appropriate educational tasks for the handicapped or slow-learning child was recorded as early as 1795 by Itard in *The Wild Boy of Averyon*. However, most of these unique approaches have traditionally been applied in a single or small group setting within the special education classroom or psychoeducational clinic. Now we are beginning to see their application in the regular classroom as well.

Certainly, good teachers have always attempted to meet the needs of their pupils. But the reality situation of large classes, insufficient funds, and even at times an indifferent public or administration has made it nearly impossible to implement innovative approaches even when successful pilot studies and models are available. In recent years our educational system has been stimulated to change from many different sources. The development in many states of educational programs for children with specific learning disabilities and for those with neurological, behavioral, and emotional disorders has had a profound impact on what goes on in the "regular classroom" as well. In addition, the infusion of Federal funds into new compensatory and experimental programs for the disadvantaged and culturally different child has drastically effected the entire system. At the same time, increasing awareness of the importance of early childhood education during the vital preschool and primary years has prompted many new proposals for changing our educational system. As a result some experienced teachers and many new ones have been motivated to attempt to integrate the information now available to them and to apply it to their work in the normal classroom. Such an undertaking is exceedingly demanding of time and energy and requires a highly motivated and talented teacher. The author of this book is such a person.

A few years ago I taught some courses on Learning Disabilities through the University of California Extension. In these classes I attempted to present research and some models which I integrated into six developmental levels of gross motor, sensory motor, perceptual motor, language, cognitive, and social skills and abilities. This was the first presentation of the material in my book *The Remediation of Learning Disabilities*. One of the very few regular teachers enrolled in these classes was Mary Lu Kost. I can still recall how surprised I was to discover that she was a first grade teacher who had no intention of entering "special education." Later on, when I had the opportunity to offer her a position as a special teacher of a primary class for the educationally handicapped, I was stunned by her rejection and explanation that she preferred to remain with the first grade and to apply what she had learned in developing a more effective program for all children just entering formal education. Although I admired her aspirations, I did not think it likely that she would be able to accomplish such a formidable task! But I was wrong. She continued to persist and gradually her innovative work with disadvantaged first graders became known throughout Central California and has now been successfully culminated in this remarkable book which should serve as an excellent guide to others.

The intent of the book is to provide specific information useful to the teacher of first year pupils. It is written so that the programs, schedules, and techniques can be applied to a normal-sized classroom. But the real impact will be much broader in that what the author has presented here is actually an outstanding model for early childhood education. Kindergarten, transitional, and primary teachers should all profit from this book as should special educators, psychologists, and therapists. I hope that this book reaches the broad audience that it deserves and that it influences their educational practices accordingly.

Within these pages the reader will find numerous excellent

descriptions of classroom learning problems and their resolutions. The fact that academic and social-behavioral failures often accompany one another is amply illustrated. Those readers interested in clearly understanding the characteristics and etiological basis of learning disabilities together with early identification procedures and diagnostic techniques applicable to the classroom will find them here. The outstanding contribution of this book, however, is in the chapters which present actual developmental and remedial techniques which can be adapted to the regular classroom. An outstanding series of developmental physical education sequences is presented in Chapter Six, which correlates numerous gross motor, sensorimotor, and perceptual skills. Those teachers and others interested in the Engelmann books and materials for the systematic instruction of fundamental language, reading, and arithmetic skills will find these chapters, with their many practical suggestions, to be invaluable. The recognition of the critical importance of developing the basic auditory decoding and sequencing abilities in children with language and reading problems is fully presented here as well. Those teachers interested in devising their own approaches to the development of these basic skills will find numerous possibilities from the examples given. Also, those who wish to experiment with newer programs such as DISTAR cannot help but be encouraged by the author's significant reports of "no failures" with this system.

I was very glad to find that the final part of the book had included an introduction to the development of social and behavioral skills through the use of several behavior modification techniques. The "traffic ticket" system is worthy of special attention and the reader will undoubtedly be very interested in some of the ramifications for teaching cooperative behavior that are presented. After all, the real success of education is determined by the degree to which the child is able to live happily and successfully with self and others in our evolving society. In my opinion, these skills should and must be taught on all levels of education and are second in importance to none.

Mary Lu Kost has written, "Teaching is exciting—enjoy it."

The excitement and challenge of teaching children with learning problems will be apparent to the reader of this book. If the regular teacher is also inspired to try to apply just some of what can be learned from this book to her own classroom, I believe she will be amply rewarded for her effort.

ROBERT E. VALETT

Preface

As a first grade teacher, I am primarily concerned with that percentage of our children who *fail* first grade. OR HAVE WE FAILED THEM? That is the question! We do not really *teach* our bright, perceptually gifted children from stimulating homes. They learn in *spite* of us, rather than because of us.

But what do we do with the child who does not mature according to behavioral age norms? What do we do with the child who does not progress according to grade level norms? Do we demote him a grade? Do we simply let him vegetate in our classrooms and then retain him for the next year in hopes that he will have matured? Or do we pass him on to the next grade because—well, "his siblings did not do very well in school either, he does not really have much going for him"? Or: "He seems to be so bright verbally, that even if he isn't reading, it is just because he does not try. Maybe he will outgrow it." What do we do?

Actually, our whole bottom reading group consists of failures. And the middle group really is not that good either, only by comparison to the bottom. They seem as though they should do better! They just do not seem to *try* hard enough!

In our teacher's colleges we have been taught to *provide for individual differences.* (Trite and meaningless educational jargon.) Translated into the *how*, the only answer we received was the formation of three reading groups. It is heresy to define these as *individual* instruction. We were taught to observe the behavior of the child to determine where he was in relation to his age norm. But then we were never taught what to do with the child who was a year or two *behind* the norms. We could not recognize or diagnose problems. The only testing we knew consisted of total readiness or achievement scores and these were invalid. We never really understood the function of testing. We did not have the tools, the measures. We had been given too

xi

much theory and subject matter, and not enough experience with our real subject, *children*. We expected too much of them. When they did not measure up, we failed *them*. We were filled with Freudian theory and learned to blame everything on the child's emotional problems, or his parents' treatment of him. Parents were too strict! Or they babied him, never *made* him behave!

Our educational objectives were unrealistic subject-matter goals rather than child-learning goals. We progressed through books, not children. (Some archaic school districts still specify which page or lesson each reading group should be on by certain dates.) We were chained to the state texts which were inadequate. We had no materials at the operating level of the immature child. Our whole curriculum was inadequate for the needs of our children. We took background learnings for granted without teaching them. We used a classroom structure that stifled the children and disguised their lack of learning. We never had enough feedback from the children to begin to understand them. The children learned early that the best way to beat the system was just to *appear* to do and say what the teacher wanted with as little effort as possible and remain fairly quiet and passive in the process.

Doctors bury their mistakes! Teachers deny theirs. Investigate the histories of delinquents and upper grade and high school children who have failed, and you will find that their failures *began* in first grade. Teachers must take the responsibility for *teaching* the child, not psychoanalyzing him or looking for excuses for his lack of learning. THE CHILD MUST BE TAUGHT!

For fourteen years I have struggled with the problem of the failing child. At first I just tried to identify the child, to predict his possible failure, and then to gain insight into his difficulties. Then the field of learning disabilities opened up new directions. I began to read extensively in this area, attended symposiums and workshops, and visited private schools. Although most of the early work of the pioneers on learning disabilities was done on severely handicapped children, it was not difficult to recognize degrees of the same symptoms in the children in my classrooms.

The biggest problem was to revise the techniques used individually or in classes of four to six children, into workable regular classroom methods for twenty-five to thirty children.

In this book I have attempted to translate and to capsulize a total picture of the work on learning disabilities as it is applicable in a regular classroom for the prevention of failure in first grade. We need not and must not wait until a child has failed for several years and has a broad emotional overlay before we diagnose his problems and provide him with the proper instruction to alleviate his difficulties. As Strauss and Lehtinen* say, "Education is the best therapy!"

The purpose of this book is to give first grade teachers the insight they need to understand the problems of our failing children and to provide the methods with which to teach these children. The value of these methods has been proven in their successful use in the teaching of immature, neurologically handicapped, and disadvantaged children. There are no theories here that have not been verified by the learning behavior of our children. So I have marched our children before you that they may teach you as they have taught me.

I have included in this book detailed lists of methods in each subject area. The lists are comprehensive in order to provide an extensive pool of ideas for even the limited facilities of the regular classroom. We must have a variety of methods at our fingertips to guide our children in a programmed, step-by-step progression, and to keep our lessons lively and interesting. For my own easy reference in my classroom, I keep these lists either on a clipboard or on 5 x 8 cards.

This has been a very difficult book to complete because there are continually so many new findings concerning our problem learners. My family jokingly calls this "the 57th Revised Edition." That may not be too far off! Just as I am attempting to close this book, neurologists, allergists, and biochemists are coming forward with revelations of behavior changes through regulation of diet and of vitamin therapy. This is an exciting new breakthrough!

---

*Strauss, A. A., and Lehtinen, Laura E.: *Psychopathology and Education of the Brain Injured Child*. New York, Grune & Stratton, 1947.

As we learn more of the physical causes of learning disabilities, such as prenatal and postnatal problems and chemical imbalances, we can look forward to the day when fewer of our children will be so impaired.

I only hope that this book, with its techniques, will not be taken as the one *final* answer to all children's learning difficulties, but as a beginning, an opening door to a brighter future for problem learners in our classrooms.

MARY LU KOST

Acknowledgments

THE RESEARCH AND experimentation necessary for this book were made possible by the foresight of the administration, which allows innovation in our classrooms, and by a retinue of supportive principals and vice-principals, especially Thelma Clark, Dave Vaca, and Jay Baumgartner.

I must credit the teachers in my University of California Extension courses with affecting the organization of the material in this book and the methods of presentation.

Actively working with me developing our program, guiding my thinking, and greatly influencing my decisions were my team teachers, Gloria Cox and Joan Fields.

A list of the lecturers and authors who have stimulated my work would be extensive and impressive. Probably those who exerted the greatest influence were G. N. Getman, Newell C. Kephart, A. Jean Ayres, Ray Barsch, Marianne Frostig, Katrina deHirsch, Beth Slingerland and Siegfried Engelmann. I am especially indebted to Jeanne Bartelt for her instruction in the use of movement exploration techniques and for her developmental steps in the teaching of specific physical education skills. Also, I must thank Sharon Pritchard for her demonstrations in the use of her unique and excellent drawing techniques.

I offer my heartfelt thanks to my many patient and loyal friends, including Lillian Stillwell, Joan Smith, Dolores Cook, Joan Fields, Ruth Ann Gardner, and Jeanne Bartelt, who so graciously preread and constructively criticized certain chapters.

I must also extend thanks to my editor, Morris Val Jones, and to my typist, Edith Bleyl, who did such a superior job of deciphering my confusing code.

Finally, to my wonderful family goes my love and eternal thanks for their tolerance of me, especially during these last three harassing years.

Contents

		Page
Foreword—ROBERT E. VALETT		vii
Preface		xi
Acknowledgments		xv
Illustrations		xix

Chapter

ONE	LET'S START WITH THE CHILDREN	3
TWO	SYMPTOMS ASSOCIATED WITH LEARNING DISABILITIES	16
THREE	CAUSES OF LEARNING DISABILITIES	33
FOUR	DIAGNOSTIC TESTING AND EVALUATION	62
FIVE	SENSORIMOTOR DEVELOPMENT AND FIRST DISCRIMINATIONS	97
SIX	DEVELOPING TACTILE AND KINESTHETIC SENSES	132
SEVEN	PERCEPTION OF SPACE AND FORM	159
EIGHT	TRAINING IN GROSS MOTOR SKILLS	200
NINE	READING AND WRITING	273
TEN	ARITHMETIC	334
ELEVEN	LANGUAGE	367
TWELVE	MODIFYING BEHAVIOR	414
Index		465

Illustrations

Figure   *Page*

1. Auditory Discrimination Test 68
2. Reading Tests 69
3. Winter Haven Perceptual Forms Test 71
4. Bender Figures 72
5. Immature Forms of Bender Figures 73
6. Immature Forms of Perceptual Forms Test 73
7. More Bizarre Distortions of Bender Figures 74
8. More Bizarre Distortions of Forms—Perceptual Forms Test 74
9. Test of Visual Sequence 82
10. Class Profile 85
11. Pupil Profile 87
12. Photomicrograph of Synaptic Knobs 109
13. Activity Chart 121
14. Sorting Tiles for Color and Design 127
15. Matching Fabrics from the Feeling Box 128
16. Figure-ground Worksheet 129
17. Immature "Man" Drawings of First Graders 142
18. Using Fingers to Aid Placement of Features 144
19. Kephart's Diagram of Feedback Mechanisms in Perception . 156
20. Hierarchy of Sensory-Motor-Perceptual Development 174
21. Traversing the Beam With a Bucket of Beanbags 178
22. Children's Errors in Executing the Equalateral Triangle .. 189
23. Scoop Throw and Catch 226
24. Throw and Catch Against a Wall 229
25. Crossing the Beam with Different Limbs 238
26. Scat Scoota 241
27. Walking on Coffee Cans 242
28. Bouncing On An Inner Tube 244
29. Jump Wall 249
30. Crawl-through Culverts 251
31. Circle Kick Ball Game 257
32. Experimental Study, 1964-66 288
33. Team-teaching Schedule 302

34. Letters for Visual-Memory Flashing Exercise 308
35. Graphs for Flashing X's and O's 310
36. Lazy Eight 316
37. Rainbow Tracing 321
38. Frostig Box Writing 326
39. Writing Practice; Three-inch Lines 328
40. Name Tracing on Lines 330
41. Sequence of Math Packets 351
42. Rockets to the Moon 353
43. Place Value Cards 355
44. Tens and Ones Benches 358

Success or Failure
Begins in the Early School Years

Chapter One

Let's Start with the Children

THAT FIRST DAY

ON A BRIGHT September morning, parents troop up the halls of the school, holding the chubby hands of their precious progeny. The fathers beam with pride and assurance of the innate ability of their own. The mothers leave with lumps in their throats and often come back for the last-minute peek at their cherubs. The little faces glow with expectation. Their own desks! And today they're going to learn to read!

Those eager, hopeful faces look toward the teacher to open that magical door to learning. So, in the traditional American classroom, you get out the chalk and write an experience story. Every first grade teacher knows that's when you put the words in the children's mouths, and then twist their sentences around to the king's English, write them on the board, and read it back to them while you point at the words. You do this over several times to encourage memorization, the iron curtain to reading.

Then you pass out the lined paper and have them laboriously copy the blackboard story. Their heads bob up and down as they verify each letter, eye muscles strain with the constant near-far accommodation problem. They squint, lose their place, leave out words, weave all over the lines, reverse the letters and whole words, or write the whole thing backwards. They quit in complete frustration, scribble over their work, or tear it into shreds.

Later you pull the books off the shelf and say, "This is Susan. See her yellow curls?" Then every page after that when they see a picture of a girl with yellow curls and a blur of ink blots about the right size, they say, "Susan." This is fine until you come to the words *see, sun, come, not,* and others. Eliminate the pictures and they are *really* lost. In your bottom reading group they drop their books, lose the page, don't pay attention, squirm all over their seats. They make wild guesses and inadequate substitutions. After they have struggled through a passage, they have no idea what they have read.

In spelling, these children are completely lost. They may show some understanding of the math concepts if you can decipher enlarged numerals, one on top of the other, and persistent reversals. And there is Eric, who simply cannot recognize the numerals, and Tommy, who cannot seem to match one-to-one. Yet these same children shine in a discussion of weather or transportation. They remember all about the animals they saw on the zoo trip.

FRUSTRATION AND FAILURE

In spite of their insatiable curiosity and desire to learn, they fail again and again, day after day, because reading and writing are the mainstays of the curriculum. The papers are not acceptable; the work is too hard; the goals too unattainable; the frustrations too great. They have but three choices. They can rebel and withdraw through disappointment and disillusionment into their respective shells, and become silent and negative, or they can rebel and man the battle stations of belligerence and defiance toward you and toward their enviable peers. If you listen with your feelings as well as your ears, you can almost hear them say, "I'm no good and I know it, but you're no good either and I'm not going to let anyone get the best of me."

The third alternative belongs to the child with superb auditory memory. He will simply memorize every word of each story with the aid of picture clues, and not only fool himself but the teacher as well, thus closing the door to any help from her. This is probably the most damaging solution. One child might read all three pre-primers with rare errors, and his subterfuge would not be detected until he was asked to read flash cards. He would not even know the names of the characters he so glibly recited.

So now we have a hard core of wily, withdrawn, negative, rebellious children. What have we done to them? What happened to those eager faces? When we pulled those books and lined paper off the shelves, and imposed the traditional curriculum on them, we thereby pulled the magic carpet to learning out from under them, and they fell into the abyss of failure. From now on, perhaps all through school (as most records of problem learners show) they will be the underdogs, in the lowest reading groups, the remedial readers, the children thought to be mentally retarded, or dull-normal.

Some children overcome their initial disability by the fifth grade, but the emotional problem may be so deep that rehabilitation may take years. Even the eventually adequate achiever has such a low opinion of himself that he still doesn't know that he *is* capable. If a child is barely able to hang onto the shirttails of his classmates, he is labeled a *slow learner* and receives no special attention—is excused from achievement. He is doomed to mediocrity! A life sentence by his first grade teacher!

As a first grade teacher, I am primarily concerned with the large percentage of children who *fail* first grade, or fail to find success. Or have WE failed THEM? That is the question! We don't really teach our perceptually mature, language-affluent, ready children. They learn in spite of us rather than because of us. Just give them a book, tell them a word once, and they're off. They have the visual perception and memory to recognize the word when they see it again, the auditory discrimination and memory to make the necessary sound associations, the receptive language ability and integration to perceive its meaning, and the expressive ability to answer comprehension questions. They are stimulated by their reading and can thus learn much of the information they need. We often gauge our classes by these children, move rapidly to keep them interested and to stimulate our own egos, proud of the progress of our class. We speak lightly of individual differences and expect all our children to learn by the same visual-memory and multiple-sound-association methods.

SUCCESS VERSUS FAILURE

My deep concern is that we are shortchanging our children who do not learn so easily. Instead of inspecting our own methods, we blame the child's innate ability, or his home training. It's time to stop "passing the buck," to admit our failure to teach these children, and to find the methods and the techniques that will do the job. Let's start with the problem children and not with a preconceived curriculum. Let's not wait for them to fail for five years, three, two, or even one. Let's diagnose the problem child and analyze the tasks required of him. Does the work we give the child really help him to learn? Or is it a waste of his precious learning time? Is it *busy work*? Let's search for methods to help these children their first year of school, BEFORE those smiles are wiped from their faces! Before their first failure!

Anna Gillingham, who has done extensive work retraining children with learning disabilities, speaks of such a program:

> These children who have never failed are wonderful to observe. Their assurance and joy in achievement are even more thrilling than is the happiness of the remedial cases who have failed and are now realizing success. Those who have once failed bear deep in the shadowy places of their thoughts the lurking fear that some new demand may be made upon them which they cannot meet. They have deeply ingrained in their unconscious minds that most devastating of all lessons—that failure can follow earnest effort. (Gillingham, 1965, p. 21)

SHALL WE WAIT?

Some teachers and administrators advocate simply retaining the immature child in kindergarten another year. This would be advisable if the child's specific immaturities were diagnosed and trained, but another year of time and play-therapy will not help him overcome his disabilities. Researchers like deHirsch, Frostig, and Kephart have shown this. Dr. Frostig feels that seventy-five percent of the children with learning disabilities in the early grades will not outgrow their problems. DeHirsch studied a group of boys eleven to fifteen and found persisting deficits in spatial organization, oral language, and writing, much like their first grade counterparts (deHirsch, 1966).

I sat on the crest of the Sierras one summer and gazed at the twisted pines in that Hudsonian life zone. As a teacher who never really forgets her charges, I thought of withdrawn Ty, and aggressive Bill, and also of confused and disorganized Timmy. Then my eyes again rested on those bent pines. A heavy winter snow buries the tender young saplings under ten to twenty feet and bends them downward on the steep slopes. If the snow melts early, the young tree curves back up toward the sun, and with favorable conditions, may yet grow strong and tall and survive the subsequent long winter snows—though it never loses the telltale curve of the trunk. But the mountain tops are dotted with trees which were never quite able to pull themselves erect, though they may yet grow, pointed downhill. Or trees that were so buffeted by winds that they resemble corkscrews. Or those that did not survive at all as their wind-smoothed, white, dead trunks testify. So might our children survive our present educational system without special methods. But what of those children who are so twisted and torn by their early failure that they forever feel inadequate and carry their subsequent emotional problems to adulthood? Or those who fall by the way completely, never learn properly, are erroneously dubbed retarded and/or drop out of school? I think of those scarred and dead trunks and know that we dare not sit by persisting in our old methods, and WAIT for the child to outgrow his disabilities.

Radler and Kephart say:

> Fortunately we can do more than wait. During the past two decades a great deal of research and clinical experience has proven that the basic skills acquired in the first half-dozen years of life are not entirely the result of maturation. Instead, they can be significantly improved— even supplied, where entirely missing—by learning. We now know the "readiness" is not only preparedness to learn, but also, to a significant extent, the result of learning. (Radler and Kephart, 1960, p. xiii)

The psychology and philosophy that readiness to learn can be taught is reflected in the titles of the newer books that have been written for parents on the education of young children: Radler and Kephart's *Success Through Play;* Avery and Higgins, *Help Your Child Learn How to Learn;* and Getman's *How to Develop Your Child's Intelligence.*

In 1964–65 we pretested and posttested first graders with the Kuhlmann-Anderson test. Children in a control pre-first with traditional methods had a mean deviation IQ of 82 in October and 88 in May. The children in the experimental pre-first who had been taught through language, sensorimotor, and perceptual training scored 88 in October and 103 in May. Waiting would not have helped these children. Education for their specific deficits certainly did.

Anna Gillingham felt strongly the right of these children to be provided for in our public school system:

> Skilled teaching is provided at public expense for blind and deaf and crippled children. These children whom we are discussing, normal, often highly endowed with artistic, scientific, or social understanding, and constituting ten to twenty percent of the school population, are expected to pull themselves up by their boot straps by "trying," or their parents must pay large fees to have them taught.
>
> If the majesty of the law can hold all children in school throughout their childhood, then it is the obligation of the law to provide this not inconsiderable proportion of the school population with instruction adequate for their needs.
>
> This is a challenge to the school not to be lightly shrugged off. (Gillingham, 1965, p. 23)

LET'S LOOK AT THE CHILD

To understand the child's feelings, let's go back to that first day again and take a better look at those problem learners. Generally, these children enter school as eagerly as all the other children. True, there are some whose parents are aware that this child is not as quick as the others, or that he does at least have some *social* problems. But most parents think that their children are bright and ready for school and that their behavior is within normal limits. But then, they've had little opportunity for comparison. And often the other siblings developed at about the same rate. Or else the parent really can't remember.

The unhappy, emotionally unstable child is afraid of all new environments and is pushed in the door by parents who figure that today is the day for him to grow up. Or the overly protective parents hover around the classroom door almost hoping the child will cry to return to them. But probably ninety-five percent of the future problem learners enter with the same bright, eager faces of their classmates.

The kindergarten teacher wanted to retain Eddie, but that was ridiculous! Mother wasn't going to have him just *play* another year. How can you flunk kindergarten anyway? That teacher was just too young and didn't understand him. Besides, the principal said that it was all up to the parents whether Eddie should be retained or not. So she shoves him into the first grade classroom.

The first few days or even a week pass like a charm. The child is enthralled by all the new equipment, his own new box of crayons, his own desk, the smiles of that lovely teacher, and so many friends with whom to play.

Then the teacher shows them how to write their names. Eddie just can't figure out all those crooked lines. The good papers are put on the bulletin board. They didn't want his. And the teacher raves about Joan's lovely picture. Why didn't his turn out like that? His is just a scribble, no matter how hard he tries. He tried it four times, but his teacher just scolded him for wasting paper. He knows how he wants it to look, but it just won't turn out the way it should. And those color words! *Red, yellow,* and *blue* weren't so bad for at least he could guess. But now there are so many, and they all look alike! He *could* get it all right if the teacher wouldn't nag him about staying in his seat, and let him look at Joan's paper. Besides, he can't find his crayons. Someone must have taken them. And that writing on the blackboard! There is so much of it and it all looks the same!

Then the teacher is getting crabbier every day. She's always telling him to "Turn around!" "Stop talking!" "Pay attention!" "Go back to your seat!" He doesn't know just what they're doing in that class anyway! They never want *him* to talk. They just don't like him. Besides, he doesn't want to sit in an old seat all day.

Out on the playground the boys won't let him play catch or football just because he can't seem to catch the ball. And if he tries to play four-square or tetherball, they put him "out" right away because he can't hit the ball. Then he has nothing to do. So he just ambles alone around the playground. He was running to get a drink and all of a sudden there was Timmy on top of him. Then Timmy was pounding him with his fists! Timmy blamed it on him and said that *he* had started the whole thing by knocking him (Timmy) down. He was just going to get a drink! But the teacher was on Timmy's side and he (Eddie) didn't care! Anyway, he doesn't like Timmy, or any of those other kids, or that crabby old teacher, either. She just picks on him! He'll tell his mother! (And she'll be *sure* the teacher is picking on her baby!)

So all the problems mount. In the morning he dawdles with his dressing and his breakfast. Maybe if he is too late, his mother won't make him go. His stomach doesn't feel good anyway. Maybe he's sick. (He is! He's sick of *failure!*)

As Radler and Kephart say:

> When Johnny and Suzie enter the first grade at the age of six they are expected to bring into the classroom with them a background of experience and achievement, a complement of skills, that make a list a good deal longer than Suzie's braids. . . .
>
> But for the child who is lacking some or all of the skills he is assumed to have, the first grade is nothing short of a tragedy. The child finds it impossible to understand and assimilate the material presented by the school. Since each grade level assumes adequate learning at all previous levels, the child falls farther behind each year. (Radler and Kephart, 1960, pp. xii, xiii)

WHAT ARE THE PERCENTAGES OF FAILURE IN FIRST GRADE?

How many children in our classrooms are we discussing? How many children fail in the first grade? Some would consider only the severest *failures,* that bottom five percent who completely fail in *every* academic area. Other teachers would list mostly their bottom reading groups, a fourth to a third of their classes. Other teachers would say that their middle groups were *passing,* but were not achieving up to what they thought the children's potentials to be. (Probably judging their performance against their verbal ability.) The percentage would be lower in a high socioeconomic area, and higher in a disadvantaged area. When I taught in an area where the least expensive home was $25,000, there were only about seventeen percent failures or strugglers. In my present teaching position in a low socioeconomic area, using a version of deHirsch's Predictive Index, we found forty-two children out of sixty to be potential failures. This would be close to seventy percent. These high percentages might be found in other big city slum areas.

Turning to deHirsch's research of estimates:

> One of today's major social problems is the enormous number of
> children who, as a result of severe reading, writing, and spelling dis-
> abilities, are unable to realize their intellectual and educational po-
> tentials. The incidence of reading difficulties has been reported to be
> as high as thirty percent of the school population. More conservative
> estimates put the figure between five and fifteen percent. According to
> the National Council of Teachers of English this would mean that at
> least four million elementary school children in the United States are
> disabled readers. (deHirsch, 1966, p. xi)

RECOGNIZING CHILDREN WITH SYMPTOMS OF POTENTIAL LEARNING PROBLEMS

Observe a group of potential problem learners in a pre-first
class and the evidences of their disabilities wave like red flags.

The bell rings and the children filter in from the playground.
Billy runs all the way. He must be first in line. Anyone who
beats him is liable to a sharp kick in the shins. In his animal-like
home environment he has had to fight even for his share from
the grocery bag. "My first!" he shouts. Richard ambles in swinging his jacket in a circular orbit over his head. The tip of the
zipper hits Susan on the side of the head and a wail erupts from
her. She's glad for an excuse to cry. She loves sympathy. Chris
and Frank come in arm-in-arm in a newfound friendship. Ted
walks so very reluctantly as though molasses underfoot slowed
his pace. Timmy can't be content with one mode of locomotion. In fifty feet he walks, hops, dances, jumps, turns, twists,
looks back between his legs, gives another twirl and rams smack
into a hall support pole. (A month later he will run out in front
of a car and be mortally injured.) Mike is happily kissing the
girls whether they like it or not. Joyce objects, gives him a
shove into the growing line of boys, knocking Steven into Bill.
Bill comes up swinging at Steven and the fight is on. Not a word
of language accompanies any of the action.

Eric and Bobby, with sand in hair and eyes, complain of each
other's atrocities in the sandbox. Oh, yes, they are using language!
They are both saying, "Her started it!" "Her threw it first!" "No,
me didn't!" "Him knocked my tunnel in!" And they really don't
know how it started. Eric may have lost his balance and sat on

Bobby's mountain accidentally. And since he never even *saw* Bobby's creative masterpiece, he is at a complete loss as to the reason for the assault.

Inside the classroom it isn't much better. Debbie is in someone else's seat. Bill can't get from the door to his seat without handling everything on his way. Teresa heads for the bathroom again. Eric is draped over the top of his desk. Billy is slyly tripping children as they go by. The teacher commands her trickiest techniques and by sheer willpower and perseverance, gets them into order and begins her math demonstration.

Teacher: ONE APPLE PLUS ONE MORE APPLE . . . . "Three!" yells Mark, who can never keep his mouth closed. "Is it lunch time?" asks chubby Timmy.

Teacher: NO, TIMMY. NOW, LETS TRY AGAIN. ONE APPLE IN THIS SET, AND ONE APPLE IN THIS SET. PUT THE TWO SETS TOGETHER. . . .

"There's an eagle!" shouts Dwain, as an unwary seagull soars outside the window.

Now it's music time and Timmy sings how "Jack and Jill went down the hill to petch a pail of water." Pitches vary, sometimes resulting in harmony. Billy sings faster to finish the song first. Mike is again repeating the last line when the others have finished.

Reading is a frustrating tragedy of errors. Mike has memorized the whole book, but can't read one word by itself. Billy can get the context and picture clues, so he makes up the words he doesn't know. The children call *help, play; surprise* is *airplane; kitten* is dubbed *Frisky; My* is *Mrs.; saw* is *was,* and ad infinitum. Yesterday Mark knew every word and read beautifully. Today he stumbles on *Tom.* Jimmy reads, "Susan said, 'Bow-wow, bow-wow.'" His eyes have skipped down a line in the middle of the sentence. Kandy knows all the flash card words, but stumbles hesitantly as her eyes jerkily try to follow the line of print across the page.

Attention is everywhere except on the reading. "Her gots my pencil." "How many more recesses?" The children care only about reading solo. When another child is reading, chairs are tipped and books fall on the floor. "Where are we? I can't find it!" You try, "Find-the-line-that-says." "I found it first!" "No, you didn't,

I did!" You try to discuss the plot, such as it is, while children thumb through the pages and more books drop. "There's my brother!" (going by the window). You get their attention back to the book, help them find the page again, bring them back up-to-date on the story, and "Recess time!" announces Timmy, as the custodian's bell rings.

Meanwhile, back at their seats with the rest of the class, Eric has made a crayon mark on Dwain's desk, and the latter is loudly indignant. "Who stole my crayons?" demands Carolyn. They slipped to the floor as she opened her slant-top desk to get a pencil.

Seatwork is greatly limited. They can't read the color names to do a color-word paper. You enthusiastically build them up to a theme for a picture-story. They scribble a one- or two-color blob, and copy a series of words from their books as best they can, disregarding all lines. "My all done!" announces Billy in three minutes flat, and he sits with no inclination to think of anything constructive to do. You try simple math papers. Timmy puts numerals at random on the blanks on the page without considering even one problem. Then he slips the paper into his desk and goes off to find the noisiest puzzle or game available. Carol just cries, "I can't do it!" tears the paper, mashes it in her hands, and throws it on the floor. By this time a half-dozen children have followed Timmy to the game shelf and Linda is standing over by the window absorbed in watching the kindergarteners play outside.

"Well," says this clever teacher, "they are just restless, tired of sitting inside. I'll meet their needs by taking them outside to P.E." She tries to herd them into a circle game, but the boys consider holding hands a game of tug-of-war. The result resembles a burst balloon accompanied by wails from the girls, "He hurted my hand." A running game is next, but they are confused as to who is to chase whom. The result? A collision!

Timmy tries to race across the lawn, but runs in a diagonal and is the last to reach the fence. Susan is afraid of the rings and of heights. She will run up to the raised jump rope held for *building blocks* and then stop dead, as a horse at a jump.

Eric can't skip, nor can many of these immature children.

Kandy hops only once before falling forward. Jimmy can't stand on one leg without falling. Ronnie can't do jumping jacks. His arms and legs just won't work together. Susan and Kandy don't want to participate in anything. Ronnie says, "I can't do it," without having ever made the attempt. Timmy just sits or lies down, "I'm tired." Ted finds a ball and wanders off with it alone.

NO SINGLE SET OF SYMPTOMS OF LEARNING DISABILITIES

No two children with learning problems are alike. They are not *all* poorly coordinated, nor *all* lacking in language ability. And they don't *all* have the same visual or other perceptual or behavioral problems, either. What they do have in common is frustration and failure.

Richard is well coordinated and wins almost every race. But he cannot identify colors and perseverates when we play a game of sequence directions. When told to "stand on the left side of his desk, tap his head twice, and sit down", he will jump up on the right, change to the left, clap, jump, turn around, change to the right side and perform again en total.

Mark has bizarre visual perceptual problems. He is hyperactive and distractable. He jumps up and says, "I can spell *are—a-r-e.*" Then he writes *r-a-e*, and misspells every word on his spelling test. But just listen to his vocabulary! He expresses himself dramatically. The children love the vivid stories he tells them at sharing time.

Billy may say, "My got none," and be unable to describe things, but he's the only one in the class who remembers that camels have humps and that this strange-looking sea creature is a sea anemone, and how the Russian cosmonaut was killed. Of course, he lacks the command of language to explain it to you, but piece together his broken efforts and you'll realize he has the understanding.

Susan has a good auditory memory, but a poor visual memory. She can discriminate tones and remember sounds and their names, but she can't remember that the visual configuration *c-a-t* is *cat*.

So it is impossible to set up a pat list of symptoms to be found in every case of learning disability. Instead, we'll list possible symptoms, watching especially the child who has more than one or two, and especially noting the child with three or four or more. As Katrina deHirsch has found in her research and noted in her book *Predicting Reading Failure:*

> The diagnosis of reading disability does not depend on any single pathognomonic sign, but on an appraisal of the whole configuration of dysfunctions. (deHirsch, 1966, p. 42)

Thus, if a child has but one or two specific handicaps, he may learn well through his strengths in other areas. However, if, for example, he has deficits in both auditory and visual perception, or in visual perception and fine motor coordination, or in auditory memory and decoding and conceptualizing, he is in for a hard time, and a miserable school life.

REFERENCES

Avery, Marie L.; and Higgins, Alice: *Help Your Child Learn How to Learn.* Englewood Cliffs, N. J., Prentice-Hall, Inc. 1962.

deHirsch, Katrina, *et al.: Predicting Reading Failure.* New York, Harper & Row, 1966.

Getman, G. N.: *How To Develop Your Child's Intelligence.* Luverne, Minnesota, Getman, 1962.

Gillingham, Anna: *Remedial Training for Children with Specific Disability in Reading, Spelling and Penmanship.* Cambridge, Ed. Pub Service, 1965.

Radler, D. H., and Kephart, Newell C.: *Success Through Play.* New York, Harper & Row, 1960.

Chapter Two

Symptoms Associated with Learning Disabilities

PHYSICAL

Poor Gross Coordination

THE CHILD FALLS frequently and is an awkward runner. He doesn't participate in a variety of activities of coordination like tetherball, rings, or four-square. His poor posture is especially evident at a desk where he slumps on his back. Outside he has accidents frequently and runs into other children. At recess time he climbs the monkey bars, or the slide, or just runs or walks aimlessly around the playground. There is the danger here of thinking that the child who has a *splinter skill* (e.g., ability to ride a bike, or to play baseball, or to play tetherball) is well coordinated in all areas. Watch his running, crawling, hopping, jumping jacks, high jump, etc., and his ability to imitate a position or movement, or to change movements or directions.

Poor Balance: Static or Dynamic

He can't hop more than a few times in succession. He may lean too far forward and fall, or else stiffen backward to keep from falling and thus lack the necessary forward momentum. He has poor balance on a beam, continually stepping off or running across it to avoid balancing. He either can't ride a bike or has frequent accidents. He can't stand easily on one foot, while swinging the other more than five times.

Lack of Rhythm of Movement

He has a poor skip, or skips only on one leg. He can't bounce a ball against a wall and recatch and throw it in rhythmic movement. He can't jump rope. He has an awkward walk, perhaps lacking alternation of arms and legs. He has difficulty clapping a rhythm, or in singing lacks feeling for the time, the rhythm, often singing a phrase or two behind or ahead of the class.

Poor Fine Motor Coordination

The child's cutting is poor, as he slashes or tears the paper rather than actually cutting it. He has difficulty picking up small objects at will. He is slow or awkward at placing clothes pins on a line or pegs in a peg board. He is at the scribble or naming stage (he names or identifies the scribbles after he has finished) in drawing—which is often done in only one or possibly two colors. He has difficulty manipulating buttons or zippers or tying shoe-laces or holding a pencil.

Poor Eye-Hand Coordination

He can't bounce a ball repeatedly or play catch. He can't color between designated lines. Timmy tries to place a small block on top of a tower of blocks. The whole thing collapses. Each time Vicki places a puzzle piece, she disrupts the other parts and has to reposition them also.

Mike tries a dot-to-dot paper. He starts on Dot (1) but moves off in the wrong direction and then has to keep correcting his line as his eyes jump back and forth from the (2) to his pencil. The result is a wobbly, wandering line rather than "the shortest distance between two points." Carolyn is never able to *stop* on a line because of lack of visual-motor control, so that her writing slices *through* the lines.

Lack of Adequate Eye-Movement Control

Ronnie tries to follow the plastic cricket on the end of a pencil with his eyes only. The teacher holds his chin in her hand, but he still tilts and turns his whole head. Mike's eyes water as he tries to follow-the-cricket. They tire too easily of the task. Kandy's eyes give quick spasmodic jerks with each movement. Her reading is slow and jerky. She skips from a phrase on one line down to a phrase on the next line, stairstepping down the page. Carolyn's eyes wander away repeatedly.

Jerri has difficulty adjusting from distance vision to near vision. Thus she tires quickly of board-to-paper copying. Ronnie's left pupil jumps away when he tries to converge on a pencil at near point. Eddie slumps in his seat, doing all his seatwork on an eye-level with the page. Shirley writes with her eyes only three inches from her work. Joyce holds the kaleidoscope out to the side of one eye to look through it, while Billy flips it back and forth over the bridge of his nose, not knowing how to focus through the lens.

There is a lack of peripheral vision also—a lack of awareness of the visual fields to the sides of the body. Rene appears to have a *tunnel* vision. She comes in the door, sees a piece of new equipment at the far side of the room, and makes a beeline for it. She falls over everything and everyone who happen to be in the way or approach her line of travel from either side. Debbie invariably looks sideways when walking in from the playground, and runs into children in front of her. The ball rolls away from him, and as Timmy tries to retrieve it, he collides with a child walking a path perpendicular to and between him and his ball. At the zoo Timmy zeros in on Monkey Island, heads straight for it, unknowingly passing by the alligators, penguins, and leopards.

SENSORIMOTOR
Poor Body Image, Concept, and Schema

The child is unaware of all of his body parts, their functions in relation to each other, and in the size of area his body requires in space. He is unable to control his balance or his actions in space, or to coordinate different parts of his body. Teddy tries to go under the table, but bangs his head on the edge. Cindy tries to go around the pole, but hits it instead. (Those hall support poles are booby traps for these children.) Kandy and Susan are afraid to jump over a raised rope; Mary Ann is afraid of heights and falling; Timmy hangs limply from the rings, afraid to try to swing his body or to let go with one hand to reach for the other ring. "Catch me!" he yells.

In the classroom you say, "Put your hands on your shoulders." Eddie looks around to copy his peers. He knows only arms, legs, head, eyes, and mouth. His nose runs unnoticed. You know the lunch menu by the food left on the children's faces. They seem to lack some tactile sensations of the body. Ronnie jumps stiff-legged, unaware of how his knees could bend and give him thrust. Mike draws a picture of himself: a head, vacant eyes, and mouth, with arms and legs extending from the head. Their frequent comments are "I can't" and "I'm afraid." Ted just withdraws. Billy puts his hat on backwards, his jacket inside out. His collar has one side tucked under.

Lack of Laterality

The child lacks feeling for the sides of his body and their relationships. When he leans to one side, he may not know how to shift his weight and use his arms and legs to keep his balance. So he falls! He is often unable to use one side of his body without seemingly also using the other side. Thus we see the child placing pegs in holes with his right hand, while the left hand is *mirroring* the movement, bending up toward the board and following the activity of the right hand. Or while writing on the board with the right hand, Amy's left elbow is bent and her left hand is making similar circular movements in the air.

The opposite case is Mike, who tries to write with his right hand without any aid from his left hand in holding the paper still. Thus his paper moves and wrinkles, and his writing is very difficult to control. Still, he does not seem to see the need to use his other hand to remedy the situation. In fact, his left hand may hang quite limply down at his side. In cutting, he may or may not hold the paper with the left hand, but even if he does, he will not use it to turn the paper to simplify the movement of the scissors in the right hand. Thus, he tries to cut the left side of an object by turning and pointing his scissors back toward his body. The scissors may even end up, up-side-down.

Laterality is not dominance or handedness according to Kephart, but ". . . an internal awareness of the two sides of the body and their difference." (Kephart, 1960, p. 44)

After the child learns laterality, he probably stabilizes this learning by developing a dominant side.

Lack of Directionality

The child lacks an adequate feeling for the space beside, behind, above, and below him. He has no understanding of the position of objects in relation to his body. The spatial terms *above, below, under, over, up, down, right, left* are confusing to him or appear unstable. He transfers this confusion to objects in space to his reading and writing. Thus, *L* is a *7*, *u* is *n*, *W* is *M*, *Z* is *N*, as their only difference is in relation to his body in space. The opening of the *u* is upward toward his head; the opening of the *n* is downward toward his feet.

The children make many letters and numerals reversed because of this lack of feeling for the sides of the body. Numerals *2, 3, 6,* and letters *s, a, d, e, b, c, g, j* are especially frequently reversed. There are total confusions of *d, b, p,* and *q.*

The problem of directionality is evident in the lack of left-to-right sequence in reading and writing. Charles writes *dog* as *god.* The word is read as if it began on the right. So *help* becomes *play.* Even auditory sounds are reversed because the spatial confusion relates to the temporal confusion of the sound in time. Teacher: WHAT ELSE STARTS WITH P LIKE PAT? "Stop?" says Timmy. Eddie has his shoes on the wrong foot. Mark can't find the stapler *on the right side* of the desk.

In writing, many of their lines lack direction and preciseness. Alan cannot plan his first line in a slanted direction for his *A,* so he makes it straight. Then he makes the second line slanted to the right and the result is an *A* standing on its left leg and on the verge of falling over. Many letters are ill-formed because they are not *started* at the correct point. Two-place numerals are reversed so that the child writes *01, 11, 21, 31, 41, 51, 61, 71,* etc. for the teens.

Lack of Spatial Relationships

The child is unable to understand the relationship of one letter or word or object to another. Eddie doesn't know where the *front of the room* is. He also puts his jacket on inside-out. Carol can't find the school office, though she has been there before. Remember Mark's *r-a-e* for *are?* Then there are all the word reversals with which we are all so familiar: *was* for *saw,* and *on* for *no.* And the inconsistencies within words might also be termed spatial problems: *children* is mistaken for *chickens,* or *what* for *want.*

The child has difficulty following directions: PUT IT ON TOP OF MY DESK. PUT YOUR BOOK INSIDE YOUR DESK. DELBERT, GO AROUND THE PUDDLE. Then he splashes through the *middle* of it. Eddie put his raincoat on *first,* then struggled to put his jacket on over the raincoat.

Timmy is getting ready to go home. He piles his papers on top of his desk, opens the slanted top, and the papers swirl to the floor in all directions. "Who threw my papers all over the floor?" Or he gathers his papers precariously in his arms, grabs his coat, and then just can't figure out how to get his coat on. So he juggles all until, again, the papers scatter to the floor.

These children have extreme difficulty reproducing designs with blocks or pegs, or in specific art projects. They cannot figure out the relationships of the parts to the whole. They place the chimneys on the houses usually at angles to it, rather than in erect positions. The *witch's hat* may have the brim up on top of the point, rather than on the witch's forehead. The cat's head is placed with chin side up, and ears down on the body.

Much of this behavior resulting from lack of understanding of spatial relationships is *very* often misinterpreted by the classroom teacher. You may think his inability to follow directions, to understand prepositions to be deliberate misconduct or negative behavior. The accidental scattering of his papers is often judged deliberate irresponsibility or lack of home training. The problem in writing and following directions are sometimes considered a sign of mental retardation. Thus the child's real problems go undiagnosed, misunderstood, thereby increasing his frustrations and adding resentment and rebellion, an emotional overlay of his original perceptual problem.

Lack of Perceptual Constancy

A letter, symbol, or word, etc., does not always look the same to the child at all times. It may change with position, size, or vary from day to day because the original perception was inaccurate. Mike recognizes the word *Mother,* but not *mother.* Or he recognizes it on a chart, but not in the book, or can read it off a flash card, but not in a sentence. A square ceases to be a square to him when it is turned on its points, or when it forms a house or a furnace register. He may see a door as a rectangle, but not a table or the blackboard. Or the small electric receptacle may not be identified as a rectangle because of its size, or because of the shapes within it. This child cannot make realistic drawings because he is unable to perceive the basic shapes involved in the subject to even begin the project. Thus, he wails "I can't," scribbles up his paper, tears it, and throws it down.

Figure-Ground Confusion

The child is unable to perceive an object for its overpowering background. Carolyn can't find her scissors. She has five pair in her messy desk. Eddie can't see the red ball out among the children on the playground. Timmy can't find the word *airplane* in the sentence.

Some teachers like to use a multitude of decorations in their rooms to make them colorful and happy. This impresses the parents with feelings that the teacher likes children and is providing a pleasant environment; but to the child who is easily overstimulated and has difficulty sorting stimuli, the result is confusion. The child cannot discriminate a letter with a shadow background, or a numeral mounted on wallpaper, or too many of anything mounted too small or too close together. This can, in fact, be very distracting to the children. It has been researched that a figure-ground confusion sometimes causes the hyperactivity, the distractability, the lack of ability to sustain attention toward a single stimuli.

Some lined paper causes confusion because there are too many lines, or they are too close together. Board-to-paper copying can be most frustrating to these children because they are unable to focus on the one single word or letter which they are writing, and they keep losing their place.

We showed the colorful film *Los Tres Osos (The Three*

Bears, in Spanish). The background for this cartoon film was a wall of flowers drawn large and childlike. Afterward, the children were asked to draw pictures about the film. Most of the products emerged with brilliant wallpaper flowers covering the whole page. No bears! The children had been so entranced with that brilliant wallpaper that they saw little else.

Blackboard instruction can become too confusing to the child when the board is not first cleared of all other writing, marks, etc. He cannot concentrate on what the teacher is writing on the board, or on that to which she is pointing, because there are so many previous problems and notations all over. Or half-erased chalk marks may blend into the new letters or numerals and cause frustrating distortions.

General Disorganization

Because perceptions are poor or faulty, or inconsistent, because the child has problems of association and integration of the information he receives from his senses, or because he has poor or incomplete language facilities, and/or because of some insult to the central nervous system, the child with learning disabilities often appears terribly disorganized. He cannot hold many ideas or directions in his mind. He cannot organize his time or plan his actions. He cannot organize his possessions or keep track of anything.

Carolyn's desk is stuffed full of everything she has ever touched. At one count she had ten pencils, five pair of scissors, six paste jars (all without lids), eight library books, three dolls, piles of papers (new and used), and a myriad assortment of toys, pieces of plastic, iron, seeds, keys, old flowers, etc.

Timmy will dash off to do an errand for the teacher only to return and ask for what he was sent, or reenter with a confused look and empty hands. Dwain may do one paper or one puzzle on specific instruction, and then be at a loss as to what else to do. He may sit idle, or mischievious, or he may just wander absently around the room with no plan of action. Or he may simply copy the actions of another, whether they are good or bad, constructive or destructive.

Much of what these children do is left incomplete. If given several papers at once, they may do just a couple of items on one page and then go on to another. They take a book off the shelf and then just throw it back. Kenny takes puzzle after puzzle off the shelf, dumps it out, manipulates the pieces a few moments, and then goes off to another.

LANGUAGE
Poor Auditory Discrimination and Decoding

The child can't discriminate the sounds or tones that he hears even though the auditory acuity is good. *Reading time* might sound like *feeling fine; string* sounds like *thing, cut* like *cuff; sit* like *set*. Thus he misunderstands directions or continually asks you to repeat instructions. This child fails at phonics exercises, giving totally unrelated responses.

Words and sounds may be scrambled. *Me and the King* might emerge for *The King and I; spaghetti* might come out *pasketty; hamburger* is often *hangaburg*. Words are misinterpreted and therefore later mispronounced. Children with good auditory decoding and discrimination ability enjoy jokes of mispronunciations and *plays* on words, such as are found in children's joke books. (Of course, vocabulary plays a large part here, also.) But a classroom of problem learners is almost completely immune to simple children's jokes and riddles. Even after careful explanation of the point, blank eyes stare back uncomprehendingly.

Poor Auditory Memory

The child has difficulty following sequence directions or remembering names of things. He returns from an errand saying, "What did you send me to get?" He may discriminate colors or numerals, but be unable to identify them by name. Thus he is also unable to remember that this word is *cat,* even though his visual perception of the word might be precise.

Poor Vocal Encoding

Speech is limited in quality and quantity. Grammar is poor, articulation faulty, sentence structure is abbreviated. Billy says,

"My all done." Shelly, "Her gots it." Lacy, "It broked!" Her goes." "She runned." Often they'll leave off the subject of a sentence, or the small words, conjunctions, etc. In telling the story of *The Three Bears,* Wayne said: "Mama tasted. Too hot. Daddy too hot. Baby too hot.'

Poor Visual Decoding and Visual Memory

The child is unable to identify parts of a picture. Or he can identify objects or details, but lacks the point, the idea. This, of course, is also due to problems in conceptualizing or integration of ideas. These children might have particular difficulty noting the feeling from a picture as being *fear* or *surprise.* Sometimes, not one child in a pre-first class can correctly explain the pictoral escapades of Happy in *My Weekly Reader,* Grade 1.

The children can't recognize familar names, numerals, and letters. Or the symbols and words are unstable. Yesterday, Mark seemed to be reading well; today, he can't seem to get one line right. Or he remembers the meaning of a word, but not its name. Therefore, *kitten* is deciphered as *Frisky.*

COGNITIVE
Lack of Information

The child doesn't know the names of things. The dogcatcher is described as "the thing that takes the dogs." (Auditory memory is a factor here, too.) He doesn't know his father's name, his address, his parent's work. He is unaware of local events or geography. Actually, he is unaware of almost everything in his environment, except that which affects him very directly. He is often unable to name even the food he has eaten, the family car in which he has ridden, or the television program he has watched.

Disorganized Temporal and Spatial Sequence

At every bell, the child asks, "Is it time for lunch?" "Can I go home now?" "What is today?" "Is today our field trip?" He is unable to organize thoughts. He tells a story or event out of sequence: "The three bears goed for a walk. Papa Bear tasted his porridge."

He is unable to see relationships in a sequence of beads. Teacher: RED, YELLOW, BLUE, RED. WHAT COMES NEXT? This child often has poor number sequence and problems with spelling and writing words and letters in correct sequence. It is the horizontal sequence which is most often disturbed. Horizontal equations are difficult, vertical problems are less confusing.

Inability to Integrate, Organize, or Classify Data Received

The child may have a good rote memory for facts, but be unable to see the relationships involved. He may know number facts, but be unable to solve problems. He is unable to call on the correct data from his memory which will help him to reason out a problem or question, e.g. Teacher: WHY DID THE THREE BEARS GO FOR A WALK? WHY DOES HAPPY HAVE THAT MAD LOOK ON HIS FACE? WHAT IS A HAMMER? A SAW? A SCREWDRIVER? WHAT IS BIG AND ROUND AND HAS NUMERALS ON IT? WHY DOES THE LION HAVE CLAWS? The child might know that a tiger is fast and has sharp claws and teeth, but be unable to answer the question HOW DOES HE GET HIS FOOD? This thought process is referred to as convergent thinking, and also as integration of data. The child must sort and classify data learned and make proper associations to come up with the answer. This is a higher process than simply cognitive memory of information.

SOCIAL-EMOTIONAL-BEHAVIORAL
Self-Centered, Egotistical

These children have no awareness or concern for others, a trait typical of much younger children. "That mine!" "I want it." "Me first." "I don't want to." They never wait for another to finish talking. They are unable to delay gratification of their wishes. "Teacher! Hey, Teacher!" (Accompanied by taps on her back or tugs on her arm.) "I gotta tell you sumpin'!" If you are unwary enough to tell them of a coming event beforehand, you are besieged with queries constantly. "Is it time yet?" "Do we get it now?" "Is it today?" Of course, this is a temporal problem, too. Then there is the frequent wail of the child you just helped a moment ago, "You forgot me!"

Dependency

You hear the desperate cry: "I can't unbutton this! Help me!" And after every small effort they want reassurance: "Is this right?" You show the children specifically how to do a simple task. Susan just sits, making no attempt. "I can't do it!" You go back to the instructions for the first step, reassure her, guide her gently, ensure her success with your hand over hers, praise her efforts, start her on the second and third steps, and go to help another child. A moment later, Susan: "Is this right? What do I do now? Help me!" For two months, withdrawn Ted made not a single mark on a paper without my hand on his. The intense desire and need of these children for constant reassurance, praise, support, makes independent seatwork extremely limited, and conduction of a small reading group almost impossible.

Hyperactivity

These children are a bundle of uncontrolled, undirected energy. They are always moving, tapping, fingering, talking, sliding around seats, leaving seats, wandering, striking out, etc. Now Eric is on his knees, now sitting backward, now lying arched over seat with his head on the floor. He teases, acts silly, clowns, laughs too loud and in an uncontrolled way. Then there is Mike, perpetually kissing the girls. Dr. Payne's description accurately portrays my pre-first children:

> Hyperactivity . . . involves ready overstimulation, a seemingly obligate response to every new stimulus of whatever nature, a tendency to become overstimulated, overactive, and frequently silly. Behavior is often inappropriate, as though the child either did not foresee the consequences of his act, or else was powerless to control it. Such children usually have poor relationships with their peers and are frequently overaffectionate or indiscriminately affectionate. They are often regarded as gullible by classmates. Inability to perform as expected (actual or anticipated) is associated with a low tolerance for frustration which may be compensated by a quick attempt to change the subject, a temper tantrum, or by complete withdrawal from effort. . . .
>
> . . . .The child's behavior is typically hectic and disorganized and is notoriously variable from one day to the next or even from one half-hour to the next. (Payne, 1965, p. 5)

Hypoactivity

When we suspect only the hyperactive of disability, we are missing another group of children who are almost the opposite. These are the quiet, rather inactive, hypoactive ones. They may be inattentive, nervous, and fidgety with frequent squirming and hand, leg, foot, and head movements. But they are not so grossly or noisily or boisterously moving as are the *hyper*active children, and thus are often missed by the teacher. Sometimes in their quietness, they might be thought to be emotional problems, withdrawn. Or you might think that they are understanding or achieving because they don't object, they don't ask questions.

They slowly, quietly try, or else copy someone else's work. There is no dishonesty involved in this. They simply want to please, to succeed, and this is the only way they know how to do it. It must not be overlooked that these children might also have physical causes for their lack of energy or interest. A referral to the medical profession might turn up something like hypothyroidism or iron deficiency or a hearing loss.

Dr. deHirsch says of some of the reading failures in her research:

> (They) were hypoactive, had difficulty maintaining a sitting posture, and tended to slump. Their throwing was hypotonic; some of them could hardly hold a pencil. Both hyper- and hypoactive youngsters showed a considerable tendency to fatigue. (deHirsch, 1966, p. 47)

This latter point, too, must be remembered in reports referring these children to physicians. You must be quite specific. Some doctors might think that the teacher is being ambiguous in describing a hyperactive child on the one hand, and then also telling of the same child's periods of inactivity, or lack of participation. Super-hyperactive Timmy, for example, might rarely be still, verbally or physically. Yet when the class is engaged in physical education, he has less than a fourth of his peer's energy. He can run only about twenty-five feet before slowing to a walk. Or he may do only one jumping-jack before sitting down. In fact, although he perpetually wants to play running games, he will collapse at the onset. And often, during exercises and games, he will "sit it out." Two of our children with these symptoms have been medically diagnosed as having poor lung capacity, and it has been recommended that we build up their capacity with very active physical exercise until the child is actually tired, but not exhausted. The time, the distance, or the number of exercises is then increased very gradually to build up the child's endurance and lung capacity.

Another cause for a child to sit out physical education in spite of usual hyperactivity is due to his awareness of his poor condination. He is afraid to *fail* in front of his classmates.

Impulsivity

This child does not plan his actions. He rams into peers and furnishings, knocking things over. He swings objects around, unaware of what or whom they might hit. Bill grabs Ted's car and smashes it under his foot. Mike sees a child's ball coming toward him on the playground. He draws his foot back and kicks it as hard as he can. Dwain can't resist opening the piano and playing a few notes. Eric grabs the paint brush as he goes by the easel and splashes up someone's paper or clothes. Sweet Roxanne smashes all our prize Monarch butterfly larvae. Danny can't resist water. He turns it on as he goes by, splashing it on anyone within range. Someone accidentally shoves Ray. He explodes, pummeling the child with his fists.

Mary Ann, with all the money she needs, gathers all the children's lunch money into her purse. Everything small and colorful disappears from the classroom: scissors, paste jars, pencils, plastic toys, even bits of intriguing junk. And they don't know why they do it. It isn't all desire or kleptomania. They're too naive to be consciously dishonest. Sometimes it is an attention device or a tease, but most often, more of an unexplainable impulse.

Richard's father was fixing the roof when he realized that his six-year-old son was there beside him. "You get yourself right off this roof this instant!" "O.K." said Richard. And he walked to the edge of the roof, squatted, and jumped off. No broken bones! Boys like Richard have personal angels sitting on their shoulders. One day Richard stood in the hallway deliberately emptying his milk carton on the sidewalk and smashing his banana. Teacher:

RICHARD! WHY ARE YOU DOING THAT? Richard shrugged, "I don't want it!" Then he gave me that blank stare as if he, too, wondered why he did it.

This impulsivity leads them to mimic their peers. One child says, "I don't want to" and several follow suit. Billy starts to sing a song faster than the rhythm as a joke, and soon a number of his peers have followed his lead and are rushing the song. Teresa stops to look out the window on her way back from the bathroom. Soon several children join her. One child leaves his seat to get a puzzle, and the lemming run is on. Or Debbie squeezes into the cubbyholes for coats. Immediately, all the cubbyholes are filled with children. One boy in a line will teasingly lean back on the child behind him, that child follows suit, and then another, until the whole line collapses like Alice's deck of cards.

Perseveration

This child is unable to leave a stimulus and so continues the same behavior or response repeatedly. In taking the Kuhlmann-Anderson test, perseverative Susan marked the third box or object in every item on every page of the test. Remember Richard trying to follow a sequence of three directions? He was supposed to stand on the left, tap his head twice, and sit down, but he was able to recall more clearly that the former instruction in the previous game was to *jump* two times. Too, he probably remembered it better because he saw all the children jumping. So now, this time, he jumps! But then, seeing the other children's response, he copies them too, and taps his head and adds several other motions just for good luck. Or if he is asked to clap once, he perseverates by clapping over and over many times. He paints a wide ribbon of red across his paper, and then continues to paint similar ribbons until he has covered four 18" x 24" papers with red ribbons. Another day he will paint only green balls. In writing, he may go over and over a letter many times. This child might be said to be stimulus bound.

Lavada has trouble with *a*'s and *d*'s. So one day she writes her name *L-a-v-a-a-a*. YOU FORGOT THE D IN YOUR NAME, VADA. So she corrects it, *L-d-v-d-d-d*. She is free-cutting a piece of paper.

Soon her desk is littered with tiny pieces. There is nothing left of the original sheet of paper, and no purposeful shape has resulted.

Short Attention to a Task: Distractability

These children have very short attention spans, even to a task of high interest. Attention to group instruction is especially brief. Even in individual speech therapy, Ronnie's eyes and mind wander. The only way I can be sure that premature Mike hears the instructions is to cup his chin in my hand while expressing myself as simply and concisely as possible. Then I have him repeat the instruction word by word, step by step.

The child is constantly subjected to a multitude of stimuli—visual, auditory, olfactory, and tactile. He must be able to screen out a majority of these stimuli continually in order to concentrate on a selected object or detail or stimulus. The child who is very distractable has the problem of attending to too many different stimuli and is unable to screen out the irrelevant.

These children often seem to be "on a pink cloud," out of contact with the present. This is true of the hyperactive children who are so easily distracted by movement or sound or complexity of the visual field, as well as of the withdrawn, quiet, shy child whose attention wavers to his inner thoughts. The hyperactive child's inattention may first be a lack of control, of ability to concentrate on a task, a nervousness, or of an overpowering consciousness of himself and his thoughts. Then, as his mind wanders away from the class, he is often brought back to reality by a sound or a movement or a memory of something vital to him.

Thus hyperactive Timmy's mind wavers from the math lesson and he stares off into space. Someone goes by the window or a bell rings, which jerks him back. Since he has been out of contact, he is confused by the movement or sound, and often misinterprets it. Thus in his sudden return to consciousness of the present, he sees one or two children outside on the playground and thinks that everyone is out. He recalls the sound of the bell (the telephone) and shouts "Recess!" And he dashes for the door. Or the memory that jerked him back was of Dad's promise. So in the middle of teacher's HOW MANY DO I HAVE NOW? he announces, "My Dad's gonna take me fishing."

Lack of Social Skills

This child grabs, pushes, hits at any interference with his individual or parallel play. A child touches him by accident and he comes out swinging. Lacking the language, the words, or the tolerance, for him there is no alternative. Children with a better language facility and self-concept and impulse control can discharge their problems, their tensions, with words. Problem children just *think* that they have been deliberately touched, and they will pummel the startled "attacker." They are often highly sensitive to touch by another. Ray would yell, "You hurted me!" when I just held his arm.

There seems to be a "pack" instinct with some of the disadvantaged children today. Sort out the cause of a fight before a large audience, and it will often boil down to a wrong that was done to someone's brother or friend the day before.

These children are unable to share toys or take turns. Thus they don't invite others to join them in play. Or they don't know how to react to a peer's taking of a toy. Ted will merely hide his head and pound his desk when someone takes his truck. While Timmy throws his seventy-five pounds on top of fifty-pound Tony, and regains HIS toy fast.

The most common complaint on problem learners is social. "He just can't get along with other children." This is probably due to the fact that it is the most evident, the most volatile trait of the child. You HAVE to notice him beating up a peer. But it is too often thought to be only a social problem in itself or evidence of a primary emotional disorder. Instead, this is a signal to us to question the cause of the aggression. Why is he so touchy? Why doesn't he talk out his problems? Why is he so immature? Why does he feel inadequate? Why is he so frustrated? Could it be the result of his inability to perform in school?

REFERENCES

deHirsch, Katrina, *et al.: Predicting Reading Failure.* New York, Harper & Row, 1966.

Kephart, Newell C.: *The Slow Learner in the Classroom.* Columbus, Ohio, Merrill, 1960.

Payne, Richmond S.: Organic neurological factors related to learning disorders. In *Learning Disorders,* Hellmuth, J., Editor. Seattle, Spec Child, 1968, vol. 1.

Chapter Three

Causes of Learning Disabilities

WHAT IS INTELLIGENCE?

NOW THAT WE HAVE a vivid picture of these children, the next question is, Why? Why do they have these symptoms, these traits? Is it because they are deliberately naughty? Do they simply not want to learn? Is it laziness? Is it lack of motivation?

Negative! All children initially *want* to learn, to succeed. From the age of two on, they want to be self-sufficient, to do it themselves, to do it the right way. They want to get praise from the teacher, to get a pat on the back from Dad, a hug from Mom. But more than the reinforcement from elders, they want that inner feeling of accomplishment, the exhilaration of success, the feeling of their own worth.

The old fear of parents is that their children's learning problems are congenital, a lack of inherited intelligence, and therefore a reflection on their own intelligence. What is that elusive element we call intelligence? One psychologist suggested we test the parents, add the scores, and divide by two to determine the child's intellectual capacity—synonymous with achievement capacity. If this is true, all educators are wasting their time and children can simply assimilate all learning with their inherited intelligence without being taught. And if they lack intelligence, there is no hope for them. They'll never learn anyway. But is this true? What is intelligence?

Binet's original task was to determine what traits were typical of children who achieved well, not what traits the child had before the learning process began. Examine each item of an intelligence test. Try Binet's two-year level. Did the child inherit the words *tree, scissors, arm, legs?* Or did someone have to supply these words to him at the proper time? And would he have learned it from but one or a limited number of auditory inputs, or did it have to be repeated many times, reinforced day after day?

Then examine the child's ability to place a square piece into a square hole. Does this ability come automatically or did he have to learn it through hundreds of manipulations and trials?

Intelligence is often defined as "the ability to reason, to understand". But before you can reason, you must have a store of accurate information. If the child's environment has been devoid of sufficient sensory stimuli to build a storehouse of knowledge, and if he was not given the language to describe and explain that which his senses received, or if his bizarre sensory distortions were due to some insult to the central nervous system, then his initial information is too inaccurate to allow him *to reason, to understand.*

Correlations *are* found between intelligence and reading ability. This is true. But these statistics may be more due to the fact that children who read very well also score higher on IQ tests, rather than at the other end, that children who do not read well, lack initial innate ability. How a nonreader scores would depend more on the weight of perceptual factors in the test. Higher correlations have been found between tests of perception and reading achievement, than between IQ tests and reading achievements.

Problem readers often score high in verbal ability but low in performance. In fact, the very performance factors that lowered his IQ score, such as coding, digit span, auditory discrimination, and visual-motor, may be the very ones that he also needs for reading. And if these skills can be taught him, then not only his reading ability but also his IQ will improve.

The good psychologist today does not rely on one test of intelligence such as the WISC or the Binet, and the sanctity of the total score. Instead, he utilizes a variety of measures such as the Bender Gestalt, the Slausen, Wide-range Reading, Wepman, I.T.-P.A., and Spraing's Multiple Choice Bender Gestalt. He looks for specific weaknesses which may be hampering the child's ability to learn. He then considers that the child's potential is toward that of the higher scores, and endeavors to help the teacher devise a program to use the child's intact abilities and reinforce his deficiencies to achieve his potential. The child is considered mentally retarded only if he is uniformly deficient in all areas, showing no potential in any of the tests.

It used to be thought that the IQ was static, an unalterable characteristic. Some psychologists still cling to that old security of the total IQ score. Now we know that the child is not only the product of his parents, but of his environment. IQ can and does change. As understanding increases of how children learn, the average IQ may well be closer to 130 by the year 200.

We know that a genius can become an imbecile through a sudden trauma, but we are not at this time able to help a child of very low overall potential to become a genius. We can, by teaching the specific weaknesses discerned in the testing, raise a child's achievement and total potential at least twenty IQ points. In an experimental class, when twenty-one experimental pre-first children were pretested and posttested with the Kuhlmann-Anderson Test, the mean IQ gain for the year for the class was fifteen points. Eight children gained from nineteen to forty-one points.

Professionals involved with presently diagnosed mental retardates are finding an amazing number of these children with remediable physical, emotional, or neurological impairment. It takes only thirty IQ points to raise an Educable Mental Retardate of 70 to that golden average of 100. Yet often the teacher's first and only reaction to a child who can't seem to learn by *her* methods is that the child *must* be mentally retarded. Education has relied much too long on IQ scores to label children. If the scores are high, the teacher expends tremendous effort on the children or "rides" them for being lazy. If the scores are low, she just gives them busy work to keep them out of her hair. After all, they aren't going to launch any sputniks! And they certainly won't! Not if she doesn't teach them!

Many have decried the gap between research in learning and child behavior, and the present widespread practices in education. So let's examine some of the causes of learning problems that the other disciplines have researched.

CHRONOLOGICAL AGE

There have been many attempts to discover at what precise

chronological age a child is ready for school. Several countries outside the United States do not allow children to enter a comparable first grade class of academic emphasis until the child is seven years old. However, in the United States proud parents and determined teachers have pushed the entrance age back further and further. School entrance ages for first grade vary according to law from state to state, and sometimes, from one school district to another. Mainly, the entrance ages vary from five years seven months to six years of age. Doctors Ilg and Ames are much concerned about this:

> If chronological age alone must be used as an entrance criterion, our experience favors the older age allowed by a September 1 date line. However, even this does not allow for the fact, generally accepted, that the development of boys in this age range is lower than that of girls. (Ilg, 1964, p. 16)

In deHirsch's study of beginning school children, she notes that:

> When they entered first grade, all the Superior Achievers were older—six years, five months or above— than were the Failing Readers and Slow Starters, thus apparently confirming Hall's and Ilg and Ames' findings of generally better achievement among overage pupils than among underage ones. The Superior Achievers were specifically described in the protocols as "mature" or "physically well developed." (deHirsch, 1966, p. 51)

If school entrance age is the only criterion we are to consider in subjecting children to academic subject matter, then in my own experience with these children and their parents, the September deadline is much more realistic than the later dates and would certainly help the present situation. Perhaps our education associations would do well to push legislation for these changes. It would save a tremendous number of parent egos and parent-teacher "head-ons." In California, with our December 1 deadline, and first grade entrance age of five-nine, our six-six to six-nine children most often make up the bulk of our top achievers. The children under six conversely are predominantly in the lowest group of achievers and often are not reading by the end of the year. Of course, there are so many factors involved, the chronological age must *never* be the sole factor considered. A class usually has at least one child who is six-six or above, who is failing to learn. At the other end, in my own classes, I have known only one child entering school *before* age six who achieved at the top level of my class. Today in the sixth grade, his IQ is judged as around 145. With an exceptionally fine home environment and excellent health, he had many factors in his favor to compensate for his early entrance age.

So generally, as traditional classrooms are today, we can conclude that the average child is developmentally more mature, more ready to learn; while the younger child, particularly the child under six or even under six-three, really needs more time to develop, to mature, to gain in readiness to learn.

I present this consideration of chronological age only because I realize that it is of prime importance to such a large number of educators across the country in setting up their programs. However, since I am concerned with teaching the environmentally deprived children, I feel very strongly that we must get these children into our schools *much* earlier, as early as three or four years, to provide education for them during their prime language and perceptual readiness years and to compensate for the great void in their homes. I would advocate a good compensatory preschool program for these children. I also cannot condone retaining an immature child in kindergarten unless specific methods to fill his particular needs are utilized. It is much too risky. Time alone is a healer of less than twenty-five percent of our problem learners.

THE SLOW BLOOMER
The Behavior Norms

There are many children of chronologically older ages (at least six at entrance) who appear young and immature and who have problems with school achievement. If we compare their behavioral traits with Gesell Institute norms, we find them several months or a year or more behind in development. When we first see a child like this we might say "Ah ha! A fall birthday!" We dash to the records for his birthdate and are chagrined to find that he is actually six-three or over, a summer or even a spring child. Yet he appears to have more of the characteristics of the five-year-old. Is this abnormal? Is he mentally retarded? Ilg and Ames say of the child development norms:

> The fact that any of these standards are only averages means that in the first year of life a variation even of several months from this average—at four or five years of age a variation of even a year—can be quite within normal limits. (Ilg, 1955, p. 192)

All schools have noted that children of certain families seem to be a little slow in development in primary. But Father is an engineer and Mother a teacher, and the children pick up speed in the middle grades or in high school.

We have all heard many cases of children who were presumed to be slow learners who later bloomed and became top achievers. There have been several articles in newspapers and periodicals describing such eminent leaders as Churchill, Edison, and Darwin as "late bloomers." Who knows? That immature little Johnny in your class might be another Einstein preparing to emerge. Several recent studies have shown that certain learning problems are indeed inherited, but they can be overcome by good teaching, and often are, unless the child has suffered too severe an emotional overlay.

Terms frequently used in the literature today are *developmental lag* and *maturational lag*. This maturational lag is the reason the child is a slow bloomer. The lag can be of unknown origin, or have been caused by an insult to the central nervous system (according to who is defining the term). He is simply behind in development according to the norms with which we are familiar. The Gesell Institute has been concerned for some time with a process of testing children to determine their developmental levels (definitely not their intellectual levels) and then placing them in a grade level or classroom commensurate to their operating levels. They have thus *replaced* hundreds of children a year or two behind their present grade placements. They have found this system highly successful in decreasing the number of emotional and social problems in the schools. When you have status in your classroom, there is less to fight about.

Boys as Late Bloomers

Boys especially are likely to be late bloomers or at least slow

achievers their first years of school. There has been extensive research to determine the reason or reasons for the predominance
of boys in slow-achiever or remedial reading groups. It has been
thought attributable to larger size of head and thus a longer
birth process and possible lack of oxygen during delivery; skeletal
age—J. M. Tanner found six-year-old boys to be twelve months
behind girls in skeletal age (Tanner, 1961) ; slower maturation of
males; some sex-linked genetic factors; or to varying social expectations of males. No research has been conclusive thus far to
my knowledge. It may be found to be a combination of various
factors such as these or there may yet be some undiscovered cause.

ENVIRONMENTALLY DEPRIVED
The Welfare Home: Care Versus Neglect

We hear more and more of the disadvantaged child and the
culturally deprived environment. The latter is generally too
loosely used to describe the home that is poor economically. In
our own school attendance area, which is considered a depressed
area, the deprivation may not be so much that of economics but
of love, of care, of concern, of intelligent goals.

Compare Jimmy's home with Billy's. Jimmy's father is frequently absent, drunk, in jail for petty thievery or drunkenness.
The family, mother and three boys, is on welfare. The rented
home is four small rooms about 10' x 10' each. There is no lawn
or planned landscape, but a few iris grow near the house. They
have no operable car. The yard is littered with old wagons, junk,
boards, boxes, and an old car. Inside, the furnishings are sparse
and threadbare. There are fingerprints on the walls and doors;
the curtains are limp from handling; but the floor is swept, the
clothes are washed, the dishes done. The boys play outside making
roads in the dirt or forts with piled-up junk. They "race" in the
old jalopy, find polliwogs in the undrained puddles, bugs under
boards, and ride their old, rusty bikes up and down the road
with the other children in the neighborhood.

Visit the home and you'll find the boys very dirty from all
their digging and crawling around outside. But when the school
bell rings, the boys enter with clean, shiny faces from daily baths,

and fresh clothes carefully inspected by Mother. In the evenings Mother reads to the boys, plays games with them, or helps them with their homework. They are tucked into their small cots with a hug and a prayer. When they are ill, Mother keeps them home in bed, or asks a neighbor or friend to take her to the county hospital. They might not have the expensive toys, candy bars, and soda pop of other children, but their diet is stable and filling. Mother can't afford school hot lunches, but she makes the boys hearty sandwiches and homemade cookies. At parent conference time, Mother will walk the two miles to school to keep appointments with her sons' teachers. She knows the importance of her sons' educations.

Now picture Billy's home. It is a makeshift construction, bigger than Jimmy's, but then it houses seven children and both parents. Father is deferred from work because of a heart condition. The family is on welfare. The home is filthy! The bathroom is inoperable half of the time. The stench is overpowering! The parents are absent from the home much of the time via the family car. The children attend school sick or well, with filthy bodies, and angry infections from untended cuts and abrasions. The menu is from grocery bag to mouth. He who grabs first is best fed, with generous amounts of hot dogs, soda pop, and candy bars. Money is no real problem. The children always have lunch money. They roam the neighborhood, taking what appeals to them. When the neighbors complain to the father, he just answers with a volley of unprintables, cursing the children. When the children are tired they just collapse on old, filthy mattresses, fighting each other for the blankets. Language in the home consists of "Ge' ow' a 'ere!" "No!" "Don' gi' me none a that," all interspersed with choice descriptive adjectives.

The two boys come to school, Jimmy happy and secure in his mother's love; Billy, sad, negative, morose, ready to start a fight on any excuse, craving attention at any cost. Jimmy's language is adequate, though poor in grammar and articulation. He can count, knows his colors, his name, but has perceptual problems. He responds well in the classroom, participating and cooperating. By second grade he may be at the top of his class.

Billy's four older siblings are in classes for the educably mentally retarded (EMR). Billy's speech is extremely poor in construction and grammar. He speaks in phrases rather than sentences. His severe speech articulation problem makes it very difficult to understand him at all. He cannot name colors, count, or recognize any letters or numerals. He has problems in concentration and motivation. His visual perceptions are grossly distorted; his drawings are just scribbles. It will require two years of special training before he will be ready for second grade. Without training he would likely join his siblings in EMR.

Language

Much of the child's environmental handicap is due to lack of the type of care and concern which would give the child the good physical and mental health, the body image, the confidence in himself which he needs to succeed in school. The other most important factor is language, without which little learning takes place. In a poor home I watched the mother of a two-year-old fondle the child and say, "One, two, three," while we all enjoyed the child's faltering attempts to imitate her. Then the family mongrel pattered into the room and Mother said: "Tipper!" (which the child repeated) "Come on, puppy dog. Nice Tipper. Gary loves Tipper." Then as the child stroked the dog, his mother said, "Tipper is so soft. Feel how soft he is." Much of which baby Gary attempted to repeat. And so, at two, hearing daily repetitions, Gary gained names of things in his environment, an awareness of details, adjectives and sentence structure that Billy never heard until he started school.

Sensory Perception

Then there are the spatial concepts, but it is most often language which is the tool to learning these concepts, also. Mother lifts baby Gary up and says, "Up, up, up you go! High in the sky! Now we go down, down, then up in the air again!" As she dresses him she says, "Right foot now. This is your right shoe. No, not that foot. The other one. This is your right foot." "Right foot," echoes Gary. She talks to him about things *near* and *far*.

She sends him for things that are *in* the cupboard or *on top of* the table. He learns *big, little, under, over, behind, hot, cold, sweet, sour, soft, furry, smooth,* and *hard* just from his mother's everyday conversations with him, and his own explorations. She allows him to crawl around the house after Tipper, and he gains a feeling for the space which his body needs to crawl under or over something. He plays with pans, measuring cups, an old coffee pot. He learns which things are smaller, which fit inside others, how many cups of sand are needed to fill this pan.

The neglected child from a deprived home may miss all of these perceptual experiences, besides the language and the love and care. He may never be taken on rides and trips, never visit zoos or museums, never hear or sing music or move to rhythm. In central California, without family excursions he may never watch the waves wash the shores of the ocean just two hours west of us, or know the big evergreen trees, the mountains, the rivers, the snow, the smooth pebbles and trickle of the mountain streams just an hour to the east of us.

J. McVicker Hunt believes that the environmentally deprived child is not hampered in development the first year of his life because he encounters a larger variety of stimuli in his crowded living conditions. However, in his second, third, and fourth years he is hampered in his locomotor and manipulative development; in addition he seldom is given names for things or answers to questions. Hunt implies that if the deprivation continues through the fifth year, the damage done may be irrevocable (Hunt, 1964).

The Economically Stable Home

The child may be environmentally deprived in an economically secure home by overly strict limitations in his boundaries which keep him from exploring his spatial world. As an infant he is belted into a modern version of the Indian cradleboard where he might remain from one nap time to the next. He is not able to turn and twist and learn to turn himself over. He does not learn to maneuver his body and creep to reach objects to inspect. Later, he is kept in a play pen with an assortment of toys wherein he just sits or pulls himself to an upright position. Again he misses the experiences of crawling under and over things. He may be loaded with toys at which he might look or shake, but he doesn't get to fit things one inside the other, or take things apart, or experience a variety of textures and sounds which he would encounter in the various rooms of any home, or in a better selection of toys.

Then there is the fearful parent who won't allow her child more than an arm's length away from her. Won't let him climb for fear he'll fall. The child who has never been allowed to play in dirt or sand is truly deprived of a fine experience; or to create a building out of odds and ends of boards; or to wander through fields, vacant lots, woods, listening to birds, watching toads, discovering insects. The poor country child may be rich in these experiences. But city children and apartment house dwellers are deprived of these learning experiences. The ghetto child is thus doubly deprived.

If, as a teacher, you ever visited a home with white carpeting and satin brocade upholstery, you might well have been in a home as environmentally deprived of perceptual learnings as the economically poor home. Teachers must be careful not to overrate cleanliness. It is not always "next to Godliness." If you must judge the child's parents, do so on the criterion of the degree that they foster the child's growth of experiences and language.

MINIMAL CEREBRAL DYSFUNCTION
Terminology and Symptoms

Terminology and definitions are so varied in this field that we will need a working definition to put us on common ground. We are concerned with any insult to or impairment of the central nervous system. Other terms used might be *central nervous system disfunction, neurological impairment, neurological handicap, minimal brain damage,* or probably most frequently now *minimal cerebral dysfunction* (MCD), this latter being the term of the medical profession. I prefer this term, MCD, for the medically diagnosed and will hereafter use in this context.

However, physicians debate just what is *minimal.* Minimal signs might be due to severe lesions of the brain, or conversely, only a mild lesion might be found in the brain of a child with major language and motor and physiological symptoms. Neurologists use the terms *hard* and *soft signs* of MCD. Generally, the soft signs refer more to the behavioral and learning problems of these children. The hard signs refer more to the medically tested and diagnosed disabilities, such as pathological change in the brain, an abnormal electroencephalogram (EEG), depending on the tests which the individual neurologist utilizes, and on his estimation of their relative importance.

We cannot always be sure that a child with severe disability and hard signs will have learning problems. Dr. Robert Cohn describes a hypothyroid patient:

> . . . was unable to roll over until the age of nine months, she sat at sixteen months and walked at about two years of age. She produced many unintelligible verbalizations, but did not speak recognizable words until the age of six or seven years. (Cohn, 1964, p. 182)

She had a moderately abnormal EEG and other hard signs of MCD. At thirteen her family was headed for France, and it was predicted that she would never learn French. However, in spite of her slow motor development "she has become an effective linguist with hopes of being an interpreter." Conversely, he tells of a male patient with only the *soft signs* of disability who "had a delayed acquisition of, and a distorted language function; yet he had relatively few neurological abnormalities." (Cohn, 1964, p. 183)

Diagnosis of MCD

We may have children with quite severe learning disabilities, a multiple of known symptoms of MCD, but may or may not be able to obtain from the parents a case history with any likely cause. Subsequently, when referring this child for medical evaluation or drug therapy there is the definite possibility that the doctor will not be able to discover any overt symptoms or neurological hard signs to his own knowledge. In fact, if he is not aware of the research in this field, he may come out with a flat statement that the child positively has no neurological etiology. Further, he may retort with some very uncomplimentary descriptions of the teacher for her intrusion into the sacred field of medicine.

If even the well-qualified neurologist still can't turn up any

case history of MCD or any hard signs, what then? Dr. Richmond
S. Payne eases that dilemma:

> Physicians must admit, too, that of a group of children with closely
> similar symptomatology, probably no more than half will have his-
> torically plausible cerebral insults of the type which one encounters
> in cerebral palsy clinics, for example. The learning and behavioral
> characteristics of those without such histories are more or less identical
> to the others. This suggests that we are in part dealing with potential
> causes of damage to the brain which are not currently recognized as
> harmful, and perhaps in part with irregularities in maturation of cer-
> tain types of cerebral function. One suspects that if the brains were
> available for inspection and for histological examination, we might
> nevertheless fail to find definite abnormalities in many instances. This
> may to a large extent reflect the limitations of present neuropatho-
> logical methods . . . even in average C.P. clinics, in which one is
> dealing with grossly damaged brains, there remains a substantial mi-
> nority of perhaps one third in which the causative factors remain
> entirely obscure. (Payne, 1965, p. 7)

Previously, the EEG was thought to be the only final indicator
of MCD. Every child who was referred for a medical evaluation
because of his learning problems was routinely given an EEG.
Now doctors feel that the EEG is useful only when petit mal or
certain other type seizures are suspect.

Dr. Payne feels that:

> Except for circumstances in which seizures are suspected, the electro-
> encephalogram usually contributes little of practical value in the diag-
> nosis or management of cases of the type considered. An abnormal
> record may appear to document an organic component in a child's
> difficulties of learning, but it is well to remember that many epileptics
> with grossly abnormal EEG's are highly intelligent and have no par-
> ticular educational difficulties. (Payne, 1965, p. 17)

There are children with abnormal EEGs and/or medical histories of insults to the brain who do not have continued extensive
learning problems, as Dr. Cohn pointed out. There are children
with known MCD, who have learning problems and abnormal
EEGs.

So we are left with a "does he or doesn't he have MCD?"
and we sound like an ad for hair dye. This puts education in the
position that we must for simplicity's sake term all our children
in regular classrooms who have a multiplicity of learning problems as *learning disabled,* at least until we do have a more

specific, more accurate diagnosis of each case. Perhaps we would still use the term *learning disabled* as a general label (if we must have labels), but then as we obtain diagnosis, qualify it by adding *due to MCD,* or *from a maturational lag,* or *due to a primary emotional problem,* or *from environmental deprivation.*

History of Knowledge of MCD

Research into MCD and/or learning disabilities has been conducted only in this century, although there was some work on aphasia in the nineteenth century. First, there was a British physician, James Hinshelwood, in 1917, tracing reading difficulty to organic defect. Then there was a neuropathologist, Samuel T. Orton, 1928, who worked in this field until his death in 1948. He was succeeded by Marion Monroe and Lauretta Bender. Next were Strauss, a physician, and Lehtinen, a teacher, who worked with MCD children for twenty years before publishing their book in 1947. The rest of the major work in learning disabilities had been done and published since 1960, with Kephart, 1960; Cruickshank, 1961; Frostig, 1961; deHirsch, 1966; Barsch, 1967, and Valett, 1968, the number increasing monthly. Many researchers on learning disabilities have been too busy investigating the problem and testing and designing methodology to write books. They meet and lecture at conferences and symposiums so that these have become the seedbeds of enlightenment and the source of multidisciplinary enrichment on the problem. The publications of these lectures, then, provide us with rich insights on the learning disabled child.

Symptoms of MCD

All of these disciplines, all these researchers have searched for clues, for causes, methods of diagnosis, medications, methods of education, etc., but they have never found one consistent set of symptoms or causes or remedies which would hold for all MCD children. Often referred to is the Strauss syndrome of symptoms including perseveration, perceptual-spatial disturbances, hyperactivity, and distractability. However, this is only a part of the picture. According to A. Jean Ayres, there are many other syndromes, and more than one might be found in a single child (Ayres, 1964).

Actually, the emerging compilations of learning and behavioral characteristics of MCD in the literature resemble closely those of very young and emotionally disturbed children. The list would also be similar to those described previously in Chapter Two. The behavior of normal but immature children is often different only in degree from that of the child with MCD. The differences in the behavioral symptoms of MCD children and others with learning problems are mostly in the realm of gross distortions and more bizarre behavior.

The MCD child might be more easily provoked into an outburst. Other children sense this, and thus the child is often tormented, his weakness exploited. He may be extremely aggressive and destructive, even cruel and sadistic. Yet he wants to be a leader. He wants the other children to follow HIS idea, HIS game. He may be filled with hostilities toward his parents, peers, teachers, baby-sitters, and all authority figures.

The MCD child may be supersensitive to touch. He doesn't want to be cuddled or rocked. If the teacher puts her arm around him or holds his hand, he may pull away. He may be startled by a touch and react as to an injury or a burn. He might have a heightened fear of being burned.

This oversensitivity may be evident in the other sense modalities, also. Although he may be very loud himself, lack control of his voice, and be unable to hold to a whisper, he complains that the other children are too noisy. He often covers his ears to strain out the noise. In the midst of a confusion, Timmy screams out, "QUIET!"

Bold colors, vibrant designs, flashing lights, a fast-moving film might cause him to cover his eyes to escape. He might also reject spicy foods and unknown flavors.

Many of the hyperactive and/or supersensitive children are constantly overly warm. They may strip off clothing even on cool days. You'll think that it is all "show" but look around his hairline for beads of perspiration and feel his wet back. He is perpetually thirsty, likes to soak his head under the faucet, loves waterplay.

The impulsivity of these children is especially dramatic. We have already discussed this in Chapter Two. There is also an inability to delay gratification. The child wants everything immediately, NOW! He may seem completely ungrateful for gifts or kind deeds. He desperately wants to play with other children, often bribing them to join him. If this won't help, then he quickly turns to slugging them. When you inquire as to why he hurt them, he'll say, "They won't play with me."

Even though he is aggressive, he may be extremely affectionate, hugging, kissing, and stroking peers, relatives, teachers, and even strangers. He may want you to hold his hand all the time, or he pulls your arm around him, or he practically climbs up you in a tenacious bear hug, even wrapping his legs around you, or he hangs on your arm, often pulling you off balance. Some of his spats with his peers may be due to their annoyance at his affection, overpowered by his tenacity. Susan complains about Mike chasing her. "I just want to kiss her!" wails Mike.

Many of these problem children are prone to certain physical problems such as allergies to foods and pollens, infant colic, constipation, lack of bladder control, bed-wetting. In percentages of the school population, these children also have more hearing and vision problems, particularly farsightedness, astigmatism, poor ocular motility, and labored convergence.

The lack of control of behavior is also evident in inability to control the voice. The MCD child might talk incessantly. The voice is often overly loud; with girls, sometimes high pitched. The pitch and intensity often rise gradually until the child is shouting or screaming.

The child with MCD often has severe perceptual problems in at least one modality. He may have impaired auditory discrimination ability, marked body image deficiencies, and/or be extremely disorganized. The visual-perceptual impairments may be the most bizarre, particularly his perception of space. He may struggle with the simplest puzzles, being unable to see the relationships. He is often able to discriminate shapes and match them but is particularly handicapped when he tries to reproduce a simple line drawing. He is unable to translate the message his eyes perceive, to the directions of movement his fingers must make. He therefore is prone to make particular errors in drawing, such as extra points or elbows on diamonds, rotations and reversals of figures, perseverations or multiple repetitions of parts. He is unable to stop a movement, to relate parts of figures correctly, to connect lines properly, thus his drawings may be particularly bizarre.

There are also certain learning characteristics that are evident, especially in the area of convergent thinking, reasoning, integrating ideas. This child can memorize separate facts, but be unable to relate them to attain a concept. He may see the parts of something, but not the whole. He points out the separate elements in a picture, but is unable to relate them to explain the action or mood of the total picture. Thus he sees the sun, the blossoms, the baby animals, but does not know that this depicts spring. Or he sees one character chasing another, but can't tell by the action, the facial expression, whether it is a game in fun, surprise, anger, or terror.

He may make the same mistake in behavior repeatedly, unable to learn by his previous error. He lacks understanding of a cause-and-effect relationship. He hits a child and then can't understand why that child won't play with him. He runs with a liquid in an open container and is surprised when it spills on him. He is extremely rough with a lunch pail or toy, and then can't understand why it breaks.

The MCD child may be unable to coordinate what he sees, hears, feels, etc. and express it with an imitation of the movement or sound. He recognizes a shape, but can't draw it. He hears a tone, but cannot match it. He sees a movement, but can't imitate it.

He may overgeneralize a concept. Because something looks like chocolate, he may eat too much of it before he realizes that it is not. Because the sun is out, he presumes that it is hot, so he discards his jacket and runs out into forty-degree weather.

The MCD child may have difficulty in remembering and following sequence directions. His poor sense of time and space complicate even the simplest directions. His memory may be short for some things, yet he may recall very distant events in his life.

He may have motor difficulties with everything from the co-ordinations of the large muscles, through the fine finger movements, to speech articulation and eye movements. Or he may have just one or two of these disabilities. On the other hand, the hyperactive child may learn to stand, walk, or ride a bike earlier than his peers.

All of the core scholastic-achievement abilities may be disturbed, or only one might be a problem. Thus he might have excellent verbal ability, but be unable to read or spell. He may be able to read and spell very well, but not understand. He might be excellent in math, but not operating well in any of the language areas. He may be able to read, but not to speak, to express himself. Or his reading might be excellent, but his writing and drawing atrocious. Spelling, the translating of the sounds in time to the sequence of letters in space, is a frequent handicap of these children. The child might write all the correct letters, but completely scramble their sequence. A complete contrast to this was dramatically demonstrated to me by Jan, the daughter of a psychiatrist and author. As we drove by a large shopping center Jan, with her careful articulation, read every sign in sight. Her spelling was excellent, too. Yet she is severely handicapped in so many other ways.

Causes of MCD

The teacher should be aware of some of the known historical cases of MCD. Many are attributed to prenatal or delivery injury to the brain through lack of oxygen. Some causes are considered to be due to anesthesia, anoxia, Rh negative, German measles (during pregnancy of mother), a long labor or a very fast delivery, and premature birth. Theodore Irwin gives more details of medical causes of MCD at birth, as does Payne (Irwin, 1967; Payne, 1965).

Then there are the accidents, falls from cars, bikes, etc. These could be seemingly quite minor, yet cause severe disabilities, even seizures. Also included as causes are circulatory problems and infectious diseases, such as meningitis, encephalitis, and bronchitis. Prolonged high temperatures may be dangerous, as are poisons, convulsions or seizures, revival from drowning, brain tumors, and serious operations (e.g. changing the position of an organ).

Premature Births

The incidence of learning difficulties in premature children is well known. These might be mild, seemingly a maturational lag, or severe enough to expect some brain damage. Some doctors feel that the premature child is often one month behind in development for every week of prematurity. This gauge is useful in helping parents of the premature to better accept the child's difficulties.

Some of the learning problems of prematures are related to actual neurological damage and some to a severe maturational lag. As deHirsch says:

> The two may be related since clinically, non-focal brain injury may manifest itself primarily in disruption of or interference with crucial maturational processes. (deHirsch, 1966, p. 67)

She studied the learning problems of the premature, and found that:

> . . . while they showed some indications of "catching up" during the years between kindergarten and the end of second grade, significant lags persisted well into the eighth year of life. Prematurely born children, therefore, have to be regarded as an academic high-risk group. In view of the fact that at the very least four percent of school age youngsters in the United States are prematurely born, the findings reported here have more than theoretical relevance. (deHirsch, 1966, p. 69)

The medical team at Columbia Presbyterial Hospital have also been concerned with brain damage of the premature child. There they have established the Neonatal Intensive Care Unit to try not merely to save the lives of high-risk babies but to endeavor to act so quickly and so precisely as to prevent brain damage (Irwin, 1967).

Many feel that the marked rise in the number of children with learning disabilities in the past two or three decades is due to the saving of infants from prenatal and postnatal fatality, without the understanding of the resultant damage to the child's central nervous system. Several parents have told me of their children's birth problems and how they were reassured by their physicians at the time that the children had not been damaged. Yet the children struggled all the way through school with the typical symptoms of MCD.

Recording Clues to MCD

In conferencing and in obtaining case histories from parents, it would be well to note any of the above, or any time the child was possibly without oxygen to the brain. Remember that it takes only a very few minutes of lack of oxygen, possibly three or four, to reduce a man to a vegetable state.

It is very important for future reference that the teacher note on the child's records any of his past physical history which may be pertinent. School registration forms should be revised to help obtain such information. Even though the mother's description may not be clear or clinical, it might be invaluable to you or to the doctor or the psychologist at some later time. For example, hyperactive Teddy's mother said that her child had never had any physical problem. Then as she was leaving she said, "When he was little, he had a hole in his head. If he fell on it, he would pass out. One time he turned a funny black color before we could get him to breathe."

A year after she had been questioned for a case history, the mother of hypoactive, confused Chucky finally revealed how her son was born "with his lungs under his diaphram," and how the doctor operated to save the child's life. Then Timmy's father described how "when he becomes overexcited or cries too hard, he can't catch his breath. Then he gets blue around the mouth." Don't try to translate their descriptions into medical terms, just record their words. This information may be helpful in a multi-disciplinary conference concerning school placement of the child.

Referrals to Doctors

Some teachers new in this field grasp at any composite of symptoms, with an "Ah ha! Brain damage! I'll refer him to a neurologist for an EEG." In the first place, all of this costs the parents considerable money, and unless the doctor then has something concrete to offer (e.g. medication) , they come back at the teacher often in a most aggressive and hostile manner. Since treatment and/or medication for these children is very infrequent, the teacher should carefully analyze the purpose involved before making a referral. First, discuss with the school nurse and the psychologist, and their observation of the child would be an important guide; especially watch for staring and daydreaming, which might be signs of petit mal. Dr. Payne says:

... episodes of inattention, daydreaming, or staring which impress the physician as involuntary, or as reminiscent of petit mal seizures, an electroencephalogram is, of course, indicated. Properly speaking, of course, petit mal refers to a brief, incomplete depression of consciousness associated with fixed staring of the eyes, or more often with the eyes rolling upward, often accompanied by rapid, rhythmic blinking. The episodes last only a few seconds in most cases, although they occur many times per day. Their brief duration often leads to a false impression that someone is able to "snap the child out of it," or that he can stop the inattention at will. This is the one type of seizure with which the electroencephalogram (if including overventilation and photic stimulation) is probably always abnormal in a characteristic way and when petit mal is suspected, an EEG thus has obvious value in either substantiating or ruling out the possibility. (Payne, 1965, p. 17)

The teacher should also note the characteristics of temper tantrums, watching for involuntary or stereotyped or bizarre movements, which might be clues to more obscure types of seizures.

When a child appears sleepy, hypoactive, yawns repeatedly, or daydreams, then you might inquire of his physical health of the parent. If he has not had a recent physical examination, then you, or the nurse, might want to suggest a physical examination to ascertain that the child is not hypothyroid, allergic, malnourished, or does not have any other chronic illness.

In the case of the parent whom you cannot get to accept the fact that the child is having learning disabilities, that he isn't *just lazy,* or that you *just haven't been trying to teach him,* or you *don't like him,* or you *just don't know how to handle him,* or you *just are not making him pay attention,* or your class just *is not interesting enough,* then perhaps it is time to scream for the doctor. If the parents do not respect your interpretation, they might accept the doctor's. At least he is a chance for some understanding from the parents. He may support you and add considerable weight to your efforts to try to teach the child—if you do not prediagnose.

Writing a letter about the child's school behavior and your own findings for the parent to take to the medical appointment will ensure that the doctor will understand the reasons for the referral. Use your notes and pupil profile to describe the child's total behavior. Do this as objectively as possible. Describe actual incidents. Avoid opinionated and nondescriptive phrases like "strange behavior," "naughty boy," "spoiled child." Put down specifics like "scores low on tests of visual perception," "breaks peers' toys," "tears their papers," "fights frequently," "poor fine motor coordinations," "often yells out in class." If this is a Strauss syndrome child, mention the child's "hyperactivity," "distractability," and "impulsivity." This will cue the doctor toward the child's needs. If you must make an observation or conclusion without a specific illustration, preface it with "seems to . . . ," or "appears to . . . ." "He *appears* unable to refrain from talking." "He *seems* to be in perpetual motion."

It is probably best to tell the doctor what you suspect—petit mal, a neurological base for explosive behavior, or a need for drug therapy. Never diagnose, or you will turn the doctor against you immediately. State the facts and ask his opinion. Ask him for a report on his examination. He can give this only if the parents agree. Offer your cooperation with his diagnosis, and with future progress reports or observations.

When you have worked with a child, diagnosed his learning problems as well as you can, tried specific methods to help his disability and he is still very difficult to manage and very hyperactive, then a referral to a doctor might also be in order. The child might have hypoglycemia or food intolerances (Von Hilsheimer, 1970). There are also certain drugs which are being used today to calm these hyperactive, distractable children so they can be taught. (Tranquilizers seem to have an opposite effect on these children and key them up even more.) Doctors are using drugs in the amphetamines, stimulant group such as Dexedrine,® Benzedrine,® deanol, Ritalin,® and dexiamphetamine. These have to be carefully administered by a doctor who is familiar with this type of drug therapy. The school nurse may have a list of possible doctors to suggest to the parent, or you might consult your local chapter of the Association for Children with Learning Disabilities, or the Mental Health Association.

The Multidisciplinary Approach

It is very difficult to pull together all the pertinent information of value to teachers on MCD into a few short pages. In attempting to do so here, I do not mean to minimize the importance of any one phase of this vital work.

We are most fortunate in having so many of the different disciplines working to enlighten the subject. The quality and quantity of the work in the last ten or twelve years and the professional willingness to share their knowledge in symposiums, conferences, and compilations are most encouraging to us in education, who feel so strongly the responsibility for the emancipation of these children.

The best treatment or diagnostic centers today use the team approach, including the pediatrician, neurologist, psychologist, audiologist, psychiatrist, optometrist, *and* the teacher. Those of us in education who are working with these children feel that this is an excellent approach, and only hope that such a team, such facilities, may someday be available to all the children in our public school classrooms who need this help.

EMOTIONALLY HANDICAPPED

Some children with learning difficulties have emotional problems. They might be insecure, frightened, unhappy, aggressive, unaware, suspicious, rebellious, or withdrawn, but unable to make a satisfactory adjustment to their peers, the teacher, and/or the classroom.

Rebellion with Aggression

There is rebellious Richard, whose mother left him, whose father gave him no boundaries, no guidelines, whose stepmother demanded the impossible of him, whose eight brothers and sis ters added to his feeling of entrapment. He just couldn't suppress his feelings. He had to explode! He had to rebel! The school had to give him the understanding, the room in which to operate, to learn to control his feelings. Without it he would never be able to learn even though he is a very intelligent boy.

Leonard was from a $40,000 home with loving parents, but something was wrong! He was so sadistic toward the other children! He would hit and kick them unmercifully for no apparent reason. They were well-adjusted, well-controlled children. They would just stand there with tears rolling down their faces, saying, "Mrs. K., Leonard is hitting me again." One day he brought a new guitar, a rather expensive toy, to school. He shared it calmly at show-and-tell time, but later used it to strike several children so viciously that it was shattered to pieces and five children were crying before I was able to reach them.

Randy had a confused home life, and now a new stepfather. He cried every day in a regular first grade. He didn't want to go to school. "I can't do it!" he would cry. "It's too hard!"

Cindy, from an unhappy home, was rebellious, negative. "I won't do it!" "I don't want to!" Then she crumpled up the paper and threw it down. Or she grabbed other children's papers and tore them. She made big crayon marks on their papers and desks and broke their toys.

Rebellion with Withdrawal

Then there was Teddy—hurt, withdrawn. He had two loving parents, and an adoring grandmother. But he came to us from four frustrating months of a regular classroom. He would sit sprawled at his seat, negative, and a nonparticipant. When approached, he would pull in his arms and head like a turtle fearing reprisal. He withdrew at any physical contact, or at any assumed injury. Finally, he would let the teacher touch him, but no one else. Even then his only paper work was produced with the teacher's hand on his. As soon as she lifted her hand, his fell limp at his side with the objection, "I can't do it!" He never volunteered anything, but remained in his shell. He rarely spoke, never communicated with anyone. On his own, in a free period, he enjoyed blocks, alone.

Later, we found that he knew his colors and could recognize some numerals. He could not retain words or do the simple number papers of his classmates. His writing was at angles, irrespective of lines. All fine and gross coordinations were poor. As we came to know him, we found him very sensitive and extremely immature, but with ability to form concepts, to integrate ideas. He was possibly a slow bloomer with some perceptual and coordination problems, lacking the maturity, the self-confidence, the emotional stability to accept his lack of ability.

Primary and Secondary Emotional Problems

We have here basically two types of emotional problems in these disabled learners. Either the problem in social-emotional adjustment is primary, basic to the learning difficulty, causing it; or the emotional problem is secondary, caused by the child's repeated failures, his lack of confidence in himself. In the latter case the child might turn from his failure and in his disappointment in himself, either withdraw completely from all activity and sometimes from all contact with others, or become aggressive, striking out at the world for his failure. Arthur Gates notes in one study that seventy-five percent of the children with specific reading problems had marked signs of maladjustment. The child may have guilt feelings from having disappointed his parents. He may become negative, refuse to conform, rebel (Gates, 1941).

These cases are rarely clear-cut, either absolutely a primary emotional problem or positively a secondary problem. Often, the unhappy home life is simply made more unbearable by the failure. Or the insecure child feels even more depressed, more cheated, or more rebellious, and this results in the emotional upheaval.

Katrina deHirsch tells of two children who, in spite of major family upheavals and great emotional strain, managed to succeed in school:

> For these two youngsters, the academic area must have been relatively conflict-free; in fact, they may well have found in the school setting a source of satisfaction and support. (deHirsch, 1966, p. 76)

Violet Spraings (1967), of the Northern California Diagnostic

Center in San Francisco, tells of an extensive study of children in classes for the emotionally handicapped. Many of these children had had from one to four years of therapy for their emotional problems. Yet when these children were studied carefully, all but two of the three hundred were found to have some neurological involvement or impairment. This would lead us to believe that with the greater proportion of our emotionally handicapped children, the problem is secondary. They probably need extensive diagnosis, therapy, and training to overcome the neurological cause of the basic learning problem.

Dr. Riley W. Gardner discusses the hyperactive internal thoughts of the severely anxious child which distracts his attention from the learning. The child is so absorbed by his internal distress that he is unable to concentrate on the classroom activities and therefore is not able to profit measurably from the instruction. Again, of course, the anxiety could have been caused by emotional upheaval or instability, or by previous repeated failure (Gardner, 1967).

THE SEARCH FOR A DIAGNOSIS

Previous to studies by the medical profession (beginning with Hinshelwood in 1917) almost all children with learning problems were considered to be either mentally retarded or emotionally disturbed. Thus the bulk of the study of these children for many years has been by the behavioral scientists. The parents, anxious to have a diagnosis different from that of incurable mental retardation or mental illness, have tromped from psychologist to psychiatrist to neurologist, handing out hundreds into thousands of dollars for one word of solution. Parents have wondered what they have done wrong, where they have failed. They are willing to try anything, to do anything to help their child. Often the whole family situation, the marriage itself, is on the verge of collapse because of this one disruptive child.

Parents have been told that they are overprotecting their children, spoiling them, not using enough discipline, or are too harsh, too demanding of them or, the crowning insult, that they do not love them enough. Parents have been referred to private residential schools or therapy sessions for either or both parents and child. They were given suggestions for control and management of the child, often with extremely discouraging results.

The situation is changing today as psychologists and psychiatrists themselves have made some excellent studies on how children learn, and on the complexities of the emotional problems of these children. Dr. Jampolsky reports that:

> . . . the majority of children who are over two years retarded in their reading have emotional problems that inhibit their total adjustment to life, regardless of whether one considers these emotional problems to be primary or secondary. (Jampolsky, 1965, p. 64)

Damerau found that even removing the reading disability did not seem to improve the behavior in some children. It may be that the child still felt inadequate, that his defeat was too severe (Damerau, 1934).

There was the high school boy who received intensive perceptual training and special reading instruction, and began reading more and more of easy-reading fiction. When asked if he felt he had improved in reading, he answered in the negative. He was retested and was amazed when he was told that he was now above his grade level in reading. Not only must you reteach and convince the learning-disabled child of his own worth, but often the problem is so involved that the whole family must be included in the counseling in order to bring about the desired changes in attitude and behavior.

REFERENCES

Association for Children With Learning Disabilities, 2200 Brownsville Road, Pittsburg, Pennsylvania, 15210.

Ayres, A. Jean: *Perceptual-Motor Dysfunction in Children*. Monograph from the Greater Cincinnati District Ohio Occupational Therapy Association Conference, 1964.

Barsch, Ray H.: *Achieving Perceptual-Motor Efficiency*. Seattle, Spec Child, 1967.

Cohn, Robert: The neurological study of children with learning disabilities. *Except Child, 31(No. 4)*:179–185, Dec. 1964.

Cruickshank, William M., et al.: *A Teaching Method for Brain-Injured and Hyperactive Children*. New York, Syracuse U Pr, 1961.

Damerau, R.: Influence of treatment on the reading ability and behavior disorders of reading disability cases. *Smith College Studies in Social Work,* 5:160–183, 1934.

deHirsch, Katrina, *et al.: Predicting Reading Failure.* New York, Harper & Row, 1966.

Frostig, Marianne, and Horne, David: *The Frostig Program for the Development of Visual Perception.* Chicago, Follett, 1961.

Gardner, Riley W.: Some effects of severe disequilibration on the cognitive functioning of the child. *Academic Therapy Quarterly, IX (No. 4)*:205–213, Summer 1967.

Gates, Arthur: The role of personality maladjustment in reading disability. *J Genet Psychol,* 59:77–83, 1941.

Geortzel, Mildred, and Geortzel, Victor: *Cradles of Eminence.* Boston, Little, 1962.

Hunt, J. McVicker: The implications of changing ideas on how children develop intellectually. *Children, 11(No. 3)*:83–91, May-June 1964.

Ilg, Frances L., and Ames, Louise Bates: *School Readiness.* New York, Harper & Row, 1964.

—: *The Gesell Institute's Child Behavior.* New York, Dell, 1960.

Irwin, Theodore: In most newborn babies, brain damage can be prevented. *Look,* Sept. 5, 1967, pp. 61–70.

Jampolsky, Gerald G.: Psychiatric considerations in reading disorders. In *Reading Disorders,* Flower, Richard M., *et al.,* Editors. Philadelphia, F. A. Davis, 1965.

Kephart, Newell C.: *The Slow Learner in The Classroom.* Columbus, Ohio, Merrill, 1960.

Payne, Richmond S.: Organic neurological factors related to learning disorders. In *Learning Disorders,* Hellmuth, J., Editor. Seattle, *Spec Child,* 1968, vol. 1.

Pither, Marjorie S.: Is our child a late bloomer? *Family Weekly,* Apr. 9, 1967.

Spraings, Violet: From a lecture in Sacramento, California, on Dec. 14, 1967.

Strauss, A. A., and Lehtinen, Laura E.: *Psychopathology and Education of the Brain Injured Child.* New York, Grune & Stratton, 1947.

Tanner, J. M.: *Education and Physical Growth.* London, U London Pr, 1961.

Thompson, Lloyd J.: Language disabilities in men of eminence. *J Learning Disabilities, 4(No. 1),* Jan. 1971.

Valett, Robert: *Remediation of Learning Disabilities, a Handbook of Psychoeducational Resource Programs.* Palo Alto, California, Fearon, 1967.

von Hilsheimer, George: *How to Live With Your Special Child.* Washington, D. C. Acropolis, 1970.

GENERAL FILMS ON LEARNING DISABILITIES

Bright Boy, Bad Scholar. (28 min.) Contemporary Films, 1211 Polk Street, San Francisco, California.

The Case Against Rubella. (10 min.) Smith Kline and French Laboratories, 1500 Spring Garden Street, Philadelphia, Pennsylvania, 19101.

Cerebral Dysfunction in Children. (25 min.) Available from your local CIBA drug representative, and from Association Films, 25358 Cypress Avenue, Hayward, California, 94544.

Early Recognition of Learning Disabilities. National Medical A.V. Center, Chamblee, Georgia, 30341.

Film Series: Children and Learning Disabilities. Bucks County Public Schools. Available from Federal Program Coordinator, Bureau of Special Education, Dept. of Public Instruction, Harrisburg, Pennsylvania 17126. Education: A Program of Habilitation (52 min.); Neurology: Aspects of Neurological Assessment (55 min.); Ego Development: A Psychiatric View (28 min.); Etiology: What a Child Brings to the Classroom (41 min.).

Gesell Development and Neurological Examination in Infancy. (28 min.) Ohio State University, 56 West 19th Avenue, Columbus, Ohio, 43210.

The Hyperactive Child. (34 min.) Newer CIBA film available as above.

Identifying Learning Disabilities. (30 min.) Franklin County Board of Education, 46 East Fulton Street, Columbus, Ohio, 43215.

Infantile Autism, The Invisible Wall. (27 min.) Behavioral Sciences A.V. Laboratory of Oklahoma Medical Center, 800 NE 13th Street, Oklahoma City, Oklahoma, 73104.

The Learning Series. Contemporary Films, McGraw Hill, 338 West 42nd Street, New York, New York 10036: Teaching the Way They Learn (28 min.); Old Enough But Not Ready (28 min.); It Feels Like You're Left Out of the World (28 min.); I'm Not Too Famous At It (28 min.)

Portrait of a Disadvantaged Child. (17 min.) University of Illinois, Visual Aids Service, 1325 South Oak, Champaign, Illinois, 61820.

Public School Programs for Learning Disabilities. (16 min.) Cook County Special Education, Chicago Civic Center, Clark & Washington Streets, Chicago, Illinois, 60602

The Puzzling Children. (20 min.) CANHC Movie Distribution, P. O. Box 1526, Vista, California, 92083.

Thursday's Children. (34 min.) Swank Motion Pictures, Inc., 201 South Jefferson, St. Louis, Missouri, 63166.

Why Billy Couldn't Learn. (26 min.) CANHC Movie Distribution, P. O. Box 1526, Vista, California, 92083.

Chapter Four

$\mathcal{D}$iagnostic $\mathcal{T}$esting and $\mathcal{E}$valuation

DIAGNOSIS

IN AN ANCIENT dictionary, I found "diagnosis" defined as "Scientific discrimination of any kind." That is just what it used to be, a mere discrimination between illnesses, so that they could be named. But now the new Random House Dictionary says: "The process of determining by examination the nature and circumstances of a diseased condition." (Stein, 1966, p. 397)

So now, we are compelled to go further than naming. We must gather data with which to examine the nature and circumstances.

Previously, in education—perhaps we should say before learning disabilities were recognized—diagnosis was more for labeling. If the child couldn't read, he might have been labeled a *non-reader, retarded,* or more recently, *dyslexic.* Later, the reading was further diagnosed as *lacks comprehension, lacks skills, unable to retain words.* Then they began to look at the errors the child made and define them with terms such as *makes substitutions, omits words, misses word endings, makes reversals, misses vowels.*

By now it is, Why? Why does the child make the substitutions? Is it really an error in reading or in memorizing? And why does he miss parts of the words? Is he unable to perceive all the letters in the word? Or is he confusing their order? Is it a contextual guess, a substitute for his inability to read at all? Is it merely an attention problem?

Karl Menninger defines skillful diagnosis in the medical and psychiatric sciences:

> But this means diagnosis in a new sense, not the mere application of a label. It is not a search for a proper name by which one can refer to this affliction in this and other patients. It is diagnosis in the sense of understanding just how ill the patient is, how he became ill,

and how his illness serves him. From this knowledge one may draw logical conclusions regarding how changes might be brought about in or around the patient which would affect his illness. (Menninger, 1963, p. 6)

So we, too, in education must attempt more skillful diagnosis according to all we can find out about a child, his history of growth and development, and his present behaviors, abilities, and limitations. We must make use of all the research and all the studies by the various disciplines on learning disabilities and keep abreast of the constantly new developments to increase our ability to diagnose. To really SEE the child, we must make a composite picture of all facets of his life—environmental, historical, physical, and behavioral—adding each new symptom as it appears, or as we come to understand it. Only when we discover the really basic deficit of the child can we take steps to help him. Then we start with what the child knows that he knows, so that he experiences complete success, and we move in precise steps, according to the degree of his disability.

Testing proves to us (if we're willing to learn) that abilities vary considerably more than we had expected and that there is a tremendous span of abilities in one child. But we must use a variety of instruments to discover this. Total scores, such as those obtained from standardized reading-readiness tests, are rarely of any value. The emphasis must be on perceiving the low trends of the subtests of standardized tests, and the details of the child's errors, rather than just numbered scores.

INDIVIDUALLY ADMINISTERED TESTS

The awesome, often revered, intelligence test—the Stanford-Binet and the WISC, or Wechsler (1949)—are probably of the least value as diagnostic tools to the classroom teacher. Yet, in the hands of a competent psychologist, they could offer many clues to learning difficulties, but it is up to the psychologist to translate the findings into specific deficits and methods which the teacher can use. If he fails to do this, the scores lack any implication for the child's future; in fact, they will remain about the same or even lower in the succeeding years. The child's IQ is static, a true prognosis of his ability ONLY if he is not taught.

Most children can be taught to overcome some of their disabilities, thus raising future IQ scores.

Particularly with reading problems, the tests of visual and auditory perception, memory, and language are most valuable. A diagnostic reading test—for above first graders—such as the Wide-range (Jastak, 1965), might yield more clues. Tests of retention, such as Memory for Sentences (Spencer and MacGrady, 1964), and Digit Span (from the WISC or Stanford or Chambers, 1967), give clues to the child's memory ability. Tests of visual perception which might be given by the psychologist (or the teacher, with some help) would be the Frostig Developmental Test of Visual Perception (Frostig, 1963), the Bender Gestalt, or Beery's Developmental Test of Visual-Motor Integration (Beery, 1967). The Wepman (Wepman, 1958), a test of auditory discrimination, can also be given by a teacher but must be administered individually.

For language the Illinois Test of Psycholinguistic Abilities (Kirk, 1961), or ITPA, is good although lengthy and should be administered by trained personnel. For the child with expressive disabilities, the Peabody Picture Vocabulary Test (Engelmann, 1967) is compact and easily administered by the teacher. In language it is especially important to ignore total scores and find out which particular language skill or skills the child lacks.

Carefully select your series of tests for your class so that you have some measure of each different ability: visual perception, auditory perception, language skills, memory span, and sensorimotor. If you find that the child's problem is evident or questionable in one area much more than the others, you may want to choose a second test in that area to make a more specific diagnosis and be able to initiate effective training.

Dr. Robert Valett has devised A Psychoeducational Survey of Basic Learning Abilities (Valett, 1966), an excellent comprehensive individual diagnostic device which could be used to pinpoint a child's specific weaknesses and levels of development. It includes tests in motor integration and physical development, tactile discrimination, auditory discrimination, visual-motor coordination, visual discrimination, language development and verbal fluency, and conceptual development.

A simple screening test for parents or teachers to administer to determine readiness for first grade (and perhaps to convince a parent of the child's disabilities) is School Readiness Survey (Jordon, 1967). This is in a small booklet which can be sent home with the parent. This test is not comprehensive enough to be diagnostic.

THE DEHIRSCH PREDICTIVE INDEX
The Study

Pointing the way to diagnostic testing of children's specific abilities utilizing a variety of media is the deHirsch Predictive Index. In the book *Predicting Reading Failure* the authors tell of their research with fifty-three kindergarten children who were tested with a battery of thirty-seven tests. The tests used included a variety of motor, perceptual, language, and reading surveys; some standardized tests, and results of careful observations. The children were then retested at the end of second grade with the Gates Advanced Primary and the Gray Oral Reading tests. The pretests were then evaluated for their ability to differentiate between the children who subsequently failed the reading tests in second grade and those who were successful with reading. They found that:

> It was not, however, failure on any single task that distinguished the Failing Readers from the other subjects (some of the superior achievers also showed isolated failures), but rather the accumulation of deficits . . . the diagnosis of reading disability does not depend on any single pathognomonic sign, but on an appraisal of the whole configuration of dysfunctions. (deHirsch, 1966, pp. 52 and 54)

Therefore, after careful statistical analysis, the authors chose a battery of ten tests (some of them parts of tests) which would best predict the possibility of reading failure and with them formed The Predictive Index. According to their research then, the child who fails not just one but three or more of these tests is a potential reading failure.

The ten tests are Pencil Use, Bender Visual-Motor Gestalt (Bender, Illustrations A, 1, 2, 4, 6, 8) ; Wepman Auditory Discrimination (the odd-numbered items) ; Number of Words used in telling the story of The Three Bears; Categories, Horst Reversals, Gates Word Matching, Word Recognition I and II, and Word Reproduction. Thus the elements of the index include a variety of the skills essential to reading:

Visual perception: The Horst Reversal and Bender tests

Auditory perception: Wepman and Number of Words

Visual Motor: Bender and Pencil Use

Language Ability: Categories, and Number of Words

Integration of skills needed for reading: Gates Word Matching,
Word Recognition I and II, and Word Reproduction.

As a result of their study, the authors made the following recommendations:

> . . . our findings suggest that it is possible to predict end of second grade achievement on the basis of kindergarten functioning. We, therefore, recommend that a predictive index of the kind described in Chapter 4, be administered to all children during the second half of their kindergarten year, and that the decision as to first grade entrance be based by and large on the child's score on this index. . . .
>
> Rather than being a substitute for observation, the index should assist the teacher in translating her often excellent, but sometimes impressionistic, judgment of the child's readiness into a more specific assessment of his perceptuomotor and linguistic functioning. (deHirsch, 1966, pp. 84 and 85)

The Predictive Index is a large step forward in the attempt to diagnose and predict and remediate learning disabilities on the preventive level. It not only is valid as an instrument of identification and prediction, but it also provides an extremely valuable profile of the child and his specific disabilities which we have never had heretofore. The tests are simple to administer by any teacher or teacher's aide. This element, too, is invaluable because psychological help is rarely available for a whole classroom of children.

Adapting the Index to the Public School Classroom

The greatest problem confronting us in the public schools in the use of the Predictive Index is that of individual administration. This requires about thirty minutes per child, and means about fifteen hours of individual testing for thirty kindergarten children. There are various solutions to this problem. One would be to have all the testing done by someone outside the classroom, e.g., high school or college students, or P.T.A. personnel (who are discreet). The other solution is to shorten the tests and to do as many of the tests as possible in a group testing situation. For example, the Horst Reversals Test and the Bender can be done with the whole class with some help in proctoring. Of course, you won't be able to note where each child begins each figure as you would with individual testing, but better partial results than none at all. Some noticeable mark, or the child's name, could be made to designate the top of the paper. If the child moves his paper to make a figure this should be noted, and the paper returned to the correct position before the next figure is presented to him.

The Pencil Use (ability of the child to hold a pencil without losing it or tearing the paper) could be noted in any group pencil and paper exercise. Still, the Categories, Words in a Story, Auditory Discrimination, and Reading would have to be individual. Whatever the solution to individual testing, it will by needs have to vary according to your own situation. The great advantage of the deHirsch Predictive Index is its adaptability.

Our use of the test might be of help to you. The tests were dittoed, with the instructions for each subtest and spaces for the scores. This was necessary and convenient because several people helped with the administration of the tests. We added two other measures, the Winter Haven Perceptual Forms Test, and the Goodenough Draw-a-man. The former is an easier test of visual perception for younger children, and the latter is a test of body image. I've tried a number of other scoring measures for the drawing of a man, but found that the Goodenough scoring is more precise and provides a wider spread.

A tape recorder was used to record the telling of the story of The Three Bears for the teacher to study later. This latter test was the most time-consuming of all the tests in administration and scoring. We used an abacus to count the words; we also noted speech articulation problems, lack of sequence, and sentence structure. The Wepman Auditory Discrimination Test was not available to us, so we devised a short substitute of just twelve sets of words (Fig. 1). We especially chose words with which the

"I am going to say two words. I want you to tell me whether I say the same word twice or whether I say two different words: 'cat, hat'; 'fun, fun'; 'bed, bet'. Now, turn around so you can't see me. Are these the same or different?"

1. thick
   stick
	2. dot
	   got
		3. shot
		   shop
			4. wish
			   wish
				5. sit
				   set
					6. cut
					   cuff

7. thing
   sing
	8. man
	   Nan
		9. bake
		   bake
			10. with
			    whiff
				11. wing
				    ring
					12. bath
					    bash

VII score: (number of sets that are different, but are heard by the child to be the same).

0–10

Critical Score: 1

Figure 1. Auditory Discrimination Test.

children might be familiar, because our children have very poor vocabularies and we wanted to be sure we were testing auditory discrimination and not an environmental language condition. We also wanted to give the children every advantage in the test. A few weeks later we retested the children who failed the test to find they failed exactly the same items the second time.

The reading tests used by deHirsh were too time-consuming, so we substituted the recognizing and naming of colors, reading letters and numerals, and reading of the names of the classmates (Fig. 2). The children had been exposed to the names of their classmates during the year through a Helper's Chart, so we felt that the recognition of these names would give us some indication of their present reading abilities. Later, we changed from the telling of the lengthy story of The Three Bears to the singing of two of the class's favorite songs which had been sung many times over all year. We also asked the child to recall his address and phone number to give us additional clues on his memory and sequence ability. We found a high correlation between Reading Letters and Numerals and Reading Names of Classmates.

Only four children knew the letters and numerals but *not* the names of their peers. I understand that the deHirsch team have now also added a test of letters to the Predictive Index.

When using the Distar Reading I Program, which teaches single

1. RECOGNIZING AND NAMING COLORS:

Point at a colored paper. WHAT COLOR IS THIS? Put an "X" on colors missed. Repeat those on which the child hesitates. If he misses it a second time, mark it.

red   blue   green   yellow   (Score: Number missed)
orange   brown   black   purple

0–8

Critical Score: 0

2. RECOGNIZING AND READING LETTERS AND NUMERALS:
   The child is to READ these! No prompting! Put an "X" on those missed:

J 2 a T r m P 8 n 5 L K e 4   (Score: Number missed)
C 6 B f g o 3 y R S b N i 7

0–27

Critical Score: 10

3. READING NAMES OF CLASSMATES:
   Put an "X" on names the child is unable to READ.

Sandy	Glen	Terry	Jerri	Dale	David
Mike	Frank	Brian	Nora	Kenny	Roger
Debbie	Del	Eddie	Jane	Willie	Tommy
Johnny	Jeff	Sandy	Tena	Rhonda	Shirley
Julie	Mark	Alice	Bobby	Neal	Michael

(Score: Number missed)

0–30

Critical Score: 12

Figure 2. Reading Tests.

sounds and single skills a step at a time, we found that the reading of numerals and letters was the sole test needed to place the children into reading groups according to their potential ability. If the child failed this test AND was not able to name the colors, he subsequently had great difficulty learning the sounds and retaining sounds and words in reading. There is a memory factor tested here that is vital to reading.

The value of the consistent testing over teacher judgment was sometimes dramatically apparent. A child who had seemed to be so bright in the classroom was thought by the kindergarten teacher to have been able to read all of the names. She knew only two. It is extremely easy to make these kinds of errors in judgment when you are busy with the responses of thirty children. It is often the verbally expressive child who is misjudged and thought to be ready for the fine skills and visual perceptions and integrations necessary for reading. It is often a shock to the parents and to the kindergarten teacher to realize the next year this child does not have these skills and is not able to succeed with his classmates. Therefore, individual responses, comparative scores, and adequate notes are essential to an accurate evaluation and prediction of children.

Results of the Adaptation

We computed critical scores on the substituted subtests and charted the scores. In our low socioeconomic area one year, only eighteen children out of fifty-nine failed in two or fewer tests and were therefore judged fully ready for first grade skills. Our twenty-five lowest achievers failed in six to nine of the subtests. This is a very high percentage of failure compared with deHirsch's subjects, but our second and third grade reading scores have been extremely low, too. So the test does appear to predict a potential of future below-grade-level achievement in reading.

All but six children out of the forty-one potential failures had already failed in three areas, namely visual and auditory perception, *before* their ability in the reading was assessed. Considering the large number of children with visual and auditory perception problems in the top thirty-three children, it is an injustice to these children to expect them to read before they have the mechanics, the tools they need to learn to read. This indicates to us that ALL first grade classrooms should do perceptual training exercises in some degree according to the needs of their children.

Using the Bender Gestalt

The test failed by the greatest number of children was the Bender. To obtain further information on these children's visual perception, we also gave them the Winter Haven Perceptual Forms Test (Fig. 3). We found high correlations at the extreme ends with the very high or very low scores, but considerable discrepancies with the middle scores. A child can pass the Per-

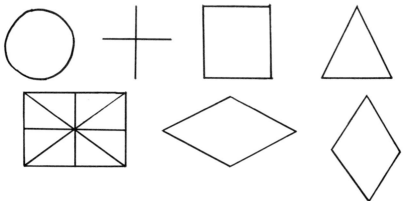

Figure 3. Winter Haven Perceptual Forms Test.

ceptual Forms Test and yet (using the Koppitz ratings) fail the Bender. There are several reasons for this. A kindergartener can fail the diamonds in the Perceptual Forms Test and still pass according to his age level. Yet there are two Bender figures, A and 6 (in the deHirsch test), which contain diagonal lines and thus make him fail the test according to deHirsch's critical score of *one* (Fig. 4). At the kindergarten level, it was a rare child who used any counting to determine how many dots to place in a row (Bender figures 1 and 2). Most often they seem to perseverate and make the dots clear to the side of the paper. This may be due to the stimulus of their peers noisy dot-making and their enjoyment in making this sound themselves. Another problem that is apparent in the Bender is the child's inability to intersect lines and to make curves (Bender figure 6). These kindergartners tend to make zigzag sharp spastic movements instead.

The Bender figures are much more complicated than the Winter Haven Perceptual Forms, utilizing more than one form in each figure. Therefore, the Bender requires considerably greater ability to integrate the forms in relation to each other, thus more directionality and spatial relations problems appear. A child might score high on the Winter Haven but fail the Bender. In both tests, the immature child often rotated the figures or left them incomplete (Figs. 5 and 6). This did not seem to predict

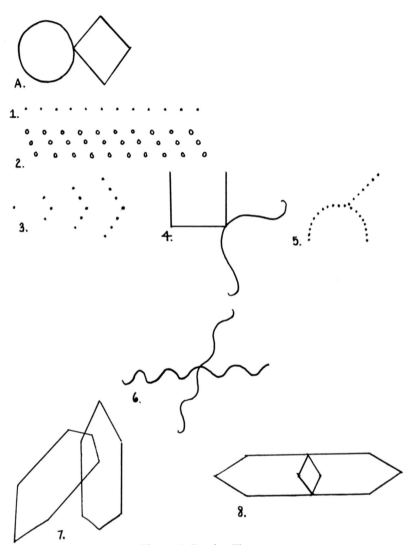

Figure 4. Bender Figures.

later failure in school. On the other hand, the child with dramatic behavior and control problems (e.g., Strauss syndrome) often made bizarre distortions of the figures and this appeared to be more of a prediction of later failure than the rotated or incomplete figures (Figs. 7 and 8). Reproduced by permission of The American Orthopsychiatric Association, Inc.

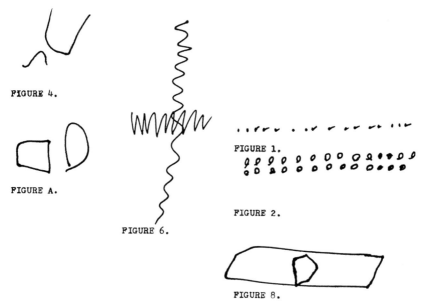

Figure 5. Immature Forms of Bender Figures.

Katrina deHirsch does not describe any scoring of the Bender to determine failure on a figure. Thus we used the Koppitz Ratings (1968) with certain allowances for the early ages of our

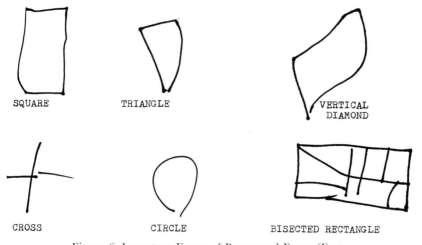

Figure 6. Immature Forms of Perceptual Forms Test.

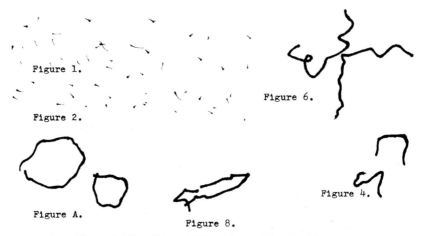

Figure 7. More Bizarre Distortions of Bender Figures.

subjects (five years, six months to six years, five months). On Bender figure A, we allowed forty-five degree rotation and one-half inch between figures. On Bender figure 1, we allowed more than the fifteen dots, and on figure 2, more than fourteen columns. Some of our children were still making just two rows of dots, a five-year level. On Bender figure 4, we allowed one-half

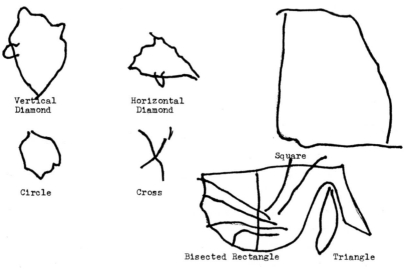

Figure 8. More Bizarre Distortions of Forms—Perceptual Forms Test.

inch between figures and some rotation. The curve was often incomplete. On Bender figure 6, there were sharper angles allowed on the horizontal lines especially. Developmental norms for the Bender are found in *A Visual Motor Gestalt Test and Its Clinical Use* (Bender, 1967). It is suggested that the teacher study this text thoroughly before attempting to administer the test, or else enlist the aid of the school psychologist.

A few comments are necessary on administering the Perceptual Forms Test, if it is to be a supplementary or substitute test. This test allows ten points for left-to-right progression. To be sure that the child does *not* turn the paper around after each figure and destroy the sequence, put each child's name on the top *center* of the paper. Thus you can check the position of the classes' papers at a glance before presenting each new figure. Placing his name on the right or left might influence his starting point and again invalidate the test. Before you give the test, briefly shuffle through the cards to show them how many you are going to ask them to make. YOU ARE GOING TO MAKE ALL THESE DIFFERENT SHAPES, SO BE SURE TO LEAVE PLENTY OF ROOM ON YOUR PAPER FOR ALL OF THEM. Be sure that you then present the forms in the correct sequence, giving the children no auditory clue or name to identify them. Just say: MAKE THIS FORM. He may erase if he desires. He is given all the time he needs to make each form. Always reassure the frustrated child: THAT'S FINE! YOU DID A GOOD JOB.

CLASSROOM TESTING
A Format

Diagnostic testing of children need not rely solely on formal or standardized tests. There are numerous simple testing devices which may be used to better understand your children, to determine *where they are* in development, and to intelligently plan a training program which will help to overcome their disabilities.

A good testing program for the classroom teacher might include some formal tests with standardized or critical scores, along with individually performed tasks (such as rote counting), and with comparison of scores on sample daily seatwork. The criteria for choosing the tests will depend on the individual classroom situation. The selection must include some measure from each area of ability or disability, as with the deHirsch Predictive Index. You should generally consider at least one measure of each of the following: visual perception, auditory perception, memory, gross motor, sensorimotor, fine and visual motor, expressive language, sequence, number concepts (meaning, numeral recognition, rote counting, addition), and reading (letters and words in isolation). When there is any question on a child's disability in any one area, then do more thorough testing in that particular area.

For a teacher who is newly discovering the skills behind the learning of the three R's, the testing will have to be quite comprehensive and the gathering of sample papers and data extensive. Some testing which yields individual scores both pre and post would help to delineate the problem and to evaluate the effectiveness of your training program. The inexperienced teacher would need to score the deHirsch measures and the Winter Haven Perceptual Forms Test and the Goodenough Draw-a-man in the fall, and possibly the last two again in the spring.

The standard readiness tests common to kindergarten and first grade classrooms are usually of little value because they do not pinpoint specific disabilities, but give only *total* scores, percentile ranks, and trends, or rank the child with his classmates. You must diagnose and pinpoint specific weaknesses and train these if you are to help the child overcome his disabilities. To lump perceptual, motor, language, and integrative abilities into a total readiness score is useless. Thus the child can be high in verbal ability, low in perceptual, average out as *ready to read*, and fail reading because of his inability to perceive and integrate visual and auditory stimuli. It is rather like saying that the child has one foot on a hot stove and one in a refrigerator, but on the average is quite comfortable.

You will want to keep a folder of each child's work, with an individual profile of his varying abilities, and a class chart of scores. Request help of your principal, psychologist, consultant, or teaching partner in planning your testing program and in evaluating your results.

A Testing Schedule

You will need to begin testing the first week of school and continue collecting data so that by the November parent conference date you will have enough information to be able to form a profile of the child's abilities to discuss with the parent. You would then want to readminister certain tests and check new work in January for the end of the semester report to parents. Carefully recheck or retest the slowest children as needed the third quarter to be able to make intelligent recommendations for these children for the next school year. Then you will want certain end-of-the-year testing for a final report of the child's progress. Where the emphasis at the other testing periods was on diagnosis of problems, this last would be on academic achievement and growth on specific abilities. Generally, if you save papers, score and chart them, and test and evaluate just these four times in the year, this is sufficient. It is too likely that you will overtest or overconcern yourself with evaluation if you try to keep weekly or monthly scores. Remember your main function is to teach, and your greatest percentage of effort should be in that direction.

The Experienced Learning Disability Teacher

The teacher experienced in the area of learning disabilities, who has scored the same tests many times in the past, and who is able to thus diagnose problem areas readily, will require less *formal* testing. She can use more *scoreless* measures and collections of papers, and making notes. However, the quarterly testing schedule outlined above would apply to all teachers. No one is capable of evaluating children and remembering all their little problems without some tests, notes, and records. Certainly, if you are not doing diagnostic testing, you are not doing diagnostic teaching to specific disabilities, either.

If you intend to train your whole class in, for example, visual perception, you would want to pretest but not need to score certain tests, merely note the problems involved and save them for comparison with later tests. (If you are going to train only the children with *low* scores, you will have to score the tests.) You could give both the Bender and the Winter Haven Perceptual Forms tests three times a year without scoring them. The same would go for the Draw-a-Man Test. If you are going to train your whole class in body image, simply have the children make their drawings three times a year, without scoring, for subsequent comparison. You would then judge their drawings not only according to maturity but also on the child's own growth. Or, if there is a particular question on a certain child, then score just *his* test.

Generally, follow deHirsch's pattern of using small measures of several different skills. Put these together to form a profile. When there are still questions of a child's ability, use more exacting tests in just the problem areas.

Battery of Informal Classroom Tests

There are a number of simple measures which the classroom teacher can use to give her a diagnostic profile of each child's ability. These measures can be much more revealing, often delineating the child's problem better than the more formal tests.

Gross Motor

1. DYNAMIC BALANCE: Walk on the beam, heel-toe fashion, forward and backward. Or hop on the preferred foot (note which foot) the perimeter of the room.

2. STATIC BALANCE: Stand on one foot for ten seconds. Change feet.

3. FLEXIBILITY AND CONFIDENCE IN SPACE: Jump and kick yourself with both heels.

4. COORDINATION: Do four or five rhythmic jumping jacks in sequence. Note if rhythm is poor or if arms or only legs are coordinated. If you have rings, a horizontal ladder, or climbing poles, note the child's ability on these.

Fine and Visual Motor

1. CUTTING: Cut out a simple shape with straight lines, such as a house. Note hand used. The lines on which the child is to

cut should be thick and dark so that there is no possibility that he can't see where he is to cut.

2. VISUAL-MOTOR DITTO: Stay on the lines of a ditto first with a pencil and then with crayon. Note hand used. Use a simple widely spaced dotted line with a ball at one end and a box or house at the other. Use straight and curved lines and several changes of direction. A commercial ditto may do. Directions would be: TAKE YOUR PENCIL AND START ON THE BALL. STAY RIGHT ON TOP OF THE DOTS, COVERING THEM UP, AND GO ALL THE WAY TO THE HOUSE. GO SLOWLY AND CAREFULLY. THEN TAKE YOUR YELLOW CRAYON, START ON THE BALL AND GO TO THE HOUSE. THEN DO THE SAME WITH YOUR RED CRAYON. Demonstrate each step on the board before handing out the paper. Note the child's ability to stay on lines. Note motor control, smooth or spastic.

Ocular Pursuit

Place a small object (such as a plastic bug) on the end of a pencil. Move the pencil slowly in an arc about twenty inches from the child's eyes. The child must hold his head still, moving only his eyes to follow the target. First use a horizontal arc, then a vertical, then a circular, and both diagonal directions. The child should be able to fix his eyes on the target and follow it smoothly and easily. Note any slight jerking of the eyes, tilting of the head, inability to sustain contact with the target, the straying of one eye, or watering of the eyes.

Sensorimotor

1. DOMINANCE: Have the child look through a kaleidescope or through a hole in a piece of paper. Note the eye used. Note the hand which the child uses to write, draw, and throw. Ask the child to kick a ball as hard as he can, and to hop all the way around the room on one foot. Which foot does he use?

2. BODY IMAGE

a. *Draw-a-Man Test:* Use Goodenough Scoring (available in Sutfin, 1964, pp. 60–61).

b. *Give directions to group:* PUT YOUR HANDS ON YOUR HEAD, YOUR EARS, EYES, NOSE, MOUTH, NECK, SHOULDER, ELBOWS, HIPS,

KNEE, THIGHS, ANKLES, FEET. Note children who are unsure and look to copy the others. Recheck individually as needed.

3. VISUAL PERCEPTION

a. *Tests:* Use both the Bender and Winter Haven Perceptual Forms tests as described earlier.

b. *Directionality:*

(1) Give directions like: PUT YOUR RIGHT HAND ON YOUR RIGHT EAR. First do several that do *not* cross the body line. Then: PUT YOUR LEFT HAND ON YOUR RIGHT EAR. Use well-known body parts for this so that you are not confusing skills.

(2) Spatial directions on a flat plane: Separate children so they cannot copy. DRAW A RED CIRCLE AT THE TOP OF YOUR PAPER. Give aid in the selection of the correct color so that you are testing direction only and *not* knowledge of colors. DRAW A BLUE CIRCLE ON THE RIGHT SIDE OF THE PAPER. MAKE A YELLOW CIRCLE IN THE MIDDLE OF YOUR PAPER. Also use *left side* and *bottom.*

(3) Note frequency of reversals of letters, numerals, and names on all papers.

c. *Spatial relations worksheet:* Use a ditto with four or five different simple patterns or designs made by connecting dots. Demonstrate carefully on the board. Directions would be: SEE THE DESIGN AT THE LEFT? SEE HOW THE DOTS ARE CONNECTED TO MAKE THE DESIGN? NOW LOOK AT THE DOTS AT THE RIGHT. SEE IF YOU CAN CONNECT THOSE DOTS TO MAKE A DESIGN THAT LOOKS EXACTLY LIKE THIS ONE ON THE LEFT. Call on children to complete the design on the board. Then pass out the papers.

d. *Distractability or figure-ground difficulty:* Note the child's inability to pay attention or stick to a task. Note any confusions on paper work or inability to find an object surrounded by other objects. Use a sample Frostig figure-ground worksheet or make one up.

e. *Draw-a-house:* There is a lot of visual form perception and integration demonstrated in a child's drawing. Elicit suggestions from the class about subjects the child might use. Discuss possible details to be included. Having every child draw a picture of his home gives him plenty of leeway with details and gives you a basis for class comparisons between children's work.

The house is one of the first realistic objects the child is able to draw and the execution of the shapes involved and their placement in relation to each other can be very revealing. Do NOT suggest the details he should add, but ask leading questions: HOW DO YOU GET INTO YOUR HOUSE? HOW DO YOU SEE OUT? WHAT IS OUTSIDE YOUR HOUSE? *Label all the details the child names* so that you have a record of the child's intent. If you fail to do this you may misjudge his work. A rectangle beside a house, for example, may appear to be the garage, but the child may have intended it to be a window of the house.

The papers may be scored or judged and recorded according to the various drawing stages. If his effort is a mere scribble, mark an *S* in your records. The child who says, "I don't know what it is," is honest. His picture is probably in the *scribble stage*. If it is an indistinguishable blob and he calls it something, or if he made it first and named it afterward, call it the *naming stage*, *N*. If the picture is more a design, a framing of the page in colors, or intersecting horizontal and vertical lines with the blocks colored in, call it the *design stage*, *D*. This is a step ahead of the naming stage, as the movements are controlled and planned. The realistic stage is not far off. In fact, the child who organizes a balanced, intricate design might be quite mature. If it is a realistic representation of a house or truck, call it the *realistic stage*, *R*. Count the details, e.g. a house with a roof, chimney, and smoke would be *R3*. Count all windows as one single detail, and all flowers as one. A tree, sidewalk, sun, garage are additional details. Note size and position relationships between the details. Is the window in proper position? Are the flowers larger than the house? Is the house firmly balanced or floating at an angle in space?

4. AUDITORY PERCEPTION

a. *Discrimination:* Does the child confuse your verbal directions, misunderstand words, substitute incorrect words in songs and stories? If so, give him at least part of the Wepman, or a substitute.

b. *Recall:* Note the child's recitation of his address and phone number, his singing of songs, reciting poems. Each child could have a turn singing a song or reciting a poem to the class. If a child is too shy for this, try using the tape recorder for him, or simply tune in on him during group singing or flag-saluting.

Expressive Language

Tape record or take notes of each child's ability to express himself at sharing time. Again, if he is too shy, note his personal conversations with others. Note length and completeness of sentences. Does he omit the small words, prepositions, verbs, articles? "He home." Does he destroy the sequence of words in a sentence or distort the verb, or misuse pronouns. "Why come you my house?" "Her goes."

Conceptual Development

1. SEQUENCE: Teach sequence of large objects such as floor blocks, using the chalk rack of the blackboard. I'M BUILDING A FENCE. A TALL BLOCK, A SHORT ONE, A TALL ONE, A SHORT ONE. . . . WHAT SHOULD BE NEXT? WHO CAN DO IT? Then draw a sequence of circles and rectangles on the board and have different children complete the pattern. Finally, when the children understand what you want them to do, ditto about four to six simple sequences for them to complete (Fig. 9) .

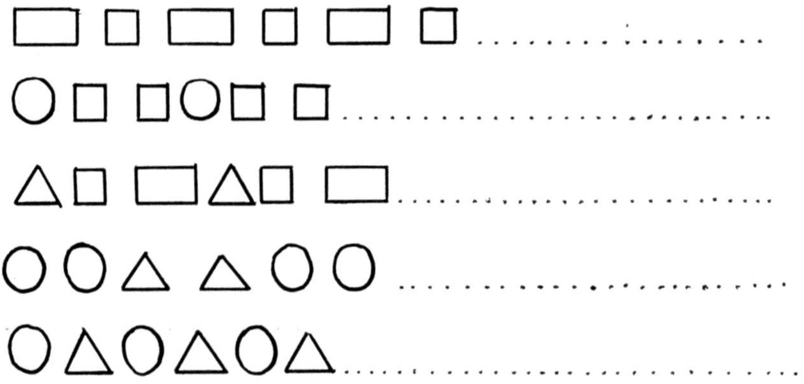

Figure 9. Test of Visual Sequence.

2. CLASSIFYING

a. *Class exercise:* Use four pictures in a pocket chart, one of which does not belong in that category. Use toys, animals, furniture, or vehicles. WHO CAN FIND WHICH OBJECT DOES NOT BELONG HERE? A second task notes expression and further cognitive ability. CAN YOU TELL ME WHY THAT DOES NOT BELONG?

b. *Ditto:* Make up a simple ditto of pictures. The child cuts out the pictures on their rectangular frames and pastes all the animals in one category, all the clothing in another, the toys in another, foods in another.

3. MATH CONCEPTS

a. *Number meaning:* Give each child about fifteen counters or bottle caps or sticks and a paper plate. PUT SIX COUNTERS IN YOUR PLATE. PUT TEN COUNTERS IN YOUR PLATE.

b. *Rote counting:* Have each child count as far as he can. There is probably no need to go past 50 or 60. At least, stop at 100. Our problem learners have difficulty with the teens, or even before. Others are unable to make the transition from 19 to 20, from 29 to 30, or from 39 to 40.

c. *Numeral recognition:* Make a large 9 x 12 card with two-inch flow-pen numerals in mixed order. The child names them.

d. *Numeral writing:* Have the child write the numerals one to ten from memory. If he can't do this, see if he can copy the numerals from the board. Remember that this latter is a test of visual-motor perception and ability, rather than just a math concept.

e. *Relating the numeral to the number of objects:* Use a ditto of sets of pictures (sums up to ten) with several numerals under each set. The child counts the objects and circles the correct numeral. The difficulty noted here is twofold: the inability to count objects in a precise, rhythmic, one-to-one manner, and the inability to recognize numerals.

f. *Integration of counting, number meaning, numeral recognition, and visual-motor ability:* Use a ditto of sets of pictures (sums to ten) with an adjoining box, wherein the child writes the numeral which tells how many are in the set. If he is able to do this without any errors, he is ready for independent seatwork requiring the writing of numerals. If not, then before he is given such work he must be *taught* numeral recognition and writing, counting, and number meaning.

g. *Addition:* Ditto a simple addition page of vertical and horizontal equations using sums up to six or ten. Use no zeros for this initial test.

4. READING

a. *Letters:* On a 9 x 12 card write in mixed order about fifteen of the most common letters. Have the child identify them by either name or sound.

b. *Words:* Have the child identify a list of words or names to which he has been previously exposed.

KEEPING SCORE
Class Profile

The effectual teacher never relies on her memory to keep track of thirty children. The memory becomes too quickly eradicated by the multiplicity of events which crowd her life. Then she tries to think: "Now who was it whose mother said he had bronchitis?" "Who reversed everything on his paper? Was it Timmy? Or did he make just a few reversals?" "Was Richard able to do the first number papers we had, or has he just begun to find them difficult now?" "Tommy cries all the time now. Did he do that the first of the year?" Thus records are imperative, and a class chart, or profile, is the first essential step toward accurate record-keeping.

Use your gradebook to list your children (ranked according to your initial estimate of their performances or ranked alphabetically), their birthdates, scores on tests and seatwork, and as space allows, special notes on behavior. Figure 10, oversimplified for clarity, is one way of recording scores and achievement. Group like things together with spaces between for ready reference. For example, you would want to group the visual-perceptual items, the gross motor, fine-motor, auditory, reading, math, to give a clearer profile. Use a simplified scoring scale that you can decipher at a glance. I use a blue *C* for correctly done papers, with a −1 or −2 beside the *C* for one or two errors. If the child com-

	Birthdate	Visual-Perceptual			Gross Motor		Visual-Motor			Language Skills			
		Perceptual Forms test 9/18	Bender 9/20	Horst Rev. 9/20	Hopping 9/22	Balance 9/22	Visual-Motor Ditto 9/19	Cutting 9/21	Writing 9/22	Auditory Discrimination 9/19	Naming Colors 9/21	Recalling Phone Numbers 9/21	Recalling Song 9/22
Cindy	12-9	80	-1	-2	C	C	C	C	C	C	C	C	C
Jane	5-14	70	-1	-4	C	C	C	C	C	-4	-2	**O**	**O**
Jerry	2-6	30	-4	-9	C	C	C-	C-	C	C	C	C	C
Tommy	8-5	65	-2	-2	**O**	**O**	C-	C-	C-	-1	C	C	C
Mike	11-20	20	-4	-8	**O**	**O**	**P**	**P**	**P**	-6	-3	**O**	**O**

Figure 10. Class Profile (The bold-faced letters would be written in red).

pletely fails the exercise I use a red *O* or a red *P* for *poor* writing or cutting.

When there are many errors I put −6 (the number of errors) marked in red or boxed with red. If tests have letter or numeral scores, mark these. Date each column so that you can judge progress effectively.

Marking the low scores in red pencil, you can more readily see that Tommy is low in gross motor, but not in fine. That Jane is low in the language and auditory items but not in the visual, and that poor little Mike is low in everything. Thus you will be able to focus on specific children for certain activities. Therefore, if Jerry and Mike are low in the tests of visual perception, then you will pay particular attention that they have extra help as needed with these exercises. At activity time you will guide them to working with the parquetry block designs, perceptual forms puzzles, and sorting objects.

If you use wall charts to note subsequent progress in math, reading, workbooks, and physical education skills, you will probably need only the class profile (Fig. 10) for the fall to get an overall class picture and to recall where the child was at the beginning of instruction. This fall class profile is excellent for comparing the progress of different children.

Pupil Profile

To evaluate an individual child you will need some kind of pupil profile. It is easiest to first record all first of the year scores and notes on the class chart and then each quarter transfer them to the pupil profile before you do your conferences or report cards. The individual profile can be a single dittoed sheet listing health history, gross motor coordinations, fine and visual motor coordinations, sensorimotor development, and visual perception, language, conceptual development, and social-emotional behavior, with space allowed for making comments. Or it can be longer, listing each item which you expect to record (Fig. 11). This profile would then be used quarterly to discuss the child with his parents, or to make out report cards. This might seem like a lot of work the first of the year, but it is imperative in evaluating the

NAME .... BIRTHDATE .... SCHOOLYEAR ......

HEALTH HISTORY:

GROSS MOTOR COORDINATIONS:
  Hopping:
  Jumping Jacks:
  Balancing:
  Rings:
  Horizontal Ladder:
  Pole Climbing:
  Jumping Rope:
  Ball Bouncing:

FINE AND VISUAL MOTOR COORDINATIONS:
  Visual-Motor Ditto
  Writing
  Cutting

SENSORIMOTOR DEVELOPMENT AND VISUAL PERCEPTIONS:
  Laterality: Eye: ...... Hand: ...... Foot: ......
  Bender Gestalt Test:
  Perceptual-Forms Test:
  Draw-a-Man Test:

LANGUAGE:
  Therapist's Report

CONCEPTUAL DEVELOPMENT:
  Math Tests:
  Sequence Ditto
  Reading
  Letters and Sounds

SOCIAL EMOTIONAL BEHAVIOR:

Figure 11. Pupil Profile.

child and diagnosing his needs. In later quarters, it is very gratifying and encouraging to see such a clear picture of the often
dramatic growth in a child.

Date new entries on the pupil profile or use different colors
of ink each quarter. At the end of the year make any final entries
and write a few-sentence progress report and place it in the
child's cumulative folder.

Anecdotal Records

Now, we have the pupil profile of ratings on tests and sample
seatwork, but what of the child's speech and general behavior?
We must have some way of keeping track of the significant things
he says and does in the classroom. Billy is sharing for the first
time. The words tumble falteringly from his lips: "Bucky got
carpie. My got none." That is all. Ten children *share* after Billy,

and his words are quickly lost in the torrent that follows. You have no time to go to his file and write his comments on his profile. Later in excited class discussions, he suddenly comes out with bits of important information about sea anemone and camels and astronauts. Amazing for Billy with a history of environmental deprivation and whose siblings are all in EMR classes. He may have poor expressive ability, but he is certainly absorbing more information from the class than you had thought. It is too easy to forget these flashes of light in the dark if they are not recorded. Even by recess you have forgotten.

The best solution I have found yet in my very busy classroom is to simply keep a scratch pad handy. Jot down his few words, or just a couple of significant phrases to remind you of the incident. When you have time later you can elaborate on the same paper, date it, and drop it into his file folder which contains his sample seatwork and tests and pupil profile. At the end of the quarter when you are recording his scores from your gradebook onto the profile, you can also add your scraps of notes. You'll be amazed at how enlightening some of these can be to the total profile, adding insight to the child's problems.

Using the Pupil Profile for Prescriptive Teaching

Some of the diagnosis and also the training of the child will come from the task or the disability itself. Whatever the child cannot do, must be taught. For example: The child can't jump over a two-foot-high rope, so you teach him to jump over a two-inch-high rope and gradually increase the difficulty of the task until he can clear the two feet. But further diagnosis might tell you that the child lacks depth perception and balance, and therefore is afraid to jump over an object. Then you must go back to the teaching of these skills and probably body image also. This child would benefit from Getman's sensory motor training. We must diagnose to the particular task and to the *cause* that makes that task difficult for the child. There is yet so much unknown about children's learning problems that researchers and observant teachers will continually find new ways to look behind the task to find more basic causes of confusions which must be remediated.

As another example, let's take a reading problem. A reversal was previously thought to simply be that the child looked at the wrong end of the word and, therefore, to remediate the problem, you merely had to focus his attention on the left side of the word. Now we know that it is more than that. The child's visual processes are such that the word is continually changing for him. It won't stand still and be constant. This is based on the child's lacking understanding of left-and-right, up-and-down of objects, or directionality, as we call it. Yet this in turn might be due to the child lacking a feeling for laterality, or the sides of his own body. Again, this is movement oriented and the child might lack basic balance, or body image for the parts of his body, how it moves and how it functions (see Chapter Seven). A child seeming to have auditory or visual perceptual problems might in reality have more basic problems embedded in the other senses— olfactory, gustative, tactile, and motor. When these senses are trained, it then might be found that the auditory and visual problems are no longer apparent.

THE SCHOOL NURSE

The school nurse should be invited to visit and observe children. She is able to quickly pick out children with various symptoms which you are simply not trained to discern and are too involved with the total class to notice. She helps identify children with poor coordinations, spastic movements, petit mal seizures, skin diseases, low energy, symptoms of malnutrition, or deficits in auditory and visual acuity. Have her observe those quiet, withdrawn children who stand around at recess, lag behind the others, seldom run, or otherwise exert any extra energy. They could be low in iron or be hypothyroid or suffering from malnutrition. Children who seem to daydream or forget what they are doing should be observed for possible petit mal. Violent temper tantrums should be referred to the nurse, also. Any time you have a question on a child's appearance or behavior, it is wise to ask the nurse to come and observe him to see if she can discern any medical symptoms.

The nurse will make necessary doctor, dental, and optometric referrals. We have had as many as seven children in one class requiring optometric care, and usually two or three with hearing losses each year. We find it necessary to request that hearing be rechecked several times a year in certain children because it seems to fluctuate so frequently, especially with postnasal problems. When there are symptoms of vision and hearing problems, the nurse usually has a standard form which she will give the parent, suggesting a medical check on the difficulty. Or she may make a phone call or even a visit to the home to discuss the matter for you. She will probably take care of cases where there appears to be malnutrition or neglect or brutality. She knows the agencies to contact to bring about the most good for the child. Often she can get donations of clothing, shoes, and eye glasses for families in financial stress.

The school nurse may call a child's doctor to obtain a report on a recent examination. She knows which doctors will cooperate with the school and which specialize in certain types of care.

PARENT CONFERENCES

Your attitude toward the child and his problems will be reflected in your approach to the parent. The loving parent usually senses your concern for his child and appreciates it.

The fear, guilt, and rejection of some of the parents presents the problems. Then we have rebellious, negative parents of rebellious, negative children, and you wonder which came first, the chicken or the egg.

As stated before, there is always the fear that the child is mentally retarded, and parallel to this is the implication that the parents are also of subnormal intelligence. Then, since they can probably see some mistakes that they made in rearing the child (and who hasn't made plenty!) they pile on top of this their feeling of guilt and failure of their responsibility. Then some parents reject the child. Or some overwhelm the child with overprotection and smotherly love. Of course, we have all combinations, all degrees of these problems.

The first step at a conference is to get the parent to talk about the child's home behavior (as in a previous illustration). The parent's comments are often excellent clues to the child's behavior. Next, have that representative folder of the child's work to go over with the parent. Then bring on your other notes and findings as you have them noted in the class or pupil profile. You are laying the child bare to the loving parents, so tread softly, considering their feelings. Emphasize as many good, encouraging aspects of the child as you can, and state these first, if possible. If the child has a whole range of problems, try to concern the parents with only one, probably the basic difficulty, or the most urgent one, perhaps just touching briefly on some of the others. Show that you like and accept the child. Telling of some amusing thing the child said or did helps to break the ice and put the parent at ease.

Try to relieve the anxieties of the parents of the problem child. Explain that children are different. Children's readiness to learn varies just the way their heights and weights vary. These children can be as much as a year behind the developmental norms (according to Gesell) and still be normal, healthy children. Note the child's age, and if he is on the young side you can press *this* point. Tell them how some children are slow starting, but if given training in their weak areas, often catch up later. Tell them that some of our finest citizens were slow starters. They may cite family members as also being this way.

If there is a possible medical history of MCD, tell them that sometimes a difficult pregnancy, birth, or childhood disease seems to slow down a child's development and/or cause the perceptual problems. Then explain that if a child is not really seeing and hearing things clearly, he is then unable to learn. Go over the pertinent tests of the child which reflect his problem. "See, he looked at this diamond and then drew this distorted figure. He knows that his figure is not right, but he is unable to fix it. Since he distorts these simple shapes, how can we expect him to be able to read and write those twenty-six confusing squiggles we call letters, let alone put those together to make words? So we have to help him to discriminate and make simple shapes and then teach him each letter very thoroughly before he will be ready to learn to read." Explain your training program, especially your most immediate areas of emphasis.

Be cautious of terms used with parents. I have never felt that a parent would accept the term "brain damaged." This has terrible implications to them. It is too permanent, too hopeless, futile! Besides, you have no right to impose a medical diagnosis. If the child is nervous, parents might accept the possibility that he "could have a nervous condition." Thus, if you must use a term, you might call it "neurologically handicapped." It might help to explain that intelligence is learned and not all inherited; that some educable mental retardates read very well and some people with IQ's of 140 can't read at all. If you can draw a true or mythical picture of a doctor or college professor's child with learning problems, it seems to relieve the parent of defending his own IQ. If the child's main problem is attention, often you can say that the child is very intelligent verbally, has good understanding of other things, but just can't "attend" long enough to concentrate on reading. If the case is severe, suggest a medical evaluation.

The parent who won't accept the fact that his child is immature or lacks the basic skills and attention for reading is a problem. This may be a defensive mechanism, or perhaps the parent may not have had the opportunity to compare his child with a mature child. If the latter is true, you might show him some writing, etc. of children who are extremely mature, and tell of these children's other related abilities. Tell how they can sit and listen quietly, and then go to work all by themselves, or whatever behaviorisms would be a decided contrast to the parent's child. Never let the parent see the name on the paper of another child. Never compare children whom the parent knows. Also, encourage the parent to visit the class, particularly during the child's most difficult task. She will then make her own comparisons.

Having specific details of tests and papers in the problem areas is most important. For example, tell the parents the number of letters and numerals the child can name. Explain how, if the child can't recognize the letters and name them, he can't be expected to remember words and name them when they are made up of a composite of those same letters. This gives them something specific that the child needs and that they can help remediate. If the child's attention is poor, endeavoring to teach him themselves, they quickly come to understand your problem in the classroom.

On the other hand, if the parent is really convinced that the child is retarded, offer a wait-and-see attitude. Ask him to see what can be discovered, what can be taught first. Take adequate notes on this child, and as you find a possibility of potential tell the parents. They will be grateful. Concerned parents appreciate a phone call when the child has improved, has had a good day, or made some change for the first time. Don't let your phone calls home be ONLY when you're having problems with the child.

Encourage parents to visit, to ask questions whenever they wish. Offer a conference with the principal if this would help. Ask them to call you when they have a question or are anxious about the child for some reason. These children carry some amazing stories home. You might like to make an agreement with the parent that you won't take as gospel truth every word the child says in school if they'll do likewise, and to please call if they have a question.

Always conclude the conference with a positive line of action for both of you. Let the parent know on which things you will concentrate at school. Give her at least something she can do at home. This could be the eye or medical checkup, an earlier bedtime, a more stable home schedule, small responsibilities for the child, a quiet story time at bedtime, toy suggestions, or fine motor activities to aid his training. I have made different lists of some simple body image and directionality activities, and language, sequence, and memory games for parents. I give them perhaps one or two of these on which to concentrate. Of course, I wouldn't give something like this to *all* the parents. Some children are better off if the nervous, demanding parents just leave them alone.

The Ilg and Ames book, "Child Behavior" (60 cents for paperback), has an excellent chapter for parents on school readiness. (Ilg, 1960) For those who won't buy books, I lend my copy. For the interested parent of the MCD child, I recommend Radler and Kephart's *Success Through Play* (Radler, 1960).

REPORT CARDS

Report cards are an abomination, a carry-over from the Dark Ages! But at the present time, we're usually stuck with them! A conference is much better if you have your choice. Rarely do the columns on the report card relate to the problem learner. If you mark all the items according to protocol, the child is a failure and a monster, and you immediately have the parents on your back. The child is upbraided and upset by all the commotion and nothing has been gained. In fact, all might be lost!

The best we can do with the report card (if we are stuck with one) is to write in words which will change the phrasing, the negative aspect. For example, where it says *Reading,* try writing in *Readiness.* Or, if the card asks if he is reading, write in *Beginning.* Cross out irrelevant items like *Spelling* and *Creative Writing.* For the child with impulsive uncontrolled behavior, or the child who is doing his very best in an area, write no grade or mark only the word *tries* or *improving.* Make the card as encouraging as possible.

Sometimes it is necessary to bend the truth a bit. When Timmy's parents already reject him, it will do the child no good to go home with a poor report card. Some children are spanked for poor grades, or otherwise punished. However, it is helpful to the next year's teacher if you make accurate pertinent comments on the report tissue copy which goes into his cumulative record.

If a card is just impossible to write out, no matter how you cross out and write in, try writing across whole columns *Not Ready,* or *Not Yet,* and *See Comments.* Then in the *Teacher's Comments* space, state that the card is very difficult to fill out for Johnny, and "I would rather see you personally instead. Could you call me as to when it would be convenient for you?" Remember at all times with a report card, that its effect on Johnny is the most important factor to consider, not the inviolability of the instrument. It is better to go before an administrator for mutilating a report card than before God for knowingly damaging a child.

REFERENCES

Beery, Keith E., and Buktenica, Norman: *Developmental Test of Visual-Motor Integration.* Chicago, Follett, 1967.

Bender, Laurette: *A Visual Motor Gestalt Test And Its Clinical Use.* New York, American Ortho-Psychiatric Association, 1938, 1967.

Chambers, Arta Jo: Prescriptive Teaching Framework for Educating the Educationally Handicapped. "Digit Span." Santa Clara, California, Santa Clara County Office of Education, 1967.

deHirsch, Katrina, *et al.: Predicting Reading Failure.* New York, Harper & Row, N. Y., 1966.

Engelmann, Siegfried: *The Basic Concept Inventory,* Chicago, Follett, 1967.

Frostig, Marianne: *Developmental Test of Visual Perception.* Palo Alto, California, Consulting Psychologist's Press, 1963.

Goodenough, Florence L.: *Measurement of Intelligence by Drawings.* Yonkers, New York, World Book, 1954.

Ilg, Frances L., and Ames, Louise Bates: *The Gesell Institute's Child Behavior.* New York, Dell, 1960.

Jastak, J. F., *et al.: Wide Range Achievement Test Manual.* Wilmington, Guidance Associates, 1965.

Jordan, F. L., and Massey, James: *School Readiness Survey.* Palo Alto, California, Consulting Psychologist's Press, 1967.

Kirk, Samuel A., and McCarthy, James P.: *Illinois Test for Psycholinguistic Abilities,* Urbana, U of Ill Pr, 1961.

Koppitz, Elizabeth M.: *The Bender Gestalt Test for Young Children.* New York, Grune & Stratton, 1968.

Menninger, Karl: *The Vital Balance.* New York, Viking Pr, 1963.

Peabody Picture Vocabulary Test. Nashville, Tennessee, PPVT, American Guidance Service, 1959.

Radler, D. H., and Kephart, Newell C.: *Success Through Play.* New York, Harper & Row, 1960.

Roach, Eugene G., and Kephart, Newell C.: *Purdue Perceptual-Motor Survey.* Columbus, Ohio, Merrill, 1966.

Spencer, E. M.: Memory for Sentences. Ph.D. Thesis, Northwestern University, 1958, and MacGrady, Ph.D. Thesis, Northwestern University, 1964.

Stanford Binet Intelligence Scale Combined L-M Form. New York, Psychological Corp.

Stein, Jess: *The Random House Dictionary of the English Language.* New York, Random House, 1966.

Sutfin, Florence E.: *A Perceptual Testing and Training Handbook for First Grade Teachers.* Florida, Winter Haven Lions Club, 1964.

Valett, Robert: *A Psychoeducational Survey of Basic Learning Abilities.* Palo Alto, California, Consulting Psychologist's Press, 1966.

Wechsler, D.: *Wechsler Intelligence Scale for Children.* New York, Psychological Corp., 1949.

Wepman, Joseph M.: *Wepman Test of Auditory Discrimination*. Chicago, Research Associates, 1958.

Winter Haven Lions Publications Committee: *Perceptual Forms Teacher's Test Manual*. Winter Haven, Florida, Starr Press, 1963.

Chapter Five

Sensorimotor Development and First Discriminations

OVERVIEW

BEFORE WE CAN UNDERSTAND how to help these problem learners, we must know how to interpret their behaviors to determine their deficits. We must be able to diagnose their disabilities as specifically as possible. To do this we must have knowledge of the normal sensorimotor development of the child.

To understand child development thoroughly and the hazards the child might encounter through lack of maturation of environmental deprivation or neurological dysfunction, we must try to look at as much of the research, the psychological and medical groundwork as possible. We must try to meld all this conglomerate of carefully tested and researched work into some kind of outline or pattern to enlighten the whole global problem. We draw from the work of psychologists, psychiatrists, physicians, optometrists, occupational, physical, speech and aural therapists, and educators. All have much to offer toward the enlightenment imperative to this subject. In fact, the only way we can make real progress in this field is for all the professions to work together as a team, respecting the ideas, the work, the opinions, the hypotheses of all.

We cannot chop the child into segments such as physical, emotional, social, and intellectual (as education has done for centuries) and expect to be able to cure the child by treating a single phase of him separately. For years now the teacher has looked at the child and said that he can't read. That he is lazy. That he doesn't try. That he could read if he would just TRY. The doctor said that he is allergic to food, his EEG is normal, and there is no physical reason for his not learning to read. The teacher and parents just aren't firm enough. The psychologist said he's high in verbal ability and low in performance, but averages out in the normal range. Mother said that he's extremely bright. Father said the teacher just hasn't taught him. (And he was right! But she tried!) The speech therapist said he has an articulation problem. The optometrist said it's his ocular motility. The Little League team said that he's clumsy. The neighbors said that he's a spoiled brat and they won't allow him in their homes. The psychiatrist said that mother doesn't love him, or is overprotective. We as educational therapists must be able to put all of these symptoms, opinions, and comments together to form a total picture of the whole child (back to Dewey in a more thorough way). We must be able to see *through* the above comments and observations to understand the true symptoms and the causes of the child's disability.

To do this, let's look to the work of a whole spectrum of internationally known authorities in the various disciplines within the field of learning disabilities. We find some difference in terminology in their work or in the manner of expressing their hypothesis. But we also note an overall general agreement as to the developmental sequence of the child, its significance to learning disabilities and its revelations as to certain causes of specific difficulties, and the essential steps or methods toward remediation of the child's problems. I hereby attempt to compose a synthesis, or integration, of some of the work of A. Jean Ayres, Ray Barsch, Marianne Frostig, Newell Kephart, Jean Piaget, Strauss and Lehtinen, deHirsch, and others. I have tried to simplify explanations of their concepts to make them clearer to the teacher and more readily applicable to the children in our classrooms. As A. Jean Ayres says of the area of perception:

> We have to oversimplify concepts in order to grasp them and gain some kind of perspective of the whole. Be prepared to both change your ideas of perception in the future and also to make them more complex. (Ayres, 1964, p. 4)

Hopefully this composite picture will give us an understanding of the basis for the problems of our children and the methods which we must utilize to teach them. As observative teachers we have learned probably more intuitively and from basic understanding and empathy for the problem child, just how to proceed with at least *some* methods to help him. Many times we just never knew exactly *why* a certain technique or method was successful. As we learn more about sensorimotor development we will have better insight into the child's problems and thus know what training methods to employ to help him.

BEGINNING SENSORY PERCEPTIONS OF INFANCY
Random Motor Movements

The newborn infant lies with limbs flexed close to his body. When he is hungry or uncomfortable in any way, he draws his limbs in even more, with sharp spastic movements, thrashes his limbs about with no controlled or planned action. His hands might hit something but this is not deliberate. Kephart calls this random movement (Kephart, 1968). There is no separate finger action or action on one side of the body independent of the other. Both sides often move simultaneously, though not especially in unison. A nipple is placed near his lips, or the discomfort is otherwise removed, and the thrashing-around calms. The nipple initiates the sucking reflex which is essential to the survival of the infant. The first motor responses are all reflexive, the sucking and the touch reflexes.

As the infant develops he begins to notice that his needs are met by (1) the nipple and (2) by a mass of darkness and light which forms in his developing visual field. He learns to cease or decrease his crying when that globular mass appears, anticipating that it will alleviate his discomfort. This original perceptive mass has no parts, no identifying characteristics. As he nurses, his eyes stare out trying to perceive some identity to this globular undifferentiated mass in front of him. How many mothers have instinctively said "Hello!" to this tiny bundle, feeling the urge to communicate with him! And as his tiny hands patted her body, she received it as an endearment of *her*. Actually though, his first touching is merely random movement, a reflex again, uncontrolled, not planned by him.

First Sensory Differentiations or Perceptions

At first any mass of darkness that appears will lessen the child's wails, even the family dog. But if the bottle does not subsequently appear, the wail begins anew. It isn't long before the child learns that certain identifying sensations must emit from that mass for it to be his particular need-supplying mass. The sensation might be a tone of voice that could come from Mother, Father, or Grandmother, but not from Bowser. If one of the family is particularly adept at supplying his needs, then that one voice is further identified as being the one that will meet his needs (first auditory discrimination). He might come to differentiate between the feel of his mother's soft dress as opposed to his father's scratchy suit (tactile discrimination). Or the greater vibration from the floor due to father's walking (kinesthetic discrimination) might alert him. He might begin to notice a difference in the size or the shape of his rescuer (visual discrimination). Or perhaps he discerns a different odor, perfume on Mother, cigarette smoke on Daddy (olfactory discrimination).

Integration of Senses

As the child develops and his vision improves he begins making comparisons. The color and size of the mass might now better differentiate it. Then as he brings in many different perceptions which aid his discrimination—sound, smell, touch, colors, sizes, vibrations, etc.—he is able to get a more composite picture and totals it into a whole perception of Mother. This is an integrated perception. It includes emotional feelings about Mother. He can now see objects in their entirety, with all their parts, all their relationships, a total concept. Now that he has this total integrated perception, he only need to look at an object to identify and comprehend all its meanings. With this ultimate, highly differentiated perception (visual perception) he now perceives in an instant that which he had to process through many senses heretofore in order to perceive. Now that he has this visual perception, he has instant recognition of Mother. He merely notes the color and appearance of the substance in his bottle, and if it is a clear liquid or some other undesirable substitute, lets out a yell without ever having to taste it first. Visual perception has, in this specific perceptual task, eliminated the need for all the previous tactile and gustatory explorations. However, whenever he meets a new object for the first time, he must go through all the sensory explorations with it.

Mother picks up the baby and he snuggles against her shoulder instantly. But you, a stranger, pick him up and he will feel and taste your clothes, your jewelry, your body, his eyes searching you endlessly. You can just *feel* his attempt to integrate his findings and perceive the total *you*. In fact, his sum integration and opinion of you might not measure up and he will reject you for his familiar mother.

Give the child an old toy and he immediately perceives it and begins to use it intelligently. Give him a *new* toy and he must first explore its every aspect before he can begin to play with it.

Purposeful Motor Movements

As the infant lies contentedly sucking in his mother's arms his little fists inadvertently strike an object. He eventually realizes that he derives some sensation from that object. So now he purposefully strikes it again and again, arousing more tactile receptors. At first it is the little fists that are often pressed tightly against either side of the object. Finally, he touches that object (probably unintentionally at first) with his palm or his fingertips, and finds that more sensation is derived in this manner than with his fist and knuckles. Also, he now has the motor control which allows him to open and close his fist at will. So now it is more and more often that it is his fingers with which he reaches out purposefully.

He learns to control his arm and finger movements little by little and to plan them. His visual-motor control and space perception improve so that he reaches out more directly toward the object. This, too, is a planned purposeful movement (Kephart, 1968). The first sense used by the child for purposeful action is tactile. Many random and purposeful touches may identify the object as his bottle. But he does not truly understand the concept of *bottle* until he is able to explore its every aspect and integrate his findings.

Functional Movements

Now that the child has learned to control his limbs and has the visual-motor control to reach out purposefully and touch a chosen object, he goes about feeling an object in order to identify it. He brings all his senses into play to really learn about that object. You've seen a child sitting on the floor carefully inspecting his teddy. He pushes at its eyes, tastes its ear, shakes it, rubs its fur, while his eyes also work to note color, size, etc. There are also social concepts. Mother lets him have teddy at will, but not her necklace. All of this total sensory effort procures for him a total concept of *teddy bear*. Add the language of Mother saying its name and his repeating it, and now he has really learned *teddy bear*. He understands the concept of *teddy bear*. He perceives *teddy bear*. It required cognitive evaluation, integration and feedback of information. Inspecting the teddy bear then was a functional movement (Kephart, 1968). This learning made permanent structural alterations in the central nervous system. He will never forget it entirely unless he suffers damage to his central nervous system. We shall discuss this factor further later.

PIAGET'S DEVELOPMENT OF PERCEPTION AND OF SPATIAL CONCEPTS
Practical Space

Jean Piaget, of the University of Geneva, is world renowned for his research in psychology. It is his work, probably more than any other one single man's, that has shown us the importance of early sensorimotor development and has opened the door to understanding how the child first perceives form and space and develops his cognitive world. He uses the term practical space (Piaget, 1937; Barsch, 1967) to designate the period between birth and two years when the child's space world is simply *there*. Objects are not related. There is one touch of the bottle, one taste of the milk, but not deliberate investigation of the bottle and milk. The bottle relieves his hunger pangs; the milk tastes good. But not, "The milk is *in* this bottle." The child touches, sees, smells, etc. in an accidental, meaningless manner. Or he touches the blanket one minute and the satin binding the next without comprehending their relationship. He does not comprehend forms and sizes; there is no concept formation, no meaningful exploration. During this period, the child relates things only to himself. This period corresponds to Kephart's period of *random movement*.

Empirical Space

The next stage is *empirical space* (Piaget, 1937; Barsch, 1967) (2½ to 3½ years) wherein the child reaches for objects without visual control. It is a trial-and-error stage of perceptual development, wherein he is simply experimenting by trying one thing after another. He may thus solve a problem (e.g. "What shape fits into this hole?") but still not really understand or perceive the different size or shape of the object or space. He still relates things only to himself. He has no real plan of action to solve a problem and does not carry over learnings from one task to another. He is aware of only that which is in view. Thus it is exploration without cognitive feedback, control, or permanent learning. This explains to us how children can live and see and hear without learning. They are still living in empirical space. This would apply to the children with perceptual problems due to MCD, or environmental deprivation, or immaturity. Their movements are not meaningful. They are not learning from their activities. They are reacting to individual stimuli and are not learning relationships between objects.

Objective Space

The final stage is termed *objective space* (Piaget, 1937; Barsch, 1967) (about three to five years of age). The child can now systematically solve problems in form, size, and space. His behavior now depends on the object and his cognition of it, rather than its relation to him. Now he understands the relationships between objects and their properties. He notes their likenesses and differences and can generalize. He knows sizes, shapes, colors, distances, directions, positions, and their social connotations. The stove is not only big and white, but it has dials that turn it off and on, and when it is on, it is hot and it will cook his food or burn his hand if he touches it.

The child can be in all three stages during one exploration of one object. He might accidentally back into one side of the refrigerator, note that it felt hot, turn to touch it with his hand, then systematically explore it to see which sides are hot, question his parents about it, until he understands how and why certain parts of a refrigerator are hot. Thus he may never be (except in infancy) completely in one stage of perceptual and spatial development.

Each time he enters a new spatial environment, a new building, room, etc., or sees a new form or object, he may go through all three stages of spatial orientation. He will usually orient himself to the new *space* before he will to people. Thus a child entering your living room for the first time pays little attention to you, but is usually most fascinated by the room. He may move slowly around the room, methodically exploring every aspect of it before he ever turns to you. Then he carefully inspects your dress, jewelry, shoes, voice before he can relax and attend to your questions. If his social training of *don't touch* or his maturity inhibit him, then his eyes will carefully, sometimes guardedly, do the exploring. But do it he will. Even as an adult you inspect every new room you enter before you can really relax there.

FIGURE-GROUND PERCEPTION
A Description

To be able to make any of these first basic sensory perceptions, to be able to discriminate visually, auditorily, tactually, the child must be able to screen out the figure from the ground. For example, in order to be able to discriminate the difference between Mother's and Father's footsteps, he must be able to screen out all other sounds—the dog barking, cars outside, trains going by—and other stimulations—the swaying of the bird cage, the blowing of the curtains, the bright wallpaper, discomfort of the wet diaper. He must concentrate only on those footsteps and thus receive a clear, sharp perception. Or a visual example might be that in order to perceive the beautiful blue pin Mother is wearing, he must be able to screen it out from that bright color of her blouse, and the fluffy ruffles. An auditory sound too could distract him from the visual figure of the pin, so that he never really zeros in on it.

He could also be distracted from the visual or auditory figure desired, by inner thoughts or feelings. Like Timmy who was recalling a fishing trip when he should have been adding two plus two. So you ask for the answer and he comes up with, "I caught a fish." In fact, trying to carry on a discussion of some set topic with these children uncovers startlingly irrelevant comments. Bobby would start to share his fishing trip with the class; however, other thoughts kept interfering so often that he never did get to the fish. "I went fishing. My daddy's car is broke. My bike has a flat tire. I saw Jerry at the store."

The first figure-ground learning is tactile (Kephart, 1968). The child's hand sweeps over an area, then perhaps as if one sensation is suddenly different, more desirable to the child, he zeros in on that one substance. Recall the infant who seeks to find the satin binding on the blanket rather than any other part of it. Or the way his hand is feeling the bumps of the letters on the bottle, or fingering teddy's eyes while he is looking at you and drinking his milk.

Thus a mass of information is coming to the child all the time. He does not live in a vacuum. This is the ground. Many sounds are present at all times in his environment, as are a multitude of visual and tactile stimuli. He must be able to sort out all these stimuli and concentrate on one single figure in order to make an accurate perception of the figure. If he is not able to do this, his perceptions by the different senses will be confused, inaccurate. The satin might not be perceived as relating to the blanket, or different at all from the rest of the blanket. The pin might appear round instead of long and pointed, or blue instead of green. The footsteps might be completely unfamiliar, even frightening.

Hypothesized Cause

The reticular formation of the brainstem contains the mechanisms for the sorting and channeling of the messages which are received by the senses (Adler, 1968). It is this reticular system which determines which messages are to be sent to the brain for storage or processing. Stimulation of this system enhances the ability to discriminate visual stimuli.

Nerve endings do not touch each other, but have a synaptic gap between them, which must be breached. A chemical crosses the synaptic gap triggering stimuli to pass. The level of resistance of the synapses in this reticular sorting center is sometimes very low, so that these synapses transmit too many sensory stimuli at a time.

A different chemical decreases the excitability of the synapses (Butter, 1969), and thus *inhibits* stimuli from passing. Without this inhibitory action stimuli spread too easily. Thus the child is bombarded by a multitude of stimuli and is unable to focus his attention on one *figure*.

Being unable to concentrate, he perceives things inaccurately. His discriminations suffer, as does his ability to learn. If he cannot attend and discriminate, he cannot learn.

Relationship of "Protective" System

There is a dual function of the reticular system (Ayres, 1964). One, as we have mentioned, is to sort the sensory stimuli and thus aid in discrimination and learning. The other is as a protective system, which warns the child of impending danger. This protective system predominates in infancy. As the child matures, as he makes more discriminations, the protective system is inhibited and the discriminative system is enhanced. It is believed that the switch in predominant systems probably comes about through the development of the higher cortical level, which is not fully complete until six years of age. Sometimes in the older MCD child, the protective system is still predominating and thus the discriminatory system is inhibited and cannot develop properly. He is not only unable to concentrate his attention on stimuli to discriminate them, but he is much too easily triggered into defensive actions. A child touches him and he swings into action and socks the startled innocent because he is sure that he was hit on purpose and must defend himself. You reach for your pencil and he recoils as if you were going to hit him.

We also have children who are thus so oversensitive to sounds, temperatures (especially heat), sudden movements, touch, even visual stimuli that their immediate response to these stimuli is to protect themselves. You put your hand on Ray's shoulder and he immediately pushes it off or twists out of your reach or says, "You're hurting me!" A touch of a cool hand causes him to react as to a hot stove or a cut. Think of those children who strip off their wraps when others are complaining of the cold. Or the hyperactive noisy child who complains that the *others* are noisy, or a bell too loud, and covers his ears. Flashing of lights, psychedelic prints or stripes cause him to blink and cover his eyes.

Thus we have the hyperkinetic or hyperactive child who is unable to concentrate on one figure and is distracted by the multitude of stimuli around him. His synapses pass too many stimuli too easily, and the ground level is too high. He reacts with constant random movements in all directions. Then we have the hypokinetic or hypoactive child for whom the level of the figure is too low (Kephart, 1968), so that it must be stimulated and emphasized for him to perceive it. The hypoactive child is very slow moving, appears dreamy, "in a fog." He never laughs too hard or works too hard or is more than vaguely interested in stimuli around him. The world passes him by. He cannot find the figure in the first place.

Neurons

While we are discussing the central nervous system, some of the aspects of the neuron, the cell of the nervous system, are important in understanding how we learn. Our knowledge of neurons is spotty and imcomplete, but results of some recent studies throw some flashes of light in that direction.

Man has ten billion neurons, but even the most highly gifted performer, such as Einstein, uses only one small fraction of that number (Adler, 1968). Neurons do not regenerate as do other cells of the body. If you have a cut, new skin and muscle cells regenerate to reproduce their own kind and regrow those tissues. If a neuron is damaged, it is permanently inoperative, it will not reproduce itself.

When the brain lacks oxygen for even a very short period of

time, neurons are damaged. Therefore, if there is lack of oxygen for just a few minutes, so much damage is done that the organism is reduced to a vegetable state, unable to care for its own functions. You probably know victims of strokes who lost use of certain limbs, or lost skills such as talking or reading.

When neurons are damaged, other neurons in adjacent areas may be trained to take over the function of the damaged neuron. This requires immediate retraining on a systematic program of multiple repetition. Thus a person whose neurons controlling his right hand have been damaged by a stroke, may retrain his hand muscles to operate by activating other neurons. If the limb is not stimulated to action quite soon, further damage is done and retraining is not then possible. Most doctors today begin therapy in stroke patients even before they leave the hospital. Knowledge gleaned from work with these patients has been of great value in the field of learning disabilities.

If a synapse has not received much use, its resistance to impulses could be quite high. Yet with training, it has been revealed with the electron microscope that small knobs or *boutons* (Hebb, 1949; Kephart, 1960 and 1968) form on the nerve endings (Fig. 12), causing them to be in closer proximity with others. Thus there is a shorter *synaptic gap* for the stimuli to pass much more easily. The more training, the greater the size of the knob. If training stops and the synapse then comes into disuse, the knob may decrease somewhat in size, but never disappear altogether. Thus training and subsequent learning increases the size of the knobs, lowers the resistance of the synapse, and makes a permanent change in the structure of the nervous system (Kephart, 1960 and 1968). For example, as a child you practiced for hours and years to learn to play the piano. Then you left home and could not afford to buy a piano of your own. Several years later you sat down to a piano for the first time and found that although you thought you had forgotten, it all started to come back to you. Your fingers were stiff and clumsy, but you could still read the notes. With practice again, you could play as well as before.

In a study of learning in rats, it was found that training had

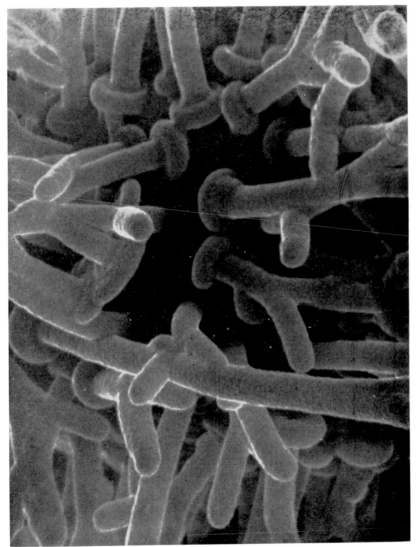

Figure 12. Photomicrograph of Synaptic Knobs.

increased both the size and the weight of the brain (Krech, 1970).
On examination it was found that this increase was due not only
to the growth of the knobs but also to the growth of new endings
on the nerves (Knutsen, 1969). Then as these reach out seeking

new connections there are many more new opportunities to learn. Thus the possibilities for training children (with or without MCD) to increase their abilities are endless.

In an exhibit at Montreal's Expo '67 we read:

> Neurons don't grow to maturity automatically. Deprived of stimulation they can fail to grow, or even die. Constant dark or complete silence has the same effect on a child as blindness or deafness. A variety of stimulation causes neurons to connect in greater variety with one another. Information can then travel by other than reflex pathways.
>
> Learning begins. The connections made between events in his environment and connections between neurons correspond. Often it is the parent who helps him make the connections in his environment. It is the parent, then, who teaches the child to perceive. (Montreal Expo, 1967)

It appears to some physicians that the tactile and digestive effectors are of those neurons first damaged by a brief period of lack of oxygen. Thus in the case histories of children with learning problems we find a larger number of infant feeding problems, allergies, colic, stomach ulcers, and migraine headaches, along with problems in tactile discrimination and form perception.

Transmission of impulses from one neuron to another over the synaptic cleft or gap is electrical-chemical as is the action of the inhibitory stimuli (Butter, 1969). Thus many of our answers to behavior problems may be in the realm of body chemistry and metabolism. Biochemists are seeking and finding organic basis for some disabilities. There was the PKU breakthrough a few years ago. Under study is a chemical treatment to prevent mongoloid traits from developing, and the discovery of an intercellular change in the blood cells of autistic children (Rimland, 1969). Hoffer and Osmond (Hoffer, 1966) have been using niacin and ascorbic acid primarily on schizophrenics with excellent results. At Oxford, England, (Hoffer, 1966) there was a successful study using vitamin B_6 (pyridoxine) on autistic children. Drs. Elizabeth Rees and Brent Campbell have been working with food intolerances. They have found children who are so allergic to certain foods that this appears to cause overt behaviors. Eliminate the guilty food and these children become happy, less hyperactive, more controlled, and even better coordinated (Rees, 1970; Campbell, 1970).

So what does all of this mean to our children with learning problems? Some of them may have suffered some subtle damage to the nervous system and thus need retraining to stimulate new neurons to take over the work of those that were damaged. Then we have our environmentally deprived children who have lacked the stimulation and the training which children of more concerned parents receive. We have to stimulate their thought processes as they should have been several years ago. First grade is not too late for these children, although nursery school or even earlier would have been better. As we have described, sensorimotor development started at birth. The period of greatest language development is from two to four years, and of perceptual development, four to seven and one-half years (Frostig, 1964 and 1967). First grade, therefore, is the child's main and perhaps only chance to use this tremendous learning period to his advantage and help him to catch up in development. To retrain these children we must begin at their developmental levels, use multiple repetition, and multisensory stimulation. Since they are already perhaps a year behind in development, we must use direct teaching methods to give them two years training in one in order for them to catch up with their classmates.

The Brain

As our knowledge of the neurons is limited, so is our knowledge of that complex of neurons, the brain. We know that various stimuli go to different parts of the brain, and that in order for learning to take place, there has to be an integration of information. This is extremely complex. The corpus callosum is the isthmus of nerve tissue that connects the hemispheres and provides the integration.

Each hemisphere of the brain receives input from the opposite side of the body, along with some input from the same side of the body. This latter is thought to be crude, not really sufficient for giving direction (Gazzaniga, 1967). Centers for certain processes or learning may be in one hemisphere only. In the child up to about the age of four, it appears that the right hemisphere is quite proficient in handling language. However, the language center for the adult is in the left hemisphere. The stroke patient with damage in the left hemisphere often has impaired speech.

In studies of epileptics who have had the corpus callosum severed to control seizures, some interesting findings have been made (Gazzaniga, 1967). Motor movements were preferred on the right side of the body, while the left side did not respond to stimulation. The patient might not know that he brushed against something with his left side, or know that he was holding something with his left hand. The examiners tried flashing words, lights, and pictures to the *left* side while the patient fixed his gaze on a central focal point. He might deny having seen anything or be unable to identify the subject or describe it. But when asked to pick up an object from behind a screen (the name of which had been flashed), he was able to do so. He might even see the humor in something that was seen, and laugh, yet be unable to tell why he laughed. Thus the patient could read and understand, but not verbalize what he had read.

When asked to arrange cubes in a design or to draw a cube, the left hand, with poorer coordination, could do it. The right could not. Though motor and language functions seem to be centered in the left hemisphere, the right hemisphere does perceive spatial concepts.

In a study in Milano, Italy, (Faglioni, 1969) it was found that "lesions to the right hemisphere are more disruptive on perceptual tasks."

In studies of the split brain of the cat it was found that one hemisphere could be taught entirely separate from the other, and that there was then no carry-over of information to the other hemisphere. The latter had to be independently trained.

It is felt that the callosum does not just transfer learning and memory from one hemisphere to the other, but that "a copy of the visual world as seen in one hemisphere is sent over to the other, with the result that both hemispheres can learn together a discrimination presented to just one hemisphere." (Gazzaniga, 1967, p. 7)

Another clue from the structure of the brain—the motor area and the sensory area of the brain parallel each other (Frostig, 1964; Kephart, 1968). The centers for the various parts of the body are adjacent, so that the motor area controlling the legs, for example, is adjacent to the sensory area receiving stimuli from the legs. Yet the motor area of the brain can be stimulated without activating the sensory area. Thus a child may move his legs without sensory feedback of the results of that movement and in this manner have physical movement without learning, or without accurate learning. The child moves, but does not learn from his movement.

Since there is yet so much to learn about the human brain, the findings are not conclusive enough to point directly to specific methods for teaching children with possible MCD. However, it would seem that we should use every opportunity to tie perceptual data together with receptive and expressive language to help the child to integrate his learnings. Thus as a child attempts to discriminate cylinders and place them into their respective holes, he should be asked to feel the shape (possibly with both hands) and then describe it and its relationships to the other shapes. Thus the learning can be better integrated. Sensorimotor training movements should be done with each side of the body, as in tracing templates, letters, and numerals, using one hand and then the other might facilitate more learning.

PROVIDING FOR THE CHILD WITH FIGURE-GROUND PROBLEMS
Identifying Children with Figure-Ground Problems

The school child who has figure-ground problems will be inattentive, easily distractable, often hyperactive, impulsive, and aggressive toward his peers. He is probably your worst behavior problem. He can't get from the door to his seat without touching, hitting, often damaging everything in his path. In sixty seconds Mike stomped on a foot, tore a paper, crayoned a desk, and stuck his tongue out at a peer. At storytime on the floor he would rock, spin around, kick children in the back, pull hair, and be upside down as often as not. At recess time he would throw sand wildly, and roll in the dirt.

Punishment does not seem to help these children at all. One day Mike put two scratches on a child's face, for which he was spanked by the principal. The next day another child arrived in tears with *four* scratch welts across the cheek which Mike had inflicted.

Then there is the quiet, distractable child who daydreams, chews on his collar, nervously taps his foot, or endlessly plays with his shoelaces. You are able to focus his attention only temporarily, and then he is off again, deep in his own thoughts.

These children are often very bright verbally. They have much to offer in class discussions and have good expressive ability. They fail when it comes to seatwork because they cannot concentrate on the task. They fail in reading for lack of attention to the instruction, for inability to keep their eyes on the words long enough to make an adequate impression, and because the reading task requires such complex discriminations. They often are unable to locate the word on the page in the mass of other words. Their eyes flit from the correct line of print even while they are reading, and they lose their place. Their discrimination of the letters may be inadequate, so that when the letters are combined to form words, they may clue in on only one or two letters of the word. Thus you will note wild substitutions, wherein every word containing an *S* becomes the most vividly remembered word, *see*.

This child may learn words printed in one form but not in another. He may read the words printed large with flow pen, but the small print in books may be too much for him. Or he may compensate for his inability to read the words, and in his impatience may memorize whole books of pre-primer stories. Or he partially memorizes and the accommodating teacher inadvertently supplies him with all the missing words. One little Mike "read" three pre-primers with errors only on a half dozen words. When the flash words for the same books were presented to him, he couldn't even read the names of the characters.

The child with figure-ground problems is often very disorganized. His desk is a rat's nest! He can't find a thing. Timmy screamed for scissors and when we searched through the piles of unfinished papers in his desk we found five pair.

Some of these distractable children compensate for their inability to find things in clutter by being extremely conscious of organization. Then everything in their desks or drawers must be exactly in a certain place or they become upset. They become meticulous for order and details and thus lose attention of the whole or final task. This child works very hard but fails to complete work because he spent so much time preparing for the task or on the first details. He is also insecure and so perseverates as a way of clinging to the known. In writing, the first words or letters must be retraced over and over.

Possibilities of Medication

A considerable amount of medical research has been in the field of medication for the hyperactive, distractable child. Generally, the tranquilizers don't work at all, and the old standby, phenobarb, makes the child less controlled (Adler, 1968). The most effective drugs have been those in the stimulant group, the amphetamines. Even a rather large dosage is used successfully with little danger of aftereffects. These stimulants are thought to increase the synaptic resistance of the neurons in the reticular formation, so that fewer irrelevant stimuli pass and the child is able to attend for longer periods (Adler, 1968). These medications help the aggressive hyperactive child and the quietly distractable child to attend. Some doctors use these stimulants in combination with other drugs for added effects, such as giving confidence or controling bed-wetting. Some of these latter drugs do have adverse aftereffects, however. Dr. Sidney J. Adler, a noted pediatrician, Clinical Professor of Pediatrics, California College of Medicine, University of California at Irvine, has participated in a double-blind study of the effect of drugs on children with learning problems. He found about eighty-five percent positive results in reducing hyperactivity with the use of one drug.

At Northwestern University Medical School, Chicago, J. Gordon Millichap, M.D., and C. Keith Connors, Ph.D., have cooperated in very interesting studies of the effects of drug therapy on performance scores of children on various tests of sensorimotor ability, such as the Bender and the Frostig. Children were tested before medication, then at specified time periods. The doctors found dramatic improvement in performances in just a few weeks.

March 1969, in San Francisco, at a CANHC symposium, a panel of eight medical doctors and two Ph.D.'s pooled their findings on drug therapy for problem learners. Their work is now under publication.

Hyperactive little Mike, previously described, showed amazing improvement almost the first day of drug therapy. Where he had produced almost no work at all previously and rarely attended in class, he became extremely attentive, his eyes glued to the teacher's face during explanations, and was the very first to begin seatwork. Discipline problems also decreased and by the end of the year he was at the top of his class.

When a medication of any kind is being tried, the teacher's observations of the child are an important part of the drug therapy. The doctor may call for her opinion on the effects of the medications. From her comments he may decide to up the dosage, or try another drug or combination of drugs. The process of finding just the right medication for that particular child may take weeks or months.

Clues from Biochemistry

Megatonic doses of certain vitamins, especially ascorbic acid (vitamin C), niacinamide, pyridoxine (B_6), and pantothenic acid, have been used to improve behavior in problem children (Rimland, 1969) and to reduce allergic reactions. This therapy does not rely on any one vitamin, but a carefully computed combination of vitamins which appear to work together to bring about the desired results (Rimland, 1968). It might seem to be not just the absence of the vitamin in sufficient quantities in the body causing the overt symptoms, but perhaps the problems are due to a faulty metabolic process wherein certain foods and/or needed chemicals are not assimilated as they should be. Dr. Bernard Rimland, of the Institute for Child Behavior Research, San Diego, is now collecting data for a research project using megatonic doses of specified vitamins on children with a wide variety of behavioral disorders.

Dr. Allan Cott, of the New York Institute of Child Development, is researching the use of vitamins B_2, B_3, B_6, C, and E, along with high-protein diets on children with learning problems. The main effect of the treatments has been to reduce hyperactivity.

Dr. Elizabeth Rees, a pediatrician in Castro Valley, California, sees a correlation between children with learning problems, food intolerances, allergies, and asthma. She has been researching the stabilizing of the diet through elimination of the allergy-producing foods to reduce hyperactivity and behavior problems in children.

George Von Hilsheimer, of Green Valley School in Orange City, Florida, finds that a large percentage of children with learning and behavior problems have hypoglycemia (Von Hilsheimer, 1970). He finds that "even if the child does not suffer from hypoglycemia, his diet may create the same functional conditions and improperly fuel both brain and body." (Von Hilsheimer, 1970, p. 24) He also feels that most hyperactive and most disadvantaged children lack sufficient proteins and eat too many sweets and carbohydrates.

Salt has been found to cause hyperactivity in rats. Hyperactive children perspire freely and are perpetually thirsty. Some learning centers reduce salt intake and water consumption in hyperactive children.

It has been found (Hoffer and Osmond) that some patients who do not test as positive hypothyroid, benefit from the addition of thyroid. It may be that our present day tests need reevaluating, and new measures of body chemistry levels must be designed. Some biochemists feel that those minimum daily requirements of vitamins and minerals, as stated by the Federal Food and Drug Administration, are invalid; that each individual's daily requirement may be different. For example, Linus Pauling, University of California, and two-time Nobel Prize winner, feels that the FDA's minimum vitamin C intake is only enough to prevent scurvy, not enough to cut down allergies or help prevent histamines from forming. Vitamin C has an antihistamine affect in the body (Pauling, 1970). Roger Williams, University of Texas, found that there are individual variations in the amounts of calcium and amino acids required by different people. Some day perhaps we will have tests to measure the nutritional requirements of individuals and thus be able to prescribe the exact amounts of food supplements needed.

Planning the Environment

The room environment should be planned with distractable children in mind. Normal children are also more attentive with these precautions. Have blackboards kept thoroughly erased except for the item on which you desire the child's immediate attention. Bulletin boards should be sparse, simple, and instructive. Eliminate decorative boards from the front of the room, or even altogether. As you use them less you will realize they only impressed the parents and the administration, not the children. Children's work may be displayed in the rear of the room. Instructional boards should have only relevant material and simple lines. Avoid wallpaper or corregated paper backing and shadowed letters with one color behind another. Especially avoid the mobiles or moving ceiling decorations. Teachers often complain of the overexcitability of their class around Christmas time, but often cause much of it with excessive distracting art projects. When children make seasonal decorations (which are often good therapy and teach spatial concepts), have them take them home daily to decorate their own houses, not clutter the instructional classroom.

Screen out the outside as necessary by painting lower windows or pulling drapes part way. Use commercial pictures or magazine pictures for instructional purposes in a pocket chart or standing in the chalkrack only as needed, not as a bulletin board display. Keep open shelves neat, and counters as free from extra stimuli as possible. Use closed cupboards for games and puzzles. Have special boxes or trays for the papers the children are to hand in to you. Some animals are too distracting, too, and should be brought into the main classroom only during certain periods. Try quiet fish and plants, rather than noisy parakeets and squirrels in squeaky exercise wheels.

Watch your own dress. Do your heels click-click around the

room? How distracting are those long dangly earrings, or those jangly bracelets, or bold stripes or some psychedelic prints? Colors and prints should be happy and pleasing but not devastating.

Reduce noise as much as possible by using rug samples under Cuisenaire rods and puzzles, and a small rug in the block-building area. Wall-to-wall carpeting would be a tremendous help. Keep your own voice quiet and calm and help the children do the same. When their voices rise, try the device of lowering yours and regaining attention with a signal.

That extra-hyperactive child should be carefully placed in the classroom. When you are giving instructions or reading a story, put him directly in front of you. When he is to do individual seatwork, place him in the part of the room that has the fewest distractions, away from shelves, windows, and peers. Be sure his seat has been adjusted to fit him so that he is comfortable.

Structuring the Program

We need not only to plan the environment around the child but also to structure the program for the overactive child. This will mean short periods of sitting or concentrating interspersed with longer periods of moving about. Intensive training in physical education is imperative. The daily program should be quite static day after day to give the child security. Thus he knows that language is after recess and math is right after lunch. He then knows where to go and what is expected of him.

For seatwork a short paper or one paper well done is worth several papers partially complete. Avoid frustration by being sure to begin with easy work, increasing the complexity very gradually. The child should rarely be in competition with his peers. Compare his work only to his previous skill and not that of his peers.

Analyze a task before you present it so that you break it down to correct sequential steps in presenting it to the child. If the child still doesn't understand, *you* erred. Show him how to do it, even with your hand on his as necessary.

When you tell a story or do direct instruction, gather the children close around you on a rug. A 10′ x 10′ rug helps keep the children in close enough to you to keep their attention and gives the hyperactive child boundaries. He must stay *on* the rug.

Allow extra chances for the hyperactive child to move around. Send him on errands and let him help pass papers. Since these children have so many problems finding things and are often extremely messy let them keep as few things as possible in their desks. Extra pencils, paste jars, and scissors could be in communal boxes on shelves. This gives restless children an excuse to move around more to get their needed materials. Show them how to organize their desks. THE PENCILS SHOULD BE KEPT HERE AND ALL THE CRAYONS MUST BE IN THE BOX. Dismiss the children by clean desks for several days to get them in the habit. Children whose desks are not clean should again be shown step by step how to do it and not be dismissed until it is done. You may be the first one to have ever tried to teach him order, so don't be impatient with him. Thereafter check desks occasionally after school. Some morning reward with a treat all children whose desks were in order.

Have them take all papers home daily. Show them how to fold them together with two folds so that they won't lose any. SHOW ME YOUR FOLDED PAPERS SO I KNOW YOU ARE READY TO GO. Don't let them leave the room with papers slipping out from under their arms. This folding also eliminates the temptation to roll papers and make a noisy horn.

These children do not operate very well with free choice, or too many choices. They end up flitting from one thing to another and accomplish nothing. Even with an art project, if you show them too many possibilities they are lost and make nothing. Show them one way of making something first. If they want to make it again, then show them a variation. With an activity period, I prefer structuring it so that the same four children paint one day, do *dough* (mixture of flour, salt, oil, and water) the next, then puzzles the next, then chalkboard routines, then balancing activities. Thus the child's choices are limited and I have ready tabs on who should be doing what. I can be sure that every child participates in all developmental activities. I am also able to

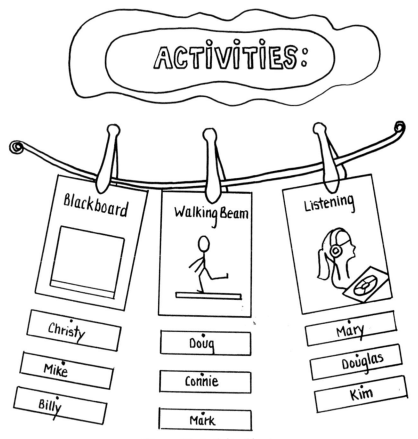

Figure 13. Activity Chart.

follow children through to see that they are responsible for the materials which they took out.

The device I use to keep track of this resembles a clothes line with cards which name and illustrate an activity, fastened thereon with clothespins (Fig. 13). The children's names are on 2″ x 6″ papers, and tacked under the cards on the clothes line. I group the children carefully, possibly two boys and two girls at each activity, spreading the real behavior problems out so that no two ever work together. This four would then work together all year, barring unforeseen changes. The activity cards on the clothesline move one space to the right each day. Thus five to seven activities change daily instead of the names of twenty-seven children.

Focusing Attention

Another possibility is to accentuate the stimulus to which you want the child to attend. Use felt figures to tell a story. Use colored chalk to differentiate things on the blackboard. For example, you might make the plus mark red. Use the board to draw illustrations rather than rely solely on verbal descriptions. Keep a file of large, pertinent pictures to illustrate concepts.

Use audiovisual aids to focus attention on the task. Sometimes the overhead projector is more effective for writing experience stories, illustrating a discussion, or demonstrating math, than the blackboard. Use the opaque projector to put reading material on the screen or to show pictures.

Record a story on tape. Then have children use earphones and the "Listening Post" (set of earphones) attached to the tape recorder. They follow the story in individual books while they listen to the tape. The earphones shut out the other classroom sounds. Also, use this tape recorder-listening post setup to instruct small groups of children as they do dittos or workbook pages. Use long-play records with the listening post for children to listen to stories or language records.

Teaching Relaxation

Teach the children to relax. They are often tense, afraid to close their eyes. Use tension-relaxation exercises: MAKE YOURSELF AS STIFF AS A STATUE! TIGHTER! TIGHTER! NOW START TO LET GO. FIRST YOUR HEAD GETS ALL LOOSE, THEN YOUR SHOULDERS, THEN YOUR ARMS, THEN YOUR BODY, THEN YOUR LEGS. AND NOW YOU'RE ALL LOOSE AND FLOPPY. They can be *popsicles* and then *melt*. Show them how to flop at their desks, letting arms hang down loose. We will discuss more of these techniques later with other exercises. The Getman Gross Coordination exercises from *Physiology of Readiness* (Getman, 1964) are especially good to teach the child to concentrate, to control his body, and to relax.

Use listening exercises such as listening for far-off sounds, or to identify what object is in the bag, or what object I drop, or *how* Jerry is moving across the room.

Grace Peticlerc has excellent suggestions on teaching concentration (Peticlerc, 1965, 1966, and 1968).

Ruth Brace (Brace, 1965) has many suggestions for teaching relaxation, plus a collection of quiet, pictorial poems, listening records, and stories.

Modifying Behavior of the Hyperactive

The hyperactive, distractable child requires a very positive approach in order to bring about changes in his behavior. Most important of all, his teacher must fully understand and accept the fact that *he* is unable to control his behavior. That his actions are not deliberate, not premeditated. Don't take his insults personally. He is lashing out at his confusing world, not you alone.

Punishment only salves your ego. It does not help to control the child. In fact, it may make him only resent you. He does not understand cause and effect. He does not believe that he did anything wrong. Therefore, when you punish him, only *you* are wrong. You are the one who is *bad* in his eye.

Train yourself to look for times when he is behaving, for the things he does well. At first this may be only the moments he is sitting in his seat, the one letter or word he writes well, the one polite word he says, the time he picks up one crayon or puts a puzzle away.

Try to ignore his misbehaviors as much as possible. This may take nerves of steel. Instead of telling him to *sit down,* praise the children who are seated: ALICE AND TOMMY KNOW WHAT TO DO! THEY GO RIGHT TO THEIR SEATS WHEN THEY COME IN. THIS WHOLE ROW IS READY TO LISTEN! WOW! LOOK AT THAT! JERRY SAW A PAPER ON THE FLOOR THAT WASN'T HIS AND HE PICKED IT UP. YOU'RE SUCH A GOOD HELPER, JERRY! When you do this, five hyperactive irresponsible children will hurry to follow suit. It works miracles! Be very sure, though, that you *do* notice when the erring child does something *right,* and give him reinforcement through praise or a treat. For the severe problems, or if you have several problem children, a pocket of tiny candies or sugared cereals is handy for immediate reinforcement. THAT'S THE NICEST PAPER YOU'VE EVER DONE! I MUST HAVE A SPECIAL TREAT HERE FOR THAT. Elaine Bruner, University of Illinois, (1969) has an excellent device for giving attention to the behaving child. When a child misbehaves, she turns to little Susan next to him, shakes the child's hand and says: "You are sitting so nicely!" Then looking at the culprit, and still shaking Susan's hand: "Isn't she sitting nicely? It's hard to sit still, but she can do it." The children love the handshaking and after succeeding with a difficult task often thrust out a hand for this physical reinforcement.

When a child is yelling out, "My turn" or is being verbally disruptive, try ignoring him first and praising the others. If he's so loud that you can't hear the child who is performing, casually go to him and physically close his mouth, or use a firm hand on his shoulder to make him sit down. Say nothing to him. You don't want to reinforce this overt behavior. You needn't even look at him while you're doing this, but continue to show that your attention is on the rest of the class. JANE KNOWS HOW TO RAISE HER HAND! LET'S LET HER BE NEXT!

Another procedure is to stop the child who is not controlling his behavior and is, for example, running around the room, and say: WHAT ARE WE DOING? or WHAT ARE THE OTHER CHILDREN DOING? or WHAT SHOULD YOU BE DOING? or GO BACK TO THE DOOR AND COUNT TO TWENTY AND THINK. Or if he is just chasing around the room during a free activity period, send him to his seat UNTIL YOU GET YOUR BRAIN IN GEAR AND KNOW SOMETHING YOU CAN DO. Later when he is calm at his seat: WHAT COULD YOU DO NOW? Don't be concerned with punishing the child in doing this, but simply in getting him to restructure his own actions. If he continues to be disruptive and to have difficulty in finding an activity for himself, help him get something and take it to his seat to remain there until the task has been completed. Thus you are structuring the task for him and giving him the limits he seems unable to make for himself.

When a child hurts another or destroys the possessions of a peer, isolate him. WE CAN'T LET YOU HURT JERRY. WE WOULDN'T LET HIM HURT YOU. Put his desk off in an isolated corner of the room with his back to the others and give him an achievable task. When he does the same type of thing again, no explanation is necessary. Just firmly move him to the isolation corner. If he does not *take* in-room isolation and further disrupts the class, then he will have to be removed from the room. This would also be true for obnoxious behavior or when you have reached your own tolerance level. Sometimes, it is simply the straw that broke the camel's back, but you feel that you can no longer put up with him, so you simply remove him with as few words as possible. It's best if you don't let him see *you* lose control. Have a pre-arranged place of isolation. Prepare ahead of time for this child. You knew you were going to have trouble with him. Discuss him with your principal so that he knows some behavioral history of the child. Then when you bring him in, the principal understands. All you need to say during the crisis is, MIKE NEEDS TIME OUT.

Sitting in the outer office does little more than relieve the classroom tension. To really help the child, there should be a temporarily unused office, first aid, supply, or therapy room where he can be completely alone. After about an hour of this and a quiet talk with the principal, the child might return to the class. He is given no fanfare on his return, but ignored until he does the first thing right, then reinforced immediately with praise. Do not hold grudges. You are the adult.

When a child becomes emotionally unstrung and explodes, try holding his hands until he stops fighting and breaks down. Restraining him from destructive behavior helps him learn control. If he will let you then put your arms around him and let him cry it out. Or if he resents the fact that you had to restrain him or is ashamed, he needs to gain face. If he goes for the door, let him go with: YOU MIGHT WANT TO GO TO THE RESTROOM AND WASH UP. YOU MAY COME BACK WHEN YOU'RE READY. Always give him the out, the excuse to leave, the reassurance that he may return. If you have an understanding principal, the child might *flee* to him and find release of his tensions.

Sometimes, restraining the child in his seat may help him to get over the tantrum. Stay with him, massaging his back and shoulders, talking softly as needed. When the worst is over he might go get a drink and wash his face. Don't try to discuss the problem when he is upset. Wait until later when he is calm and controlled. Then do it privately.

Sorting Exercises

Exercises for sorting objects and perceiving details help the distractable child to be less confused by his environment and learn to attend.

1. Begin with simple sorting exercises wherein the child needs to look for only one differential, e.g., sort squares according to size only. Then sort according to size and color. Then sort a variety of shapes into size and color. Toy stores and supply houses have puzzles of this type. Learning to discriminate the basic shapes, circle, square, triangle, etc. is a good starting point.

2. Sort all kinds of objects such as buttons, bolts, nuts, anagrams, colored toothpicks as to size and/or color. Use plastic egg cartons or fly-fishing boxes for the sorting.

3. Get sample floor tiles or plastic samples for children to sort. Again, use the tiles with the simpler designs first and with the fewest differentials to consider. Tiles may be easily cut with a blade to have two exactly matching ones. Use tiles to learn color hues and shades and to match these (Fig. 14). Begin with the main eight colors, then have a set with two shades of each color which the child has to differentiate. Increase the difficulty until you have four or five shades of each color. Read *Doctor Montessori's Own Handbook* (1965). Have different sets of tiles to match, increasing the intensity of the child's concentration. Matching different wood grains or similar splatter designs would be more difficult sorting tasks.

4. Paper paint swatches or samples may be used for sorting. Again, begin with the simplest discriminations and increase the difficulty of the task. The children prefer three dimensional materials like the tiles, however.

5. Have the child find a designated item in a box of many items. A box of plastic toys would be good for this. Or use toy soldiers or horses and ask him to find a particular one for you.

Figure 14. Sorting Tiles for Color and Design.

6. Make a closed box with a hand hole in one end. First put simple shapes or objects into the box and let the child "find all the shapes that are round like a circle," without looking. Later, put in all kinds of objects that are round, and have him identify them. Then glue matching cloth samples on tiles. The child removes one and then tries to find its match. Use velvet, corduroy, sandpaper, satin, hopsacking (Fig. 15).

Other Figure-Ground Exercises

1. Use Frostig's *Figure-Ground Worksheets,* or workbooks, Follett Publishing Company.

2. Show a picture and ask children to find details that you name or to answer questions according to the details they see. Discuss the main focal point of the picture, then the details: WHOM DO YOU SEE HERE? WHAT IS HE DOING? WHAT IS THAT BEHIND HIM? IS HE HAPPY? WHAT KIND OF LOOK DOES HE HAVE? WHAT ELSE DO YOU SEE? WHAT IS IT DOING THERE? Use consecutively more and more complicated pictures with added details.

Figure 15. Matching Fabrics from the Feeling Box.

3. As you teach letters and words provide exercises in which a child must separate the desired letter or word from a multitude. For example, you are teaching the letter *n*. Make a ditto page on which you have upper and lower case *n*'s, large and small, printed and typed, and words beginning with a variety of *n*'s. Place these in a scrambled arrangement on the page interspersed with other similar letters and words. The child finds and circles all the *n*'s and words beginning with *n* (Fig. 16) .

4. After each shape has been taught, have the children find that shape in their environment. In looking for rectangles the children will find them in windows, doors, paper, the blackboard, electric receptacles, and in the shape of a house. When drawing anything, relate it to its basic shape. A Christmas tree is a triangle, eyes are ovals, the neck is a rectangle, a wheel is a circle.

As discussed earlier in this chapter, the hyperactive, distractable child is operating at a subcortical level, perhaps midbrain, and this is why he is so impulsive, explosive, uncontrolled. We are endeavoring to train him to think. The brain's ability to extract

Name:

Figure 16. Figure-Ground Worksheet.

the figure from the ground and to make discriminations is the basis of all higher cognitive processes. As you systematically develop the child's ability to focus attention and make discriminations you are training cortical processes so that the cortex in turn will then come to control behavior and the hyperactivity will diminish. Strauss found that education is the best therapy to help overcome behavior problems. Von Hilsheimer found that when children do not respond to educational therapy there is usually a physical cause of the learning problem often based on allergies or hypoglycemia.

REFERENCES

Adler, Sidney J.: Lecture in Sacramento, California, May, 1968.

Ayres, A. Jean: *Perceptual-Motor Dysfunction in Children.* Monograph from the Greater Cincinnati District Ohio Occupational Therapy Association Conference, 1964.

—: Lecture in Sacramento, California, Oct. 19, 1967.

Barsch, Ray H.: *Achieving Perceptual-Motor Efficiency.* Seattle, Spec Child, 1967.

Brace, Ruth: Relaxation. Pleasant Hill, California, Contra Costa County Schools Office, 1965.

Bruner, Elaine: Lecture in Sacramento, California, 1969.

Butter, Charles M.: *Neuropsychology: The Study of Brain and Behavior.* Belmont, California, Brooks-Cole, July, 1969.

Campbell, Brent: Lecture in San Diego, California, January 29, 1971.

Faglioni, Pietro, and Spinnler, Hans: Immediate and delayed recognition of nonsense figures in patients with unilateral hemisphere damage. *Learning Disabilities, 2 (No. 12),* Dec. 1969.

Frostig, Marianne: The Education of Children with Learning Difficulties. Santa Rosa, California, Sonoma County Superintendent of Schools Office, January, 1967.

—: Lecture in Sacramento, California, Oct. 1964.

Gazzaniga, Michael S.: The split brain in man. Reprinted from *Scientific American, 217 (No. 2),* Aug. 1967.

Getman, G. N., and Kane, Elmer: *The Physiology of Readiness.* Minneapolis, PASS, 1964.

Hebb, D. O.: *The Organization of Behavior.* New York, Wiley, 1949.

Hoffer, A., and Osmond, H.: *How To Live With Schizophrenia.* New York, Univ Bks, 1966.

Kephart, Newell C.: *The Slow Learner in the Classroom.* Columbus, Ohio, Merrill, 1960.

—: Lecture in San Francisco, California, May 10, 1968.

Knutsen, Elaine Jones: Lecture in Sacramento, California, Feb. 18, 1969.

Krech, David: Don't use the kitchen sink approach to enrichment. *Today's Educator,* Oct. 1970.

Montessori, Maria: *Doctor Montessori's Own Handbook.* New York, Schocken, 1965.

Pauling, Linus: *Vitamin C, and the Common Cold.* San Francisco, Freeman, 1970.

Petitclerc, Grace M.: Give ear: let hearing be the coordinator in learning.

Academic Therapy Quarterly, II (No. 1) Fall 1966.

—: *Stand Tall and Look Far.* Oakland, California, Goodwill Industries of Oakland, 1965.

—: Plus Factor in the Classroom. Contra Costa County, California, Contra Costa County Department of Education, 1968.

Piaget, Jean: La Construction du Réel Chez L'Enfant (The Origins of Intelligence in Children). Neuchatel-Paris, Delachaux & Niestle, 1937.

Rees, Elizabeth Lodge: Lecture in Sacramento, Nov. 1970.

Rimland, Bernard: High Dosage Levels of Certain Vitamins in the Treatment of Children with Severe Mental Disorders. San Diego, California, Institute for Child Behavior Research, Oct. 1968.

—: Lecture in Sacramento, California, Nov. 1969.

Strauss, A. A., and Lehtinen, Laura E.: *Psychopathology and Education of the Brain Injured Child.* New York, Grune and Stratton, 1947.

Von Hilsheimer, George: *How to Live with Your Special Child.* Washington, D. C., Acropolis, 1970.

Chapter Six

Developing Tactile and Kinesthetic Senses

THE TACTILE SENSE
Description

PROPRIOCEPTORS RECEIVE THE stimuli near the body with the senses of touch, taste, and smell. The latter two are chemical and interact to clarify the perception. Since the tactile sense is the first sense used by the child for purposeful action, it is vitally important to him. Without tactile stimulation, the perceptions of the other modes would be incomplete and erroneous. *Tactile* refers to the sensory receptors of the skin. They receive stimuli of heat, cold, pain, texture, hardness, weight, size, and form. The most sensitive tactile receptors are on the child's tongue, hands, face, neck, arms, legs, and feet. The infant derives pleasure from the feel of the teddy bear against his body and the soft blanket binding against his face. The child loves the sensation of a fur collar against his neck.

Tactile sensory stimulation begins in the fetus. Later the parent's touching, lifting, caressing, all stimulate these receptors. The infant's first tactile learnings are not really conscious. This mode develops very slowly over the years. Thus even the normal seven-year-old is still learning to perceive by touch. He is excited by the variations in textures of different substances. He increases his learning, verifies his visual and auditory perceptions, by feeling everything and studying it meticulously. As his language development progresses, he likes to put descriptive words to his tactile perceptions. He will feel everything to determine its relative *softness,* or weight, and begin to assign these objects relative names according to his vocabulary: *softer, softest, heavy, very light.*

Research has found that the child who is handled more in infancy is more likely to have superior motor development. Conversely, the child who does not receive such sensory stimulation is slow to develop motorically, slow to turn over, to sit, to crawl, to walk, etc. He is also likely to have a poor emotional adjustment. Lack of tactile stimulation is also related to delayed speech. Some children with delayed speech especially enjoy close physical contact with objects and with people. Others will refrain from contact. Some brain-damaged inhibited children were put in a close contact situation, a little *house,* where they would HAVE to contact each other's bodies. They began to use more movement and their body images and social behavior improved (Cratty, 1964).

The child who has not received sufficient integration of tactile stimuli is often unable to locate a specific area of stimulation. One boy received an injury on his forehead, above his eye. He ran to his mother and complained of the wound, tapping his cheekbone *below* his eye to designate the location of the insult. These children also have difficulty locating mosquito bites, or even a body part.

Some hyperactive, distractable children crave constant physical contact. They throw their arms around everyone, jump on their backs, cling to an adult's hand or arm or leg. They sit as close to the teacher as possible constantly stroking her arm or leg or rubbing their cheeks against her arm. They love to feel everything. As soon as they walk into a room they must handle everything in sight.

Tactile Defensiveness

Another phenomenon is the child whom we mentioned earlier who repulses your touch. His *protective* system is still dominating (Chapter Five). He squirms out from under your hand and is not calmed by any reassurance that you don't want to hurt him. He simply doesn't want your hands on him. He fusses if another child is sitting near him and accidentally touches him. In fact, he may react with a quick kick, or an elbow in the unsuspecting child's ribs. Jean Ayres terms this *tactile defensiveness* (Ayres, 1964). This is also related to the child's oversensitivity to heat and sounds. Actually, he is *overresponding* to the stimulation as though it might be harmful or dangerous to him.

The development of the higher cortical level is thought to bring about the dominance of the discriminative system over the protective system. It has been further hypothesized that tactile stimulation might be the fuel which sets off the mechanism (Ayres, 1964). Thus the child who has lacked the tactile stimulation, or who was unable to discriminate it because of problems with sorting function and figure-ground perception, is therefore still at the protective stage of tactile perception.

Another thing we might consider about the protective state is that when the organism is thus alerted to danger, an extra amount of adrenalin is produced. This not only makes the child more excited and more ready to defend himself but also further inhibits the discriminatory impulses from the sensory receptors.

When there has been central nervous system dysfunction, it is often the protective tactile system which predominates. Then the hair cell receptors and other tactile receptors overrespond to a light touch. When there is unreasonable anger or belligerence, we might look to this protective tactile system.

Weidenbacker (1963) found that cerebral palsied children who did not walk, had a lower pressure-pain threshold than did cerebral palsied children who walked. Walking stimulates the tactile receptors of the feet. This would seem to bear out the above theory that lack of sensory stimulation allows the protective system to predominate.

APRAXIA

Praxis is the ability of the organism to plan his motor action. His movements are random and not controlled unless he can motor plan. *Apraxia* is the term we apply to those children who are unable to plan their movements. When you have been wearing gloves, have you ever tried to locate your car keys in a full purse, put on a silk scarf, fasten an earring or pin, or retie the bow on your child's dress? You were unable to make the necessary motor movements without the feedback from the sensory stimuli of your fingers. You couldn't tell how hard to pull the bow, where to fasten the earring, or how far to move your fingers to get that tiny pin point into that little opening. You probably yanked your gloves off in disgust.

Thus the child with *apraxia* is unable to plan the movements of his body, his fingers, because he is not getting the correct messages from the tactile stimulators to guide him. Where the gloves caused your lack of tactile feedback to know how to tie, his lack is in the confusions of his perceptions. He has trouble with the pencil because he doesn't know how hard he is holding it. Apraxia shows up in the lack of small muscle, especially finger, coordination (shoe tying is a real problem) and in the clumsy efforts of the child to move his body in a designated fashion. He may be able to walk forward quite well, but stumble awkwardly when he attempts to go sideways or backward.

Actually, everything we ever learned to do motorically, we once motor planned. The infant has to plan how to stand up, how to walk, although he is not cognitively aware of it. As he learns the skill it becomes automatic. Just as the first grader's writing is arduous and deliberate, until he has beautiful controlled letters. Then as he gets older, his writing becomes automatic, so much so that it becomes more and more careless, and finally, as an adult, undecipherable.

Consider yourself as an experienced driver, long accustomed to automatic transmissions. You get into a car with "stick shift" and find that you have to plan every move. You might even say it out loud to yourself. "Let's see. I have to press in this pedal and then push this gear shift over here. Whoops! That's reverse!" You are so busy planning your moves, that you cannot converse with your passenger. In fact, it isn't until your actions are automatic, that you can converse.

A. Jean Ayres suggests that the reason tactile functions have been so closely associated with visual motor control could be that the nervous system of the embryo is formed from the ectoderm. When the central nervous system control of muscles has been disturbed and thus visual-motor control, the tactile sense is also disturbed. This has been found to be true with cerebral palsy victims.

We should mention here, too, that weight is perceived by the tactile receptors. It is easier to perceive more exactly the weight of an object if you also move your hand up and down, or pass the object from hand to hand.

Since a child is usually so desirous of touching everything, it is often mistaken that he is receiving accurate information. As Barsch says:

> The fact that the child can use his hand to reach, grasp, and release objects does not indicate that he is tactually aware. The child may be unaware of differences in texture, substance, and shape. He may give no indication of tactual scanning for information even though he tries to touch everything in sight. The critical consideration is whether or not touch serves him as an information source. He may touch but not be consciously aware that he is touching. He may be touched and be either unaware that such touch has taken place, or, being aware, be unable to interpret the touch. (Barsch, 1967, p. 213)

Thus the child with apraxia must have his tactile receptors stimulated and receive training in body image and movement exploration.

TRAINING THE CHILD WITH TACTILE PROBLEMS

The first step is tactile stimulation.

1. CLAP YOUR HANDS. HARDER! HARDER! WHAT HAPPENED? HOW DO YOUR HANDS FEEL NOW? SLAP YOUR CHEEKS. SLAP YOUR THIGHS. STAMP YOUR FEET. HARDER! NOW TAP YOUR ARM LIGHTLY. EASY. HOW DOES IT FEEL?

2. Give each child a piece of material: sandpaper, velvet, lace, or satin. Do this every day or so the first of the year. Begin with an enjoyable material such as satin. Each child is given a piece. CLOSE YOUR EYES AND PUT YOUR ARMS BEHIND YOU. I'M GOING TO GIVE YOU SOMETHING TO FEEL. DON'T PEEK! HOW DOES IT FEEL IN YOUR HANDS, ON YOUR ARMS? NOW RUB IT ON YOUR CHEEK AND SEE HOW IT FEELS. RUB THAT INSIDE PART OF YOUR ELBOW. RUB YOUR WRIST. RUB YOUR NECK. PAT YOUR LIPS WITH IT. WHERE DOES IT FEEL BEST? DO YOU LIKE IT BEST ON THE BACK OF YOUR ARM OR ON THE INSIDE OF YOUR WRIST? TRY IT AND SEE. DO YOU LIKE THE FEEL OF IT? DO YOU LIKE IT MORE THAN THE MATERIAL WE FELT YESTERDAY? Help them to find which parts of their bodies are most sensitive.

3. Let the children experiment with a vibrator or back

scratcher. Often the tactile-defensive children seem to get the most out of this and want to use it for long periods.

4. Since the soles of the feet are good tactile receptors, do lots of jumping, hopping, and running exercises. Any exercises where parts of the body touch the floor or lawn or rug are excellent. Try rolling in various ways, somersaulting, crawling, and squeezing under.

5. Use the feeling box described in Chapter Five.

6. A relaxation exercise: JUST RELAX, CLOSE YOUR EYES. FEEL YOUR ELBOW. FEEL ALL AROUND IT. FEEL THAT BUMP THERE? FEEL THAT LOOSE SKIN THERE? PINCH UP SOME OF IT WITH YOUR FINGERS. FEEL THAT SHARP BONE COMING UP FROM YOUR ELBOW AND GOING DOWN YOUR ARM? Another day feel another part of the body.

7. Tasting parties: The children have eyes closed and hands behind them. Don't press this point or deny the child who can't keep his eyes closed. To the child without secure perception of stimuli, closing his eyes and eliminating vision can be very threatening to him. His visual perception might not be good either, but it is all he has any faith in. Holding their hands behind them helps them to keep from looking at the objects in their hands. Put a cracker into each child's hands. KEEP IT A SECRET AND DON'T SAY WHAT IT IS. HOW DOES IT FEEL? WHAT SHAPE IS IT? FEEL EACH SIDE. FEEL THE EDGES. NOW TASTE IT WITH YOUR TONGUE! CAN IT MAKE A NOISE BY YOUR EAR? BREAK IT BY YOUR EAR. HOW DOES IT SOUND? SMELL IT. BITE IT. HOW DOES IT TASTE? HOW DOES IT FEEL IN YOUR MOUTH? WHAT IS IT? OPEN YOUR EYES. WHAT COLOR IS IT? WHAT SHAPE IS IT?

When children name the object or look at it before they should, ignore them, praising children doing it the right way. TOMMY CAN TASTE IT WITHOUT LOOKING AT IT. HE'S SMART!

Help them to integrate the perceptions they note by tying them in with language. GOOD, JERRY! "CRISPY" IS A GOOD WORD FOR IT. CAN YOU ALL FEEL HOW "CRISPY" IT IS? LET'S ALL SAY THE WORD "CRISPY". WHO CAN THINK OF ANOTHER WORD? Summarize all their descriptions at the end while they are eating. WE FOUND THAT THE CRACKER WAS ROUND, BUMPY, ROUGH, SALTY, CRISPY, AND YEL-LOW. Often it is valuable to give each child a second cracker perhaps with eyes open so that he can reevaluate his first perceptions of it and now sense the differences which the other children noted. Thus he receives a firmer, more integrated perception of the food.

Use a large variety of crackers, finger foods, nuts, cold cereals, and special foods like Japanese tidbits and Chinese fortune cookies. Introduce new foods to them such as avocados, fresh pineapple, coconut, and sugar cane. We're digressing here from the tactile sense to the gustatory, but what we want to achieve is a total integrated perception of all the senses.

Teach the children to discriminate flavors. Begin with sugar cubes. Then another day, sprinkle cubes with cinnamon, nutmeg, or allspice. Use a straw to put just one drop of vanilla or other extract on the cubes. After they have initially experienced the flavors, they'll be better able to describe the flavors of cookies, cupcakes, and candies. Use spice and fruit-flavored candies and let them try to guess the flavoring used. Help them to learn to discriminate the cereals as to whether they were made of corn, oats, wheat, or rice. Sometimes it helps to pass out two differently flavored cereals at the same time so that they can compare them.

The tasting party could later be a special treat time when you bring marshmallow bunnies or jelly chicks for the children to feel and taste. Tasting parties are an excellent reward device. Keep a variety of future tasting treats on hand. Then: YOU'VE ALL BEEN SUCH GOOD WORKERS TODAY I THINK WE SHOULD HAVE A TASTING PARTY! Hyperactive children often enjoy salty foods more than sweet candies. Some seem to crave salt; I tried rock salt in beanbags, and the children tore holes in them to get at the salt.

8. Use the desire to feel things as a teaching tool. Have them feel smooth-washed pebbles, coins, leaves. Collect sea shells to feel the differences. Sit in a circle and pass around the shells, rocks, cocoons, twigs sealed-for-the-winter. The children learn better if you use a smaller variety of things at first, or a certain classification. One day use carpentry tools and other mechanics' tools. One day have broken versus water-smoothed granite. Being a rock hound I'll have igneous rocks one day, later metamorphic, then fossils.

Whatever you are trying to teach them, if they can feel it they will learn more and remember it better. Make it open season on feeling things. Do not put things out in the room that cannot be felt. Science objects are a natural. An activity period is a good time to put new things out on a counter or on a rug for the children to feel. However, if you don't want them to be feeling them at other times, don't fight it. Simply put them away in a cupboard until the next period. Keeping these items on easily removed small snack trays makes them more mobile.

9. When children have trouble finding the right puzzle pieces they are still at the trial-and-error stage of perceptual development, Piaget's *empirical space* (Chapter Five). Show them how to *feel* the shape of the space and of the object. Hold the child's hand, showing the use of the first and second fingers to feel accurately. Help them to *feel* the differences in size and shape to stabilize their visual perception of the objects. FEEL THIS HOLE HERE. NOW FEEL THIS PIECE. IS IT THE SAME SIZE AND SHAPE OF THIS HOLE?

10. Sometimes churches and other charitable organizations make *quiet books* or *feeling books,* into which they put many types of fabrics and textures. You can make one using a binder and strong cardboard on which you will glue textures. Different types of screening would be interesting to feel, as well as sandpaper and fabrics. Or sew familiar objects into small cotton bags. The only drawback to the latter is that the child wants so much to verify his perception with his eyes, that he may rip open the bags. Thus small zippered or snapped bags might be better. You might like to read Shower's book *Find Out By Touching* to your children.

BODY IMAGE
A Definition

Body image is the child's feeling for and understanding of his body parts, their relationships to each other, how he might use them, and finally, an emotional evaluation of himself. Some authors divide these various aspects of body image into separate terminology as *body concept* and *body schema.* For clarity here we'll use the all-encompassing term of *body image.*

deHirsch says:

> A child's body image results from integration of his proprioceptive, sensorimotor, emotional, and social experiences. It does not actually represent a figure seen, but reflects rather the child's awareness of his own body, its parts, and their relationship to each other. (deHirsch, 1966, p. 36)

Kephart says that body image arises from tactile and kinesthetic perceptions when the body moves (Kephart, 1968). He adds a further dimension to the concept of body image when he includes the perception of the size of the space around the body as it moves. Notice the child who pushes through an area too small for him, knocking down objects and peers. He has never learned the size of space necessary for his body to move. Have you ever entered your car with a new high hair style, new hat, or curlers and hit the top of the doorway? You learned from that experience and remembered to compensate when you exited. The child with body image problems often does not learn from his collisions, but will repeat the same performance again. He often blames the accident on another child, thinking someone ran into *him* or tripped *him*.

Description of the Problem

Body image is extremely important because everything else in the world exists only in relation to the individual's body image. Objects are behind *him,* in front of *him,* far away from *him,* coming toward *him,* to *his* left. Everything, too, has an emotional relationship to him: *he* likes it, *he* hates it, *he* can ride it, it hurts *him,* it is too heavy for *him*; also, they like *him,* they don't like *him.* He is the center of his universe, nothing else is more important to him than himself. If his perceptual, sensory, and/or space world are confused and misperceived, then he may have a poor body image and a distortion of the world outside himself. With perceptual distortions of himself and his world, he is unable to operate successfully in that world and his emotional opinion of himself collapses. "I can't do it," he wails. "The kids don't like me!" And he doesn't like himself. He rebels either by withdrawing from that world or by aggressive defiance.

The child's lack of understanding of his body parts may come from lack of tactile integration. Without balance he cannot learn his body's relationship to space. He must have a clear body image in order to act effectively on his environment. He may have made the movements in the past which you take for granted would give him a body image. But the motor initiators in the brain can act independently of the sensory. Thus the child can move without perceiving the movement. He is unaware of the senses which should arise from the movement. The final visual perception of the body must match the tactile and kinesthetic information. Again, it is a lack of total integration of sensori-motor stimuli. Clear body image is acquired through his sensory receptors and through the feedback he receives from his purposeful motor movements. He cannot learn it intellectually, through your simply instructing him on the subject. It must be received through the senses.

Identifying the Child with Body Image Problems

The child may be able to cognitively recognize and name body parts on another but not on himself, or he may just know the names and locations of the main parts. He must know not only where all parts are on himself, but be able to touch and activate them. The child might be able to name and locate his elbow, but not be aware of how he uses his elbow, or not be able to move it on command. He may not even be able to close his eyes on command, and if he does close his eyes, he is most insecure without the vision. He will probably wink and blink them in a strained manner. Even though a child has poor visual perception, since his other senses are so confused he might be very frightened without the use of his eyes.

The child's difficulties in body image may be evident in his drawings of human figures. These are usually distorted or extremely immature for his age. Eyes are vacant holes (Fig. 17). Legs emerge from the head. The body may simply be a colored-in area between the legs. Arms often are attached at the waist. Limbs and fingers are sticks. The number of digits is irrelevant. The Goodenough scoring provides a wide-range scale on which to evaluate the child's drawing of a man (Chapter Four).

Figure 17. Immature "Man" Drawings of First Graders.

The problem of poor body image will also be evident in the child's behavior. Being unaware of the space his body requires, he runs into peers, posts, and puddles, trips and falls, knocks things down. He might appear confused and restless. He is often insecure, worried, requiring much reinforcement for every small step of every task. He might appear to be "in a cloud" or in a foggy state. He is not really aware of what is going on around him. He is often unaware of the results of his own behavior. He might swing his jacket around him feeling only the stimulation of the movement itself. When little Susan wails that he hit her with the zipper, he is innocence itself. He is thus accused of many ill deeds of which he is so totally unaware that he really believes that others are picking on him.

TECHNIQUES FOR TRAINING BODY IMAGE

1. Locate and name the parts of the body on themselves and others. Discuss the function of each part. Draw each other. Draw the teacher.

2. Say body parts in order from top down, and vice versa. WHAT IS ON TOP OF THE BODY? FEEL IT. YES, HEAD. Or begin with hair. WHAT IS NEXT? (NECK). FEEL IT! IT GOES STRAIGHT DOWN. FEEL ALL THE SIDES OF THE NECK. WHAT IS THAT BUMP ON THE FRONT? After first exploring the parts in order, then have the children name and touch them more quickly in sequence.

3. Exploring uses of body parts: LET'S SEE HOW MANY DIF- FERENT WAYS YOU CAN MOVE YOUR ARMS. TOMMY IS SWINGING HIS ARMS. LET'S COPY HIM. NOW FIND ANOTHER WAY. JERRY IS BENDING HIS IN AND OUT. CAN YOU DO THAT? TRY IT! NOW TRY BETTY'S WAY OF TWIRLING HER ARMS IN FRONT OF HER. Use this type of activity with each movable part, with each joint, beginning with the smallest part of the body and progressing to controlled move- ment of the whole body. HOW CAN YOU BEND YOUR WRIST? JOE BENDS HIS FORWARD. LET'S TRY THAT. SUSAN IS ROTATING HER WRIST AROUND AND AROUND. TRY IT. CAN YOU BEND YOUR HAND BACK- WARDS? HOW FAR WILL IT GO? IF YOU BENT IT FURTHER WHAT MIGHT HAPPEN TO IT?

4. Sing songs with motions indicating body parts: *Under the Spreading Chestnut Tree*; *One Day One Foot Kept Moving*; *Put Your Finger in the Air*; *Where is Thumbkin? Dem Bones.* (Learning Language III)

5. Children help draw a large man on the blackboard, part by

part as they explore their own bodies and find what comes next; e.g., one child says that the head is on top, so he draws the head. Someone else says *eyes* or *nose* and draws that. If they make sticks for limbs, have them feel the limb with two hands. HOW MANY SIDES ARE THERE?

6. Use large cardboard ovals for the face and cut out features of construction paper. Have children feel themselves and look at each other to decide on placement of features. Use a child with a long forehead to show children how the eyes are not at the top of the head but about halfway down. Show them how to use their fingers to feel the distance between their hairline and eyebrows, chin and lips, and then to measure where to place the features on the cardboard head. HOW MANY FINGERS CAN YOU GET ON YOUR FOREHEAD BETWEEN YOUR HAIR AND YOUR EYEBROWS? GOOD. THEN PUT THOSE THREE FINGERS ON YOUR MAN'S FOREHEAD UNDER HIS HAIR. NOW WHERE WILL YOU PUT HIS EYEBROWS? (Fig. 18.) They find that they must leave a one-finger space between the nose and the lips and a two-finger space below the lips for the chin.

Figure 18. Using Fingers to Aid Placement of Features.

7. Ditto a simple man with scattered easy-to-cut-out parts. Identify each part. Include thigh and upper arm. The child cuts the parts out and then pastes them together on another paper to form a man. Encourage them to discover the different positions of the limbs that are possible. Have children imitate with their own bodies the various stances which they have made. SEE TOMMY HAS THE RIGHT ARM OF HIS MAN BENT UPWARD AT THE ELBOW. CAN YOU DO THAT TO YOURS? LOOK HOW HE HAS THE LEFT ARM. LET'S ALL STAND LIKE HIS MAN! Or use paper fasteners at the joints and then have children move the limbs to imitate your (or a child's) posture. For variety, ditto off a clown, a witch, a scarecrow, or a cat with each body part separate. The child cuts them out and pastes them together on another paper.

8. Draw or ditto a partially completed man. Children draw in missing parts. Draw, or cut out of a magazine, a vertical half of a man or other figure. The child draws in the missing half.

9. Find puzzles wherein each body part is a puzzle part in that distinctive shape and the child must put the parts together to form the whole body. Most of the wooden puzzles designed for school use are very poor, in that the shapes of the puzzle pieces bear little relationship to the shapes of the body parts. The two should be one and the same. Thus a hand is one part, the arm another, and the neck, shoulders, waistline (designated by a belt) are all separate pieces. In the first easier puzzles, perhaps have only six parts, the head, torso, two arms and two legs. Then break these parts down until you have, for instance, three parts to a leg, the thigh, lower leg and the foot. Later, have more and smaller parts, then the ankle and heel and the toes can be separate. Some of the *People Puzzles, Animal Puzzles, Job Puzzles,* and *Multi-ethnic Children Puzzles* (Developmental Learning Materials Co.) break down body parts even smaller. Thus a woman's face is divided into nose, upper lip, teeth, lower lip, chin, and neck.

10. Play *Simon Says*: SIMON SAYS, "HOLD UP YOUR RIGHT HAND." SIMON SAYS: "PUT YOUR HANDS ON YOUR HIPS." SIMON SAYS, "BLINK YOUR EYES." "WRINKLE YOUR FOREHEAD." Do not eliminate the child with the incorrect response. He needs the *most* practice.

11. Dramatize the expressions of a story: "The bear frowned." CAN YOU FROWN LIKE THE BEAR? "He sighed a deep sigh." CAN YOU GIVE A DEEP SIGH?

12. Opaque pictures of children in various positions on a screen. Children imitate with their bodies.

13. Have a child assume a position in front of the class. Others imitate.

14. Play Freeze: Children dance or skip around in any direction until the teacher blows the whistle. Then they freeze in position. LOOK AT THE FUNNY POSITION JERRY HAS! CAN YOU COPY HIM? WHICH FOOT IS UP? WHICH HAND IS TOUCHING THE GROUND?

15. RELAX! CLOSE YOUR EYES. Lying down or heads on desks. FEEL HOW HEAVY YOU ARE. YOU ARE SINKING, SINKING, DOWN, DOWN. NOW YOU ARE LIGHT AND AIRY, FLOATING ON A CLOUD, FLOATING OVER THE TREES. FEEL THE WIND BLOWING YOU. FEEL YOUR BREATH- ING, YOUR HEART BEAT. FEEL YOUR TOES; MOVE THEM. FEEL YOUR FINGERS; MOVE THEM. FEEL YOUR ELBOWS; MOVE THEM. CAN YOU FEEL YOUR HEAD WITHOUT TOUCHING IT? Find feeling in each body part, then try moving it. Use the above routine with eyes open and closed, and in different postures—standing, sitting, and kneeling.

16. Use many stretching and relaxing exercises. CAN YOU STRETCH YOUR BACK BY BENDING WAY BACK? CAN YOU STRETCH YOUR LEGS BY STANDING ON TIPTOE? HOW CAN YOU STRETCH YOUR ARMS? CAN YOU STRETCH YOUR NECK TOO? NOW CAN YOU GET ALL LIMP AND SOFT? NO BONES, ALL LOOSE AND DROOPY. NOW BE ICE CREAM AND FREEZE ALL STIFF AND HARD. THE ICE CREAM IS OUT OF THE FREEZER NOW. IT'S GETTING ALL SOFT. NOW IT'S MELTING. Other tension-relaxation comparisons are a metal soldier, a soft cuddly toy dog. Blow up a balloon, let the air out slowly, let it out fast, prick it with a pin. Light candles, melt as they burn. A stiff wooden puppet, a limp rag doll, hard like a tree trunk, soft like cotton.

17. YOU'RE IN A TALL, THIN BOX, ALL PRESSED TIGHTLY TO- GETHER! NOW HOW WOULD YOU BREAK OUT OF THE BOX? YOU'RE IN A LITTLE, LOW BOX, ALL CURLED UP IN A BALL. BREAK OUT OF THE BOX.

18. Make an obstacle course in the room. Place a yardstick across the top back of two chairs and children go under it. Put it across two seats and children go over it. Put hand and foot prints on square cardboard, or linoleum tiles, and make a trail with them for children to follow, going under and over things, on hands and feet, hands and knees, walking, hopping, and cross-stepping.

19. Barrel race with waste baskets, stakes in the ground, highway cones, or sticks lying on the ground. Children must run in and out around these objects to reach a goal.

20. Use rolling exercises in various positions, body outstretched or curled up; arms clasped above heads or down at sides; forward, backward, and sideways somersaults.

21. Play *Peas Porridge Hot*, and other clapping games.

22. Use crawl-through equipment such as barrels or culverts. Mover's packing barrels are great to roll on top of or inside. Move through hoops or tires or tubes.

23. Children with body image problems especially need the on-floor routines (Chapter Eight), and the chalkboard routines (Chapter Nine).

24. If you have a chance to work individually with children, use eye-movement exercises from Getman, Frostig, or Kephart.

25. Practice many balancing activities, jump board, balance board, tubes, walking beam, and stilts (Chapter Eight).

26. For daily physical education, use directed calisthenics as well as movement exploration (Hackett, Diem, and Mosston).

27. Use activities to give children a feeling of being free in space. Jump down from heights, jump over a raised bamboo pole or a rope. Vary the heights required so that the child must learn to adjust his body to accomplish the new task. Have the child climb a rope ladder and swing free, or climb a knotted rope or a pole.

28. After children have gained some movement control, teach creative rhythms. LISTEN TO THE MUSIC. SEE HOW YOU CAN MOVE TO THIS MUSIC. JERRY HAS FOUND ONE WAY TO MOVE TO THE MUSIC. TOMMY KNOWS ANOTHER WAY. Call attention to real freedom of

movement and creativity. Gladys Andrews has excellent techniques for using body movements in rhythms.

29. The Stegal, or Lind Climber, consists of sawhorses, beams, a ladder, and a slide. It can be used in a variety of ways indoors and outdoors for a whole class to explore body movement.

30. After the children have explored body parts and the different ways they can move, try the record *The Beat Goes On*. In this they pose in various unique individual positions and change poses at a signal in the music. At first, the changes are far apart; then the rhythm quickens and the poses contract into an original modern dance. The children love it!

INTEROCEPTORS

Whereas the stimuli for the olfactory, gustatory, visual auditory, and tactile senses come from *outside* the organism, the kinesthetic and vestibular stimuli come from *inside* the organism. The nerves bearing these messages are called the interoceptors. These are located in muscles, joints, tendons, fascia (e.g. in the semicircular canals of the inner ear), in the muscles of the eyes (ocular muscles), the tongue, and other oral muscles used in speech.

Thus when the child is making his first sounds, he is feeling the sensations from his mouth and throat interoceptors, telling him how he is making the sounds, while at the same time the auditory receptors in his ears are telling him the results of that movement, the ensuing sound. The child learns through the interoceptors in his extraocular muscles that he can move his eyes way over to the sides, and his visual receptors tell him that he can thus increase his field of vision.

Kinesthetic Sense

To feel an object more thoroughly, the kinesthetic receptors direct the organism in the movements of its hands and arms. In form perception, kinesthetic impulses from extraocular muscles help to discriminate form. Even to taste or smell something, the kinesthetic impulses from the muscles of the mouth and nose are utilized. In hearing, too, the organism learns to turn the head to better catch the soft sounds or cover the ears to tone down the loud ones. There is an integration, therefore, of the senses for the child to learn to speak and to see, and the receptors of the organism's kinesthetic sense play a most important part.

The infant learns the kinesthesis of the movement of turning over, by repeating it many times, and by experimenting many different ways. Each time he does it he reduces the number of errors and thus becomes more efficient. Multiply the steps of this one learning task times the hundreds of other movement patterns he performs to realize the tremendous multiplicity of the kinesthetic impulses that must be activated. Thus in infancy the child achieves his basic efficiency in kinesthesia, the degree of which may well carry on into his adult life. If his kinesthesia is inefficient, he may be one of those inept adults with inefficient movement patterns. This degree of efficiency may be noted in the organism's cognitive approach to a new task, and the skill and speed which he utilizes.

We talked before of apraxia, the inability to motor plan, in its relationship with the tactile sense. This problem is often more pronounced, more noticeable in gross muscle movements, in inefficient kinesthesia. Still, even here, you may have to look closely to recognize it. The child may appear to be well coordinated in walking, but when asked to walk in specified manners like sideways, backward, or for dance steps, his clumsiness and inability become obvious. Parents are often shocked at a diagnosis of "poor coordination" because little Ronnie has been riding his bike for years, or is on a little league team. He may have performed an isolated task repeatedly and achieved efficiency in that one task, without developing an overall efficiency of kinesthesia. Physical education people often refer to this as a *splinter skill*. Don't let a splinter skill be a basis for an overall estimate of general coordination. Always check a variety of gross motor abilities by posing movement problems which the child must solve.

A child might have good gross motor coordinations but poor fine motor. Or his visual-motor control is good for tetherball, but poor for writing and drawing. The child with poor fine and/or gross motor control may produce good writing copy, grasping the pencil tightly, working only with his finger tips, and straining very hard. He thus produces a splinter skill of writing, but lacks an efficient motor control.

Efficiency of kinesthesia is noted in our great stars of the world of sports, whose movements are a symphony of grace and control. It is in the crucial moments of their play that their superior cognitive control is most evident.

Barsch says, "Only when the young infant purposefully moves a body part and *cognitively* directs that movement can we properly assume that kinesthesia is present." (Barsch, 1967, p. 221)

Thus the child does not learn through kinesthesia when the movement is random. Nor is the learning actually taking place when the movement is automatic. It had already been learned. When the child first learned to walk, each movement had to be carefully planned, kinesthetically tested. Later, the movement is automatic and there is no cognitive kinesthesia. Practicing an automatic movement does not enhance kinesthesia. But when the child must alter the movement in order to change directions, positions, speed, and cognitively does so, then there is kinesthetic learning. Speech therapy recognizes this when it teaches the child to *think* where his tongue and teeth should be to make a particular sound.

Another quote from Barsch:

> Kinesthesia does not just happen. The perceiver must make it happen. According to this view, a teacher, parent, or therapist can only provide muscular opportunities which may lead to a kinesthetic experience only if the performer perceives it thus. (Barsch, 1967, p. 223)

The term *tactile* and *kinesthetic* are often lumped together into the term *haptic*. Actually, however, these sensations are not performed in unison but rather reciprocally, one, then the other.

The Importance of Kinesthesia

There have been many research studies that contribute to our knowledge of the importance of kinesthesia to accurate visual perception and to normal child development. Richard Held, of Massachusetts Institute of Technology, did a study with litter mates of kittens. They were in the same visual and auditory environment. The only difference is that one kitten was constantly pulled along in a wagonlike apparatus, while the other kitten walked. After a certain interval, the kittens were tested on visual discrimination tasks. The kitten that walked passed; the one that rode, failed.

In another study in Vienna in 1890, lenses were used that turned the world upside down. If the patient sat, the world remained upside down. If the patient walked, his visual world reversed to an upright position within twenth-four hours. In both these studies, the kinesthetic stimuli from movement, feeding into the brain, resulted in the improved visual perception.

In a study with monkeys a furred bleach bottle was used as a mother substitute. One bottle-mother was stationary while the other swung in a pattern around the cage. The infant monkey reared by the "stationary mother" was extremely fearful, would not allow itself to be touched, and crouched in a fetal position. The baby monkey raised by the "moving mother" was not as fearful and would let itself be petted. It still had withdrawn behavior, but not to the gross extent of the monkey raised by the stationary mother. The infant monkey raised by his own mother monkey was held, stroked, carried around, and encouraged to move along with her, imitating her movements. This infant developed into a completely normal monkey, enjoying the company of the other monkeys.

We have discussed how premature children are often retarded in development. When the fetus is in the mother's womb, it not only turns itself within that womb regularly, but is subject to all the movement of the mother as she goes about her daily chores. In the incubator, the premature infant lies still, and kinesthetic and vestibular (balance) stimuli are missing. In one study in New York Children's Hospital, premature babies were placed in incubators which included a rocking apparatus which moved the infant regularly. They were then tested with a series of tests for hand strength, coordination, and ability to move the face off the mattress. The infants in the rocking incubators showed superior development. Thus we find that the need to be touched and moved is as important as is auditory and visual stimulation to normal development.

The Vestibular Sense

One of the most vital roles of the interoceptors is that of balance in the vestibular system. This system includes receptors in the semicircular canals of the ears, plus large nerves in the neck, and a mass of cells as the nucleus in the brain stem. Investigators are often struck by the size of the vestibular nuclei and the relatively large percentage of the brain involved in vestibular function. It is the prime sensory system operating in the fetus through its own movement and the movement of the mother.

A Russian investigator, Boris Klosovskii, of the Institute of Depathology, did a research project with puppies who were litter mates. He put one in a centrifuge and spun him for specific time periods. Later the dog was killed and his vestibular nuclei were examined. It was found that the nuclei were bigger and that the individual nerve cells which make up the nuclei were larger. This is the effect of stimulation that we discussed in Chapter Five, under Neurons. However, not only were these nuclei larger, but also the nuclei to do with vision, tongue movement, hearing, eye movement, and facial muscles were larger, more mature, and thus more learning is possible. Thus we see that there is an intersensory effect, that when the vestibular sense is stimulated, so also are these other senses. We also learn that it is important to stimulate the vestibular sense to enhance the function of the other senses. Thus the stimulation or lack of stimulation of this sense affects the more refined senses of visual and auditory perception.

As the infant lies prone on his stomach, he presses his hands against the bed and raises his head. At first his head wobbles back and forth in a precarious manner, and he often drops it back down. He repeats the exercise until he becomes more and more adept and can hold his head in an upright, controlled, balanced position. What has taken place here is more than muscular. The semicircular canals of his ears contain a fluid which in its own process of flowing back and forth (perhaps not too unlike the fluid in a carpenter's level) sends messages to the brain concerning the organism's balance. A. Jean Ayres (1967) adds a third player to this drama, the sensory nuclei on either side of the neck. Thus with these cues from the muscles and tendons of the neck and chest, from the semicircular canals of the ears, and from those sensory neurons in the neck come the kinesthetic impulses which work together to give the organism balance.

A. Jean Ayres speaks of the *tonic labrinthian reflex*, referring to the infant in the fetal position. When the infant is three or four months old, he inhibits this reflex in the prone position (on his stomach) by stretching his legs back and up and forcing up his head and shoulders from his bed. Thus he is balanced on his curved abdomen. He accentuates this position when you raise him on his abdomen. Ayres feels that in practicing this position the child is activating not only those semicircular canals but also the nuclei in the neck, and thus building a foundation for balance and bilateral integration. The child who can perform this task easily is said to be inhibiting the tonic labrinthian reflex. Now, as he lies on his stomach, his legs are not flexed, but straightened. This phenomenon may be observed in children by asking them to rock on their stomachs and see how high they can rock. This is a simple task for most children, but for those with this particular balance problem it seems almost impossible. The tendons in the neck stand out and the child seems to be trying to lift his whole thorax by only contracting the neck muscles.

Inefficiency of the kinesthetic system can affect the efficiency of the other senses. If the child has a problem in any of these other areas we have mentioned (i.e., body image, figure-ground, tactile, balance), it will affect the efficiency of the kinesthetic system, and vice versa. The hypoactive child who barely drags himself along has probably not been able to achieve an efficient kinesthetic system.

THE KINESTHETIC APPROACH TO EDUCATION

We hear a lot today about using a kinesthetic approach to teach children. It has helped some children, but not others. Barsch says:

Whether or not a child can benefit from a so-called "kinesthetic approach" to anything depends upon his level of kinesthetic sophistication. For some such an approach becomes a magic formula to learning; while to others it becomes a psychologically depressing experience laden with errors. The performer is the critical variable, not the approach. (Barsch, 1967, p. 224)

Audiovisual methods of teaching are faster and more efficient. The kinesthetic approach should be complementary. If a child has difficulty learning to recognize and name a numeral through an audiovisual approach, try the kinesthetic. Have the child trace the numeral or letter very large (six to eight inches) over and over, saying its name. Or he can trace a large, commercially beaded or sandpaper letter.

Try writing the numeral with chalk on a rug sample. Have the child trace it with his fingers. Trace it on his back. Have children sitting train fashion, tracing it on each other's backs, always saying it out loud as they do it.

Write the letter with a felt-tipped pen on the palm of his subdominant hand. Have him trace it with the first finger of his other hand and say it. Prompt children to ask him what it is repeatedly. WHAT'S ON YOUR HAND, MIKE? Reward him everytime he names it correctly.

Sometimes when a child has difficulty forming a letter and even tracing it does not seem to help, take him to the blackboard. He holds the chalk. Hold one hand gently over his eyes and the other on his hand while you make the letter over and over in the same spot in a smooth rhythm. Verbalize the direction of the movement for him. To make an *A*: START ON THE RIGHT. GO UP AND AROUND, CONNECT IT, THEN UP AND DOWN. Repeat this several times until you feel his hand starting to relax and take over the movement. NOW, THINK WHAT YOU ARE FEELING BECAUSE I AM GOING TO TAKE MY HAND AWAY AND LET YOU DO IT ALL BY YOURSELF. Repeat the movement a couple more times and then release his hand. After he has made it successfully, praise him, and let him see the tracings, and then do it all by himself several times. Erase it all and have him make it large and small. From here then, he can usually go to the tracings again and the Frostig box-writing, which we shall discuss later (Chapter Nine).

The child who has difficulty with integration of kinesthetic data will be clumsy and poorly coordinated. To overcome problems with apraxia and coordination, a strong physical education program is imperative. Because this program is so vital to the problem learner we shall devote a whole chapter to methods of organizing and implementing such a program.

PERCEPTUAL-MOTOR MATCH
Description

When the child has learned to discriminate the figure from the ground, and when he has good control, his responses are planned, structured. Now he reacts in a systematic, knowledgeable way to his environment. Kephart refers to this response as a *perceptual-motor match*. This response is cognitive. It is directed by the cerebral cortex.

If the child's perceptions have been inaccurate for some reason (e.g., he lacked the figure-ground sorting ability or he lacked the reception of the tactile sensory stimulation, or the experience), the total perception is inaccurate or incomplete. He knows what elbows are on someone else, but not on himself. He sees the triangle, differentiates it, names it, matches it to another, sees the three sides, the three angles, but cannot reproduce it. He cannot put those parts together to make the whole. The inability to draw is often mistaken as simply a lack of muscular coordination or visual-motor control. But give him three sticks or pegs for a pegboard and see if he can now reproduce the triangle. If he cannot, then it is more than visual-motor, he lacks a perceptual-motor match. Again a child might be able to do all of the above with the triangle but cannot recognize it if it is upside down, or if it is larger or smaller or part of another object, such as a Christmas tree. Thus he might also be able to read some words according to one factor, like configuration, or in one type of print, or according to beginning consonant only, or according to length only, or only in context with other crutches. Or he might be able to differentiate and act on letters individually, and be totally confused when those letters are placed together to form words.

If the child can combine and match all the visual-tactile data, past and present, with control, he is able to make a perceptual-motor match. The child who can read the book but not write the story may fail not only because of lack of motor control but also because he is so involved motorically (because of lack of motor ability) that he is not free to think things through, put the thoughts into sentences, and then write them. The lack of motor control inhibits his ability to write the story. The motor act must be subconscious for the child to concentrate on composing sentences.

When a child is asked to copy a shape, he must perceive it as a whole. Then in order to make it he has to be able to take it apart visually into its component parts, to see where to start it, how to proceed, how the lines relate to each other. Thus he makes the parts one at a time, matching, using his visual perception to determine whether he is doing it correctly. This is termed the *feedback* from his previous perceptions (Fig. 19). With any confusion of perception, the resulting figure may be distorted. The child will not have made a perceptual-motor match. Thus a child may be *exposed* to perceptual experiences, but if he does not achieve a clear perception and a perceptual-motor match, he does not have an integrated concept. As A. Jean Ayres says:

> Just because there is an environment acting on an individual and that individual's receptors seem to be responding to the stimuli, doesn't mean that the individual is really interpreting his world in a meaningful manner or with the same meaning that we might expect. One of the first things we need to learn to do is to avoid taking perception for granted. (Ayres, 1964, p. 1)

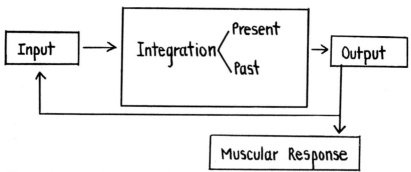

Figure 19. Kephart's Diagram of Feedback Mechanisms in Perception. Reproduced from Kephart's *The Slow Learner in the Classroom* by permission of author and publisher.

Techniques in Training for a Perceptual-Motor Match

When the child lacks this perceptual-motor match, he is not receiving the same information or verifying information from all of his senses. You might say that his eyes are sending him one message and his past experience and feedback system another. Thus he is confused and the responses of his hands, muscles, voice, etc. are inadequate. The developing vision might be poor because the ocular control and feedback are poor, and vice versa. Ebersole and Kephart explain it this way:

> However, the young child is only now developing a stable visual world with which to evaluate the present perception. Therefore, the body of information which should provide the criterion for ocular control is not yet present. On the other hand, without ocular control the incoming contributions to the body of visual information are inconsistent and spotty. Thus a continuous dilemma exists: control of the eyes is hampered by lack of a stable visual world, and, at the same time, the stability of the visual world is impaired by lack of ocular control. (Ebersole, 1968, pp. 45-46)

The solution then lies in sensorimotor and perceptual-motor training through having the child explore each concept motorically, visually, and with as many different senses as possible. Thus the child must learn through a very thorough examining of the concept from every angle. For example, if you are teaching him *round*, he would feel round balls, make round balls of clay or dough, discriminate round balls from square boxes and blocks in a tray, then in a feeling box. He would use a circle template to trace *round*, feeling the sides of the template, then removing the template and tracing over the visual circle. He would run on a circle drawn on the blacktop, to the right and to the left. Then he would make his own circle floor-pattern by running in large and small circles. He would then draw circles, large and small, with his pencil and crayons. He would find circles in his environment (the clock, a wheel, a plate) and then turn his drawn circles into these objects by making them into balls, balloons, wheels, and clocks. He could make pictures of nothing but circular objects. Bilateral chalkboard circles would aid the motor, kinesthetic, and visual integration of the concept. He could even learn to move his eyes in a circle following a target. Then, with his eyes closed, you would give him new objects to feel, taste, smell, listen to, to discover their identity. Thus you would teach him to explore his environment systematically until motor and perception mean the same. He would later be able to eliminate the need for the motor and rely on his vision for an accurate perception.

REFERENCES

Andrews, Gladys: *Creative Rhythmic Movement for Children.* Englewood Cliffs, New Jersey, Prentice-Hall, 1954.

Ayres, A. Jean: *Perceptual-Motor Dysfunction in Children.* Monograph from the Greater Cincinnati District Ohio Occupational Therapy Association Conference, 1964.

————: Lecture in Sacramento, California, 1967.

Barsch, Ray H.: *Achieving Perceptual-Motor Efficiency.* Seattle, Spec Child, 1967.

The Beat Goes On. Palo Alto, California, Peek.

Cratty, Bryant J.: *Movement Behavior and Motor Learning.* Philadelphia, Lea & Febiger, 1964.

deHirsch, Katrina; Jansky, Jeanette, and Langford, William S.: *Predicting Reading Failure,* New York, Harper & Row, 1966.

Developmental Learning Materials, Chicago, Illinois, 3505 N. Ashland Avenue.

Diem, Liselott: *Who Can . . .* Frankfort, Wilhelm Limpert, 1962.

Ebersole, Marylou; Kephart, Newell C., and Ebersole, James B.: *Steps to Achievement for the Slow Learner.* Columbus, Ohio, Merrill, 1968.

Engelmann, S. *et al.: Learning Language III.* Urbana, U of Ill Pr.

Hackett, Layne, and Jenson, Robert G.: *A Guide to Movement Exploration.* Palo Alto, California, Peek, 1966.

Held, Richard: Plasticity in sensory-motor systems. *Scientific American,* Nov. 1965.

Kephart, Newell C.: Lecture in San Francisco, California, May, 1968.

————: *The Slow Learner in The Classroom.* Columbus, Ohio, Merrill, 2nd Edition, 1971.

Klosovskii, Boris: *The Development of the Brain and Its Disturbance by Harmful Factors.* Long Island City, Pergamon, 1963.

Lind Climber: Evanston, Illinois. Lind Climber Company, 807 Reba Place.

Mosston, Muska: *Developmental Movement.* Columbus, Ohio, Merrill, 1965.

Showers, Paul: *Find Out by Touching.* New York, Crowell, 1961.

The Stegel: Plans available from Orinda Union School District, Orinda, California.

Weidenbacker, Rheta, *et al.:* Sensory discrimination of children with cerebral palsy. *Percept Motor Skills,* 71:608-610, 1963.

Chapter Seven

Perception of Space and Form

VERTICAL SPACE

W ITH A SECURE body image and accurate discriminatory perception, the child is then ready to explore the world outside his body. The first spatial concepts are vertical.

We consider the *up and down* of everything in our world, including ourselves, in relation to the earth. When we are close to the earth, we are *down*. When we are far away from it, we are *up*. Thus the gravity pull of the earth gives us the basis for our vertical world. When the infant in the prone position, on his stomach, raises his head and achieves a balanced head position, he is also achieving a static *up-down* vertical space. If his head is not balanced in relation to the center of gravity, his vertical space is distorted. *Up* might not mean straight up from the earth, but rather over at an angle, toward the upper right or left. A distortion like this could develop out of an inefficient roll-over pattern which is never corrected. If the infant is unable to turn his body completely over, becomes twisted with one arm under him, or has poor kinesthetic sensations from his muscles, then again his basis for static balance and, therefore, a clear vertical perception of space would suffer. As the child learns to propel himself forward in the many variations of the creep-crawl, he is traveling in the horizontal, but in doing so, he is further establishing his balance, his center of gravity, and this, too, affects his vertical world (Barsch, 1967).

Then the child begins to pull himself up into the vertical position, and all his previous learnings contribute to his erect vertical balance and to his locomotion in space. He probably has to relearn many of his balancing skills now as he applies them to himself in the upright position. He may have learned to control his balance well in crawling, but upright he is further from the floor, his own body's center of gravity has changed, and he must compensate for these changes. The heavy, infantile head, and his collapsible legs add to his problem. He now finds that his body's center of gravity has changed to a much higher point, rather like a bottle or vase standing on its neck. He must now learn that in order to balance himself in a variety of positions he must use counterbalance levers. For example, in order to reach far out front and away from his body, he learns that he must put one foot out to keep from falling. Or that if he wants to lean out to first one side then the other, he must spread his feet more.

As the child is now organizing his vertical space, he seems to have a compulsion to organize everything else that way (Gesell, 1949). He builds high towers piling all kinds of things one on top of the other, and often then climbing up on top of it in triumph. Thus as he is determining his own balance in space, he is also relating to objects in space and how they, too, might balance. The child is learning *upness* before *downness*. He often climbs up on a chair or up the stairs, but can't get down. The young toddler gets himself into many predicaments up from the floor in which he must howl for help. Downness is much more difficult. One study by McCaskill and Wellman (Wellman, 1937) found that children were thirty-three months old before fifty percent of them could jump from an eight-inch height, with forty-six months needed for balanced descent from a twenty-eight-inch height.

HORIZONTAL SPACE
Laterality

Balance of the body in vertical space is also the basis for the child's beginning awareness of horizontal or side space. Initially, the infant utilizes both of his sides in unison, unaware of any motion originating from one side only, or of any reciprocal action between the sides. That is, both of his arms may be flailing the air at the same time, but not in cognitive control of movement.

Then the child starts to learn balance through his rolling, crawling, and walking, and thus discovers how he must use one side of his body to counterbalance the other. He finds that now he can reach out with one hand only, and that by using his other arm and his leg in a counterbalancing motion he can keep from falling over. Now he is developing what we call *laterality,* the feeling of the awareness and the difference between the two sides of his body. It is never just the identity of right and left.

The child learns to use these two sides reciprocally. He can hold an object with one hand as he explores it with the other. He must learn to integrate the sensations arising from both sides of his body into a total perception; e.g. he is feeling both sides of an object at the same time with his two hands. If his total perception is to be accurate, he must be able to fuse the perceptions from the stimuli of both of his hands into the overall generalized perception of the totality of that single object. He is really learning three different aspects of his body: that he can use one side without the use of the other, that he can use both sides together, or in a reciprocal action to help the other.

You will often see the child who lacks laterality *mirroring* the action of one side of his body with a similar action on the other side. He is writing on the board with the right hand, while the left elbow is bent and that hand is bouncing through the air in a similar rhythm. Or there is the child who tries to write using ONLY the right hand. The paper moves all over the desk, while the left hand hangs limply at his side, making no effort to assist. When the child has learned both the reciporocal action and the singular action of the two sides of his body, we might say that he has achieved *bilaterality.*

The child achieves this bilaterality through the tactile and kinesthetic stimuli which are continually telling him the position of each of his sides. In learning different ways to creep and crawl, he is experimenting with bilaterality. He learns (1) *unilateral activity,* activation of all of one side without the other, as crawling by reaching out with right arm and leg in unison (bear walk) ; (2) *bilateral activity,* when both arms reach out, and then both knees work in unison also, as with a *frog jump* or *puppy run,* and (3) *alternated activity,* when the right arm swings out with the left knee and the left arm moves with the right knee in a rhythmical crawl.

Thus the child learns *laterality* through balance and the movement of his muscles in a variety of postures giving him an inner secure feeling of the symmetry of his own body and his control over it. To learn this laterality, he must have accurate discrimination and integration of the stimuli from his senses—tactile, kinesthetic, vestibular, and visual. Thus it is easy to see how any distortion or misperception in any of these areas could cause a problem in the child's concept of horizontal space. The resulting problem is reflected in the child's inability to discern right from left in his reversals of words, letters, and numerals. He may be able to spell orally, but not write the letters in the correct sequence. He may add vertical columns accurately, but not horizontal equations. This child's problems are most pronounced in school achievement because both arithmetic and reading are presented horizontally.

A laterality problem might also be evidenced by poor horizontal ocular movements, poor balance (either static or dynamic, or both), or in the inability to inhibit the tonic neck reflex and do a sustained head lift in the prone. Static balance is achieved when the child can stand on one leg for ten seconds, or longer. Dynamic balance is tested by having the child walk a ten- or twelve-foot-long 2″ x 4″ board on the two-inch side. We discussed that tonic neck reflex under *Vestibular Sense* in Chapter Six. Observe the child's ability to do a *rocking horse*. He lies on his stomach, lifting both legs and thorax, and tries to rock his body. Some children have difficulty even getting the chin up off the floor, while others can lift the whole thorax.

A secure feeling of laterality and a firm bilateral control are essential ingredients of an established body image. Without these elements the child is insecure, confused, often even afraid, because he cannot control his body in space. He may walk up the ladder of the slide, but is afraid to come down. He may make only small jumps into the air, needs help to jump down from even a one- to two-foot height, and is afraid to even try to run and jump over a low obstacle. He may show fear in walking or running down a hill or across a snowbank. A small child may especially show his inadequacy of his body in space by being afraid to traverse a slotted board walk where there is an inch or so between boards. This child tends to immediately revert to crawling to solve the problem. This is good. He can then reestablish his balance on this new terrain and thus teach himself to walk it. However, the parents often discourage this, or shame the child for being fearful and wanting to crawl. Thus his inadequacy is further deepened.

It is thought that eleven years is the average for learning a thorough left-right on one's self and others, but many adults continue to have this problem. Just try to give directions to some people, as to how to get to your home! Some children may acquire an understanding of right and left handedness without being also able to identify a right foot or left elbow, or right ear. When the child has a laterality problem it is necessary to go back to vertical space, balance, and motor planning to help him to achieve in horizontal space.

Midline Problem

As the body's own center of gravity is the basis for balance in space, the vertical midline of the body (a hypothetical line drawn vertically dividing the body) is the basis for the relationship of objects in their approach toward or retreat from the body. All objects which approach the midline of the body are coming *toward* the body. Objects which are retreating from the midline are going *away* from the body. If an object approaches from a right-left direction from the right of the midline, it is coming *toward* the body. If it continues in the same direction, it crosses the midline of the body, and then is progressing *away* from the left of the body. Thus a right-left direction contains both a movement *toward* and a movement *away from* the body, actually appearing to the confused child, who has not established a firm laterality, as if it had changed directions in the middle of the body. The child must learn from which side the activity arises and how to cross the midline. A. Jean Ayres calls this a *midbrain function*.

If a child has this midline problem, he may display it in a number of subtle, or even bizarre, ways. Randy would seem to be simply ambidextrous, using sometimes one hand and then the other. But upon closer observation, it was found to be more dramatic than that. He drew a large house on the board. When he was using his left hand he moved his body to the right so that he never crossed the midline of his body at any time. Then he proceeded with the windows. The left window was drawn with his left hand. Now this time, without moving his body (as he had done with the house), he changed the chalk to his right hand and placed a window on the right side of the house. He wanted the door in the middle of the house. Since he had the chalk in his right hand now, he simply moved his body to the left so that he could make the door without crossing the midline. There was no sign of his problem in the finished picture, but only in its execution.

For this reason it is most important to watch a problem learner (and particularly an ambidextrous one) when he is performing such visual perceptual tasks as the Perceptual Forms Test, the Purdue Perceptual-Rating Survey, and the Bender (Chapter Four). Watch for these three things especially: the body moving to the side, the paper being moved to one side, or the changing of hands. At Dr. Newell Kephart's San Francisco, California, visit in 1967, one happy, mixed-up five-year old solved the problem of connecting two X's placed on either side of his body. He giggled, picked up a piece of chalk in each hand, and simultaneously drew lines from the two X's until the two small fists met in the middle. He had succeeded in the task without crossing the midline. And he was triumphant!

Pouring from a pitcher might also be awkward for this child. He has problems deciding how to do it. Even if he is right-handed he may be unable to consider putting the glass on his right side where it would be easier for him. He may place the glass on his left, and next to the edge of the table, and then lean his whole body into pouring away from him in such a manner that he has to raise his whole torso to do so, and cannot readily direct his pouring. Or even if he does have the glass on his right side, he still uses the same exaggerated body movements to pour away from him where he cannot see what he is doing.

The midline problem can also be noted during horizontal eye movements. Have the child follow a small plastic bug which you have pinned to a pencil eraser. Hold the eraser about eighteen inches from the child's eyes and move it slowly across the midline of his body. Watch very carefully to see if he uses any means to prevent crossing the midline. He may just show a moment's hesitation at the midline, he may look away, or at you, or blink. His eyes might make a very rapid jerk or backward movement. He may have difficulty using both eyes together. One eye might take over on one side of the body. Or he may simply be unable to follow many consecutive crossings of the midline without the eyes watering profusely.

Larger gross motor movements may also identify the problem. In mirroring the movements of the teacher, the child may have trouble crossing his body and putting his right hand on his left ear, or left hand on right knee. One boy accomplished the task of right hand-left ear, by reaching over the top of his head.

Dominance

As the child experiments with various motor movements on either and both sides of his body, he eventually comes to favor one side over the other. One side becomes the leader in activities; the other, the follower. One hand becomes the holder, the other, the manipulator, as in cutting. One eye becomes preferred when looking through a kaleidoscope, aiming a gun or arrow, using a microscope.

Don't confuse this with the *sighting eye* that fixes on an object in the distance and which may change from one moment to the next. Look at a far corner of the room, then bring a tube of paper up and sight that corner through the tube. Then close first one eye, then the other. When the corner is no longer visable through the tube, then you have closed your *sighting eye*. This, however, is not as stable as the *dominant eye*. One day your right eye might do the sighting, the next day, the left.

As one hand becomes dominant and one eye the dominant and controlling eye, also one leg becomes stronger, preferred for hopping, kicking, stepping up, or starting out. This consistent choice of one side of the body over the other is termed *dominance.* You have a dominant hand, eye, leg, and, some believe, even an ear. They may not all be on the same side of the body, although usually they are. You might be right-handed and left-footed. The term *unilaterality* is sometimes used to designate the situation in which a person's dominance of hand, eye, and leg are all on the same side of the body. Then there are the confusing terms of *mixed dominance* and *crossed dominance,* to designate an ambidextrous nature of eye, hand or leg and to classify the person with the right-hand-left-leg preference. The two terms are not consistently defined the same way. Since there is no known educational importance to these categories at this time, I see no need to add to the controversy by attempting to define them.

It was previously believed that all stimuli received by the right side of the body went to the left hemisphere of the brain, and vice versa. More recent research with the vision of cats has led us to believe otherwise. One eye of the cat was trained to a discrimination while the other eye was occluded. When the cat was confronted with the task with the first eye occluded, he was able to perform. The visual impulses entering one eye go to both hemispheres via the optic chiasm (Butter, 1968). If this is severed, the impulses still go to the other hemisphere but now via the corpus callosum. Thus since both eyes receive the same stimuli and it goes to both sides of the brain, a double integrative process is essential for the organism to receive a clear fused picture (Ayres, 1964).

Dominance seems to develop between the ages of two and six. However, of twenty-seven children in one class of deprived problem children, five-years-nine-months to six-years-nine-months of age, nineteen children had not yet established dominance in hand, leg, or eye. This is especially apparent in the contrast of the cutting hand versus the writing hand. With sensorimotor training, most children had established dominance by the end of the year. It is thought that the organism develops dominance to help him keep laterality straight and is, therefore, often a sign that laterality is developed. Thus a bilaterality is thought to be required before unilateral dominance is possible.

Barsch describes the emergence of dominance:

His first task in defining side space becomes a matter of achieving a hand preference. Some authorities believe he has no choice in this matter—his preferential side has been genetically predetermined. Other authorities feel that his preferred side is trained by parental treatment. Still others believe that it emerges from his personal experiences. Whichever may eventually prove to be the true cause of preference it must nonetheless be achieved for efficiency. His earliest efforts at manipulating his world are bilateral and from this initial bilaterality one side becomes the leader, and one side becomes the follower. (Barsch, 1967, p. 144)

There is a preponderance of left-handed, ambidextrous, and mixed and crossed-dominance children in the ranks of those with learning problems. This has been a subject of considerable study and of heated controversy. It is felt that these things are symptoms of the disorganization of the problem learner, but not necessarily the cause of the disability, much as a rise in temperature is a symptom of an illness, and not a cause.

In the controversial Doman-Delacato program, the advocates feel that the child with learning problems who lacks dominance and unilaterality, lacks neurological organization. (Read *Human Neurological Organization* by Edward LeWinn.) Authorities who have worked with these problem children do agree that they are very disorganized and operate at a subcortical level, but have some reservations about the theory of unilaterality and sequential development. However, the basic sensorimotor techniques used to help overcome the child's problems are relatively similar in the learning disability centers throughout the country.

The Doman-Delacato program differs in its emphasis on the *patterning* of the child's crawl and on the establishment of unilaterality or dominance. Above all, though, it is a complete program directed by a staff neurologist which concerned parents can follow working with the child at home. The child is then reevaluated at the clinic at regular intervals and the home program altered according to the child's progress. Some children for whom there was no help or hope from any other source have made remarkable progress under this program. Others made limited progress, and some none at all. I personally know several children who have made gains under this program; one was the child of a highly qualified neurologist.

Actually medicine probably knows less about the nervous system than any of the other body processes, but there have been recent breakthroughs. There is the *new neurology* today, just as there is the *new math*. Hopefully with the medical research which is progressing in this field, and education's new interest in neuropsychology, we will know more in the future about how the child's brain operates. Meanwhile, the more intelligent course is to remain open to new theories, findings, and treatments, being more concerned with children than with defending a single narrow viewpoint. It is said that "theories don't die, only people who advocate them."

DIRECTIONALITY

Directionality is the relationship of objects to the body of the organism. Thus a pencil is on *my* right, my manuscript is on *my* left, and the typewriter is in front of *me*. The ceiling is over *my* head, the rug is under *my* feet. These terms all refer to the position of an object in relation to the body. We learn the relationship of objects to us through body contact. I can best reach my pencil with my right hand, because it is closer, while my left hand can most easily reach my manuscript. If there is any confusion of laterality, then there will be confusion in directionality. If I am not sure of the position and use of my right hand, I am also unsure as to which hand is closer to my pencil. Thus the direction from my body of the pencil is confused also.

I like Radler's definitions:

"Laterality" is the inner sense of one's own symmetry: "leftness" and "rightness," or "two-sidedness" . . . . We might call it the map of internal space.

Directionality is the projection into space of laterality—the awareness of left and right . . . in the world around you. We can call this the map of external space. . . .

Thus directionality is the counterpart in the world outside your skin of the sensations you feel within your skin—one man's up is another man's down; my left is your right when we are facing each other. (Radler, 1960, pp. 33-34)

Objects do not have directions within themselves except in

their relations to gravity and the earth. Thus an object can be *up* or *down* in relation only to the earth. But even that direction changes in relation to our bodies. If the typewriter is on the desk and I am standing, then it is *down* on the desk. If I am sitting on the floor, then the typewriter is *up* on the desk.

The other directions of *right, left, behind, in front of* are in relation only to our bodies. The directions of *inside of, on top of, under, over,* and *beside* may be in relation to us or to another object. If it is in relation to us, "The blanket is *over* me," then this is *directionality.* If it is in relation to another object, "under the chair," then we are in the realm of *spatial relations.* If there is a problem in laterality, the child will also have directionality problems. If there is confusion of directions, the child will also have difficulty with spatial relations. This sequence of laterality to directionality to spatial relations has been outlined by both Piaget and Gesell.

Directionality problems show up in reading and math because these activities are mainly horizontal, and if the child lacks bilaterality and, therefore, has directionality problems, he has gross confusions of left-right sequence. Thus *on* looks like *no,* *b* is like *d,* and Billy writes his name *ylliB,* and letters and numerals are reversed in execution.

A. Jean Ayres believes that:

> Visual perception of form involves much the same process as visual perception of position in space. Thus, recognizing the difference between "b" and "d" is not so very different from differentiating between a square and a triangle, nor so very different from finding a point on one piece of paper that corresponds spatially to a similar point on another. Adequate functioning of one central nervous system mechanism is probably essential to all three types of visual perception.
>
> This same mechanism, however, also is responsible for integrating kinesthetic information bearing information about position of the hand in space (without benefit of vision) and also of manual perception of form. It would seem that perception of form and position is an intermodality function, at least by ages six and seven. (Ayres, 1964, p. 10)

Control of the eyes is very important to directionality. Our eyes have to give us the same accurate information as did our tactile sense. We know the direction our eyes are pointing because we have gone through thousands of experiences of touching and looking at objects at the same time. We made a match of information from our eyes and the movement of our hands. If we learned well the laterality of our own bodies, the direction our eyes are pointing, then we need merely look at an object in space and know its position in space, whether it is right or left, behind or in front. There had to be an accurate matching of the information between the tactile, kinesthetic, and visual senses previously to result in a clear visual perception.

DEPTH PERCEPTION

The infant learns depth in his first crawling. He kinesthetically measures distance by the effort it requires for him to reach an object. If an object is little more than an arm's reach away, then it is *near* and requires very little effort to obtain. An object across the yard takes him considerable time and energy to reach. Thus it is *far*.

Forward space and a more efficient depth perception seem to begin emerging at about six to seven years of age. This might be noted in throwing, catching, jumping, hopping, and skipping, which are done in forward space. In first learning to throw, the child uses only the arm, then the arm and foot on the throwing side of the body, and finally at about seven or so he perfects a cross-diagonal throwing pattern involving the throwing arm and the opposite foot.

Jumping develops before hopping, the child first learning the vertical jumping in space. Then he finds that to move ahead through space he must use a forward propulsion or body thrust. Jumping limits his forward movement, so he develops the hop, by which he can cover ground more quickly, thus also hurling through space with more freedom, more exhilaration. The child that is still operating on the vertical plane will rely on jumping, or will have a very inefficient hop, lacking the forward propulsion. The child who has achieved static and dynamic balance and a firm laterality will find it relatively easy to hop on the forward plane. This is why we find that the child's ability to maintain balance and propulsion on a sustained forward hop is a significant indication of his physical development and his efficient laterality.

Skipping has often been used by teachers as an indication of the child's physical proficiency. It is true that a graceful rhythmic skip does indicate good bilateral control. Some children do manage to learn to skip without having first achieved adequate balance and bilateral control. The resultant skip, however, lacks the smoothness, the timing, the rhythm, the bilateral balance of the efficient skipper. Often the child with bilateral and balance problems uses only a one-sided skip, or is inefficient in distributing his body weight from side to side. He tires easily; cannot skip a distance. Thus you must look for these things in evaluating a child's skip.

Another skill on the depth plane is *catching*. If the child has good depth perception and the visual convergence to enable his eyes to follow the ball, and the bilateral control, he will be able to reach or step out of his way to get in line with the ball and successfully catch it. If he can catch the ball only when it is thrown directly at his midline, then he has not achieved efficiency in the depth plane. The child who has problems throwing and catching does not know how to coordinate his vision with his movements. He must be trained to use his eyes to aim and to follow the ball.

Barsch says that the development of visual fusion coincides with the development on the horizontal plane to give the child efficiency of movement, and a synthesis of his other senses.

> He now fuses visually, auditorily, kinesthetically, and tactually. He no longer simply looks at something but now looks *into* things. He is now better prepared to understand the howness and whyness of his world. He has an appreciation of depth and can efficiently employ it in both his physical and cognitive explorations. . . . His fusion on a kinesthetic level contributes to a coordinative efficiency which makes a graceful performer. His tactual fusion now gives him a *deeper* and profound comprehension of texture and quality. His auditory fusion makes him an efficient listener capable of comprehending the probing questions and directives which he encounters. His visual fusion allows him to perceive the profundity of graphic symbols. Having now reached the fusional point with all three axes organized to his advantage, his geometric training period for space is finished. His future can now be dedicated to expanding upon those basic efficiencies in acquiring wider and wider ranges of skills, refinements and precision in

movement—the pursuit of knowledge can now become his full-time oc-
cupation. (Barsch, 1967, p. 138)

THE MYSTERY OF BEHIND

In infancy the child's awareness of space is limited to that
directly in line with that moment's vision and within arm's reach
of his body. When his vision shifts to another side, his awareness
also shifts, and the former visual field is forgotten. Light from a
distance (e.g. a window) is just an unidentifiable blob. He
might be alerted by sounds behind him and out of his visual
field, but he cannot locate them.

The crawler is aware of everything in the visual field directly
in front of him with more distance vision. Everything exists only
in the forward plane. He is unaware of the space behind him,
and is quite vague about his periphery also. Thus if you enter a
room behind him and make a noise, he may be rudely startled,
confused, unable to locate you.

The toddler and beginning walker is now aware of the shape
of the room all around him and the location of the doors and
significant (to him) items of furniture behind him. But he is
not aware of other rooms, or of upstairs, or outside. The forward
visual field still has the greatest immediate importance to him,
and its details are the most pronounced.

When the child's spatial concepts are fully developed, he is
aware of space all around him, within and without his vision,
inside and outside the house. He has developed a visual memory
of his familiar habitat, where he keeps his toys, where he left his
bike, what Tommy's house and the store look like.

Awareness of the space behind him helps him to localize sounds
coming from that area. He knows that his mother has come into
the room by the sound of her voice. He does not have to turn
around and see her to ascertain this. He can judge the space
behind him, knowing how many steps he can safely go backward
without turning around to check, or before he must check. He
can back into a seat without having to feel for or hold the seat,
because he knows just where it is in space.

Children who have not developed an awareness of the space
behind them encounter many difficulties in space. They turn

suddenly and slam into a pole or wall. They are unaware of other children or objects approaching from directions other than frontal. Thus they run into the projectory of balls, and the paths of their peers, and think that they have been struck on purpose. This is the basis of many of the battles into which these disorganized children are thrust.

TUNNEL VISION

Some children may appear to have use of only a tunnel vision. I took Loreen to a children's *fairyland*. She came over the Three Billy Goat's Gruff bridge, and without seeing the three appealing baby goats on the ground to her right, she spied Snow White's castle one hundred feet ahead and headed straight for it. From there she zeroed in on the Crooked Mile, some four hundred feet away and bypassed Mary's lamb and Hiawatha's deer. This lack of awareness of side space is perhaps the reason for, or the outcome of, some of the disorganized hyperactivity. The child is unable to explore space in an organized manner, because he is too unaware of *side, rear,* and *down* space.

These same children are often unaware of *down* space even in front of them. Thus they splash right through mud puddles, fall over their toys, walk on their coats, and run into smaller children. Although *down space* is organized early, *up space* requires all their attention once they are erect. Thus particularly if their ocular motility is inefficient, they may never have perfected *down* space, which is used for stairs or ladders, jumping off, crawling through, or climbing down.

HIERARCHY OF SENSORIMOTOR-PERCEPTUAL DEVELOPMENT

In the last three chapters we have traced the sensorimotor-perceptual development of the child. He first had to learn to discriminate the figure from the ground in all sense modalities before he could begin to perceive anything (Fig. 20). The development of his tactile and kinesthetic perceptions gave him the basis for his gross coordinations and his understanding of his own body image. As he developed vertical space he learned the up

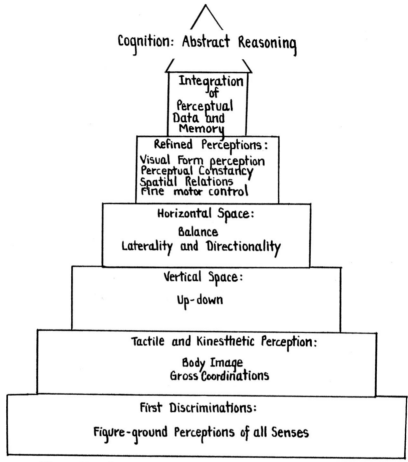

Figure 20. Hierarchy of Sensorimotor-Perceptual Development.

and down of his world. As he learned balance he attained knowledge of horizontal space, laterality, and directionality. All of these stabilized his perceptions and gave him accurate data with which to make more refined conclusions from his incoming stimuli. Understanding of lines, directions, sizes, and their relationships gave him visual form perception. Accuracy of data gave him perceptual constancy so that he could recognize a form in any position, size, or location. He has a clear understanding of the relationship in space of different objects. Ocular motility and convergence have been refined so that he now has fine motor control, depth perception, peripheral vision, and visual memory.

Finally, the child learned to integrate the information of all his senses, to compare data, to recall details, to classify, to sequence, to use language to reason and to express himself. And now he is at the pinnacle of sensorimotor-perceptual development and is capable of higher cognitive processes, convergent and divergent thinking, and abstract reasoning.

If any function at a lower level of his development is unstable or inaccurate, then the whole hierarchy is disturbed. We must keep this hierarchy in mind when testing and diagnosing a child's disabilities. A child with visual form perception difficulties might have an unstable basis because of poor balance or figure-ground problems. These basic difficulties must be eliminated before the child is ready for refined perceptions or cognition. This may be the reason we have seen so many dramatic changes in children's academic abilities after perceptual training. There was Mark who could not spell a word and after six weeks training with balance and with templates suddenly got one hundred percent in spelling. Then there was Linda, who couldn't remember more than ten words; after various perceptual training exercises, she declared she could read a primer. She could! She did!

Education in the traditional classroom has failed our children because it has concerned itself only with the final pinnacle of the developmental hierarchy, that of cognition and abstract reasoning. We tested children to see if they had the skills essential to cognition: sequence, memory, coding, classifying, spatial relations, vocabulary, directionality, visual form perception, and auditory perception. If the child was lacking in any of these, he simply scored low in total ability and we crossed him out as not having a worthwhile potential to society. We did not attempt to teach any of these basic skills which the child lacked. We failed HIM in first grade because of our own failure to TEACH him.

THE CHILD WITH LATERALITY AND
DIRECTIONALITY PROBLEMS

The child who has no clear feeling for the different sides of his body may have a variety of problems. He may not have an established dominant side, or he may be ambidextrous. He may not know which is his right or left side. He may lack feeling for the midline of his body and may change hands or body position when writing from one side of the paper or blackboard to the other. He may mirror the movement of his one arm by following or copying that movement with the other, or he may not use one side to aid the other. That is, when he writes, his nonwriting hand may hang limply instead of helping to hold the paper. His sitting and walking postures are often poor. He reverses letters, numerals, and words in reading and writing. He has difficulty following directions. He may appear to be disobedient because he does not understand the teacher's directions. He may resort to copying the work of his peers because he has no faith in his own ability. He may have difficulty finding his way around the school or finding the paper "in the top, left-hand drawer." He demonstrates rotations and reversals of figures in the Frostig, Beery, Bender, or the Perceptual Forms tests (Chapter Four). His pictures and forms lack a solid baseline. He is unable to plan space. Thus he may begin writing in the middle of a page and then run out of room to finish. This child's balance is often poor; hopping is difficult.

LATERALITY TRAINING

Laterality is an inner feeling or awareness for the difference between the two sides of the body, how one side may operate independently of, or cooperatively with, the other. The child must establish an awareness of his body (Body Image, Chapter Six). Simultaneously, he must learn to balance his body in space. Balance must be taught in a variety of ways so that the child establishes a feeling for the differences between the two sides of his body. He must learn both static and dynamic balance and how to compensate when his body's center of gravity is changed by body position or by an added weight on one side. As the child learns to balance and to feel the differences in his two sides, he usually begins to establish a favored, or dominant side. This helps him to keep these relationships straight. As you see this preference developing you may further reinforce it by stressing the use of this dominant side. Following are some suggestions for developing laterality:

1. Static balance: CAN YOU STAND ON YOUR RIGHT FOOT AND COUNT SLOWLY TO TEN WITHOUT FALLING? NOW TRY YOUR LEFT FOOT. STAND ON YOUR RIGHT FOOT AGAIN, BUT THIS TIME CLOSE YOUR EYES. TRY THE LEFT FOOT WITH YOUR EYES CLOSED. WHICH IS HARDER, WITH YOUR EYES OPEN OR CLOSED? LOOK STRAIGHT AT THIS POLE AND TRY STANDING ON YOUR LEFT FOOT. DOES IT HELP YOU? Check the posture of children with balance problems. Teach them to use visual steering to keep their balance. HOLD YOUR HEAD UP AND LOOK AT THIS TARGET WHILE YOU BALANCE ON ONE FOOT! KEEP YOUR EYES ON THE TARGET AND COUNT TO TEN. DID YOU DO BETTER THAT TIME? Change the body's center of gravity: CAN YOU LEAN WAY OVER, STAND ON ONE FOOT AND BALANCE TO TEN? CAN YOU SWING YOUR RIGHT FOOT WITHOUT BENDING YOUR KNEE WHILE YOU BALANCE ON YOUR LEFT AND COUNT? CAN YOU SWING ONE LEG IN A CIRCLE WHILE YOU BALANCE? CAN YOU WAVE YOUR ARMS OUT TO THE SIDE AND BALANCE? CAN YOU BEND YOUR KNEES AND BALANCE? CAN YOU LOOK UP AT THE SKY AND BALANCE? CAN YOU BALANCE WHILE YOU HAVE TWO BEANBAGS IN YOUR LEFT HAND? CAN YOU BALANCE HOLDING A POLE OUT TO YOUR RIGHT? CAN YOU BALANCE UP ON YOUR TOES? CAN YOU BALANCE ON YOUR HEELS? CAN YOU BALANCE WITH BOTH FEET ON THE GROUND WHILE YOU TWIST YOUR BODY AROUND AND AROUND?

2. Dynamic balance: CAN YOU WALK WITH A BEANBAG ON YOUR HEAD AND NOT LOSE IT? CAN YOU WALK LEANING SIDEWAYS WITHOUT FALLING OVER? CAN YOU WALK CROSS-STEPS WITHOUT LOSING YOUR BALANCE? CAN YOU HOP ON YOUR RIGHT FOOT? CAN YOU HOP WHILE HOLDING ONTO YOUR OTHER FOOT? CAN YOU HOP SIDEWAYS? BACKWARD?

3. Dynamic balance on the walking beam: Use an eight foot long 2″ x 4″ board, braced on both ends and in the middle. Teach the four-inch side first, walking slowly forward, backward, and

Figure 21. Traversing the Beam With a Bucket of Beanbags.

sideways. Teach the use of a central target on which the child might focus to use his eyes to guide him straight forward and backward. (Just cut a red X from construction paper.) Discover different ways to traverse the beam. CAN YOU CROSS THE BEAM WITH THREE POINTS OF YOUR BODY? WITH FOUR? Two hands, two feet; or two hands, two knees. CAN YOU GO SIDEWAYS ACROSS THE BEAM CROSSING YOUR RIGHT FOOT IN FRONT OF YOUR LEFT? NOW TRY CROSSING YOUR LEFT FOOT BEHIND YOUR RIGHT. Give the child a bucket of beanbags to carry in one hand while crossing the beam (Fig. 21). Or, have him balance a bag on his head. Put obstacles on the beam over which he must step. (More balancing activities are given in Chapter Eight.) Also use balance board, scat-scoota, stilts, and tubes—described in Chapter Eight.

4. Rolling, somersaulting, and crawling activities with a lot of body contact with the floor help him to gain awareness of his sides. The On Floor routines described in Chapter Eight are excellent for establishing control of the two sides of the body.

5. Do extensive experimentation with exploring body move-

ments in a well-balanced physical education program (Chapter Eight).

6. Template training described later under Visual Form Perception helps to teach the child the concepts of *straight, horizontal, vertical, left, right, up, down, across,* and to cross his midline.

7. Use a weighted wrist band on the dominant wrist during physical education and/or during writing or template work. The wrist band is made by sewing two square lead drapery weights into a strip of red cotton three inches by nine inches. The slack is taken up by a six-inch piece of elastic. Thus the wristband is easy for the child to put on and remove.

8. Jumping and hopping exercises stimulate feeling in the child's feet. Work on having the child jump, keeping both feet together. Jump frontward, backward, sideways, over a line or rope, into and out of a space. Jump high. Jump low. Jump from low heights, over obstacles. Hopping is taught on both feet. As you are able to determine that, for example, the right side is dominant in eye and hand, it helps to establish a greater feeling for the laterality of that side if you encourage the right foot's use in hopping and kicking. Then for long distance hopping have right-handed children hop on the right foot and left-handed children hop on the left foot. Every child (barring a physical disability) should then learn to hop all the way around the room (or about fifty feet) on his dominant foot without putting his other foot down and without touching anything. Have hopping contests and relays.

9. Another way to strengthen the use of the dominant foot is through kicking exercises. Each child should have a large rubber ball. They all put their balls on a line outside and at a signal run and kick it with the dominant foot. They try to see who can get his ball all the way to the fence first.

10. Stimulate the dominant hand. Each child squeezes and flexes his dominant hand until it tingles. NOW CLOSE YOUR EYES AND FEEL YOUR HAND TINGLE. Have the child swing or push the arm up and down until he has feeling in it. Squeeze clothespins with that hand. Or have them use the clothespins to construct

fences around the periphery of shoe boxes. Or pretend that the clothespin is a puppet and have it talk. Have each child crumble a piece of newspaper with one hand without the help of the other. Teach the use of the subdominant hand to help. Wind thread onto a spool. Sew yarn onto burlap. Hold a paper and show them how you turn it with your left hand while you cut it with your right. Teach them to use the subdominant hand to hold the paper while they are writing. Sew string on sewing cards. Fiberboard cards are more stable.

11. Use this pencil exercise daily until the children all have easy writing positions: Grip the pencil (or crayon) in the fist. Then swing it up into writing position with three fingers under it. Repeat as an exercise. FIST, THREE FINGERS UNDER; FIST, THREE FINGERS UNDER. Show them how the pencil is not gripped tightly, but slides between the fingers easily. FIST, THREE FINGERS UNDER! SEE HOW MY PENCIL IS JUST RESTING ON THAT THIRD FINGER. SEE, I CAN PULL IT IN AND OUT EASILY. CAN YOU DO THAT? Later: FIST, THREE FINGERS UNDER, THEN PRETEND YOU ARE WRITING. WIGGLE YOUR PENCIL!

DIRECTIONALITY TRAINING

Directionality is the outer expression of the inner feeling of laterality. Directionality is the understanding of the position of objects in relation to the body. The child must have a stable laterality in order to establish a stable directionality. Now that the right side feels different from the left, the child can quickly identify an object as being to his right or left, or being up in relation to his head (when standing) or down in relation to his feet. Try these activities to teach direction:

1. At flag salute time, emphasize standing on the *right* side of the desk, *right* hand on the heart. Use the right side of the desk for standing for other purposes also, e.g. to do stretching exercises, and to be counted.

2. Give directions in form of a game: *Simon Says:* PUT UP YOUR RIGHT HAND! TOUCH YOUR LEFT EAR WITH YOUR LEFT HAND. Establish sides and terms *right* and *left* before you start to give directions *crossing* the body line, e.g. PUT YOUR RIGHT HAND ON

YOUR RIGHT KNEE. PUT YOUR LEFT HAND ON YOUR LEFT FOOT. Later: NOW THIS IS GOING TO BE TOUGH! PUT YOUR RIGHT HAND ON YOUR LEFT KNEE. Say it slowly, accenting the names of the sides. Help every child to get it right. You are teaching, not testing. These directions can also be in the form of Who can . . . ? Play the game with eyes closed also.

3. Give directions for position of the body: STAND ON THE RIGHT SIDE OF YOUR DESK. JUMP OVER YOUR CHAIR AND STAND ON THE LEFT SIDE OF YOUR DESK. STAND IN FRONT OF YOUR DESK AND CLAP YOUR HANDS ONCE. STAND BEHIND YOUR DESK AND JUMP THREE TIMES. CRAWL UNDER YOUR DESK. Begin with but a single direction. Say it only once. Then give two commands ending with AND SIT DOWN IN YOUR SEAT. When giving a series of commands, say: WAIT UNTIL I SAY "GO!" Give directions, then say, Go, and whole class responds in unison.

4. In physical education calisthenics, have children verbalize the names of the directions as they do them, e.g. BEND YOUR KNEES AND GO DOWN. SAY "DOWN" WHEN YOU ARE DOWN. In toe touching, REACH HANDS WAY UP AND SAY "UP," NOW DOWN TO YOUR TOES AND SAY "DOWN." SWING TO THE RIGHT AND SAY "RIGHT." JUMP TO THE WEST, SAY IT. JUMP TO THE SOUTH. JUMP TO THE EAST. SAY IT.

5. In using form templates, after first experimenting with different directions, give specific directions. In tracing the square say, BEGIN AT THE TOP LEFT CORNER AND GO DOWN, TO THE RIGHT, UP, TO THE LEFT. SAY IT WITH ME: DOWN, RIGHT, UP, LEFT. In doing the triangle, say: BEGIN AT THE TOP AND GO TOWARD YOUR LEFT ELBOW. SAY "LEFT," "RIGHT," "TOP!" With the circle say: LET'S BEGIN AT THE TOP OF THE CIRCLE AND GO TO THE LEFT. SAY "LEFT" AS YOU GO AROUND! NOW LET'S REVERSE THE DIRECTION AND GO TO THE RIGHT. SAY "RIGHT."

6. Ditto off right and left hands, both sides. Designate the back of the hand with finger nails. WHICH HAND IS THIS? TRY THE OTHER HAND ON IT. WHAT IS WRONG? WHICH SIDE OF THE HAND IS THIS? LOOK AT THE BACK OF YOUR HAND. WHAT CAN YOU FIND? Nails, knuckles, wrinkles. WHAT HAPPENS TO THOSE WRINKLES WHEN YOU BEND YOUR FINGERS? STRETCH YOUR FINGERS BACK. SEE THE

TENDONS? CAN YOU PUT YOUR HAND ON THIS PAPER HAND THE SAME WAY AND TRACE IT? CAN YOU DRAW A RING ON THE RIGHT FINGER AND A WATCH ON THE WRIST?

7. A child stands in front of the class in any position he chooses. Children imitate him and tell on which foot he is standing, which hand he has up. Or let him be a windmill, stand with his back to the class, and place his arms straight out in any pattern he chooses. Have children imitate him. Have him turn and face class and see if they can translate his motions now. He turns his back again for them to verify their positions.

8. Play *Freeze.* Children dance or skip around. When you blow your whistle they freeze into position. Choose a child who is in an interesting position. LOOK AT JERRY! LET'S SEE IF WE CAN GET INTO HIS POSITION! WHICH HAND IS UP? WHICH KNEE IS BENT?

9. Sitting at desks: CROSS LEGS WITH THE RIGHT LEG IN FRONT; THE LEFT LEG IN FRONT. In physical education: MOVE SIDEWAYS WHILE YOU LOOK STRAIGHT AHEAD! CROSS YOUR RIGHT LEG OVER YOUR LEFT LEG AND GO LEFT. NOW LET'S GO THE OTHER WAY. THIS TIME CROSS YOUR LEFT LEG BEHIND YOUR RIGHT LEG. On the walking beam: WALK SIDEWAYS CROSSING AND UNCROSSING THE LEGS, FIRST IN FRONT AND THEN IN BACK. Alternate. WALK SIDEWAYS WITHOUT CROSSING LEGS. HOW CAN YOU DO IT?

10. Children have red wrist bands on dominant hands. Right-handed children stand in a line two by two, holding right hands. Ask them to turn and look at each other. NOW WHERE IS YOUR RIGHT HAND: WHAT HAPPENED? Repeat until children understand how the right hands are on opposite sides when facing each other.

11. Learning directions of a horizontal surface: FIND THE TOP OF THE BLACKBOARD. NOW FIND THE BOTTOM OF THE BLACKBOARD. WHICH IS THE RIGHT SIDE? WHICH IS THE LEFT SIDE? WHO CAN MAKE A CIRCLE WAY UP ON THE TOP OF THE BLACKBOARD? WHO CAN MAKE A SQUARE AT THE BOTTOM OF THE BOARD? Use a portable blackboard to continue the exercise, finding and making things on the top and the bottom of the board as you step-by-step alter the board until it is in a horizontal position. Now: FIND THE TOP OF YOUR DESK; THE BOTTOM OF YOUR DESK; THE TOP OF YOUR PAPER; THE

BOTTOM OF YOUR PAPER. MAKE A RED CIRCLE AT THE TOP OF YOUR PAPER. MAKE A BLACK SQUARE AT THE BOTTOM OF YOUR PAPER. Have children verbalize the directions. *Top. Bottom.*

12. Teaching *direction* of letters to avoid reversals: In teaching writing of letters and numerals, use the blackboard and very large forms. Emphasize where each letter starts and which direction it goes. AN *l* BEGINS AT THE TOP WAY UP HERE AND THEN GOES DOWN TO THE BOTTOM. Demonstrate several times, using the whole height of the board. I MAKE A *2* BY STARTING NEAR THE TOP LEFT SIDE OF THE BOARD! THEN I GO TO THE RIGHT TO MAKE A HALF-CIRCLE, STOP, AND THEN MAKE A STRAIGHT LINE TO THE RIGHT. Repeat while children watch. Then have children stand, clasp hands together, and *write* the letter in the air using the movement of the whole body. The top of the letter would be as high as they can reach; the bottom down as far as they can reach. Repeat. A SMALL *r* STARTS IN THE MIDDLE, AT THE WAIST AND GOES ALL THE WAY STRAIGHT DOWN TO THE FLOOR. THEN IT GOES BACK UP AND JUST BEFORE IT GETS TO THE WAIST, IT CURVES TO THE RIGHT. Have the children begin their writing at the blackboard using long strokes and very large letters as far as they can comfortably reach. Then have them make smaller and smaller numerals as they understand where to begin and the direction of the writing.

13. Crayon one large letter on 12″ x 18″ manila drawing paper. Have the children trace over and over it with a fast, sweeping movement saying its name. Or use "rainbow tracing" with the child using all different colors of crayon to trace the letter.

14. Note the children's errors in executing letters and demonstrate the correct formation on the board. The error should be pointed out, but not accentuated or the child will further learn the error. Have him make the letter over several times on the board to reinforce the correct construction. Emphasize the starting point and the direction of the movement. Help him to verbalize it: WHERE DOES IT START? SAY IT!

15. For further practice of letters, make dittos of each letter with one-inch squares in which to write the letters. Put an *x* in each box as a starting point to ensure that the child starts on the

correct side. Make a dittoed row correctly and teach the children to trace over your letters first before making it themselves in the rest of the boxes on the page. Emphasize their starting with the top left square and going to the right, then back to the left of the second row. WHERE WILL YOU START? Also have the children verbalize the letter name as they make it.

16. Avoid board-to-paper copying with these children. When writing a sentence or a story, you might do it step-by-step with the children first watching you making a letter on the board and then the children writing the letter. This is especially important in first teaching writing of words, sentences, and spacing. When they erroneously copy from the board, they have reinforced errors which may be hard to unlearn.

17. Do chalkboard routines (Chapter Nine). Alternate directions: BOTH HANDS GO IN; REVERSE AND BOTH HANDS GO OUT. BOTH HANDS GO RIGHT; REVERSE AND BOTH HANDS GO LEFT.

18. The rolling push-ups, hands-and-feet roll, and bottle-capping machine are especially good to teach directionality (Chapter Eight).

19. One day when the wind is decidedly a north wind, teach the directions of our hemisphere. WALK TO THE SOUTH AND FEEL THE SUN ON YOUR FACE. TURN AROUND AND WALK NORTH AND FEEL THE COLD WIND BLOWING FROM THE NORTH POLE. Repeat this in various ways. JUMP NORTH. JUMP SOUTH. RUN NORTH. STOP WHEN I BLOW MY WHISTLE AND RUN SOUTH. Also, teach *east* and *west* by having children watch for sunsets or by noting position of the sun when they first come to school in the morning. Note that when the wind blows hard from the south, they have to close the windows on the south side of the room. Or vice versa for the north wind. Note direction the flag is blowing. Have children carry pieces of cardboard or scarves in different directions on windy days.

TEACHING LEFT-TO-RIGHT DIRECTION

After the child has learned directionality, the third step necessary before reading is the training of the child to look to the left to start a page, a word, a sentence. So first he must learn all directions and then he must learn to direct his attention to the left consistently.

1. Get into the habit of standing to the left of the class so that their attention is directed *to the left*.

2. Have the flag held on the left front of the classroom.

3. Place left-handed children on the left side of the room.

4. Count the calendar numerals daily with children having turns pointing at the numerals as they are said. When they have come to the end of the row: NOW WHERE DO YOU GO? YES, BACK TO THE LEFT!

5. In all class work have the children write their names on the top left-hand side of the paper to avoid reversals, and emphasize the left-to-right direction.

6. In writing a story or sentence or word on the board, emphasize beginning on the left. WHERE DO I START JERRY'S STORY?

7. Have a child hold a pinwheel at the left of the classroom. The children follow the pinwheel with their eyes as the child walks toward the right of the room. The child then drops the pinwheel down, and the children's eyes must return quickly to the left of the room to see the pinwheel of the second child. The first pinwheel holder hurries around the back of class to be ready at the left of the room for his turn again.

8. Follow the pointer from the left of the blackboard to the right. Sometimes move it along the top of the board, sometimes along the middle and sometimes along the bottom of the board.

9. Use Getman's Follow the Fly routine for left-right eye movements (1964).

10. Tape stories from books. Have children use earphones of a listening-post to hear the story and follow it in their books. Use story books, not *readers*. The dialogue directions would go like this: TURN THE PAGE. SEE THE PICTURE OF BILLY AND THE DOG ON THE RIGHT HAND PAGE? NOW LOOK ON THE LEFT HAND PAGE. IT TELLS WHAT BILLY IS SAYING. SEE THOSE WORDS THERE? WE START READING IT UP ON THE TOP LEFT WITH BILLY'S NAME. "BILLY SAID, 'I LIKE MY PUPPY!'"

11. In teaching the letters and numerals, first teach the ones

that begin on the left and go to the right; e.g., *b, h, n, r, 2, 3, 4, 5.*

TRAINING VISUAL FORM PERCEPTION

The child with poorly developed visual perception may have a very unstable perception of his world. He may be made anxious by the unreliability of objects to his vision. He may learn to recognize a word or letter today, in one context or color or size, but be totally unable to recognize it later in some other position or size. He is constantly deceived by his senses. Therefore, reading is an extremely frustrating experience for him. To train a child to overcome this disability we go back to the simple shapes and gradually vary their sizes and positions, and later their complexity. We teach many aspects of each shape with a variety of activities and materials so that the child learns the shape thoroughly and makes a perceptual-motor match.

Template Training

Use $\frac{1}{4}''$ fiberboard to make 8" x 12" boards. Make a set of templates for each child. (You can share them with another class.) Thus each child will have a circle, a square, a rectangle, a triangle, and a diamond template.

Cut the shape to the right of center of the board in order to leave an area for holding it which is large enough for the child's hand. Allow only one template in his desk at a time. Begin training with the simplest form, the circle. Each child has a piece of 12" x 18" manila drawing paper. He places it horizontally on his desk. Teach him to place it straight along the bottom edge of his desk. Give him the template and he places it horizontally, straight along the bottom of his paper. The child holds the template on the holding side with his subdominant hand while he traces around the inside of the circle many times with his pencil in his dominant hand. Tell him to feel the sides of the circle with his pencil at all times. He can then look at his tracings to see if he adhered to the circle or if he crossed through the inside of the circle. IS YOUR CIRCLE HOLLOW LIKE A DOUGHNUT?

Have them put the templates away inside their desks while

they take a crayon and trace around and around the penciled circle. Work toward fast, free sweeping movements of the arm. Be sure the subdominant hand is holding the paper well. Don't let them bend their wrists to go around the circle, but use the whole arm. BEND YOUR ELBOW. KEEP YOUR CRAYON POINTED UP-WARD. KEEP YOUR ARM SLIDING EASILY OVER YOUR DESK. Good control will be evident in smoothly rounded circles. They don't have to stay right on the line. Tell them it's a race-track or a doughnut or a deep tunnel.

The next time have them learn to make the first circle over to one side enough to leave room on the paper for another circle. Then each day repeat the template tracing and crayon tracing twice. Now try some variations: EVERYONE START AT THE TOP AND LET'S ALL GO TO THE RIGHT AROUND AND AROUND! STOP! EVERYONE START AT THE TOP AND GO TO THE LEFT, AROUND AND AROUND. STOP! RIGHT! LEFT! THIS TIME LET'S USE YOUR OTHER HAND TO TRACE THE TEMPLATE! CAN YOU TURN THE TEMPLATE AROUND SO THAT THE HOLDING SIDE IS READY FOR YOUR HOLDING HAND? Some days when the crayon tracing is finished, have the children turn their circles into something. WHAT COULD YOUR CIRCLE BE? Some will simply color the circle in a design fashion. Others will turn them into clocks, or plates. Another time when the tracing is finished: NOW SEE IF YOU CAN MAKE SOME CIRCLES ALL BY YOURSELF ANY-WHERE ON YOUR PAPER. MAKE SOME BIG AND SOME LITTLE. Teach them to make a single circle joining it correctly without a space or overlapping. The trick is to teach them to stop at the right point. Let each child judge his work for himself. WHAT SHAPE DID YOU MAKE? IS IT ROUND LIKE A CIRCLE OR OVAL LIKE AN EGG? TRY IT AGAIN. FIND YOUR VERY BEST CIRCLE ON YOUR PAPER AND I'LL PUT A BLUE STAR IN THE MIDDLE OF IT.

You will probably need to do each shape at least two days. Immature children will require much more practice. Children who have learned to make the shape well could be allowed to use the templates to make original designs, while you work with the rest of the class on the template training. Use the rectangle template as the second shape that you teach. This time, to trace the template without going through the middle, say: HIT THE

CORNER! HIT THE CORNER! When children cut across corners, help them to say: HIT THE CORNER! at each corner. Demonstrate on the board what happens if you don't *hit the corner* and cut across it instead. (The rectangle turns into an oval.) In retracing with the crayon, the child must learn to stop at each corner. It helps to have them say: STOP! at each corner. After they have learned to stop, help them to feel the difference of the sides. You might have them say: LONG, SHORT, LONG, SHORT as they trace it. Teach the use of the rectangle in both vertical and horizontal positions. Again the children can turn them into something. Thus they learn the difference between a door and a chalkboard, vertical versus horizontal. Now they can make their own rectangles, some vertical, some horizontal, some large, some small, some thin, some fat.

In tracing the square, the child must learn the equality of the sides. Use the square in different positions so the child can see that it does not change its shape. Use a diagonal position, also. In tracing it, sometimes have them START AT THE TOP LEFT AND GO DOWN, OVER, UP, ACROSS. START AT THE LEFT CORNER AND GO RIGHT, DOWN, ACROSS, UP.

The child should have a good understanding of baseline and of the first three shapes before beginning the triangle. The diagonal line crossing the midline is very difficult for some children. In tracing the triangle, be sure the child has both arms on his desk. Then have him notice how that slanted line goes toward his elbow. The directions might be: START AT THE TOP AND GO TOWARD THE LEFT ELBOW, STRAIGHT ACROSS YOUR BODY TO YOUR RIGHT, AND UP TO THE TOP. Reverse directions. Count the sides while tracing them. LET'S COUNT THE SIDES: ONE, TWO, THREE! LET'S COUNT THE CORNERS. ONE, TWO, THREE! HOW MANY CORNERS? HOW MANY SIDES? IS ONE LONGER THAN THE OTHER? THEY ARE ALL EQUAL!

The most frequent error made in executing a triangle is that a vertical line is made instead of a diagonal (Fig. 22). Stand behind the child at his desk and show him how this straight vertical line if continued would strike him in the middle of his body. Have him trace and feel this movement. Then show him how

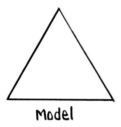

Model

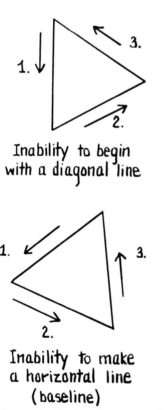

Inability to begin
with a diagonal line

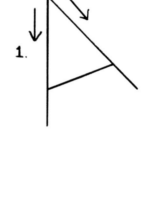

Inability to make
a horizontal line
(baseline)

Figure 22. Children's Errors in Executing the Equilateral Triangle.

the line must go instead toward his left elbow which is on his
desk. Have him feel the differences in these movements several
times. Then have him make several triangles while you watch,

helping to guide his hand as needed. Have him vary the sizes of his triangles.

The second error with triangles is that the children tend to slant the baseline downward into a diagonal (Fig. 22). Emphasize that the baseline of the triangle is horizontal: STRAIGHT ACROSS YOUR BODY AND DESK.

The diamond is a difficult shape. With immature first graders we don't even attempt it until they are at least six. Again, teach it in both the horizontal and the vertical positions.

Perceptual Constancy Exercises

1. As each shape is learned, have the children find it in the environment. They notice that the clock is a circle, as are the doorknobs, the intercom speaker, the wastebasket. If there are not enough circles or squares or triangles in the room, place a few cardboard or construction paper ones strategically around the classroom.

2. On walks, find the shapes in trees, leaves, houses, and lawns. When discussing any object thereafter, compare it to the basic shapes. Add more complex shapes like the hexagon, the oval, the heart shape. Thus a leaf may be heart-shaped, or long like a rectangle, but pointed. The body parts are examined as to their shapes. The eyes are oval with points, they have two round circles inside that. The neck is a rectangle. The fingers are long rectangles, the thumb a short rectangle with rounded end. Let the children *discover* the shapes. Ask them the questions. Let them formulate the conclusions. WHAT SHAPE IS THIS? DO YOU SEE ANY OTHER SHAPE HERE, TOO?

3. Read to the children: Sullivan's *Round as a Pancake*; Schlein's *Shapes*; Wolff and Owett's *Let's Imagine Thinking Up Things*; Budney's *A Kiss Is Round*; Robert's *The Dot*; and Emberley's *The Wing on a Flea*.

4. Have squares, rectangles, triangles, and circles which children can sort as to sizes. Begin with only the one shape and three or four different sizes. The shapes may be cut out of construction paper or cardboard and sorted into a sectioned box or egg carton. Shapes could also be cut of plastic or fiberboard or rubber tile

and piled according to size and shape. There are some commerical sets such as this in the school supply houses. *Jumbo Shape Sorting Board, Wooden Graduated Shapes, Fit-A-Space, Fit-a-Shape.* Simplex puzzles have graduated sizes of objects such as apples, pears, pigs. They also have variations in houses, windmills, sailboats, flowers, and chickens.

5. Collect many small boxes with lids and place in a large box. Remove the lids. The child tries to match lids with boxes.

6. Use the tactile and kinesthetic sense to reinforce children's understanding of forms. Begin with objects in a feeling box that are circles and squares, such as buttons, jar lids, small boxes. The child feels the shape of the object in the box, guesses its shape and possibly its identity, and then brings it out of the box for verification. He might then place all square objects in one pile, and circular objects in another pile.

7. Have children act out *floor patterns* of circles, squares; e.g., a child might run in a circle. He might walk four steps, turn right, repeat three more times to make a square. Or he could jump at the corners. Read Gladys Andrew's *Creative Rhythms.*

8. Have a child make a circle in the air with his hand. MAKE TWO CIRCLES WITH TWO HANDS. MAKE A SQUARE WITH BOTH HANDS TOGETHER. DRAW A CIRCLE ON THE FLOOR WITH YOUR RIGHT FOOT. HOW LARGE A CIRCLE CAN YOU MAKE WITH YOUR FOOT? HOW SMALL A CIRCLE CAN YOU MAKE IN THE AIR WITH YOUR POINTER FINGER?

9. Use a variety of sizes of felt squares. Have a child find THE LARGEST SQUARE, THE SMALLEST SQUARE, ONE THAT IS LARGER THAN THIS ONE, ONE THAT IS SMALLER THAN THIS ONE.

10. Have the children collect objects of different shapes to bring to school. They put all the square shapes in this box, all the circles in this box.

11. Make a picture of nothing but circles. WHAT COULD THE CIRCLES BE? Balloons, lollipops, flowers, wheels. MAKE A PICTURE OF NOTHING BUT RECTANGLES. CAN YOU MAKE BUILDINGS OF NOTHING BUT RECTANGLES AND SQUARES?

12. Use Child Guidance's magnetic board and their Geometric Forms for the child to form objects and designs. Hammer-and-nail sets are also good for this.

13. Cut construction shapes in a variety of sizes and colors. Have children manipulate them to form objects and designs, and paste them on paper; e.g., a large rectangle becomes a wagon with a thin rectangle for a handle, and circles for wheels. Teach the trimming of the corners of squares to form circles, diagonal cutting to make a triangle. Teach the forming of designs by repeating the same shapes.

14. Teach *short, tall, narrow, wide.* Compare objects wherein one is larger than the other because it is taller. Compare other objects when one is larger because it is wider. Do the same with *smaller* objects.

15. Teach the apparent changes in size of objects according to distances from their vision. Have children hold balls that are the same size at various distances, at least ten feet apart. Note the size appearance of the balls. Have the farthest child advance slowly while the class observes the change in the ball size. Have a nearer child retreat gradually for the class to see his ball diminish in size. Then place different sizes of balls in different positions to compare size appearances. Do the same with boxes. Sit on the lawn somewhere and look off in the distance to compare sizes of buildings, cars, and telephone poles. IS THAT TELEPHONE POLE DOWN THE BLOCK SMALLER THAN THIS ONE HERE NEAR US? HOW BIG IS THAT CAR OVER THERE? USE YOUR FINGER TO MEASURE IT. IS IT AS BIG AS YOUR FINGER? Find a taller object behind a smaller one. THAT WHITE BUILDING THERE! IS IT THE SAME SIZE AS THAT GREY ONE? HOW DO YOU KNOW IT IS BIGGER?

16. Art projects: Teach the forming of a square from a rectangle of paper. Make an oval jack-o'-lantern by turning a rectangle into an oval. Make a double basket by folding a square diagonally twice, and then stapling two of the creases together. Use all the simple art projects wherein the child starts with a basic rectangular paper and with cutting and folding, forms an interesting new shape. Teach him folding to make figures which are identical on two sides, e.g., trees, hearts.

Spatial Relations Exercises

1. Now the child can make the basic shapes but he has never been able to project these into his world to draw realistic objects.

Have a directed drawing lesson like this: MAKE A MIDDLE-SIZED CIRCLE TOWARD THE TOP PART OF YOUR PAPER. You also do so on the blackboard. MAKE A LARGE HORIZONTAL RECTANGLE TOWARD THE LOWER PART OF YOUR PAPER. PUT A WIDE TRIANGLE ON TOP THE RECTANGLE. MAKE A SMALL VERTICAL RECTANGLE INSIDE THE LARGE ONE, AND TOUCHING THE BASE. MAKE A TALL, THIN VERTICAL REC-TANGLE BESIDE ALL THIS. PUT AN OVAL ON THE TOP OF THIS. Coach the children step-by-step through the making of the picture. Now that they are catching on to what you are doing you could ask: WHAT ELSE COULD WE MAKE? WHAT SHAPE DO WE NEED TO START MAKING IT? WHAT CAN YOU DO TO THAT CIRCLE TO MAKE IT MORE LIKE THE SUN? WHAT CAN YOU DO TO THOSE RECTANGLES TO MAKE THEM MORE LIKE YOUR WINDOWS AT HOME? Following the di-rections for *beside, behind, in front of, inside* are important concepts in spatial relationships of one object to another. Give directions for other pictures but don't help them by making one on the board. The child must listen and follow the spatial di-rections to make the picture turn out correctly. This is not an art lesson!

2. When the children have learned to make squares, have three-inch squares of different colored felt. Also cut enough colored squares of construction so that each child has a similar set of three identically colored squares. Place your felt squares in a horizontal row on the felt board. Ask the children to do the same with their construction squares at their desks. WHICH COLORED SQUARE IS ON THE LEFT? WHICH IS ON THE RIGHT? WHICH IS IN THE MIDDLE? CHECK TO BE SURE YOURS ARE RIGHT. Arrange your squares vertically and proceed in the same manner as be-fore. Change the sequence of the colors. Form simple designs and have the children imitate them. Make it a game. CLOSE YOUR EYES AND DON'T PEEK. I'M GOING TO MIX THEM ALL UP AGAIN. NOW, OPEN YOUR EYES AND MAKE THIS! When they are proficient placing them with level baselines, place the squares on their points, vertically, horizontally, and then diagonally. Finally, ask the children to make their own designs that you may copy. TERRY HAS A NICE DESIGN. LET'S SEE IF WE CAN MAKE IT. THERE. DID I DO IT RIGHT? NOW YOU TRY IT! As the rectangle and the triangle are

learned, use the same procedure with those shapes. Also teach the different kinds of triangles.

3. WHO CAN COME AND STAND IN FRONT OF ME? NOW WHO CAN STAND ON MY RIGHT SIDE? ON MY LEFT SIDE? BEHIND ME? Choose a child. WHO CAN STAND IN FRONT OF TOMMY? Then use a portable felt board or blackboard. WHO CAN STAND IN FRONT OF THE BLACKBOARD?

4. SEE HOW QUICKLY YOU CAN DO AS I SAY. EVERYONE, STAND ON THE RIGHT SIDE OF YOUR DESK. STAND IN FRONT OF YOUR DESK. CRAWL UNDER YOUR DESK. JUMP OVER YOUR SEAT. WHAT CLOTHES ARE IN FRONT OF YOU? WHAT PART OF YOUR CLOTHES IS BEHIND YOU? WHAT PART OF YOUR BODY IS IN FRONT OF YOU? (chest) WHAT PART OF YOUR BODY IS BEHIND YOU? (back) FIND THE FRONT OF YOUR NECK. THE BACK OF YOUR NECK. FIND THE BACK OF YOUR HAND.

5. Give each child a large and a small block (or have them use any two objects you desire). PUT THE SMALL BLOCK ON TOP OF THE LARGE BLOCK. PUT THE SMALL BLOCK UNDER THE LARGE BLOCK. PUT THE SMALL BLOCK ON THE RIGHT SIDE OF THE LARGE BLOCK. Continue with *in front of* and *behind* and continue the exercises until the children are proficient in quickly placing the blocks correctly.

6. Use the Frostig worksheets in Perceptual Constancy, and Spatial Relations.

7. Have the children form a 6" x 9" paper into a square, and then fold it twice in each direction to form twelve boxes. TOMMY, CHOOSE A COLOR. ALL RIGHT, LET'S ALL COLOR THE TOP, LEFT-HAND BOX TOMMY'S COLOR. NOW FOLD THE PAPER STRAIGHT ACROSS. SEE THE SQUARE THAT YOUR COLORED SQUARE IS TOUCHING? COLOR IT THE SAME COLOR. NOW FOLD IT DOWN. SEE THE SQUARE IT IS TOUCH-ING NOW? COLOR IT THE SAME COLOR. Do the same to all four corners, so that they are all the same color. Now have a child choose another color for another particular square and have them mirror it across, and/or up or down and make the same color on the matching squares. Continue until the colors form a balanced design on the paper. Make another paper and this time use the diagonal fold also and teach the mirroring on the diagonal. Let

the children then make their own designs in like manner. Another day you make the twelve squares on the board and color in certain ones on the top left side with colored chalk. Have the children do likewise on their papers, and then *mirror* these colored squares onto the other three sides of the paper.

8. Place three or four colored blocks or Cuisenaire rods in a particular order. Have the children imitate the order with their own rods.

9. Doll house furniture could be used to form an order to be imitated: Have one chair facing the left, one facing the right, and another facing the right also, all in a row. The child copies the pattern with similar furniture. Or place three or four school chairs in a row design and have a child use four more chairs to copy your design.

10. Block Buster blocks. These blocks are dovetailed together in groups of two, three, and four. Place one of these groups of cubes in a certain position before the child. Give the child separate cubes which he can use to imitate the block construction. Change the position of the group of cubes, and see if the child can also change the position of his blocks. Begin with the simpler groupings of blocks and continue with the more complex as the child gains skill.

11. Make six-hole square pegboards of fiberboard sheets of pegboard material. They need not be framed. You need have only one-inch boards on two undersides to hold the pegboard off the desk. Use only one color of golfing tees for pegs, cutting about a half inch off the points with cutters. Place a peg in each of the four corners of the pegboard. Have the children imitate. Place two pegs in each corner for them to imitate. Form rows of pegs, horizontally, diagonally, and vertically. Ask the children to form a large "+", and a small "+" with their pegs. Place pegs diagonally in from each corner, then diagonally across the corners. The designs may become increasingly complex as the child gains skill. First use only a definite pattern of placement. Later use random placement. Then place pegs on one-quarter of the board only. Have children mirror the design to the other four corners. Ask them to make a large rectangle, a small rectangle, then a

large and a small square. As the concept of equal sides develops, ask them to make a square with two pegs on a side, then three pegs on a side. This pegboard work really synthesizes the concept of squareness. Increase the difficulty of the pegboard tasks by adding a second color of pegs, more pegs, and later even a third color.

12. Place colored marbles on a board in a pattern similar to the use of the pegboard. Let the child duplicate your design with marbles on his board.

13. Form a design with Color Cubes. Child reproduces your design. Or make designs with colored construction paper on cardboard. Child copies design with the color cubes.

14. Form a design with Parquetry Blocks. Child duplicates it. Let the child first form designs on top of a picture of the design, then later, beside the picture. Large sets of parquetry block designs and cube designs are available from Developmental Learning Materials.

15. Form toothpicks or matchsticks into squares, rectangles, triangles, and multiple designs. The child duplicates your design with his matchsticks (Kephart). If you wish this to be a whole class activity, glue your matchstick design onto tagboard to stand in the chalkrack.

16. Utilize pictures of designs with various blocks, pegs, etc. and let the child then manipulate the objects to form that design. Always begin with the simplest designs. Color Cubes, Parquetry Blocks, lighted pegboards, tile boards, include pictures of designs. Have the child reproduce these with his materials. Drawings of peg and marble designs may be simply drawn on the blackboard, using colored chalk to designate different colors of objects.

17. Teach the manuscript letters as related to the basic forms. Teach like-shapes together, beginning with the easiest. After the children have learned a straight line, stopping, and a baseline from work with the square and rectangle templates, then teach the *L, l, T, t, I, i, F, E, H,* and *4.* Teach letters and numerals curved to the right in sequence, *2, 3, 5, B, b, P, p, D,* and *R.* Teach letters with slanted lines after the triangle template has been

used and the children can make slanted lines: *A, N, M, K, k, X,* and *Z.* Teach letters and numerals curved to the left in this sequence: *O, o, a, d, g, q, e, c, s, 6, G* and *Q.*

18. With Cuisenaire Company's *Geoboard,* the children use colored rubber bands to place on the pegs and form shapes either adjacent to each other or interposed one on the other.

19. Use the feeling box now to learn to discriminate many different and more complex shapes, both solids and planes. It may also be used to increase kinesthetic sense in discriminating objects, such as small plastic toys.

REFERENCES

Andrews, Gladys: *Creative Rhythmic Movement for Children.* Englewood Cliffs, New Jersey, Prentice-Hall, 1954.

Ayres, A. Jean: *Perceptual-Motor Dysfunction in Children.* Monograph from the Greater Cincinnati District Ohio Occupational Therapy Association Conference, 1964.

Barsch, Ray H.: *Achieving Perceptual-Motor Efficiency.* Seattle, Spec Child, 1967.

Budney, Blossom: *A Kiss is Round.* New York, Lothrop, 1954.

Emberley, Ed: *The Wing on a Flea.* Boston, Little, 1961.

Frostig, Marianne, and Horne, David: *The Frostig Program for the Development of Visual Perception.* Chicago, Follett, 1961.

Gesell, A., and Ilg, Frances L.: *Child Development.* New York, Harper, 1949.

Getman, G. N., *et al.: Developing Learning Readiness.* Manchester, Missouri, Webster Division, McGraw, 1968.

Getman, G. N.: *Physiology of Readiness.* Minneapolis, PASS, 1964.

LeWinn, Edward: *Human Neurological Organization.* Springfield, Thomas, 1969.

Radler, D. H., and Kephart, Newell C.: *Success Through Play.* New York, Harper & Row, 1960.

Roberts, Cliff: *The Dot.* New York, Watts, 1960.

Schlein, Miriam: *Shapes.* Eau Claire, Wisconsin, Hale, 1952.

Sullivan, Joan: *Round as a Pancake.* New York, Holt, Rinehart, Winston, 1963.

Wellman, B. L.: Motor achievement of preschool children. *Childhood Education, 13*:311-316, 1937.

Wolff, Janet, and Owett, Bernard: *Let's Imagine Thinking Up Things.* New York, Dutton, 1961.

PERCEPTUAL-MOTOR TEACHING AIDS

A. Daigger & Company, Teaching Aids Division, 10 Tenth Street, Richmond, California, 94802.

Child Guidance Toys, P. O. Box 113, Bronx, New York, 10472.

Creative Playthings, Inc., Princeton, New Jersey, 08540.

Cuisenaire Company of America, 12 Church Street, New Rochelle, New York, 10805.

Developmental Learning Materials, 3505 Ashland Avenue, Chicago, Illinois, 60657.

Eye Gate House, Inc., 146–01 Archer Ave., Jamaica, New York, 11435.

I.D.A. Perception Blocks, P. O. Box 55, Cirtus Heights, California, 95610.

Lakeshore Equipment Company, 1144 Montague Ave., San Leandro, California, 94577.

Teaching Resources, 334 Boylston St., Boston, Massachusetts, 02116.

Warren's Educational Supplies, 980 W. San Bernadino Road, Covina, California, 91722.

FILMS ON SENSORIMOTOR FUNCTIONS AND TRAINING

Children Lost in Space. (30 min.) Society for Brain-Injured Children, 744 North 4th Street, Room 332, Milwaukee, Wisconsin, 53205.

Gateways to the Mind. (60 min.) Bell Telephone Film Library, San Francisco, California.

Learning is Observing. (27 min.) Bradley Wright Films, 309 North Duane Ave., San Gabriel, California, 91775.

Movigenic Curriculum. (40 min.) University of Wisconsin, Extension, Bureau of A.V. Instruction, Madison, Wisconsin, 53701.

Newell C. Kephart's Series of 20 films on Perceptual-Motor Development and Training, Purdue University Film Library, A.V. Center, Lafayette, Indiana, 47907.

Perception and Communication. (32 min.) Ohio State University, Dept. of Photography, 156 West 19th Avenue, Columbus, Ohio 43210.

Perceptual Development I and II. (37 and 43 min.) Bucks County Public Schools, Federal Program Coordinator, Bureau of Special Education, Dept. of Public Instruction, Harrisburg, Pennsylvania 17126.

Perceptual Motor Training and Developing Visual-Motor Skills, from I Can Learn Series, Franklin County Board of Education, 46 East Fulton St., Columbus, Ohio 43215.

Sensoritonic Readiness Program. (22 min.) The Pathway School, Resource Center, 162 Egypt Road, Box 181, Norristown, Pennsylvania 19404.

Visual Perception and Failure to Learn. (20 min.) IMCSE, 2120 West 8th St., Los Angeles, California, 90057.

Visual Perception Research. (25 min.) U. C. Extension Media Center, 2223 Fulton St., Berkeley, California 94720.

Visual Perception Training in the Regular Classroom. (23 min.) AIMS Instructional Media Services, Inc., P. O. Box 1010, Hollywood, California 90028.

We Hold These Truths. (30 min.) The Doman-Delacato Institute for the Achievement of Human Potential, Philadelphia, Pennsylvania.

World We Perceive. (30 min.) U. C. Extension Media Center, 2223 Fulton St., Berkeley, California 94720.

Chapter Eight

Training in Gross Motor Skills

GOALS OF THE PHYSICAL EDUCATION PROGRAM

F OR CHILDREN WHO are confused and disorganized, the physical education program may be the most important period on the school day. Here the child might experience his first successes, his first conception of how he might control his destiny, his first "I-can-do-it!" Until he is able to focus his attention on the control of his own muscles, he may find it difficult to attend to any other instruction which comes from outside stimuli. Until Johnny can bounce a ball or know how to put his right hand on his left foot, he can't be expected to follow the teacher's involved verbal instructions and write his name on the top left-side of the paper, or write a story all correctly sequenced and spaced about what he did at the beach.

In chapters Five, Six, and Seven we have explored the sensorimotor development of the child, the known and the hypothesized. Even though our knowledge of the intricate workings of the central nervous system is still inadequate, we do know that we must incorporate into the school program sufficient sensorimotor training to make the child fully aware of, and in control of, his own movements. The physical education program can give him a feeling of self-worth, of self-confidence essential to his behavior, his acceptance of the teacher and of her teaching. Our goals in the physical education program will not be to make a few outstanding athletes, but to help each child develop his ability to move in a cognitive fashion, fully aware of the many ways in which he can move his body, and of where he is in space. We must train all children, not just the agile and not just the clumsy. Every child can make gains with a comprehensive program. Even the controlled can be more controlled.

Into the physical education program we must incorporate the sensorimotor training in body image, laterality, directionality, tactile-kinesthetic stimulation, ocular motility, and motor-planning. This training must tie into the classroom exercises in visual and auditory perception and into the pencil and paper visual-motor activities. A primary purpose of this physical education program is strenuous daily physical exertion to the extent that the children are tired. Secondary to these are the traditional goals of dexterity, agility, speed, endurance, and social interaction.

Every activity must begin where the child is, not where he should be at his age level. If he can't jump rope, we go back to teaching him jumping, *period.* If he can't play catch, he must be taught to bounce the ball by himself or against a wall. If he can't skip, we go back to various ways of hopping and galloping. We will discuss these developmental steps in teaching coordination skills later in this chapter. As with the sensorimotor perceptual training in the previous chapters, we take no learning for granted. We begin with the very basic coordinations required of the child and build the components of a skill. A skill is not complete until a child can do it rhythmically, easily, and with many variations.

Every child must participate. No one is allowed to sit out unless there are specific health reasons. If a child has a sore arm, he can still do the leg exercises. If he has a blister on his heel, put an adhesive bandage on it and let him participate in the arm and thorax activities. If a child has a cough, he should be restricted from high exertion, especially running. Also, be cautious of exerting asthmatic children outdoors, especially those allergic to grasses. Impress the children with the importance of the program. Keep records on their developing skills so that you have concrete evidence of their progress to stimulate them to new skills. The child who is allowed to sit out may never learn control of his own body, may never know the exhilaration of a fast, free run. Every child should exercise daily until all muscles have been stimulated, until he is breathing deeply, until he is tired, until he has really exerted himself.

Although I have collected a voluminous file of materials on physical activities, I have found that the most usable are those compiled and/or designed by Jeanne Bartelt, Program Specialist for Physical Education, San Juan Unified School District, Carmichael, California. She has developed special programs for all children, including trainable mental retardates and learning disability groups. She has extended the use of many types of equipment in exploration of movement. We are especially indebted to her for teaching us the developmental skill sequence to use in teaching children such things as skipping, jumping rope, and ball throwing, catching, and bouncing. Thus I must accredit much of the material in this chapter to her knowledge and insight in training children with learning problems.

FUNDAMENTAL PRINCIPLES OF MOVEMENT EXPLORATION
Basic Movements

The basic locomotor movements are the walk, run, jump, hop, and leap, with the combination movements of the slide, skip, and gallop. From a stationary position the child might bend, twist, stretch, collapse, shake, or turn. These can be done at various levels such as standing, lying, sitting, hanging, or kneeling, or can be combined with locomotor movements. With real or imaginary force or equipment the child can push, pull, lift, carry, throw, strike, punch, climb, or hang. If balance or weight is moved from one point to another, the movement becomes a rock, roll, swing, or sway. All of these movements can be explored individually, in a group, or with a partner.

Movement Components

The above movements can be varied according to eight different components:
1. Size of movement: large or small.
2. Speed of movement: fast or slow.
3. Direction: forward, backward, sideward.
4. Level: high or low.
5. Force of movement: strong-weak, heavy-light.
6. Path or pattern: straight, curved, zigzag, spiral, etc.

7. Design or shape of motion: changing position of parts of the body, i.e., knees, elbows, head, wide or narrow.
8. Use of external objects.

Combining Movements and Their Components

As an example of how these movements can have infinite variations according to these components, let us take the basic locomotor movement of walking.

1. Vary it in size: WHAT IS THE BIGGEST STEP YOU CAN TAKE?
2. Speed: HOW FAST CAN YOU WALK?
3. Direction: CAN YOU WALK SIDEWAYS WITHOUT CROSSING YOUR FEET?
4. Level: HOW HIGH CAN YOU WALK? HOW LOW?
5. Force: CAN YOU WALK LIKE A VERY BIG, HEAVY ELEPHANT? LIKE A FAIRY?
6. Path: CAN YOU WALK IN A CIRCLE? IN A SQUARE? HOW WOULD THE CROOKED MAN WALK?
7. Design: CAN YOU WALK WITH YOUR LEGS SPREAD OUT TO THE SIDES? CAN YOU WALK FRONTWARD WHILE YOU ARE LEANING SIDEWAYS?
8. External objects: CAN YOU WALK ON THE BEAM? AROUND THE POLE? OVER THE BOARD? THROUGH THE LADDER?
9. In group: CAN YOU WALK ALL TOGETHER SHOULDER TO SHOULDER IN A LINE WITHOUT ANYONE GETTING AHEAD OR BEHIND?
10. With partner: CAN YOU WALK HOLDING HANDS WITH YOUR PARTNER AND KEEP THE SAME RHYTHM WITH HIM? WALK BACKWARD WITH HIM? WALK IN A CIRCLE?
11. With imaginary force: CAN YOU WALK AS IF YOU WERE PUSHING A WHEELBARROW? PRETEND THAT IT IS VERY HEAVY AND HARD TO PUSH!

Now let's take a stationary movement, the twist, and vary it according to the above components. Vary it by using different positions and levels:

1. Standing: WITHOUT MOVING YOUR LEGS, TWIST YOUR BODY TO THE RIGHT, LEFT.
2. Lying: LIE ON YOUR STOMACH AND TWIST YOUR SHOULDERS

TO THE RIGHT, LEFT.

3. Sitting: SPREAD YOUR LEGS, STRETCH AND TWIST YOUR RIGHT ARM OVER TO TOUCH YOUR LEFT FOOT.

4. Kneeling: SPREAD YOUR ARMS AND TWIST YOUR BODY TO THE RIGHT, LEFT.

Combined with a locomotor movement: TAKE A STEP AND TWIST YOUR BODY TO THE RIGHT. NOW MOVE IN THAT DIRECTION. STEP AND TWIST. WHAT HAPPENED TO THE DIRECTION YOU WERE MOVING?

Vary it according to the components of movements:

1. Size: TWIST TO THE RIGHT AND BACKWARD AS FAR AS YOU CAN GO.

2. Speed: LET'S TWIST FAST! RIGHT, FRONT, LEFT, FRONT!

3. Force: TWIST HARD TO THE RIGHT AND FREEZE.

4. Design: CAN YOU TWIST YOUR ARMS? YOUR LEGS? YOUR HEAD?

5. With equipment: HANG FROM THE HORIZONTAL LADDER AND TWIST RIGHT, LEFT.

6. With an object: Three children stand together each with a wand or plastic golf club holder. The middle child twists and strikes the wand of the child on his right, then twists and strikes the wand of the child on his left. He tries to work out a rhythm of movement.

ORGANIZING THE PHYSICAL EDUCATION PROGRAM

For children with problems in control and organization, a thirty minute physical education period daily is highly desirable. A shorter period will result in cutbacks of the program to such an extent that the children may be unable to make the sizable gains that are imperative to them. Remember that they may be one to two years behind in development now. Thus to bring them up to age levels they must absorb two to three years of normal training in their first year in school. Since their academic development must also be speeded up for the same reasons, the gross movement and the physical stimulation are desperately needed as time-out from the strain of the classroom. So cut down on time for almost anything but physical education. Much of our traditional seatwork, especially that copious board-to-paper copying can be eliminated. Carefully evaluate each activity for the amount of growth it provides for the child, and set aside that full thirty minutes for the child's sensorimotor, physical training.

The physical education period, daily and yearly, can be organized around the basic types of training necessary and the spaces or areas to be used for the training: calisthenics (in a limited space), movement exploration (about a fifty-foot area, can be blacktop or indoor gym), developmental skills (balls, balancing, ropes, etc.), lawn activities (tumbling, crawling), indoor on-the-floor sensorimotor training (inside only), outdoor group games, and activities for inclement weather. Subsequent sections of this chapter will deal with each of these.

The daily period can contain any combination of these activities. Plan a basic outline for the program and follow it daily so that the children know the sequence of what is expected of them. Calisthenics are best done the first part of a physical education period for better control of the children. You might have five to ten minutes of calisthenics, another ten of a group game, and the last ten minutes of training in skills. Or have a total of five minutes of calisthenics and ten minutes of movement exploration, and then divide into smaller groups for training in skills for the next fifteen minutes. The indoor sensorimotor training can be done just fifteen minutes, two or three days a week over a certain period. Keep the program interesting and stimulating. Teach a wide variety of skills.

Do some distance running or hard running for two or three minutes every day. Run with them and you will be better off, too. A period of calisthenics and/or movement explorations can be followed by a run around the periphery of the playground, extending the distance as the children gain endurance. Teach them to jog. They see boys and men jogging along the highways, so the interest is high. Tell them to bend their elbows and run easily. Don't try for speed. I might say: SEE IF YOU CAN RUN AS FAR AS I CAN. When we are all tired, I stop. Sometimes when there is reluctance to run, I line up the children as they arrive at the end of the run. ETHEL, STOP! TIME TO REFUEL! Then I give a small treat to every child that ran the whole distance. Most, if not all, of them make it!

If your playground areas or the weather are limiting factors, you may want to organize your program accordingly. For example, for inclement weather you will need to have ready lists of activities you can do in your room, or in the multipurpose room or gym. If you have the problem of sporadically mushy lawn areas from heavy sprinkling or rain, prepare lists of activities for days when you *can* use the lawn, and another list for when you will be limited to the paved or blacktop areas. In the former list you will want all the crawling and tumbling activities. On the latter list could be the calisthenics. Movement exploration of many kinds can be done in both areas. By typing ideas onto 5″ x 7″ cards you can have hundreds of activities at your fingertips. The lists should contain a large variety of movements so that you can keep the children interested. But you need never be confined solely to these. As you help your children explore the movements of their bodies you will be able to create many new ideas for movements on the spur of the moment by simply using the components of movements listed above, with every locomotor or stationary movement. Your children, too, will become adept at devising new challenges for each other.

To teach specific skills (throwing, ball bouncing, balancing) it is essential to break the group down for instruction into groups of ten to fifteen children. This can be done after your first fifteen minutes of strenuous exercise by sending part of the class off to practice on climbing equipment or with jump ropes or balls or to free play. This isn't the best solution because then half of your class is having a free play period daily. However, you have given them exercise in the form of calisthenics, movement exploration, and running already, so they have still had a good physical education program.

A second solution would be to request student aides. Ask for a sixth grader who will work with you for at least a week, preferably a month. Thus you don't have to use up too much time training aides. He need not be the sharpest child in the school, rather one who will relate well to your children and encourage them to perform. This child could teach one group tetherball, four square, jump rope, etc., or just be there to watch and encourage children to learn to traverse the rings and horizontal ladder, high jump, or other playground equipment. Or have older girls teach the jump rope and hopscotch skills, and boys teach the ball skills. Thus freeing you to teach specific skills to a small group.

The most satisfactory solution is a steady aide to take half of the class every day. This could be a paid aide, if you could be so fortunate, or a reliable volunteer parent, or a high school student. We use the latter and find this most satisfactory. The student gets a quarterly grade and credit as a teacher's aide, and the experience which may be an incentive toward a career as a teacher.

KEEPING SCORE

The first of the year make a simple 9″ x 12″ tagboard chart for each physical education group (ten to fifteen children) . You might name the groups by color names or other designation. For the last ten or fifteen minutes of your class time, keep just one group to work on skills and send the others off to a game, free play, or to work with balls.

On the charts, list the basic skills and then test each child to see if he *passes* the skill. This helps you to individualize instruction on skills. Begin with balance. The child must walk the beam forward and backward, heel-toe fashion, without stepping off. If he passes, note the date on the entry. If not, put a mark to remember that he attempted the feat and failed. Check each child for jumping jacks. His movements should be well coordinated and rhythmic. Check equipment skills such as traversing the horizontal ladder or the rings. Have each child hop fifty feet without putting his other foot down.

As the year continues add tests of new skills, each time noting the date when the child passes the skill. In this way you have a year's record of the child's gains in physical education on the one chart. One added skill would be for the child to bounce a ball about fifty feet, around a pole and back to the starting line. You could also add pole climbing, throw-and-catch, skipping, and rope jumping. The last two should be smooth and rhythmic before the child is credited with it.

These charts will give you clues to the needs of the children. You will want to choose the children with deficits to work on specific skills. One day after the whole class has had fifteen to twenty minutes of calisthenics and movement explorations, choose just the children who could not pass hopping and balancing and have them work on these skills on the beam, a large tube, or other equipment. Another day, take just the children struggling with jumping jacks and skipping, and work with them on various ways of motor planning the use of their legs. For instance: BOUNCE FEET APART TEN TIMES. BOUNCE FEET TOGETHER TEN TIMES. NOW BOUNCE FOUR TIMES WITH FEET APART AND FOUR WITH FEET TOGETHER. Finally, get down to one bounce in each position. Children with difficulties with ball bouncing and throw-and-catch will need extra help in these skill areas.

CALISTHENICS

Here, for convenience of organization, we use the term *calisthenics* to denote exercises which are performed in one designated spot. Calisthenics are a valuable part of the physical education program because they provide opportunity for strenuous physical exercise in a limited area. Too many of our school playgrounds fail to provide an area large enough for long distance running and heavy exertion. Kindergarten playgrounds are especially notorious in this regard. Calisthenics can be performed inside or out, on paving, lawn, or ground areas. They are also an excellent classroom release of tension during testing or other times of deep concentration or long inactivity.

We usually think of calisthenics as a highly regimented activity as it is performed by Army recruits or West Point cadets. This is neither successful nor really possible with poorly coordinated or controlled children. Thus we use calisthenics as a form of exploration of stationary movements and of body image. We don't usually try to have the children move in complete unison, but merely to keep them moving and exploring. So we use the stimulus challenge of *Who Can?* or I CAN DO THIS, CAN YOU?

There are a few simple exercises which can be done in unison with these young children. Example: Twist to the right, as they all shout *"Right"*; twist front, *"Front"*; and twist left, *"Left."*

Some exercises teaching sequence should be performed in unison, especially when the directions are shouted out by the children as they perform. For example, The Wooden Soldier: ATTENTION!

BEND YOUR RIGHT ELBOW UP, LEFT ELBOW UP. RIGHT ARM UP IN THE AIR, LEFT ARM UP IN THE AIR. RIGHT ELBOW BENT, LEFT ELBOW BENT. RIGHT ARM DOWN TO THE SIDE, LEFT ARM DOWN TO THE SIDE. SAY IT AS WE DO IT ALL TOGETHER. RIGHT, LEFT, RIGHT, LEFT, RIGHT, LEFT, RIGHT, LEFT. Repeat several times.

Try the exercise that teaches this up and down sequence: (1) STRETCH BOTH ARMS OUT TO THE SIDES, (2) TOUCH SHOULDERS, (3) TOUCH HEAD, (4) CLAP ABOVE THE HEAD, (5) TOUCH HEAD, (6) SHOULDERS, (7) ARMS OUT, (8) AND THEN DOWN. ALL TOGETHER: ONE, TWO, THREE, FOUR, FIVE, SIX, SEVEN, EIGHT.

After the children have gained some control of balance and limbs and directions, try this one: ATTENTION POSITION. STAND ON RIGHT FOOT AND POINT LEFT TOE OUT FRONT AT THE SAME TIME BRINGING BOTH ARMS FRONT. POINT LEFT TOE TO THE SIDE AND ARMS GO TO THE SIDES. POINT LEFT TOE AND ARMS FRONT AGAIN AND THEN STAND AT ATTENTION. Then call out: FRONT, SIDES, FRONT, DOWN. Then repeat the routine with the other foot.

Include many experiences in orientation to space or directionality in the calisthenics. Emphasize the name of the limb to be used and the direction to be faced. Having the children verbalize the directions as above helps them to a better cognition of the movement. Remember that the learning must be cognitive. When a movement is automatic, it has already been learned. When the child is unaware of what he is doing, he is not learning.

Teach the directions of the compass by noting their differences in the local environment. For example, here in California the wind from the north is often very cold. Thus we jump to the north and feel the cold wind in our faces. We jump to the west where the sun sets. We jump south and feel the warm sun on our faces.

When possible have the children do the calisthenics in the same area each time. Thus they know more what is expected of them and the compass directions are stabilized.

Choose a certain area of the playground where there are three parallel lines two to three feet apart. Line the children up on these, having them find their spaces by stretching their arms out to the sides. They should place themselves so that they do not touch each other. Initiate the signal of blowing on a whistle. The children freeze at attention and thus are ready for instruction for the next exercise.

Begin each session with a vigorous exercise like jumping or bouncing to stimulate the children. Lead it by demonstrating and performing yourself or by choosing a different *child-teacher* each day. Continue a variety of exercises, some static and dynamic balance, some using whole body movement, and some exercising specific body parts, such as arms, legs, torso. Spend only about five minutes on calisthenics. Keep the children moving, challenged, successful, and happy. If they can't do an exercise, break it down to its simplest components and teach those first. I keep a steady lingo going to keep the children moving.

One Day's Calisthenics

One day's exercises might go something like this:

Leg Movements: CAN YOU BOUNCE LIKE A BALL? BOUNCE ON YOUR TOES. TOMMY CAN BOUNCE. THAT IS GOOD! YOU ARE GREAT BOUNCERS. HOW HIGH CAN YOU BOUNCE? CAN YOU BOUNCE VERY SLOWLY? ARE YOUR LEGS TIRED? DO THEY TINGLE? CLOSE YOUR EYES AND FEEL HOW YOUR LEGS TINGLE.

Arms: LOOK WHAT I CAN DO WITH MY ARMS. I CAN SWING THEM TO THE RIGHT, THEN FRONT, LEFT, FRONT. CAN YOU DO IT? SAY IT WITH ME. RIGHT, FRONT, LEFT, FRONT. Do about ten times.

Back Movement: HOW FAR CAN YOU LEAN BACK? SPREAD YOUR LEGS TO BALANCE LIKE THIS. PUT YOUR HANDS ON YOUR HIPS, BEND YOUR KNEES, AND LEAN BACK, BACK. NOW STAND UP AND RELAX. LET'S DROOP LIKE A RAG DOLL WITH NO BONES. ALL SOFT AND DROOPY! NOW TRY TO BEND BACKWARD AGAIN. STRETCH, BACK, BACK! LOOK HOW FAR SUSAN CAN LEAN BACK. Go around helping others to perform, encouraging, prompting, while the child-teacher leads the group. The child might initiate changes in the routines. If he is unable to think of things to do to keep the group moving, make the suggestions yourself rather than let the activity lag.

Balance: CAN YOU STAND ON YOUR RIGHT FOOT AND MAKE A CIR-CLE WITH YOUR LEFT FOOT? Say the limb you want them to use. Be sure to use the reverse limbs when facing them and demonstrating so that they mirror your movements. THAT'S GOOD! LET'S

SEE IF WE CAN DO IT TEN TIMES. Count in unison even though many of the children are not moving in just the same rhythm as you are. The counting keeps them thinking and moving. WHOOPS! I GOOFED AND PUT MY FOOT DOWN! I LOST MY BALANCE! OH WELL, LET'S DO IT AGAIN, BUT THIS TIME BY STANDING ON YOUR LEFT FOOT. IS IT EASIER OR HARDER?

Whole Body Movement: EVERYBODY SIT DOWN ON THE BLACK-TOP! WHEN I SAY "THREE," SEE HOW FAST YOU CAN JUMP UP. ONE, TWO, THREE, JUMP UP! WOW! JERRY IS FAST! LET'S DO IT AGAIN. Repeat four or five times. NOW TRY SQUATTING OR SITTING ON YOUR HEELS. ONE, TWO, THREE, JUMP UP! LET'S DO IT AGAIN. WHICH WAY IS FASTER, FROM YOUR KNEES OR FROM YOUR SEAT? LET'S TRY IT AGAIN AND SEE.

Suggestions for Calisthenics

Begin with the simplest movements, gradually increasing the complexity of the exercises. Do not expect multiple coordinations of arms and legs, such as jumping jacks, until all the individual coordinations have been learned. Use a variety of exercises each day. The activities on the following list are suggestions for starters. Innovate from these by changing the locomotor movements, and/or the movement components.

1. GO UP ON YOUR TOES AND DOWN. FASTER, FASTER. UP, DOWN. Increase speed until the children are bouncing on their toes. LOOK WHAT YOU ARE DOING! YOU ARE BOUNCING!

2. CAN YOU JUMP SO HIGH THAT YOU KICK YOURSELF? HIGHER!

3. NOW YOUR ARMS ARE PROPELLERS. TURN THEM TOWARD ME. SMALL CIRCLES, THEN LARGER AND LARGER. NOW REVERSE THE PRO-PELLERS AND GO BACK THE OTHER WAY.

4. STAND AT ATTENTION! BEND YOUR HEAD TO THE RIGHT, UP, LEFT, UP. SAY IT WITH ME.

5. ATTENTION POSITION. STAND ON RIGHT FOOT AND SWING THE LEFT FOOT. SWING IT HIGH. NOW STAND ON THE LEFT FOOT AND SWING THE RIGHT.

6. ATTENTION. SWING YOUR ARMS ACROSS IN FRONT OF YOU AND UP IN THE AIR WHILE YOU TAKE A DEEP BREATH. NOW LET IT OUT SLOWLY WHILE YOUR ARMS GO OUT AWAY FROM YOUR BODY AND DOWN. LET'S DO IT AGAIN AND THIS TIME GO UP ON YOUR TOES AS

YOUR ARMS GO UP. HOLD YOUR BREATH. NOW LET IT OUT SLOWLY.

7. SPREAD YOUR FEET APART, ON THE LINE. NOW GIVE A BIG JUMP, TURN HALF WAY AROUND AND LOOK WEST. KEEP YOUR FEET ON THE LINE. KEEP THEM APART. GIVE A BIG JUMP AND TURN EAST. NOW YOU ARE LOOKING AT ME AGAIN. ARE YOUR FEET ON THE LINE? JUMP WEST. JUMP EAST.

8. STAND ON YOUR TIP TOES. HOLD IT! ONE THOUSAND, TWO THOUSAND, THREE THOUSAND, FOUR THOUSAND, FIVE THOUSAND. DOWN ONTO YOUR FEET. UP AGAIN AND HOLD IT.

9. CAN YOU MOVE YOUR FEET VERY SLOWLY IN YOUR SPACE LIKE A TORTOISE? PICK UP YOUR KNEES FAST AND RUN IN YOUR SPACE LIKE A HARE, OR RABBIT. TORTOISE. HARE.

10. HANDS ON HIPS, OUT TO THE SIDES, HIPS, SIDES, IN, OUT. SAY IT WITH ME. IN, OUT.

11. ROCK FORWARD ONTO TOES, BACKWARD ONTO HEELS. TOES, HEELS.

12. STAND ON YOUR RIGHT FOOT. LEAN FORWARD WITHOUT FALL-ING. LEAN MORE UNTIL YOU ARE LOOKING AT THE GROUND. CAN YOU BALANCE THAT WAY WITHOUT FALLING?

13. HANDS ON HIPS, BEND FORWARD, UP, BACKWARD, UP. LET'S SAY IT. FORWARD, UP, BACKWARD, UP.

14. CAN YOU BOUNCE WITH YOUR FEET TOGETHER? NOW BOUNCE WITH YOUR FEET APART. BOUNCE APART FIVE TIMES AND TOGETHER FIVE TIMES. APART, TOGETHER.

15. ARMS ABOVE YOUR HEADS! BEND TO THE RIGHT, UP, TO THE LEFT, UP.

16. SIT DOWN. TWIST YOUR TORSO TO THE RIGHT, FRONT, LEFT, FRONT. LET'S SAY IT WHILE WE DO IT.

17. WE ARE CANDLES. MELT DOWN, DOWN, UNTIL YOU ARE SQUAT-TING. NOW PUT YOUR ARMS WAY IN BACK OF YOU, GIVE A BIG PULL AND JUMP UP. LET'S MELT AGAIN.

18. STAND, SPREAD YOUR LEGS AND ARMS OUT TO THE SIDES. TWIST YOUR TORSO TO THE LEFT, BEND DOWN AND TOUCH YOUR LEFT FOOT. UP AND TWIST YOUR TORSO TO THE RIGHT AND TOUCH YOUR RIGHT FOOT. TWIST, TOUCH, LEFT. TWIST, TOUCH RIGHT. Also do this in sitting position.

19. HOLD YOUR ARMS OUT FRONT. NOW THEY ARE PROPELLERS.

SWING THEM TO THE RIGHT IN BIG CIRCLES. NOW REVERSE THE ENGINE AND YOUR ARMS SWING TO THE LEFT.

20. JUMP TO THE RIGHT AND YOU ARE LOOKING SOUTH AT THE SUN. PUT YOUR FEET APART SO THAT THEY DO NOT TOUCH THE LINE, BUT STRADDLE IT LIKE THIS. NOW JUMP HALF WAY AROUND AND LOOK NORTH. FEEL THE COLD WIND ON YOUR FACES? SEE IF YOU ARE STRADDLING THE LINE. WE ARE GOING TO JUMP SOUTH AGAIN. SEE IF YOU CAN DO IT WITHOUT STEPPING ON THE LINE.

21. SIT, SPREAD LEGS. TOUCH NOSE OR FOREHEAD TO THE GROUND. SIT UP. DOWN AND TOUCH YOUR NOSE.

22. STAND, SPREAD YOUR FEET. TWIST BACKWARD, BEND YOUR KNEES, AND SEE IF YOU CAN TOUCH YOUR RIGHT HAND TO YOUR HEEL. HOW CLOSE CAN YOU GET!

23. Bear Hug: STAND, HANDS ON HIPS WITH RIGHT FOOT DIAGO-NALLY FORWARD. ENCIRCLE THIGH WITH BOTH ARMS. BACK TO ATTEN-TION. LIFT LEFT LEG OUT AND ENCIRCLE IT. RIGHT LEG OUT. LEFT LEG OUT.

24. Sprints: GET DOWN AS IF YOU WERE GETTING READY TO RACE! PUT YOUR HANDS ON THE LINE AND YOUR LEFT LEG, WAY BACK! NOW PUT YOUR RIGHT LEG WAY BACK. GIVE A LITTLE JUMP AS YOU CHANGE LEGS. RIGHT, LEFT.

25. PUT YOUR ARMS OUT FRONT. TWIST YOUR TORSO AND YOUR ARMS RIGHT, FRONT, LEFT, FRONT. SAY IT WITH ME.

26. SWING YOUR ARMS AND CLAP THEM ABOVE YOUR HEAD. DOWN AND HIT YOUR SIDES. UP AND CLAP. DOWN.

27. JUMP YOUR FEET APART, TOGETHER, APART, TOGETHER. FEEL YOURSELF BOUNCE. Later turn in circle while doing it.

28. NOW YOUR HEAD IS A BALL AND IT ROLLS AROUND AND AROUND.

29. PUSH-UP POSITION. KICK YOUR FEET BACK TOGETHER LIKE A MULE.

30. DROP DOWN AND HANG FROM YOUR WAIST LIKE A RAG DOLL. PULL YOURSELF UP BY JUST LIFTING YOUR HEAD UP. DO IT AGAIN AND SEE HOW YOU CAN PULL YOUR WHOLE TORSO UP BY JUST LIFTING YOUR HEAD.

31. Thrusts: ATTENTION! PUT BOTH HANDS DOWN ON THE LINE. JUMP BOTH FEET BACKWARD UNTIL YOUR KNEES ARE STRAIGHT. JUMP BOTH FEET FORWARD UNTIL KNEES ARE BENT. JUMP UP. TRY IT

AGAIN. HANDS ON LINE, FEET BACK, BEND KNEES, JUMP UP.

32. MAKE PROPELLERS OUT TO THE SIDES. MAKE THE CIRCLES BIGGER AND BIGGER. NOW THEY ARE SO BIG YOU HAVE TO BEND YOUR KNEES AND GO DOWN AND UP, THEN REACH WAY UP, AND DOWN.

33. BEND YOUR ELBOWS JUST A LITTLE AND SWING YOUR ARMS AS YOU ROCK FROM YOUR HEELS TO YOUR TOES. ROCK EASY, UP, DOWN. NOW PULL YOUR ARMS HARDER. PULL HARDER. BEND YOUR KNEES MORE AND PULL HARDER. KEEP PULLING HARDER UNTIL YOU PULL YOUR FEET RIGHT OFF THE GROUND. LOOK AT THAT! WHAT ARE YOU DOING NOW? YES, JUMPING. THE HARDER YOU PULL, THE HIGHER YOU JUMP.

34. Rockets: LET US GO DOWN SLOWLY AS WE COUNT DOWN. TEN, NINE, EIGHT, SEVEN, SIX, FIVE, FOUR, THREE, TWO, ONE. Squat position. NOW GET YOUR ARMS BEHIND YOU, SWING THEM FORWARD AND BLAST OFF! JUMP WAY UP INTO THE AIR. LET'S DO IT AGAIN AND SEE HOW HIGH YOU CAN JUMP UP.

35. RUN IN PLACE ON THE BALLS OF YOUR FEET. BRING YOUR KNEES UP HIGH. HIGHER! DON'T LET YOUR HEELS TOUCH THE GROUND. SLAP YOUR KNEES AS THEY COME UP. KEEP YOUR ELBOWS SLIGHTLY BENT AND CLOSE TO YOUR BODY. Try this while leaning forward, then backward, then standing straight.

36. JUMP YOUR FEET APART AND MAKE YOUR ARMS GO OUT AT THE SAME TIME. OUT, IN, OUT, IN.

37. BOUNCE AND HIT YOUR SIDES. BOUNCE AGAIN, LIFT YOUR RIGHT KNEE AND CLAP YOUR HANDS UNDER IT. BOUNCE AND CLAP SIDES. BOUNCE, LIFT LEFT KNEE AND CLAP UNDER IT.

38. HOP EIGHT HOPS ON YOUR RIGHT FOOT, EIGHT ON YOUR LEFT. HOP FOUR HOPS ON RIGHT FOOT, THEN FOUR ON YOUR LEFT FOOT. Later reduce to two and two, finally one and one.

39. CROSS ARMS AND LEGS. SIT DOWN AND STAND UP. KEEP YOUR ARMS CROSSED. This has been called the Turk stand.

40. ARMS FRONT, DOWN. ARMS OUT TO SIDES, DOWN.

41. JUMP AND REACH: FEET SLIGHTLY APART. EXTEND ARMS OVERHEAD, PALMS OUT. SWING THEM DOWN AND BACKWARD WHILE BENDING DEEPLY AND FLEXING KNEES SLIGHTLY. SWING UP AND STRAIGHTEN AND LEAP, THROWING HANDS UP.

42. On knees: LEAN BACKWARD, THEN FORWARD, BUT KEEP YOUR BACK STRAIGHT. DON'T SIT ON YOUR HEELS.

43. On knees: TWIST TO THE RIGHT AND TOUCH RIGHT HAND TO THE GROUND BEHIND YOU. UP ON YOUR KNEES AGAIN. NOW TWIST TO THE LEFT AND TOUCH THE GROUND BEHIND YOU.

44. PRETEND YOU HAVE A ROPE. PULL IT HARD, HARDER, IT WON'T COME.

45. PRETEND YOU ARE PUSHING A HEAVY BOX. PUSH HARD, HARDER.

46. NOW IT IS AT YOUR BACK. PUSH IT WITH YOUR BACK.

47. BALANCE ON YOUR RIGHT FOOT. NOW PIVOT YOUR BODY AROUND WITHOUT LIFTING YOUR FOOT OFF THE GROUND. TRY IT WITH THE LEFT FOOT. CAN YOU GO ALL THE WAY AROUND?

48. STAND ON YOUR RIGHT LEG WITH YOUR KNEE BENT. CAN YOU HOLD IT AND COUNT TO TEN. NOW BALANCE ON THE LEFT LEG.

49. Wing Stretcher: RAISE YOUR ELBOWS TO YOUR SHOULDERS. CLENCH YOUR FISTS AND PULL BACKWARD.

50. MELT. JUMP UP AND FREEZE.

51. LEGS APART, ARMS OVERHEAD, THUMBS CLASPED. BEND DOWN AND TOUCH FINGERS TO GROUND INSIDE OF RIGHT FOOT, THEN OUTSIDE NEAR RIGHT TOES, THEN OUTSIDE NEAR RIGHT HEEL. BACK TO START- ING POSITION AND DO THE SAME THING NEAR LEFT FOOT. Or, TOUCH RIGHT TOE, TOUCH GROUND BETWEEN LEGS, TOUCH LEFT TOE, UP.

52. CLASP HANDS ON TOP OF YOUR HEAD, MAKE A SLIGHT SQUAT WITH ONE FOOT SLIGHTLY FORWARD. JUMP UPWARD REVERSING THE POSITION OF YOUR FEET AND COMING DOWN IN SEMISQUAT POSITION.

53. JUMP, FEET TOGETHER FORWARD AND BACKWARD OVER THE LINE. JUMP SIDE TO SIDE ON THE LINE. TURN NORTH AND JUMP SIDE TO SIDE OVER THE LINE. JUMP FORWARD AND BACKWARD.

54. PRETEND YOU ARE CLIMBING A LADDER. LIFT YOUR RIGHT ARM AND LEG. THEN YOUR LEFT ARM AND LEG.

55. ATTENTION POSITION. ARMS OUT FRONT. OPEN AND CLOSE YOUR FINGERS. SHOOT THE FINGERS OUT HARD. OPEN, CLOSE.

56. ATTENTION. ARMS OUT TO YOUR SIDES. POINT YOUR POINTER FINGERS AT THE SKY. CAN YOU KEEP LOOKING STRAIGHT AHEAD BUT STILL SEE THEM OUT OF THE CORNERS OF YOUR EYES? WATCH THEM NOW AND BRING THEM FORWARD UNTIL THEY ARE RIGHT IN FRONT OF YOUR NOSE. WATCH THEM ALL THE WAY.

57. ATTENTION. TOUCH YOUR HEAD, SHOULDERS, KNEES, AND TOES. LET'S SAY IT AND DO IT ALL TOGETHER LIKE THE HIGH SCHOOL BOYS.

MOVEMENT EXPLORATION

Calisthenics are very highly structured exercises, whereas the movement explorations in this section are more free-moving, a discover-for-yourself method. In movement exploration the child is trained in motor-planning and the development of the basic locomotor movements as opposed to the more stationary movements of calisthenics. The exploration of these locomotor movements can be performed on either paving or lawn, or in a large multipurpose room or gym. The fifty-yard dash lines painted on the blacktop can be used for toe-heel walking, and learning to cross step.

First it is important to have a signal system so that you have control of the group. A whistle for freeze-and-listen is the most efficient. Set up controllable limits of the movements so that the children don't get carried away and end up on the other side of the playground. Allow about sixty feet between certain landmarks. For example, from the tetherball poles to the lawn; or, south to the backstop and then north to that white line over there. As with the on-the-line calisthenics, keep the children moving, experimenting.

Remember that the learning must be cognitive. He must be aware of his movements. Inane or uncontrolled movements are to be discouraged. The disorganized children tend to run blindly instead of following directions. First use copious praise for those performing well. But remember that the confused child runs inanely not because he is just being disobedient or does not want to cooperate, but because he is unable to follow your instructions, or demonstration. Stop him physically, firmly, but not angrily.

Ask him: WHAT ARE WE DOING NOW? Clarify the instructions. Show him a child who is performing well. SEE WHAT TOMMY IS DOING? SEE IF YOU CAN DO IT, TOO. Then guide him step by step, moving a limb as needed or holding his hand and doing it with him. Give him immediate reinforcement. THERE, YOU CAN DO IT, TOO. YOU'RE SMART! SEE IF YOU CAN DO THIS NEXT ONE, TOO.

One Day's Exploration

CAN YOU WALK FAST SOUTH TOWARD THE POLES? REMEMBER TO STOP AND FREEZE WHEN YOU HEAR THE WHISTLE. WALK FAST! Blow the whistle. FREEZE! TOMMY KNOWS HOW TO FREEZE. HE STOPPED RIGHT AWAY. I CAN'T CATCH HIM. NOW TURN AND GO NORTH BACK THE OTHER WAY TOWARD THE LAWN. THIS TIME CAN YOU SKIP? Blow whistle. YOU ARE GOOD FREEZERS! TURN SOUTH AND WALK LIKE A CROOKED MAN. LOOK HOW SUSAN USES THAT WHITE LINE AND CROSSES OVER THE LINE. CAN YOU DO THAT? Blow whistle. They freeze and turn. CAN YOU WALK ON A LINE WITH ONE FOOT RIGHT IN FRONT OF THE OTHER? COVER THE LINE WITH YOUR FEET. MAKE YOUR HEEL TOUCH THE OTHER TOE. SEE, I CAN DO IT. Help them to explore this movement for a minute or two. Then blow the whistle. Use five to ten minutes of these movements a day.

Suggestions for Movement Exploration

Here are some basic movement requests for starters. Innovate from these by changing the locomotor movement and/or the movement components.

1. CAN YOU SLIDE TO THE RIGHT WITHOUT CROSSING YOUR LEGS? SLIDE LEFT.

2. CAN YOU CROSS YOUR LEFT FOOT OVER YOUR RIGHT AND GO RIGHT?

3. WALK VERY SMALL. WALK VERY BIG.

4. WALK HIGH. WALK LOW.

5. CAN YOU WALK HIGH AND LOW? NOW YOU ARE A MERRY-GO-ROUND.

6. PRETEND YOU ARE A RABBIT. YOUR HANDS ARE TALL EARS. SQUAT, LEAP HANDS FORWARD TOGETHER, THEN JUMP FEET UP TO HANDS.

7. ELEPHANTS ROCK FROM SIDE TO SIDE LIKE THIS. MY ARMS ARE AN ELEPHANT'S TRUNK. LEFT, RIGHT, LEFT, RIGHT.

8. BE AN OSTRICH. HOLD YOUR ANKLES, KNEES STRAIGHT, AND WALK.

9. FROG JUMP. USE YOUR HANDS ON THE GROUND OUTSIDE YOUR KNEES. LEAP. LAND ON YOUR HANDS AND FEET.

10. BE A HIGH-STEPPING HORSE. SEE HOW HIGH YOU CAN RAISE YOUR KNEES.

11. NOW YOU ARE A CROW. SQUAT, HOLD YOUR ANKLES. WALK.

12. CAN YOU JUMP TEN JUMPS WITHOUT STOPPING? COUNT THEM AND FREEZE.

13. CAN YOU HOP TEN HOPS? COUNT THEM AND FREEZE.

14. NOW TRY SOMETHING HARDER. JUMP FIVE JUMPS AND THEN DO FIVE HOPS. Later reduce to two and two.

15. NOW YOU ARE A DADDY LONGLEGS SPIDER. WALK WITH FOUR LONG LEGS. KNEES STRAIGHT.

16. TURN UPSIDE DOWN AND WALK LIKE A CRAB ON FOUR LEGS. A CRAB WALKS SIDEWAYS. CAN YOU? TRY CRAB-WALKING FRONT-WARD, BACKWARD.

17. PRETEND YOU ARE A KANGAROO. SQUAT, KNEES BENT. KEEP YOUR BACK STRAIGHT, ELBOWS AND WRISTS BENT IN FRONT OF CHEST ARE SHORT FORELEGS. WALK ON THE BALLS OF YOUR FEET. THEN SPRING UP AND BACK TO A SQUAT.

18. WHAT IS THE BIGGEST STEP YOU CAN TAKE? THE SMALLEST?

19. CAN YOU WALK BACKWARD? CAN YOU WALK IN A CIRCLE? WALK IN A BIG CIRCLE WITHOUT TOUCHING ANYONE. WALK IN THE SMALLEST CIRCLE YOU CAN.

20. CAN YOU SKIP BACKWARD, FORWARD, SIDEWAYS? This is a difficult coordination. Work extensively on walking and running and galloping before you require this.

21. CAN YOU RUN LIKE A MONKEY? RUN ON ALL FOURS WITH HANDS DRAGGING OR HELPING.

22. CAN YOU RUN ON YOUR HEELS? YOUR TOES?

23. LOOK HOW I CAN DO A SHUFFLE-WALK. I MOVE SIDEWAYS BY PIVOTING MY TOES, THEN MY HEELS, TOES, HEELS. TRY IT.

24. PUT YOUR RIGHT FOOT OUT FRONT AND GALLOP. CHANGE TO YOUR LEFT FOOT. SEE HOW YOUR LEFT FOOT IS LEADING. SEE IF YOU CAN CHANGE THE LEADING FOOT WHEN I SAY CHANGE. CHANGE! The first few days let them go several steps before asking them to change. Later, speed up the changes until finally they change every other step. This then becomes a skip.

25. HOW CAN YOU DRAW A BOX ON THE GROUND WITH YOUR FEET BY HOPPING? BE SURE THE CORNERS ARE SHARP.

26. THERE IS A BIG BOX HERE. PUSH IT. IT'S HEAVY!

27. HERE IS A SLED WITH TWO CHILDREN ON IT. PULL IT.

28. RUN ON YOUR TOES.

29. WALK FAST, BUT YOUR WHOLE FOOT MUST TOUCH THE GROUND, HEEL AND ALL. Have children demonstrate the difference between a run and a fast walk. Note that with the run, only one foot is on the ground at one time, the other is in the air.

After the children have had some experience with the different locomotor movements, the movement components and with motor-planning movements, use more of the suggestions from Hackett (1966). This is a small booklet easy to keep on hand, and loaded with ideas for movement explorations. Now try for more cognitive contact: HOW CAN YOU GET FROM YOUR SPOT OVER TO THERE WITH THE FEWEST STEPS (skips, hops, jumps)? With a partner, HOW CAN YOU BOTH MOVE FORWARD, BACKWARD? HOW CAN YOU MOVE FORWARD AT THE SAME TIME YOUR PARTNER MOVES BACKWARD? FIGURE IT OUT.

Lawn Activities

If the teacher is able to do all the movements with the children, and the children are easy to control, then the space need not be as structured as above. Just say: LET US ALL . . . and they follow you en masse as you strike out across the playground. Thus you can do one movement, then, without using the whistle signal, just call out the next idea and they follow you Pied Piper fashion. We work with fifty to sixty children at one time, in a team-teaching situation. Our children are very impulsive and lacking in self-discipline as well as being unable to motor plan and co-ordinate body parts. We usually begin the school year with the calisthenics and movement explorations outlined above. These children require a highly structured curriculum until they learn self-control and have made gains in motor coordinations. Usually by Christmas the children have gained control of themselves and are responding well. From then on use a large lawn area, challenge the children with WHO CAN, or LET'S SEE YOU. . . . Either do the movements with them (such as skipping or jogging) LET'S SKIP TO THE FENCE! Or just give the performers lots of attention and praise, and blow the whistle to announce the next movement. Thus for the rest of the year, except for rainy days when movements are restricted, use the lawn area and this loose organization for all of the movement explorations, some calisthenics, and all the activities in the following sections.

For some exploration of movements, the lawn or indoor tumbling mats are essential to avoid injuries. Doing the chasing games on the lawn also avoids skinned knees.

Crawling Activities

1. NOW YOU ARE POLLYWOGS. LIE ON YOUR STOMACHS. YOU HAVE NO LEGS. CAN YOU MOVE BY USING JUST YOUR ARMS? PULL WITH YOUR ELBOWS. CAN YOU MOVE USING BOTH ARMS TOGETHER? NOW TRY MOVING USING FIRST YOUR RIGHT ELBOW AND THEN YOUR LEFT.

2. Seals: PUSH-UP POSITION, ELBOWS STIFF, LEGS STRETCHED OUT BEHIND. ONLY TOES TOUCHING GROUND. WALK WITH HANDS, DRAGGING TOES.

3. PRETEND YOU ARE A TURTLE. USE YOUR ARMS AND YOUR LEGS THIS TIME BUT STAY CLOSE TO THE GROUND.

4. NOW YOU ARE PUPPY DOGS ON YOUR HANDS AND KNEES. CAN YOU USE YOUR HANDS TOGETHER, THEN YOUR KNEES TOGETHER?

5. I AM GOING TO CHANGE YOU ALL INTO BIG, HEAVY, LUMBERING, FOUR-LEGGED BEARS. THEY ROLL FROM SIDE TO SIDE AS THEY WALK. USE THE RIGHT ARM AND KNEE, THEN THE LEFT ARM AND KNEE.

6. NOW YOU ARE HORSES! LINE UP FOR THE HORSE RACE. SEE WHO CAN CRAWL OUT TO THIS JUMP ROPE THE FASTEST. Use alternate movement of limbs.

7. Horse and rider: Child on hands and knees is horse. Rider sits on his partner's hips, bending knees to keep his feet off the ground. Have horse races.

Tumbling Activities

1. BE ROLLING LOGS. LIE DOWN, STRETCH YOUR ARMS OUT OVER YOUR HEAD AND ROLL LIKE A LOG.

2. SIT DOWN AND CROSS YOUR LEGS. NOW TRY TO SOMERSAULT OVER AND OVER LIKE A BALL ROLLING. Or, SQUAT, WEIGHT ON HANDS OUTSIDE OF KNEES, BEND OVER AND SOMERSAULT.

3. PUT YOUR FINGER ON THE GROUND AND RUN AROUND IT.

4. SQUAT, JUMP AND SPIN HALFWAY AROUND.

5. LET US WIND THE CLOCK. KNEEL, KEEP YOUR KNEES AND FEET FIRM. WALK YOUR HANDS AROUND YOUR BODY.

6. HANDS AND FEET ON THE GROUND. SHOOT YOUR LEGS TO THE SIDES, RIGHT, LEFT. WALK YOUR FEET AROUND TO THE SIDE.

7. Coffee Grinder. ONE HAND ON GROUND. STRETCH LEGS OUT TO THE SIDE. WALK AROUND YOUR HAND.

8. MONKEYS RUN ON ALL FOURS, WITH HANDS DRAGGING OR HELPING.

9. Egg sit: SIT WITH KNEES BENT, HANDS HOLDING TOES. ROCK BACK AND FOURTH ON BUTTOCKS.

10. Leap: LEAN FORWARD AND TAKE LARGE STEPS. PUSH YOURSELF UP INTO THE AIR. NOW YOU ARE A DEER.

11. YOU ARE A GENTLE RAIN SHOWER, VERY LIGHT. NOW IT'S RAINING VERY HARD AND YOU ARE BIG RAINDROPS.

12. Teach cartwheels. Have a child demonstrate how the movement is sideways, but that you turn completely around in the process.

13. Teach balancing with head and hands on lawn forming triangle, knees balanced above elbows. When balance is achieved, child raises his legs to a headstand.

14. RUN AND WHEN I BLOW THE WHISTLE, STOP AND SEE HOW FAST YOU CAN GET INTO A PUSH-UP POSITION. Also, RUN AND WHEN I BLOW THE WHISTLE, SLIDE. RUN AND WHEN I BLOW THE WHISTLE, SOMERSAULT.

15. Push-ups: Girls on knees, boys on toes. STRETCH TORSO, LIFT BODY UNTIL ARMS ARE STRAIGHT. GO DOWN AND TOUCH CHIN TO LAWN. KEEP YOUR BODY STRAIGHT. DON'T LET YOUR TUMMY TOUCH THE GROUND. CAN YOU DO IT FIVE TIMES?

16. Measuring worm: HANDS AND FEET ON THE FLOOR. WALK STIFF-LEGGED IN SMALL STEPS TOWARD HANDS. THEN KEEP FEET STATIONARY AND WALK HANDS FORWARD UNTIL BODY IS OUT-STRETCHED. NEXT KEEP HANDS STILL AND WALK FEET UP TO HANDS.

17. Three-legged walk: MOVE WITH TWO HANDS AND ONE FOOT ON THE FLOOR. WALK THE HANDS, HOP THE FOOT.

18. Egg roll: KNEEL, KNEES APART, ROUND BACK TO PUT ELBOWS ON GROUND IN FRONT OF KNEES. ROLL SIDEWAYS.

19. Upswing: KNEEL, BODY ERECT, WEIGHT ON BALLS OF FEET.

SWING ARMS TO RAISE BODY TO FEET AND STAND.

20. Bicycle: LIE ON BACK! LIFT LEGS OVER THE HEAD, BRACE BACK WITH HANDS ON WAIST, ELBOWS ON GROUND. PEDAL LEGS.

21. Back flip: LIE ON BACKS AND LIFT LEGS UP AND OVER THE HEAD UNTIL THE TOES TOUCH THE LAWN BACK OF YOU.

22. Backward somersault: SQUAT WITH YOUR HEAD BETWEEN YOUR KNEES. NOW ROCK BACK AND PUT YOUR HANDS BY YOUR SHOULDERS, PUSH UP AND ROLL OVER.

Partner Activities

After the children have gained some skills in movement exploration individually, try some of the same movements with partners. Thus they must learn to adjust their rhythm of movement to that of the other child, in order to move in synchrony. They also learn to work together, helping each other, giving each other support.

1. HOLD YOUR PARTNER'S HAND AND JUMP FROM HERE TO THERE. TRY JUMPING BACKWARD TOGETHER. CAN YOU JUMP SIDEWAYS? LET'S GO TO THE RIGHT FIRST. NOW LEFT. NOW HOLD BOTH HANDS. CAN YOU JUMP TOWARD THE FENCE? TOWARD THE SCHOOL? SOUTH? NORTH?

2. Do the above routines with hopping, skipping, walking, galloping, and running. Also, vary these routines according to speed, size, design, etc., as described previously.

3. Have partner races with the various locomotor movements.

4. One child is a rock. His partner tries to push him over. Change, and the other child is the rock.

5. One child is a post and his partner tries to pull him down.

6. Child places his hands on his partner's hands, fingers up. They both push.

7. Partners hold both hands and try changing position. CAN YOU SIT DOWN WITHOUT LETTING GO OF HANDS? CAN YOU BOTH STAND UP AGAIN?

8. One sits down while the other stands up. NOW CAN YOU CHANGE AND THE OTHER ONE SITS DOWN WHILE YOU STAND UP. YOU ARE LIKE A MERRY-GO-ROUND.

9. Two children stand in line holding right hands. Then front

child turns and faces partner. WHAT HAPPENED TO YOUR RIGHT HANDS? WHERE ARE THEY? DO IT AGAIN AND SEE WHAT HAPPENS.

10. HOLD RIGHT HANDS AND BRACE YOURSELVES WITH YOUR LEGS. WHO CAN PULL HIS PARTNER AWAY? TRY IT WITH LEFT HANDS.

11. STANDING, SPREAD FEET FRONTWARD AND BACKWARD. HOLD BOTH HANDS. NOW YOU ARE A SAW AND YOU PULL EACH OTHER FRONTWARD AND BACKWARD.

12. With shoes off, one gets down on hands and knees. The other partner steps over him without touching him. They change positions quickly.

13. One child makes a bridge. WHO CAN CRAWL UNDER HIS PARTNER? NOW HE CRAWLS UNDER YOU. CHANGE POSITIONS QUICKLY.

14. HOLD HANDS, LEAN BACKWARD AND SPIN YOURSELVES AROUND AS FAST AS YOU CAN.

15. FACE EACH OTHER AND HOLD HANDS IN FRONT OF YOU. TURN TOWARD THE SCHOOL, RAISE THE HANDS INTO AN ARCH. TWIST UNDER THE ARCH WITHOUT LETTING GO OF YOUR HANDS. NOW YOU ARE BACK TO BACK. RAISE THE OTHER ARMS, TURN AGAIN AND YOU ARE FACING EACH OTHER AGAIN. HOW MANY TIMES CAN YOU DO IT? CAN YOU DO IT OVER AND OVER WITHOUT STOPPING?

16. Siamese twins: STAND BACK TO BACK HOLDING HANDS! KEEP YOUR BACKS TOGETHER. WALK TOWARD THE SCHOOL. WALK AWAY FROM THE SCHOOL. CAN YOU WALK SIDEWAYS?

17. Wheelbarrows: One child stands and holds feet of partner who then walks on his hands. Have distance races.

18. STAND BACK TO BACK AND HOOK ELBOWS. SIT DOWN. STAND UP.

19. Line up with partners holding hands. Have about six partners to a line. Last couple runs forward and arches over couple in front, under the next couple, over the next, etc., until they come to the front of the line. Then they yell GO! and the last couple at the end of the line arches over and under as did the first couple.

BALL SKILLS
Beanbags

Beanbags are excellent for teaching throwing and catching. The beanbag is easier to grasp and will not bounce away from the child. Thus time is not lost in continually retrieving the ball.

Every child should have a beanbag. They should be made about child-hand size. The child should be able to grasp it easily in the palm of his hand. If it is too big he will throw it by a corner and thus have a wild aim. Fabric should be a sturdy tightly woven fabric like denim. Double layers of fabric might make the bags last longer, as the children tend to work the beans through loose threads or small holes. Using a variety of colors and patterns helps to distinguish them. Designate numerals on the bags that are of the same fabric. Thus in group throwing activities each child knows which one is his.

Throwing

1. THROW IT UP AND CATCH IT WITH TWO HANDS. KEEP YOUR EYES ON IT. TRY IT WITH ONE HAND. NOW YOUR OTHER HAND. THROW IT HIGHER. HIGHER!

2. THROW IT OUT IN FRONT OF YOU, RUN UNDER IT AND CATCH IT. KEEP YOUR EYES ON IT. CAN YOU THROW IT OVER YOUR HEAD, TURN AROUND AND TRY TO GET UNDER IT AND CATCH IT? THROW IT OUT TO YOUR RIGHT SIDE. YOUR LEFT SIDE.

3. THROW IT FROM HAND TO HAND ACROSS YOUR BODY! CAN YOU DO IT WITH YOUR PALMS DOWN? TOSS IT UP WITH YOUR RIGHT HAND AND CATCH IT WITH YOUR LEFT HAND. CAN YOU KEEP DOING IT AS YOU SIT DOWN AND STAND UP AGAIN?

4. CAN YOU PASS IT UNDER YOUR RIGHT LEG AND OVER THE LEFT? CAN YOU PASS IT AROUND AND AROUND YOUR BODY? HOW FAST CAN YOU DO IT?

5. Throw for accuracy: EVERYONE STAND AROUND THE BIG CIRCLE AND TRY TO THROW YOUR BEANBAG INTO THE LITTLE CIRCLE IN THE MIDDLE. Throw underhand and overhand. Or use two or three large circles with small circles in the center of each. All throw bags into the center circle. Team with most beanbags within center circle gets one point. EVERYONE STAND ON THIS LINE AND TRY TO THROW YOUR BAG INTO THE SPACE HERE. THROW YOUR BAG INTO NUMBER TWO HOPSCOTCH SQUARE.

6. Throw for distance (Developed by Jeanne Bartelt) :
EVERYONE STAND ON THIS LINE. TURN SIDEWAYS AND LOOK LEFT. TAKE A BIG STEP TO THE LEFT. DO IT AGAIN. THIS TIME, TAKE THAT BIG STEP LEFT AND TWIST YOUR SHOULDERS LEFT AT THE SAME TIME.

STEP AND TWIST. AGAIN. PRETEND THAT YOU ARE HOLDING THE BEAN-
BAG ON THE BACK OF YOUR HEAD. GET YOUR ELBOW UP SHOULDER
HIGH. NOW TAKE A BIG STEP, TWIST, AND THROW YOUR ARM OUT. DO
IT AGAIN AND MAKE YOUR ARM GO "SWISH." AGAIN. NOW LET'S DO IT
WITH A BEANBAG! STEP, TWIST, LOOK RIGHT TOWARD THE FENCE,
AND THROW. RUN GET YOUR BAG AND LET'S DO IT AGAIN. LINE UP
AGAIN. LET'S SEE WHO CAN THROW IT THE FARTHEST. STEP, TWIST,
KEEP THAT ELBOW HIGH, THROW! SOMEONE'S BAG WENT SIDEWAYS!
YOU HAVE TO LOOK WHERE YOU WANT THE BAG TO GO. LOOK
STRAIGHT AT THE FENCE. BRING THE BAG RIGHT PAST YOUR EYES.
LEFTIES TURN TO LEFT, LOOK RIGHT AND STEP OUT WITH RIGHT FOOT.

Other Beanbag Activities

1. HOLD TWO BEANBAGS, ONE IN EACH HAND. MAKE CIRCLES BE-
SIDE YOU WITH YOUR ARMS. FEEL THE WEIGHT OF THE BAGS. CAN
YOU THROW THEM FROM HAND TO HAND, BOTH BAGS AT ONCE?

2. With a partner, one bag each: THROW YOUR BAGS TO EACH
OTHER AT THE SAME TIME. MAKE A RHYTHM OF IT. SWING BACK,
THROW. WATCH YOUR PARTNER'S ARM SO THAT YOU DO IT AT THE
SAME TIME.

3. PUT YOUR BAG ON YOUR FOOT AND WALK. SWING YOUR LEG
FORWARD WITHOUT LETTING THE BAG FALL. CIRCLE YOUR LEG WITH
THE BAG ON YOUR FOOT. SWING YOUR LEG TO TOSS THE BAG AWAY
FROM YOU. SWING YOUR FOOT SO HARD THAT THE BAG GOES UPWARD
AND YOU CATCH IT.

4. PUT THE BAG BETWEEN YOUR FEET AND JUMP WITH IT. JUMP
AND TOSS THE BAG AWAY FROM YOU. JUMP AND TOSS THE BAG UP
AND CATCH IT.

5. With bare feet: PICK UP THE BAG WITH YOUR TOES. CARRY IT
TO THIS CIRCLE AND PUT IT IN. PUT IT IN THE BUCKET.

6. Bag on head: WALK, BALANCING BAG. RUN WITHOUT LETTING
IT FALL. MAKE IT BOUNCE FROM YOUR HEAD INTO YOUR HANDS. GIVE
A BIG JUMP TO TOSS THE BAG OFF YOUR HEAD. CATCH THE BAG. TOSS
IT FROM YOUR HEAD SIDEWAYS. WHILE THE BAG IS ON YOUR HEAD,
SIT DOWN AND STAND UP.

An Instant Ball

Individual balls can be easily made of either men's or women's hose. Simply crush a whole double sheet of newspaper into a ball and insert it into the toe of the stocking. Pull tightly so that the ball is hard and firm. Twist the sock just above the ball and turn the sock inside out over the ball. Pull tightly, twist and invert the sock again. Repeat until the sock has been all used up. The ends can be taped with masking tape for temporary use, or it may be sewn. The children can sew it themselves with a double knotted thread. This ball can then be used for most of the bean-bag activities, the passing around the body, the throwing in different directions, catching, throwing-for-distance and accuracy, and for throw-and-catch against a wall, also for indoor ball games on inclement days.

Scoop Throw and Catch

Cut off the bottom third of a gallon bleach bottle with a diagonal cut to form a scoop. Use the neck of the bottle as a handle. This scoop can then be used to throw and catch beanbags or soft balls of any kind (Fig. 23). The child uses it alone,

Figure 23. Scoop Throw and Catch.

tossing the bag up or forward or against a wall. He also uses it with a partner to play catch.

Bouncing Balls

The first rubber balls used for bouncing should be eight inches in diameter, or more. It is good to have a variety of sizes and types of balls so that the child can learn how he must make changes in position and thrust. It is imperative that every child have a ball with which to experiment by himself. It requires lengthy individual practice to learn to handle a ball for throwing, catching, and bouncing. When there are only one or two balls per class of children, no child gets enough practice to lock-in a real skill. One way of accomplishing this is to pool all the balls for the school in one caster-bottom box. Thus when any one class is out for physical education, there will be enough balls for at least half of your class to have a ball each. Teach bouncing skills in this developmental sequence which was developed by Jeanne Bartelt, of Sacramento:

1. HOLD THE BALL IN TWO HANDS. WALK FRONTWARD, BACKWARD, SIDEWAYS, TO THE RIGHT, TO THE LEFT. WALK AROUND IN A CIRCLE TO THE RIGHT, TO THE LEFT.

2. KEEP YOUR EYES ON THE BALL. THROW IT UP OVER YOUR HEAD. CATCH IT IN FRONT OF YOUR EYES.

3. HOLD THE BALL IN BOTH HANDS RIGHT AT YOUR WAIST LEVEL. DROP IT AND CATCH IT. HOLD IT ABOVE YOUR HEAD. DROP IT AND CATCH IT. HOLD IT BY YOUR KNEES. DROP IT AND CATCH IT.

4. NOW HOLD IT BY YOUR WAIST AGAIN AND TRY TO MAKE IT BOUNCE BACK UP TO YOUR WAIST. WHAT DO YOU HAVE TO DO TO IT TO MAKE IT COME UP TO YOUR WAIST? DROP IT FROM YOUR KNEE-HEIGHT. CAN YOU DROP IT HARD ENOUGH SO THAT IT COMES BACK UP TO YOUR KNEES AND YOU CATCH IT THERE? BOUNCE IT FROM YOUR EYE LEVEL. HOW HARD DO YOU HAVE TO BOUNCE IT TO MAKE IT COME BACK UP TO YOUR EYE LEVEL?

5. BOUNCE THE BALL WITH BOTH HANDS FROM YOUR WAIST. BOUNCE IT WITH BOTH HANDS AT YOUR RIGHT SIDE. MAKE IT COME UP TO YOUR WAIST. KEEP YOUR EYES ON THE BALL. NOW BOUNCE IT WITH BOTH HANDS AT YOUR RIGHT SIDE.

6. BOUNCE THE BALL WITH ONE HAND, WAIST HIGH IN FRONT OF YOU. THEN AT YOUR RIGHT SIDE, THEN AT YOUR LEFT SIDE.

7. BOUNCE THE BALL IN FRONT OF YOU WAIST HIGH. NOW TRY TO BOUNCE IT LOWER AND LOWER TILL YOU ARE BOUNCING IT AT KNEE LEVEL! CAN YOU SIT DOWN STILL BOUNCING THE BALL? KEEP IT GOING. KEEP YOUR EYES ON IT. NOW, CAN YOU START TO STAND UP, STILL BOUNCING THE BALL ALL THE TIME?

8. CAN YOU BOUNCE THE BALL WITH SOME OTHER PART OF YOUR BODY? YOUR HEAD? YOUR ELBOW? YOUR ARM? BOUNCE IT EASY WITH JUST YOUR FINGERTIPS.

9. CAN YOU BOUNCE THE BALL FIRST WITH ONE HAND AND THEN THE OTHER?

10. NOW TURN AND THROW THE BALL UP AND FORWARD, AND RUN UP UNDER THE BALL AND CATCH IT.

11. CAN YOU WALK AND BOUNCE THE BALL? GO AROUND THAT POLE AND COME BACK AGAIN BOUNCING THE BALL ALL THE WAY.

Throwing Against a Wall

1. STAND JUST TWO FEET AWAY FROM THE WALL. THROW THE BALL AT THE WALL AND CATCH IT. CAN YOU CATCH IT WITH BOTH HANDS? ONE HAND? DO IT TEN TIMES. MOVE BACK ONE BIG STEP. THROW THE BALL AND CATCH IT TEN TIMES (Fig. 24). MOVE BACK ANOTHER BIG STEP, THROW AND CATCH. When the child is far enough back that he requires more thrust, teach him to throw it sideways, changing weight from his right foot to his forward left foot. Left-handed children throw from the left side with the right foot forward.

2. THROW THE BALL AT THE WALL AND CLAP ONE TIME BEFORE YOU CATCH IT. TRY THROWING IT AND CLAPPING TWO TIMES. CAN YOU DO IT THREE TIMES?

3. Put an X on the pavement about three feet in front of the wall. CAN YOU THROW THE BALL, LET IT BOUNCE ON THE X, THEN THE WALL, BOUNCE ONE MORE TIME AND THEN YOU CATCH IT. LOOK AT THE X. THROW RIGHT TO IT. Do this about nine feet from the wall. Teach the child to use the sideways throwing position when he needs greater thrust, shifting his weight as he throws and keeping up a steady rhythm.

Figure 24. Throw and Catch Against a Wall.

Throw and Catch

When a child has good control throwing and catching the ball against a wall, then he is ready to play catch with a partner.

1. The two children stand about fifteen feet apart, with a line between them. One child stands sideways throwing the ball at the line. It bounces and his partner catches it and returns it in the same throw, bounce, catch order.

2. LOOK STRAIGHT AT YOUR PARTNER'S ARMS AND THROW THE BALL RIGHT TO HIM. KEEP YOUR EYES ON HIM AS YOU THROW IT. AIM WITH YOUR EYES. SEE IF YOU CAN THROW IT RIGHT INTO HIS ARMS. NOW HE IS GOING TO THROW IT TO YOU. PUT YOUR FEET APART, SHIFT YOUR WEIGHT SIDE TO SIDE. NOW WATCH THE BALL. KEEP YOUR EYES ON IT. IF IT GOES A LITTLE TO YOUR RIGHT SIDE YOU HAVE TO SHIFT YOUR WEIGHT TO THE RIGHT TO CATCH IT. WHAT WILL YOU HAVE TO DO IF HE THROWS IT A LITTLE TO YOUR LEFT? WHAT WILL YOU HAVE TO DO IF HE THROWS IT TOO HIGH? TOO LOW? If a child is unable to shift his position to accommodate the ball, work with him yourself, deliberately throwing the ball offside. If

you place him near a wall you won't waste too much time chasing the ball. Also, he could go back to throwing at the wall to learn to shift his position. Children having problems with this could also be lined up and asked to pretend a ball is coming at them. SHIFT TO CATCH IT ON YOUR LEFT. SHIFT TO YOUR RIGHT. NOW IT IS UP HIGH. POINT YOUR FINGERS UP. WHAT DO YOU HAVE TO DO? REACH FOR IT. NOW IT'S DOWN TOO LOW. POINT YOUR FINGERS DOWN TO-WARD THE GROUND. CAN YOU CATCH IT? Have them practice throwing from several distances to vary the thrust required and the throwing position necessary. When a child has particular problems learning to catch, practice with him yourself.

3. Bounce-hit as for two-square. HOLD THE BALL IN BOTH HANDS. DROP IT. POINT YOUR FINGERS AT THE GROUND, GIVE THE BALL A LITTLE HIT WITH BOTH HANDS AND IT BOUNCES OVER TO YOUR PART-NER. NOW GET READY FOR IT TO BOUNCE BACK. KEEP YOUR EYES ON THE BALL. KEEP YOUR FINGERS POINTED AT THE GROUND ALL THE TIME. WHAT HAPPENS IF YOU HIT THE BALL A LITTLE TO THE SIDE? WHERE DOES IT GO?

Ball Kicking

Have children practice free kicking of the ball. Encourage the use of the dominant foot.

1. To teach control of the direction of the kick, put the ball on a line. Have the child stand on the same line, touch the ball with his toe and aim it straight down the line. Kick it. Use the far part of the line as the target. THIS TIME, STAND ON THE RIGHT SIDE OF THE LINE AND KICK THE BALL. WHICH WAY DOES IT GO NOW? PUT THE BALL BACK ON THE LINE AND STAND ON THE LEFT SIDE OF THE LINE. KICK THE BALL. WHICH WAY DOES THE BALL GO? PUT IT BACK ON THE LINE, STAND ON THE LINE AND KICK IT. KEEP KICKING IT IN A STRAIGHT LINE ALL THE WAY ACROSS THE PLAYGROUND.

2. Kicking for distance: Line all the balls up at the edge of the playground. Children stand a few feet behind their balls. When you say, GO, they run and kick their balls. See whose ball went the farthest. Line up again and kick for speed. HOW FAST CAN YOU KICK YOUR BALL ALL THE WAY TO THE FENCE? THE FIRST ONE TO THE FENCE WINS.

JUMP ROPE SKILLS
Knotted Rope

Every child has a jump rope which is as long as the distance from one armpit to the ground under his feet and back up to the other armpit. Instruct the children in folding the rope in half, then half again, then tying a knot in the folded rope by crossing the ends and looping one end under and up through the middle to form a knot.

1. TOSS THE ROPE UP IN THE AIR. CATCH IT ON THE LOOP. CATCH IT ON THE KNOT. CATCH IT WITH YOUR HAND UNDER THE KNOT. NOW AS YOU CATCH IT WITH YOUR HAND UNDER THE KNOT, ALSO PUT YOUR OTHER HAND ON TOP OF THE KNOT.

2. PASS THE ROPE BACK AND FORTH FROM ONE HAND TO THE OTHER, CATCHING IT ON THE KNOT. PASS THE ROPE AROUND YOUR BODY, HOLDING IT ON THE KNOT EACH TIME. PASS THE ROPE UNDER YOUR RIGHT LEG, AROUND AND OVER IT, AND UNDER IT AGAIN. NOW PASS UNDER YOUR RIGHT LEG AND OVER THE LEFT LEG. NOW UNDER THE LEFT AND OVER THE RIGHT. KEEP IT GOING. YOU ARE MAKING A FIGURE EIGHT.

Open Rope

1. LAY IT ON THE GRASS LIKE A LONG SNAKE POINTING AT ME. NOW WALK ON IT BARE FOOT. WHEN YOU COME TO THE END, TURN AND GO BACK. CAN YOU WALK THE ROPE BACKWARD? CAN YOU WALK WITH ONE FOOT ON EACH SIDE OF THE ROPE NEVER TOUCHING IT? CAN YOU JUMP FROM ONE SIDE OF IT TO THE OTHER WITH BOTH FEET TOGETHER? CAN YOU WALK CROSSING IT, LIKE THE CROOKED MAN? CAN YOU WALK IT ON TWO POINTS? (Two feet, or one hand, one foot.) CAN YOU WALK IT THREE POINTS? (two feet, one hand) CAN YOU WALK IT FOUR POINTS? HOW ELSE CAN YOU WALK IT?

2. MAKE A CIRCLE WITH THE ROPE: CAN YOU WALK ON THE CIRCLE? CAN YOU WALK OUTSIDE THE CIRCLE? CAN YOU WALK INSIDE THE CIRCLE? CAN YOU WALK WITH ONE FOOT INSIDE AND THE OTHER OUTSIDE THE CIRCLE? CAN YOU JUMP INSIDE, OUTSIDE? WHAT OTHER WAY CAN YOU TRAVEL WITH YOUR CIRCLE?

3. WHAT OTHER SHAPE CAN YOU MAKE WITH YOUR ROPE? HOW WIDE A SHAPE CAN YOU MAKE, HOW THIN? MAKE A SHAPE WITH FOUR

CORNERS. WHAT IS IT? CAN YOU MAKE A SQUARE? WHAT DO YOU
HAVE TO DO? CAN YOU MAKE A SHAPE WITH THREE CORNERS? WHAT
IS IT? CAN YOU MAKE WAVES WITH YOUR ROPE? CAN YOU MAKE A
NUMERAL? A LETTER? CAN YOU HOLD ONE END OF YOUR ROPE AND
MAKE IT WIGGLE IN CURVES LIKE A SNAKE? CAN YOU COIL IT LIKE
A SNAKE READY TO STRIKE?

4. Tie the ends of the rope together. Two children to a rope.
One child just holds the rope in both hands and follows its sig-
nals. The other child pulls him along. CAN YOU HAVE HIM MOVE
SLOWLY? CAN YOU HAVE HIM MOVE FAST? CAN YOU HAVE HIM
CHANGE SPEEDS? CHANGE DIRECTIONS? WHAT SHAPE DOES THE ROPE
MAKE BETWEEN YOU? WHAT IS THE LONGEST SHAPE YOU CAN MAKE?
WHAT IS THE FATTEST SHAPE YOU CAN MAKE? HOW ROUND A SHAPE
CAN YOU MAKE?

Teaching Jumping Skills

(developmental sequence designed by Jeanne Bartelt)
Before you give a child a rope to teach jumping, build up the
coordination skills needed:

1. Begin with bouncing in rhythm. Then bounce one high
bounce and one low bounce, one high, one low. Saying, HIGH,
LOW, as they bounce, helps. Or JUMP ON TOES, THEN JUMP AND
LAND ON HEELS, or whole feet. TOES, HEELS.

2. Teach swinging the arms in arcs to the sides, both arms in
unison. POINT YOUR HANDS DOWN TO THE GROUND, AROUND BEHIND
YOU, POINT UP AT THE SKY, AND BRING YOUR HANDS DOWN IN FRONT
OF YOU. SEE IF YOU CAN DO IT IN RHYTHM WHILE WE SAY IT. DOWN,
UP.

3. CAN YOU BOUNCE WHILE YOU CIRCLE YOUR ARMS? NOW WHEN
YOUR HANDS POINT DOWN, TRY TO BOUNCE HIGH. WHEN YOUR HANDS
POINT UP, BOUNCE LOW. HIGH, LOW. STAND TALL, CLOSE YOUR EYES
AND SEE IF YOU CAN TELL WHEN YOUR ARM IS DOWN. FEEL THE
RHYTHM WITH YOUR BODY.

4. Give each child a rope. Use a paved area. HOLD BOTH ENDS
OF THE ROPE IN YOUR RIGHT HAND. MAKE A CIRCLE WITH YOUR ARM
SO THAT THE ROPE SLAPS THE GROUND. MAKE YOUR CIRCLE BIG AND
SMOOTH. LISTEN TO THE ROPE SLAPPING. LET'S MAKE IT AN EVEN

RHYTHM. SLAP, SLAP. MAKE IT HIT THE PAVEMENT IN FRONT OF YOU. BESIDE YOU. LOOK STRAIGHT AHEAD. STAND ON A LINE AND TRY TO MAKE THE ROPE SLAP RIGHT ON THE LINE AT YOUR SIDE. CHANGE TO THE LEFT HAND. HIT THE PAVEMENT IN FRONT OF YOU, BESIDE YOU. HIT THE LINE. CAN YOU MAKE IT HIT THE PAVEMENT BEHIND YOU? CAN YOU START TURNING THE ROPE BESIDE YOU, THEN CHANGE HANDS AND DO IT ON THE OTHER SIDE? DO IT WITHOUT STOPPING THE RHYTHM OF THE ROPE.

5. START BOUNCING. NOW TURN THE ROPE BESIDE YOU, AND BOUNCE IN RHYTHM TO THE ROPE. Wait until they have a good rhythm. NOW TRY TO BOUNCE HIGH, LOW. WHEN THE ROPE SLAPS THE PAVEMENT, BOUNCE HIGH. WHEN YOUR HANDS POINT UP IN THE AIR, BOUNCE LOW. STAND TALL ALL THE TIME. LOOK STRAIGHT AHEAD. FIND A TARGET RIGHT IN FRONT OF YOUR EYES. KEEP WATCHING IT! CLOSE YOUR EYES. HEAR THE SOUND OF THE ROPE SLAPPING AND JUMP HIGH. DO YOU KNOW WHEN YOU SHOULD JUMP WITHOUT WATCHING YOUR ARM GO DOWN?

6. LAY THE ROPE ON THE GROUND. JUMP OVER IT. LEAN FORWARD AND JUMP OVER IT. LEAN BACKWARD AND JUMP. STAND TALL AND JUMP. WHICH IS EASIEST? STAND TALL, LOOK STRAIGHT AHEAD, AND JUMP BACK AND FORTH ACROSS THE ROPE. CAN YOU DO IT SIDEWAYS? FRONTWARD, BACKWARD? BOUNCE BACK AND FORTH, BACK AND FORTH. FIND A TARGET AND LOOK AT IT WHILE YOU BOUNCE BACK AND FORTH. FIND A TARGET AND BOUNCE SIDE TO SIDE.

7. Have two children hold an eight-foot rope just an inch or two off the ground while a child jumps backward, forward, side to side. Ten children can play follow the leader and have turns doing this. When they can do this easily, try swinging the rope slowly side to side and have children practice jumping it. Can they run and jump over once, then the next child and the next? Also, hold the rope steady at varying heights while the children run and jump over it.

8. HOLD THE ROPE IN BOTH HANDS NOW. CIRCLE YOUR ARMS AND JUMP THE ROPE. It seems to be easier to run and jump over the rope until they get the arms going in rhythm. This is much easier than standing still and jumping. LOOK STRAIGHT AHEAD. THINK ABOUT YOUR ARMS. YOU KNOW WHEN THEY ARE DOWN. PICK OUT

A TARGET AND RUN TOWARD IT WHILE YOU JUMP. LET THAT TREE OVER THERE BE YOUR TARGET. RUN AND JUMP ROPE TOWARD IT.

9. After the child has learned to jump the rope one way, try variations: CAN YOU SWING THE ROPE BACK AND FORTH AND JUMP OVER IT? CAN YOU JUMP THE ROPE WITH ONE FOOT FORWARD AND THE OTHER FOOT BACKWARD? CAN YOU CHANGE FEET AND DO IT WITH THE OTHER FOOT FORWARD? CAN YOU JUMP WITH YOUR FEET TOGETHER? HOW HIGH CAN YOU JUMP AS YOU GO OVER THE ROPE? HOW LOW? CAN YOU CHANGE THE HEIGHT OF THE ROPE AS YOU ARE JUMPING? CAN YOU MOVE BACKWARD WHILE STILL JUMPING ROPE? CAN YOU MOVE SIDEWAYS? CAN YOU TURN THE ROPE BACKWARD? DO THIS AND MOVE BACKWARD, TOO. CAN YOU RUN BACKWARD? CAN YOU JUMP WITH A PARTNER?

10. One eight-foot rope for two children: When the children can jump rope easily alone, they are ready for partner jumping. HOW CAN YOU AND YOUR PARTNER JUMP OVER THE ROPE? CAN YOU JUST SWING THE ROPE AND JUMP IT? CAN YOUR PARTNER JUMP WHILE YOU TURN THE ROPE? CHANGE TURNERS WITHOUT STOPPING THE ROPE. CAN YOU TRAVEL AND JUMP TOGETHER? WATCH HOW MARY AND SUSAN ARE JUMPING TOGETHER. CAN YOU DO THAT?

BALANCE

As we discussed earlier in Chapter Seven, body balance is essential to the establishment of laterality, a feeling for the sides of the body and posture. The distortion of perceptions in some children is based on an unstable space world. The child really never learned an easy balance in space, thus his whole world is distorted. His lack of balance is evident in his clumsiness, his uneven walk and run, his reversals of numerals and words, or his nervous or contorted sitting posture. His body balance must be developed to give the child a firm laterality, an internal directionality that is basic to reading, to left-right progression, to an understanding of right, left, up, down, forward, backward, and other spatial concepts.

Static Balance

There are two basic types of balance, static and dynamic.

Static balance is performed in one spot or area, without locomotion or traveling. It is taught in connection with the on-line calisthenics or the on-floor activities. Or simply in the classroom as a change-in-activity routine when the children tire of a sitting task and need extra movement. These are some examples of static balance exercises. Some are combined with the movement of one or more parts of the body, to challenge balance. Although they are partially dynamic balance, since they are performed in one spot we will list them together.

1. ATTENTION. GO UP ON YOUR TOES. HOLD IT WHILE WE COUNT TO FIVE. ONE, TWO, THREE, FOUR, FIVE. NOW DOWN ON YOUR FEET.

2. STAND ON YOUR RIGHT FOOT AND SWING YOUR LEFT FOOT BACK AND FORTH. CAN YOU SWING IT TEN TIMES WITHOUT PUTTING IT DOWN?

3. STAND ON YOUR LEFT FOOT AND MAKE YOUR RIGHT FOOT MAKE TEN CIRCLES.

4. PUT YOUR HANDS ON YOUR HIPS AND GO DOWN TO A SQUAT AND UP, WITHOUT LOSING YOUR BALANCE.

5. STAND ON YOUR RIGHT FOOT, BEND OVER AND LOOK AT THE GROUND. CAN YOU COUNT TO TEN WITHOUT FALLING?

6. ATTENTION. HANDS ON HIPS. KNEEL ON YOUR RIGHT KNEE AND STAND UP WITHOUT LOSING YOUR BALANCE. THIS TIME CAN YOU KNEEL ON BOTH KNEES AND GET UP AGAIN WITHOUT LOSING YOUR BALANCE?

7. STAND ON YOUR TIPTOES. NOW BEND OVER AND SEE HOW LONG YOU CAN HOLD IT WITHOUT FALLING.

8. STAND ON YOUR HEELS. HOLD IT WHILE WE COUNT.

9. STAND ON YOUR RIGHT FOOT AND LEAN TO THE RIGHT. USE YOUR ARMS AND YOUR LEFT FOOT TO KEEP FROM FALLING.

10. On-floor: PUT YOUR RIGHT HAND AND FOOT ON THE FLOOR AND BALANCE. TRY YOUR RIGHT FOOT AND LEFT HAND. TRY YOUR RIGHT KNEE (NO TOES) AND LEFT HAND. WHAT OTHER WAY CAN YOU BALANCE?

11. STAND ON YOUR RIGHT FOOT. SWING YOUR RIGHT ARM. SWING YOUR LEFT ARM.

12. STAND ON YOUR LEFT FOOT. SWING BOTH YOUR ARMS SIDE TO SIDE (crossing midline)! CHANGE FEET AND SWING YOUR ARMS IN CIRCLES OUT AT YOUR SIDES.

13. STAND ON YOUR RIGHT FOOT AND STRETCH YOUR LEFT LEG FORWARD, TO THE SIDE, BACKWARD.

14. STAND ON YOUR TOES AND LEAN BACKWARD. HOW FAR CAN YOU LEAN WITHOUT FALLING?

15. Try any of the above with eyes closed.

Dynamic Balance

The balance which is achieved in the body during locomotion in space is dynamic. It is best trained through the use of various kinds of balancing equipment. The most noted of these is the balance beam, an eight or ten feet long 2″ x 4″ board, braced with end fittings to hold it stable. A center brace is also needed to hold the beam still while the child is learning initial balance, overcoming fear of falling, and gaining confidence.

The child with balance problems, unable to traverse the beam slowly without stepping off, needs to be trained in the use of his eyes to maintain his balance. As this child attempts to walk the beam, his eyes flit all over the room, up and down, side to side, and he struggles to balance. He often looks to one side, leans that way and falls off. If you let him continue to watch his feet, he simply continues falling. Holding his hands might give him initial security for his first trial, but it does not teach him balance.

Line the beam up straight with the walls and the tiles on the floor. Place a twelve-inch red X on the wall about nine feet from the end of the beam at the child's eye level. Then ask the child to LOOK AT THE TARGET while he is walking forward and backward. Standing by the target with lots of verbal encouragement helps him to concentrate on the focusing of his eyes and to be less fearful. Teaching him to use visual steering in this manner gives him the needed stability and the tool he needs to gain balance. Until he learns to stabilize his focus while balancing he will not be able to balance well consistently.

To achieve a complete relaxed balance, rather than a splinter skill, the child must learn to balance in a variety of different ways. He must be able to maintain balance in spite of changes in direction and attention. Therefore, challenge his balance in many ways: by having him carry a weight in one hand, hold a pole, or do something different with his hands and arms, or eyes. Finally his balance must be so complete that he can easily balance in any way. Then his posture sitting, standing, or moving will be relaxed and so automatic that he can now concentrate on learning.

Walking Beam Activities

1. WALK FORWARD, HEEL AND TOE. YOUR HEEL MUST TOUCH YOUR TOE.

2. WALK BACKWARD, STILL LOOKING FORWARD AT THE TARGET.

3. WALK FORWARD, WAVING YOUR ARMS AT THE SIDES LIKE BUTTERFLY WINGS. KEEP YOUR EYES ON THE TARGET, BUT WATCH YOUR HANDS OUT OF THE CORNERS OF YOUR EYES.

4. WALK SIDEWAYS TO THE END AND THEN, WITHOUT STEPPING OFF, TURN AND FACE THE OTHER WALL AND WALK SIDEWAYS BACK AGAIN.

5. WALK SIDEWAYS CROSSING OVER, ONE LEG OVER THE OTHER! CAN YOU DO IT WITHOUT WATCHING YOUR FEET? STOP WITHOUT GETTING OFF THE BEAM AND COME BACK THE SAME WAY. THIS TIME, CROSS ONE FOOT BEHIND THE OTHER.

6. WALK TO THE GREEN LINE ON THE MIDDLE OF THE BEAM, THEN BACKWARD TO THE BEGINNING, THEN FORWARD TO THE END OF THE BEAM, AND OFF.

7. WALK FORWARD TO THE END, TURN AROUND WITHOUT STEPPING OFF AND COME BACK TO THE BEGINNING, WALKING FORWARD.

8. WALK FORWARD AND BACKWARD WITH A PAIL OF BEANBAGS IN ONE HAND. CHANGE HANDS AND DO IT AGAIN.

9. WALK FORWARD, CHANGING THE WEIGHT FROM HAND TO HAND.

10. WALK FORWARD WITH AN ERASER ON YOUR HEAD.

11. CROSS THE BEAM USING JUST TWO LIMBS OTHER THAN TWO FEET. NOW TRY THREE LIMBS. FOUR LIMBS (Fig. 25) .

12. WALK FRONTWARD WITH THE RIGHT FOOT ALWAYS IN FRONT. DO IT AGAIN WITH THE LEFT FOOT IN FRONT.

13. WALK FORWARD, PICK UP THE BEANBAG AT THE END OF THE BEAM AND GO BACKWARD WITH IT WITHOUT STEPPING OFF THE BEAM!

14. WALK TO THE MIDDLE OF THE BEAM, PICK UP THE BEANBAG, PUT IT ON YOUR HEAD AND WALK TO THE END.

Figure 25. Crossing the Beam with Different Limbs.

15. Place a wand on the seats of two chairs which are on either side of the beam. The child walks the beam stepping over the wand, without losing his balance.

16. Place the wand on the backs of two chairs. The child crosses the beam, going under the wand.

17. WALK TO THE CENTER OF THE BEAM, KNEEL, GET UP, WALK TO THE END.

18. WALK TO THE CENTER, KNEEL ON ONE KNEE, STRAIGHTEN OTHER LEG FORWARD UNTIL HEEL IS ON THE BOARD AND KNEE IS STRAIGHT. STAND AND GO TO THE END.

19. WALK ONLY ON THE BALLS OF THE FEET. ONLY ON YOUR HEELS.

20. WALK TO THE MIDDLE OF THE BEAM. THROW THREE BEAN-BAGS INTO THE BUCKET AT THE END OF THE BEAM. GO FORWARD TO THE END OF THE BEAM, GET THE BAGS WITHOUT STEPPING OFF AND GO BACKWARD TO THE END OF THE BEAM.

21. WALK TO THE MIDDLE OF THE BEAM. SEE IF YOU CAN CATCH ALL THREE OF THESE BEANBAGS AS I THROW THEM TO YOU ONE AT A TIME.

22. CAN YOU HOP ON ONE FOOT TO THE END OF THE BEAM?

23. HOLD YOUR HANDS CLASPED BEHIND YOUR NECK. WALK FORWARD AND BACKWARD.

24. STEP ONTO THE BEAM. SWING ONE LEG IN A PEDALING MOTION BEFORE PUTTING IT FORWARD ON THE BEAM. DO THE SAME WITH EACH STEP.

25. TAKE A STEP ONTO THE BEAM. LEAN FORWARD, BALANCING ON ONE FOOT UNTIL YOUR BACK IS PARALLEL TO THE BEAM. PUT THE OTHER FOOT FORWARD ON THE BEAM, BALANCE ON IT IN THE SAME MANNER. CONTINUE STEPPING AND BALANCING TO THE END OF THE BEAM.

26. TAKE ONE STEP, SWING ONE LEG THREE TIMES, THEN STEP AND SWING THE OTHER LEG THREE TIMES.

27. WALK TO THE CENTER, CLOSE YOUR EYES AND SEE HOW LONG YOU CAN BALANCE.

28. HOLDING A PARTNER'S HAND OR HANDS, HOW MANY WAYS CAN YOU WALK THE BEAM?

29. WITH A PARTNER AT THE OTHER END OF THE BEAM, BOTH OF YOU GO FORWARD, PASS EACH OTHER WITHOUT STEPPING OFF, AND GO TO THE END OF THE BEAM.

30. PLACE OBSTACLES ON THE BEAM AT SEVERAL POINTS FOR CHILD TO STEP OVER: A 4″ x 4″ BLOCK AT STEP INTERVALS, OR A PILE OF 3″ x 4″ BLOCKS AT THREE DIFFERENT POINTS.

31. Removing the center brace gives the beam more resiliency and provides a more difficult balancing task. CAN YOU WALK TO THE CENTER OF THE BEAM AND BOUNCE A LITTLE?

32. WALK FORWARD FIVE STEPS AND BACKWARD THREE STEPS!

OTHER EQUIPMENT
Balance Board

A balance board is made of a sixteen-inch square of half-inch plywood. It may have a 2″ x 2″, 4″ x 4″, or 6″ x 6″ as a center post underneath. The surface of the board should be covered with ribbed rubber, or bathtub strips to keep feet from slipping. The child balances on the board in a variety of ways. As the child gains skill he is able to try higher and/or narrower posts.

1. First the child just learns to balance himself on the board.

The teacher can use her foot on the center of the board to hold it steady and give the child security. Or the child can hold onto a chair or desk. Using a target (an X cut from red construction paper) at his eye level helps him to use visual steering to maintain his balance. He can also learn to balance while sitting or kneeling on it.

2. Then he learns to tip the board side to side, front to back, without losing his balance. As he gains skill he is able to *walk* the board with a slight rotation of the ankles, and a rhythmic shift of his body weight. You might hold his hands to help him get started. He might first walk the board around a chair. Finally he is able to walk the board all over the room at will.

3. Now challenge him with more tasks where he has to think of some other object besides the board. Try bouncing and catching a large rubber ball while balancing on the board. Then try different ways of bouncing it with both hands, one hand, alternating hands. Decrease the size of the ball.

4. Use other aiming tasks while the child is balancing. He might throw a beanbag at the wastebasket, or into a certain square on the floor, or to another child.

5. Have the child touch body parts while balancing. Ask for right and left discriminations, crossing the body for right hand on left shoulder, etc.

6. Hang a ball from the ceiling, and swing it pendulum fashion in front of him as he balances. Have him reach out as it crosses his midline, and touch it. Or mark certain spots or letters on it and ask him to touch that spot. TOUCH THE RED DOT. TOUCH THE S.

7. Have the child try some simple calisthenics while balancing. He might twist his body right and left; kneel and stand up; bend down and touch his toes; go up and down on his toes; move his arms in a variety of ways, swinging, circling, in front of and beside himself.

Scat Scoota

The Scat Scoota is an excellent device for balance available from some mail-order houses and toy outlets. It consists of two pedals and four wheels, all made of tough plastic. It is almost indestructible. The child simply stands on the pedals and pushes them to propel himself forward and backward (Fig. 26). The children love this and never tire of it.

Walking on Cans

This is another enjoyable way to teach balance and arm-leg coordination. Open two two-pound coffee cans with a beer-can opener. Make the openings on the sides of the cans rather than on the tops. Remove contents. Place the plastic lids on the bottom ends of the cans as insulators to cut down on noise. Thread a loop of quarter-inch rope onto each can through the holes. The child then holds a loop of rope from a can in each hand, puts his feet on the cans, and with a lifting of the rope lifts his feet alternately to walk (Fig. 27). After he has learned to walk freely, front-ward and backward, designate a pattern over which he must walk. WALK STEPPING INTO THESE BROWN SQUARES; or WALK FROM THIS CHALK CIRCLE TO THIS ONE AND FOLLOW THE TRAIL.

Figure 26. Scat Scoota.

Figure 27. Walking on Coffee Cans.

Stilts

Stilts can be purchased or homemade. They should be taller than the child, as a ski. Try a pair about five feet tall. Make them with two footpieces each, ten and fifteen inches off the floor. Thus the child attempts the lower foot piece first. Have no band of any kind over the foot piece, as this prevents him from stepping off easily and may cause him to fall. He holds the stilt poles by wrapping his arms around the inside front of the poles, grasping the poles at his natural arm length. Stand behind the child, holding the stilts steady for him as he gets on and helping him with the first movements. Since stilt-walking is quite a difficult skill, it should be introduced *after* the child has learned balance on other equipment. Have the child look at a target, rather than at his feet. Have him take short steps at first. After he has learned to walk, he can go forward, backward, in and out of hoops, around poles, and over beams.

Twister

The twister is a piece of plywood or pressed wood which twists freely with ball bearings under it, much the way a lazy-susan swivels. It is sold as a reducing exerciser or to strengthen muscles used in skiing. The child can stand on it and by twisting his knees make it turn right, left, or side to side. Or he can lie on it on his stomach and spin himself around with his hands.

Scooter Board

This is a thorax-sized, or sixteen-inch square board with four rubber casters under it. Be sure to get quiet casters. Mostly the child lies on his stomach and propels it with his hands. According to A. Jean Ayres, it helps to have a slight incline down which the child might propel himself. In this situation he raises his thorax as the scooter gains momentum and thus gives added support to that inhibiting of the tonic labyrinthian reflex discussed in Chapter Six, under *The Vestibular Sense.* The scooter can also be used in a multipurpose room. The child might push off from one wall to gain momentum. He might try to knock over some cardboard boxes as he pushes into them. Children can also play tag on the scooter. Or use a *plumber's helper* with which to propel the scooter. The child could also sit on it and propel it with his feet. Also use it for exercise in pushing. A child sits on the scooter, crosslegged while another child pushes him. This pushing is especially helpful for the child who has an uncoordinated walk or run.

Inner Tubes

Use a very large inner tube, like one used for an airplane or heavy equipment. If the valve is scratchy, wrap it with tape. Devise ways the child can bounce on this. One child might sit on either side and they both bounce to their right, then to their left, feet inside, then outside. Straddle it and bounce forward and backward. They might bounce from facing outward on the tube, to facing inward, toward each other. They walk around the tube forward and backward, and sideways, facing in and out. A child can stand and bounce on one side of the tube while a child sits on the other side to balance it for him. You might have to hold the bouncing child's hands at first. Or two children can hold hands and jump at the same time, later jumping around the perimeter of the tube (Fig. 28). Two children can sit astride the tube, bounce around it by propelling themselves forward as they bounce. The child can jump in and out of the tube. The tube can be part of an obstacle course and the child can jump into the middle of it and then go under it. Or make a line of several tubes and the children must travel in and out of them. STAND ON THE TUBE AND JUMP AS FAR AS YOU CAN. STACK TWO TUBES, STRADDLE THEM AND BOUNCE AROUND.

Different-sized tubes can be used for rolling. Have a race rolling two tubes to a certain line and back. HOW FAR CAN YOU ROLL IT BEFORE IT FALLS OVER? WHO CAN ROLL IT THE FARTHEST? WHILE THE TUBE IS ROLLING, CAN YOU THROW A BEANBAG OR BALL THROUGH IT? CAN YOU DIVE THROUGH IT WHILE IT IS ROLLING? Roll a tube for a dodge ball game. SIT INSIDE AN UPRIGHT TUBE WITH LEGS ASTRIDE!

Figure 28. Bouncing On An Inner Tube.

PUSH IT WITH YOUR HANDS OR BODY AND MOVE IT FORWARD. CAN YOU ROLL THE TUBE AND JUMP ON IT? STAND ON THE INSIDE OF AN UPRIGHT TUBE, HOW LONG CAN YOU BALANCE WITHOUT FALLING OFF? HOLD ONTO THE TOP AND BOUNCE IT AS YOU WOULD A POGO STICK.

For dexterity and agility, have several children sit on the rim of a horizontal tube with their feet on the inside. On a signal they all scramble out. See who is the fastest. Or have them go out and then in again. STAND BESIDE THE TUBE, BOUNCE AGAINST IT WITH YOUR KNEES AND THEN BACK UP TO A STANDING POSITION. RUN TO THE TUBE, JUMP UP ON IT, JUMP ACROSS TO THE OTHER SIDE AND THEN OFF AGAIN.

Bicycle Tires

Bicycle tires can be rolled in an upright position as the tubes. This is great for eye-hand coordination, yet more available and cleaner than larger tires and tubes. Lay them horizontally in different patterns and make up a task with them. JUMP IN AND OUT OF EVERY TIRE, BOTH FEET TOGETHER. PUT YOUR RIGHT FOOT IN THE FIRST TIRE, YOUR LEFT FOOT IN THE SECOND AND TRAVEL TO THE LAST ONE. START WITH YOUR LEFT FOOT, CROSS YOUR RIGHT FOOT OVER TO STEP INTO THE SECOND TIRE AND KEEP CROSS-STEPPING TO THE END. STRADDLE A TIRE AND JUMP, BRINGING BOTH FEET INSIDE. JUMP AND BOTH FEET GO OUTSIDE AGAIN. HOP ON YOUR RIGHT FOOT FROM THE INSIDE OF ONE TIRE TO THE INSIDE OF THE NEXT.

Ladder

Lay an aluminum, or well-sanded wooden, ladder on the ground. Play follow the leader, traversing the ladder in as many ways as possible. WALK BETWEEN THE RUNGS WITHOUT YOUR SHOES TOUCHING ANY PART OF THE LADDER. HOP FROM ONE SPACE TO THE NEXT. JUMP FROM ONE SPACE TO THE NEXT. WALK WITH ONE FOOT ON EACH SIDE OF THE LADDER. WALK ON THE SIDES FORWARD AND BACKWARD. WALK THE RUNGS OF THE LADDER. WALK ON EVERY OTHER RUNG. WALK BACKWARD ON THE RUNGS. WALK SIDEWAYS. STRADDLE IT. GET TO THE OTHER END WITHOUT EVER TOUCHING THE LADDER.

JUMP BOTH FEET TOGETHER FROM THE RIGHT SIDE OF THE LADDER, INSIDE, BETWEEN THE RUNGS, THEN OUT TO THE LEFT SIDE. NOW JUMP INTO THE SECOND SPACE IN THE LADDER AND OUT TO THE RIGHT SIDE. CONTINUE TO THE END OF THE LADDER. HOP INTO AND OUT OF THE LADDER THE SAME WAY. STRADDLE THE LADDER AND JUMP BOTH FEET INTO THE INSIDE, THEN JUMP AND BOTH FEET GO OUTSIDE AGAIN. DO THIS FOR EACH SPACE ON THE LADDER AND TRAVEL TO THE END THIS WAY.

Have two people hold the ladder sideways on the ground. Children crawl in and out between the rungs. Make it harder by having the child give two jumps every time he comes out on the right side and two claps when he emerges on the left side.

Barrels

The large, modern packing barrels made of a composition material are great for rolling and crawl-through exercises. They are available from moving companies or large supply houses, or from institutions which purchase soap. A school district might have them in the cafeterias. The child sits or lies inside in various positions and propels the barrel to turn. The inside might be lined with rug material to provide more tactile reinforcement of the body moving in it. Cutting out the other end allows the barrel to be used as crawl-through with someone holding it still. Rolling in it with both ends out gives the child more freedom to attempt different positions.

Jumpboard

Some children are very fearful of their bodies in space and need some kind of practice swinging or jumping free in space. One device is made of two pieces of plywood about thirty inches square with four heavy springs between the boards. The child jumps on it until he has a free rhythmic, balanced jump in space. Use in a mat or lawn area, and be ready to assist the child.

Another type of jump board is made of a twelve-inch wide, eight-foot long board of half-inch plywood. Or better yet, use the sturdier stair-tread material. Screw on a sturdy brace of 2″ x 6″ material on each end. You might want to put rubber matting on the under side of the board where it touches the floor to cut down on noise. The child first learns to walk on the swaying board. Then he steps out onto the board and bounces, steps and bounces, steps and bounces. Or he just stands in the middle of the board and bounces. As with the spring jump board, he works to achieve a free, rhythmic jump in the upright position. The target used for the balance beam also helps to keep the child balanced in an erect position instead of in the typical bent-over one. DON'T LOOK AT YOUR FEET. KEEP YOUR EYES ON THE TARGET AND BOUNCE.

High Jump

Make two erect wooden supports or braces about three to four feet tall. Place large nails on each brace, beginning six inches from the ground, an inch apart to about twenty-eight inches up. Place the braces six feet apart on the lawn, with the nails on the side away from the children. Put a bamboo pole across the nails at the six-inch height. The children line up and run and jump over the pole, without disturbing the pole, and land on their feet on the other side. Raise the pole to the next higher level and the children jump that. Continue raising the pole as needed to spur higher jumping.

The child who is fearful of jumping over the pole will need lots of practice at the very low levels, perhaps even with someone else holding his hand and jumping with him. This child should be checked for vision problems. He might be seeing with only one eye, and for this reason lack depth perception. Children with "patched" eyes are very cautious of high jumping and of jumping down from any height.

All children with a fear of falling and of high jumping, first need practice jumping down off low heights. Use any climbing equipment, jungle gym, stairs, or piled boxes. Begin having them stand on and jump down from eight- or ten-inch heights. You might have to hold both hands at first, later one hand, later only stand there ready to assist. Have him jump from the same height many times over until he is secure and free in the jump. Then increase the height gradually as the child gains confidence. Another device would be to have the child walk up a plank from the ground to the height and then jump off. Use various ways of jumping off from heights. WHILE YOU ARE IN THE AIR, SHOUT HI!

CLAP YOUR HANDS. TOUCH YOUR KNEES. TURN IN THE AIR. Also work on jumping sideward and backward off low heights.

Stepping Stones

Outside, regular cement garden stepping stones may be placed in the ground to form an alternating walk pattern beginning with the stone for the right foot. Play follow the leader. The leader might:
1. Walk the stones, right foot first.
2. Start with the left foot so that the child must cross the right foot over to put it on the stone on the left side.
3. Jump from stone to stone. Jump, turn, jump, turn.
4. Hop from stone to stone.
5. Walk the stones backward.

For inside, use pieces of cardboard or odd floor tiles. Paint each one with the imprint of a right or left hand or foot or a circle for a knee. Then place the tiles so that the child has to plan how to traverse them using the proper limb. For example, there might be several left and right feet side by side, designating a jump, then three right feet only, designating three right-footed hops. Then two knees and right and left hands in a crawl pattern under a table or between desks. A stick across two child-sized chairs forms an obstacle to step across with a right foot on one side and a left foot on the other side.

Climbing Wall

Have two double two-inch metal pipe supports about six feet apart. Secure in the ground with cement. Into this permanently set two 2″ x 6″ boards. Have three to four other two-by-sixes, which can be slipped in or out to raise or lower the wall.

The children run to the wall and hoist themselves over it, landing on their feet on the other side (Fig. 29). Caution them to be sure to go feet first. A hyperactive child tends to get just the head over and then he flips. This could cause a very serious accident. Stay nearby, even giving the feet a push, or holding the head up until the feet are over. Remember that this child might have body image or language problems and not even understand what you mean by *feet first,* or he might be unable to motor

Figure 29. Jump Wall.

plan his action. Many instructions to these children must be demonstrated or the child must be *led through* an act before he comprehends it. Some hyperactive children have no fear of falling, or any other consequence, and so take unnecessary risks and have a large percentage of accidents.

A low wall is usually jumped by placing the hands a few inches apart on the top of the wall and vaulting the feet over without their touching the top. A higher wall might be traversed by placing one foot on the top and leaping over. Higher still, the child has to use more thrust and merely scramble over the top. The removable boards provide this variety of heights so that the child must learn to adjust to them. It also provides for the needs of all sizes and ages of elementary children. Commercial climbing walls are available from equipment companies.

When the wall is just two, three, or four feet high, use one of the two-by-sixes as a ramp from the ground to the top of the wall. The child then walks up the ramp and jumps off the other side. Have them do this in different manners. They might jump and clap their hands twice before landing on the ground. Or, JUMP, FLAP YOUR ARMS TWICE LIKE A BIRD BEFORE YOU LAND.

Hula Hoops

Use three-quarter inch polyplastic hose in coils (the type you put in the ground). Cut into eight-foot lengths and fasten into a hoop with doweling and epoxy. Use the hoops for the same tasks as the bicycle tires. Also: HOLD THE HOOP ON ONE SIDE, SWING IT BACK AND FORTH AND JUMP IN AND OUT OF IT. ROLL THE HOOP ACROSS THE PLAYGROUND. TRY TO RUN THROUGH IT WHILE IT IS ROLLING. CAN YOU ROLL IT IN A ZIGZAG? IN A CIRCLE? HOLD THE HOOP OVER YOUR HEAD. SEE HOW FAST YOU CAN BRING IT DOWN OVER YOUR BODY AND STEP OUT OF IT. ROTATE IT ON YOUR ARM, ON YOUR LEG, YOUR NECK. ROLL IT AWAY FROM YOU AS FAST AS YOU CAN. NOW RUN AND TRY TO CATCH IT BEFORE IT FALLS DOWN. WHILE THE HOOP IS ROLLING TRY TO THROW A BEANBAG THROUGH IT. Have hoop-rolling races. Roll the hoop back and forth between partners. Partners hold hands and jump in and out of the hoop. Use hoops for relays. Each child must go through the hoop until it gets to the last child. He brings it to the front of the line, goes through it, and passes it back to the next child. Or roll the hoop around a pole and back.

OBSTACLE COURSES

Use whatever equipment you have and combine with ladders, beams, bamboo poles, chairs, ropes to form an obstacle course that can be rearranged in a variety of courses. Obstacle courses can be indoors or out, elaborate or simple. An indoor course was described under *Stepping Stones.*

An outdoor task could be to go around three tetherball poles, crawl under a pole laid across the backs of two chairs, over the high jump, under a low pole across the seats of the chairs, jumping back and forth over a beam, down the slide, across the rings, balance on the edging around the sandbox, and run to the far fence. Or just vary three or four obstacles such as the high jump, chairs and poles by changing from over-the-low-pole to under-a-high-one, and over the high jump to an over-over-over or to under-over-under. Or vary the way the child is to traverse any of

Figure 30. Crawl-Through Culverts.

the equipment, or how he must travel to any point. Maybe he must walk the beam backward, or get to the fence by hopping. However you arrange the equipment, keep as many children moving at the same time as possible. Beginning and ending with a long locomotor action such as running, is ideal. Concrete culverts and stepping stones add to an outdoor course (Fig. 30).

There is a combination of indoor-outdoor equipment variously called a Stegel (plans available from Orinda School District, Orinda, California), or a Lind Climber (Lind Climber Company, Evanston, Illinois). This consists of a slide, ladder, three four-by-fours, and two large end supports. The pieces of the equipment can be used separately on the ground with ten children traversing the beam in different ways, follow the leader style, ten maneuvering through the ladder, and ten going up the slide and across the other beam. Or put the whole thing together and direct the children to go up the slide, across two beams on hands and knees, and down the ladder backward. Or go over one beam, under the second, across the third to the slide and down. There are hundreds of variations on how the equipment can be used. Innovate ways of traversing it, or have the children make up ways. They like to try to figure out different ways of doing things and this is excellent learning in motor planning. A film, *Anyone Can,* on the use of the Stegel is available from CANHC.

OUTDOOR GAMES

The best games for the physical education period are those in which *all* the children are vigorously moving. The old circle games with only one child performing at a time are boring even for the teacher, and provide little physical activity. Immature, impulsive children need games of very low organization, with few directions to remember. They become so excited by the physical activity and the movement of the other children around them that they forget all instructions and lose self-control. When asked to join hands in a circle they yank each other around, fail the responsibility of connecting the circle, and pull it apart when it is nearly complete. If a circle organization is to be used, it is best to have the use of a circle painted on the blacktop. One with a second circle two or three feet inside the first is useful for many games, such as Circle Dodge Ball.

Teach children that *tagging* is *touching,* not *catching,* and you will save wear and tear on dresses and shirts. The child who is *touched* must relent and go as directed. It might be well to demonstrate how a child's coat can be touched and thus the *tagger* feels he has tagged the child. Yet the latter is not able to *feel* the tag through his coat and therefore doesn't know that he has been tagged. IT IS JUST A GAME ANYWAY, SO IF SOMEONE SAYS HE TAGGED YOU, WHY DON'T WE BE GOOD SPORTS?

Action Games

Games are listed here in approximate order of low to higher organization.

1. *Freeze:* Children run, dance, skip, and jump around until the teacher blows the whistle. They *freeze* in a position. The teacher chooses a child in an interesting position and all the children try to imitate him. WHICH HAND IS UP? WHICH LEG IS BENT?

2. *Pied Piper:* Children follow the teacher using a movement

she suggests, or any free movement. When she stops and turns, they squat and freeze.

3. *Stop and Start:* The leader points in any direction and the children move that way. When the whistle is blown they freeze and face the leader. She points in another direction and they move off again. Children who fail to stop or follow directions form another group. See which children can remain in the star group the longest. Any locomotor movements may be designated.

4. *How Can You Get to Sacramento?* Children line up and the teacher asks a child how they can get to Sacramento. The whole group moves to the goal in the manner designated. Teacher calls on another child to tell how they will get back.

5. *One, Two, Buckle My Shoe:* Children line up and say: "One, two." Leader answers: "Buckle my shoe." Children say: "Three, four." Leader: "Shut the door." Children: "Five, six." Leader: "Pick up sticks." Children: "Seven, eight." Leader: "Run or you'll be late!" (Or *walk* or *gallop*, or other locomotor movement.) Children run to goal and back. The first one back becomes the leader for the next time.

6. *Flag Tag:* Loop colored plastic surveyors ribbon, or just rag strips, through back of boys' belts or belt loops—or tuck halfway down the back neck of girls' dresses or around a button. Beribbon half of class in this manner. Give them a count of ten to get away, then let the rest of the class run after them. Give them a minute or two and recall them with your whistle. There could be a candy prize for all children returning with ribbons. Or simply rest a bit and then have those who won be the runners and start out again.

7. *Old Lady Witch:* Children in a single line formation move up to the witches' area (fifty feet away) chanting "Old Lady Witch, fell in a ditch. Picked up a penny and thought she was rich." The witch says: "Whose children are you?" They reply: "Yours!" Whereupon they all try to run back to their home-base line without being tagged by the witch. Immature children might just stand there waiting to be caught, or else deliberately run in front of the witch, practically tripping her. Tell the witch to chase only children who are running. If the witch catches a

nonrunning child, choose a child who was a good runner to be the next witch. Or have the witch tag several children. Those tagged aid her in tagging in subsequent runs.

8. *Red Rover:* Single-base line formation. One child is *it*. He calls: "Red Rover, I dare all the boys (girls, blondes, boys in blue jeans, girls in red, etc.) to come over." They run to a far baseline. The children he catches help him to catch the rest. Game continues until all children have been caught.

9. *Scat:* Similar to above, except that the leader performs some calisthenics and the children imitate him. He suddenly yells, "Scat!" The children race to the opposite goal while he attempts to tag them. Those tagged join him in catching others.

10. *Fairies and Brownies* (Use Cowboys and Indians for older children) : Girls are fairies on one goalline, boys are brownies at the opposite goal. Fairies line up single-line formation, turning their backs to the boys and hiding their eyes. It helps if the teacher stands facing the girls and keeps them from peeking. The teacher then motions the boys to come quietly. When they are near she calls: THE BROWNIES ARE COMING! The girls try to tag as many as they can. Those tagged join the fairies. The teacher then goes to the brownies' goal. They line up and hide their eyes and she motions to the fairies. When they come up close she yells: THE FAIRIES ARE COMING! Game concludes when either side has the most children, or when the children are tired.

11. *New York:* Two teams as above, one at each goalline. One team decides an animal or a situation to act out. They then approach the other team chanting: "Here we come!" The reply: "Where from?" "New York." "What's your trade?" "Lemonade!" "Get to work and show us some." Whereupon the *it* team begin their act. The others try to guess what they are. When they guess correctly, the teacher and the children yell: "Yes, Go." They chase the *actors* home. Those captured join opposite team as in Fairies and Brownies.

12. *Red Light:* Choose a more mature child to be *it*. Children line up at goal, facing leader. Leader turns his back and says: "Green light." The children move forward. When the leader says: "Red light" and turns around, they must freeze. Those he

catches moving are sent back *home*. The game continues. The first child to reach the far goal becomes the new leader. Even though immature children do not play this game too well, it doesn't seem to matter, as they enjoy it anyway. With a large group, it helps when the teacher aids *it* in spotting those who move. Without this aid, too many children try *sneaking*, which snowballs and spoils the game.

13. *Midnight:* The children in line formation ask: "What time is it, Mr. Clock?" The leader then says an hour, e.g. "Six o'clock!" The children take that many steps toward him. Game continues until suddenly the leader says "Midnight!" whereupon all the children run to the goal while he attempts to catch them. Those caught assist the leader in catching others as the game continues.

14. *Dogcatcher:* Children decide on three kinds of dogs, and each child decides which one he wants to be. The dogs line up at one end of the playing area (the kennel) and the dogcatcher stands in the center of the area. One of the side boundaries can be the dog pound. The dogcatcher calls the name of one of the kinds of dogs and all those players run to the opposite kennel, or goal. After the dogcatcher has called all three kinds of dogs he counts up his catch, his dogs in the pound. He then chooses a new dogcatcher from one who was not tagged to begin the game again. The dogcatcher with the most dogs in the pound is the champion!

15. *Follow the Leader:* Divide into groups of six to eight. They line up and play follow the leader. When you blow the whistle, the leader goes to the end of his line and a new leader takes over. Be sure to give all children a chance to be a leader.

16. *Get the Basket:* A version of the old Steal the Bacon. Two lines of players facing each other. They are numbered from left to right in opposite directions so that like numbers will be on opposite ends. We use a plastic basket in the middle between the children. Using a rug sample to designate the middle saves a lot of argument each time a child replaces the basket. The teacher calls a number, six, and those two children try to get the basket without being tagged. The successful child wins a point for his side.

17. *In and Out the Windows:* Circle organization games usually provide for little movement except for the one or two who would be *it*. The rest of the class are merely standing. The following circle game is not spectacular, but does end up with every one moving.

Two children are *it* and go in and out the windows made by the raised hands of the children in the circle. They all sing: "Go in and out the windows." As they sing, "Go forth and face your partner," *it* children go stand before chosen partners. On the third verse, "Come follow me to London," they take their partners outside the circle and skip around. Fourth verse, "I'm sorry I must leave you," they go opposite directions from that of their partners around the circle. Four children now are *it,* and all four verses are repeated again. Game continues until all children have partners and skip around. The last children chosen become the new leaders for a repeat of the game.

Ball Games

1. *Circle Dodge Ball:* Begin with half the class in the center circle (marked on the blacktop) and half around periphery. Throw the ball sideways (be sure to show them how) to hit between the waist and the knees. If a ball touches a player, the thrower trades places with him. Use two or three balls to keep the game going. Children on the periphery cannot dash into the inside circle, or in front of another child to get the ball. The child touched by the ball cannot carry the ball out. It must be retrieved by an *outside* child. Any inside child touching the ball at all is *out.* Help the children to share the ball enough to give the shy children turns. Be sure all have a turn being *in.*

2. *Prisoner Dodge:* Rectangular playing field with center line and prisoner area at each end. Two teams on either side of center line. They throw two or three balls at each other. Children so tagged go to prisoner area on other side. Child may not catch ball until it has touched the ground once. All players remain within their own areas. Prisoners may catch the ball that comes into their area and bail themselves out by hitting others with the ball.

3. *Circle Kick Ball:* Draw a line through the center of the circle. Boys on one side, around periphery, girls on the other. All join hands except girl on the far right near center line, who is the server. She kicks the ball across the center line toward the boys and then she, too, joins hands. Boys attempt to kick it back (without letting go hands). The ball is kicked back and forth until it is kicked outside (Fig. 31). If it goes outside on the boys' side, the girls get one point. If it goes outside on the girls' side, the serve then goes to the first boy on the right near the center line. As the game continues, the old server goes to the left end of his circle and a new child becomes the server. If the ball is kicked over the children's heads or hits a child in the head, it is a score against the kicker. His team loses the serve.

4. *Swim, Fishy, Swim:* Children in single line with one or two leaders who each have a ball. Leader calls: "All fish swim!" Children run to opposite goal while leader tries to hit them below the waist with the ball. Any player so hit sits down in the place where he was tagged. He then helps to reach out and tag the runners

Figure 31. Circle Kick Ball Game.

who come near him, though he may not move away. All tagged runners sit until all are caught.

Singing Games or Dances

Use dances with little organization. Suggestions are "Hokey Pokey," "Loopy Loo," "The Thread Follows the Needle," "Seven Jumps," "Wooden Shoe Dance," "Broom Dance," "Bow Belinda," "Kinderpolka." Favorite folk tunes can be made into simple dances. "Where, Oh Where is Dear Little Mary?" can be done with couples in a line facing partners. The head couple takes hands and slides down the line, up again, down and up again for the first four lines. For "Picking up paw-paws," the head couple splits, goes behind the lines and down to the end with the children following them. Here they form an arch and all the couples take hands and slide through to the original position. The new head couple then repeats dance.

Races

Races are always excellent to get everyone moving. Use all the locomotor movements. You might divide the group into boys and girls. First the boys run to the fence, then the girls. Then the boys gallop, then the girls. Or use color groups. This keeps them active, but gives a breather between races. Race with beanbags in various positions, with hoops, or tires, or gunny sacks. Have spider races, monkey races, crab, kangaroo, rabbit, and frog races. Race on all fours, with and without riders. Also have wheelbarrow races; or a child stands with another on his back and they race to the goal.

ACTIVITIES FOR INCLEMENT WEATHER

The activity you choose for your inclement day will depend on a number of factors. If the children have been running out of doors in the morning, or have had at least one good recess, then strenuous activity might not be advisable. In fact, with hyperactive, impulsive children, it might be better not to excite them within the classroom any more than necessary. Inside, because of room echo and closeness, an activity is more stimulating than the same activity outside. In this case, choose something relaxing without being overstimulating like drawing, cartooning, cutting and pasting, playing Bingo, disassociated movements, isometrics, body image and directionality activities.

If the children have been confined much too long already, and they are ready to "burst at the seams," then choose a more strenuous activity such as calisthenics or those with large movements. Creative rhythms, activity records, and mimetics would be advisable at this time. Then, if it stops raining or snowing for a few minutes, be ready to take a good jog around the blacktop on your way to lunch, or just before bus time. Here are a few more suggestions.

Isometrics

WITH PALMS TOGETHER, PUSH DOWN WITH THE RIGHT HAND AND UP WITH THE LEFT WHILE WE COUNT TO SIX. NOW PUSH DOWN WITH THE LEFT HAND AND UP WITH THE RIGHT. ONE, TWO, THREE, FOUR, FIVE, SIX. LOCK YOUR HANDS UNDER YOUR RIGHT THIGH. PULL UP WITH YOUR HANDS, PUSH DOWN WITH YOUR LEG. Count slowly. LOCK YOUR HANDS BEHIND YOUR HEAD. PRESS BACK WITH YOUR HEAD, PULL FORWARD WITH YOUR HANDS. An inch or so ring of tire tubing makes a useful addition to isometrics. This ring of tubing can be held between the wrists and stretched out overhead or in front of the child. Or step into it and stretch it between the ankles. Loop it under one foot and pull up with a hand while you push down with the foot.

Disassociated Movements

CLAP HANDS AND TAP ONE FOOT. NOW SPEED UP THE FOOT TAPPING, BUT KEEP THE CLAPPING SLOW. CAN YOU TAP YOUR FOOT AND MAKE CIRCLES WITH YOUR HAND? STILL SITTING, CAN YOU TAP ONE FOOT THEN THE OTHER? NOW TAP YOUR RIGHT POINTER FINGER AND THEN YOUR LEFT POINTER FINGER. NOW CAN YOU TAP YOUR RIGHT FINGER AND YOUR LEFT FOOT? THEN YOUR LEFT FINGER AND YOUR RIGHT FOOT? CAN YOU TOUCH YOUR FINGERS ONE AT A TIME? TOUCH YOUR LITTLE FINGERS TOGETHER! NOW OPEN THEM AND TOUCH YOUR RING FINGERS. NOW YOUR TALL-MAN FINGERS. NOW YOUR POINTER FINGERS. NOW YOUR THUMBS. SEE IF YOU CAN DO IT A LITTLE FASTER. ONE FINGER, TWO, THREE, FOUR, THUMBS. PUT YOUR THUMB ON YOUR

OPPOSITE POINTER FINGER. DO THE SAME WITH THE OTHER ONE.
NOW PIVOT ONE THUMB AND WALK YOUR FINGER OVER TO THE OTHER
THUMB. Demonstrate. CAN YOU DO IT WITH YOUR TALL-MAN FINGER
AND YOUR THUMB? WITH YOUR RING FINGER? ONLY YOUR THUMB?
PUT YOUR FINGER TIPS ON YOUR DESK. THEY ARE PISTONS IN YOUR
CAR. CAN YOU LIFT YOUR TALL MAN AND YOUR THUMB AT THE SAME
TIME? NOW LIFT ONLY YOUR POINTER AND RING FINGERS.

Exploration of Smaller Movements

1. HOW CAN YOU MOVE YOUR WRIST? Choose one joint or one
limb or part of the body to explore each time. CAN YOU MOVE IT
FORWARD? BACKWARD? TO THE RIGHT? TO THE LEFT? CAN YOU MOVE
IT JUST A LITTLE? A LOT? JOHNNY IS MOVING HIS . . . SEE IF YOU
CAN DO THAT, TOO!

2. WHAT CAN YOU SHAKE? CAN YOU SHAKE A FINGER? ONLY ONE?
ALL YOUR FINGERS, BUT NOT YOUR HAND? YOUR HAND AND FINGERS?
YOUR FOREARM, HAND, AND FINGERS ONLY? YOUR WHOLE ARM?
CAN YOU SHAKE YOUR HEAD? YOUR TORSO? YOUR FOOT? YOUR LOWER
LEG? YOUR UPPER LEG? WHAT OTHER PART CAN YOU SHAKE? CAN
YOU SHAKE JUST TWO PARTS? CAN YOU SHAKE FOUR PARTS? CAN YOU
SHAKE YOUR WHOLE BODY? CAN YOU SHAKE YOUR EAR? YOUR NOSE?
YOUR SHOULDERS?

3. Do the same things as above with WHAT CAN YOU STRETCH?
WHAT CAN YOU RELAX? WHAT CAN YOU BEND? WHAT CAN YOU
ROTATE? WHAT CAN YOU SWING? WITH WHAT CAN YOU STRIKE OUT?
Do all of the above in different positions, sitting, standing, or
kneeling.

4. HOW CAN YOU PUSH? CAN YOU PUSH WITH YOUR RIGHT
SHOULDER? WITH YOUR HAND? WITH YOUR FOOT? WITH YOUR HIPS?
WHAT OTHER PART OF YOUR BODY CAN YOU USE TO PUSH? HOW
WOULD YOU PUSH SOMETHING LIGHT? SOMETHING SMALL? SOMETHING
VERY BIG BUT LIGHT? SOMETHING VERY HEAVY? Do the same explora-
tions with *pull.*

5. Do tension-relaxation exercises from *Body Image,* Chapter
Six.

Mimetics

To keep movements thoughtful and creative, have only half the children moving at once. Use all the animal movements under *Movement Exploration.* Pretend you are carrying a heavy load, a giant, loading a truck, making a cake, sweeping the floor, driving a car, skating, an engine of any kind, a witch, a pirate, drilling in the street, climbing a telephone pole, or riding a merry-go-round. Let children talk about how they are doing it. Ask questions to get them to feel the movement more. IS YOUR ENGINE RUNNING SMOOTHLY? HOW FAST ARE YOU GOING? CAN YOU PRETEND YOU ARE MOVING VERY SLOWLY? YOU ARE RUNNING OUT OF GAS. YOU ARE A TALL TREE AND THE WIND IS BLOWING. YOU ARE FLOWERS IN THE WINTER. WHAT HAPPENS TO YOU IN THE SPRING? CAN YOU SHAKE LIKE JELLY? CAN YOU BE AS HARD AS A ROCK? CAN YOU BE DOLLS? WHAT CAN YOU DO?

Adding Music

Add music only after children have explored all the movements of their bodies and all the locomotor movements. Have children sitting in their seats, or on one side of the room. LISTEN TO THE RHYTHM OF THE DRUM. Beat a very slow, steady rhythm. IS IT FAST? CAN YOU CLAP IN THE VERY SAME RHYTHM? VERY GOOD! CAN YOU SWAY YOUR BODIES TO THIS RHYTHM? WHO COULD GET UP AND MOVE AROUND THE ROOM RIGHT IN TIME TO THIS RHYTHM? LET'S START WITH GIRLS. WE MUST ALL MOVE TO THE RIGHT. WE CAN ONLY GO ONE WAY ON A FREEWAY. Then have girls sit down and have boys try it. Try another rhythm pattern. Be sure it is a very fixed rhythm and very different from the last. Use a fast beat for a run, a broken beat for a skip or gallop, a light beat for tiptoes (and fingertip clapping) .

After they are familiar with these rhythms and respond well, try variations. YOU ARE ROBOTS NOW AND YOU CAN MOVE ONLY THE WAY THE DRUM TELLS YOU. WHEN THE DRUM STOPS, YOU MUST STOP. LET'S TRY THE GIRLS FIRST. Begin with a walk, stop, change to skip or run, but stop between each change of movement to give the children a greater clue to the change. If you want to really get them moving, try a run and then an arpeggio on the piano to designate sliding down.

LET'S MAKE A RHYTHM WITH SOMEONE'S NAME. LISTEN TO THE DRUM AND SEE IF YOU CAN FIGURE OUT WHOSE NAME THIS IS. YES! THAT WAS TOMMY CALLIMAN. CAN YOU CLAP THE RHYTHM OF TOMMY'S NAME? WHO CAN MAKE UP A MOVEMENT TO GO WITH TOMMY'S NAME? It could be something like: walk, walk, jump, jump, jump. WHAT DOES MOTHER TELL YOU TO DO RIGHT AFTER SCHOOL? YES. COME RIGHT HOME FROM SCHOOL. LET'S USE IT TO MAKE A RHYTHM. WHO CAN MOVE TO THIS RHYTHM? Gladys Andrews, *Creative Rhythmic Movement for Children,* is full of excellent ideas for creative movements.

Some records and piano music are good for rhythmic movement. Rhythm should be clear and well accented. Spare the vocal unless the children are singing it. Newer records that are excellent are *The Beat Goes On* and the *Hap Palmer* records. Some simple folk dances are listed in the *Outdoor Games* section, and are good for inside.

Indoor Games

1. *Change Seats:* Move empty desks out of the way. Say: CHANGE RIGHT, or FORWARD. The children change seats. Children in the front of the rows, or on the right, must hurry around to the end of the rows. See how quickly they can change seats without getting lost.

2. *House Hunting:* Children are numbered in couples as they sit in their seats. The first two are *one,* the next two are *two,* etc. One extra couple sits in the front of the room in *the trailer.* They call out two numbers. Those two couples hold hands and try to change seats. The couple in the trailer try to get their home-seats while they are gone. Left over couple is without a home and must go live in the trailer.

3. *Who's Gone?* One child is *it,* and hides his eyes. Another child is designated to leave the room or hide in the closet. *It* tries to guess who is missing. Make game more difficult as desired by having children scramble into other seats to confuse *it.*

4. *Cat and Mouse:* Use this very old game with five or six players. The cats sit in the front of the room with erasers or bean-

bags under their chairs for the *cat food*. Five mice are chosen to steal the food. They creep up quietly to get it. The children all change seats to confuse the cats. Each cat is then given one chance to guess who stole the food. If successful, he remains a cat. If not, the mouse who got his food becomes the cat.

5. *Circle Beanbag Relay:* Form two circles. Beanbags are given to about every two or three children. One beanbag for each team, held by the captain, is distinctive. At a signal, they all start passing the bags around the circle to the right. The captain who gets his bag back first is of the winning team. There could be more circles, fewer children in each, more beanbags, and a greater distance between children so that the bag has to be tossed more accurately.

ON-FLOOR ROUTINES

Some of the most effective sensorimotor training techniques are those which are performed while the body is in contact with the floor. In this position, the child's control of movement is challenged and trained. His powers of concentration are deepened. He is better able to concentrate on planning his movements because he is not involved in balance or in any other movement. Supine, on his back on the floor, he sees only the ceiling and upper walls, and thus his visual distractability is lessened.

The facility essential to this training of a whole class is a large open floor space, most often available only in the multipurpose room or cafeteria of the school. These routines are not satisfactory on the lawn because the sun then shines directly in the children's eyes, and the grass, too, can be irritating to allergy-prone children. Each child requires about three square feet of space. Vinyl tape can be used to make X's on the floor in alternate three-foot spaces to designate where each child is to sit. This tape will withstand several months of scrubbing. When the floor is thus prepared ahead of time, we have worked with as many as sixty children, with two teachers and a high school aide. We take all of the first graders through all the routines until they can accomplish them easily, with good control. We might use the facility two or three sessions a week. In just a few weeks, most of the children *graduate* out of the program and one teacher takes them out to another activity. Thus we are left with ten to twenty children who have severe coordination control problems. Usually then we go back to the simplest routines, moving much more slowly through the levels, gradually increasing the complexity of the movements until these children, too, have gained control and concentration. The results of this program have been very gratifying, sometimes dramatic. One child who had severe gross and sensorimotor problems, entered late in the year and had missed all of our basic template, chalkboard, and movement exploration training. He wrote his name upside-down and backward with poor control. After a few weeks of the *on-floor* training and very little help with the specifics of writing, he suddenly wrote his name correctly to the amazement of all of us.

Then there was Mark who could spell orally but jumbled all the letters in writing a spelling word. After just four weeks of floor training he, who had missed every word every week, had all of his words spelled correctly.

The on-floor routines seem to increase the child's ability to relax parts of his body while he concentrates on the movement of other parts. Thus improvement will be noticeable in writing as the child can now relax his lower extremities to concentrate on the use of his arms for writing. As G. N. Getman says:

> The child who gains skill of mobility usually has the skill of immobility. He can sit still better—and thus pay attention better. His postures will be more balanced and thus he will be less subject to fatigue. When he moves, his direction of movement will be more direct and efficient, and thus his random, time consuming actions will be reduced. (Getman, 1964, p. 3)

Getman (1964, pp. 11-30) describes the most complete program of on-floor activities. I use a combination of these along with ideas from Kephart, Ayres, Delacato, and my own variations. I begin simply with feeling the sensations of the body against the floor, set the scene for the robots, then start with eye movements alone (Getman), gradually adding arm and then leg movements until they can complete *Angels in the Snow*. Then I go to movements on just one side of the body, then alternating the two side movements. The final tasks then require alternate bilateral movements using both the upper and lower extremities.

A Sequence of Floor Routines

TAKE OFF YOUR SHOES AND COATS AND PUT THEM WAY OVER HERE. Not anywhere near the children.

1. LIE ON YOUR BACK ON YOUR SPOT WITH YOUR FEET POINTING STRAIGHT TOWARD THE DOORS ON THIS SIDE OF THE ROOM. RUB YOUR HEELS TOGETHER. FEEL THEM? NOW KEEP YOUR HEELS TOUCHING AND RUB THE SIDES OF YOUR BODY WITH YOUR HANDS. FEEL YOUR SIDES. NOW YOUR HEELS ARE TOUCHING AND YOUR HANDS ARE TOUCHING YOUR SIDES. CLOSE YOUR EYES AND RELAX. FEEL YOUR BODY SINKING, SINKING DOWN, DOWN. JUST RELAX. NOW YOU ARE FLOATING ON A CLOUD. LIE VERY STILL AND SEE IF YOU CAN FEEL YOUR HEART BEAT. FEEL YOUR LUNGS BREATHING. SEE YOUR CHEST GO UP AND DOWN. NOW MOVE JUST YOUR TOES. CAN YOU FEEL THEM MOVING? MOVE JUST YOUR FINGERS. FEEL THEM. STRETCH YOUR ARMS. RELAX THEM. STRETCH YOUR LEGS. RELAX THEM. KEEP YOUR EYES CLOSED AND SEE IF YOU CAN TOUCH THE BODY PART THAT I SAY. TOUCH YOUR HEAD, YOUR CHIN, YOUR NOSE, YOUR CHEEKS, YOUR ELBOWS.

2. OPEN YOUR EYES AND LOOK AT YOUR CEILING SPOT RIGHT OVER YOUR HEAD. NOW YOU ARE A ROBOT AND CAN MOVE ONLY THE PART I TELL YOU. LOOK TO YOUR RIGHT, TURN YOUR HEAD TO THE RIGHT UNTIL YOUR EAR TOUCHES THE FLOOR (from Getman, 1964) AND LOOK AT THE GREEN WALL. Stand on that side of the room. THIS WAY. THIS IS YOUR RIGHT. IS YOUR EAR TOUCHING THE FLOOR? CAN YOU FEEL IT THERE? NOW TURN YOUR HEAD UNTIL YOUR EAR TOUCHES THE FLOOR AND LOOK TO YOUR LEFT, TOWARD THE TABLES. Speak slowly, keep them thinking of what they are doing. If a child turns his whole body, go to him and hold his body still while he turns only his head. The attention of distractable children will stray quickly until they are lying sideways, or have their feet crossed. Stay near these children, helping them to concentrate. If they are out of position, ask them questions so they have to think what they are doing. ARE YOUR HANDS STILL TOUCHING YOUR SIDES? ARE YOUR HEELS STILL TOUCHING? CHECK THEM. Sometimes it is advisable to divide your children into two different sessions, one group which will attend better and you can move them through the routines more quickly. The other group of distract-

able children will take many more sessions and accomplish the skills much more slowly.

3. ATTENTION POSITION. LOOK AT YOUR CEILING SPOT. NOW LOOK UP OVER YOUR EYEBROWS, UP HERE TOWARD ME. Often you have to stand above the head of each child coaxing his attention that way, touching his eyebrows to show him where they are. NOW LOOK AT YOUR CEILING SPOT. NOW LIFT YOUR HEAD, PUT YOUR CHIN ON YOUR CHEST AND LOOK AT YOUR TOES. KEEP YOUR HEELS TOGETHER SO THAT YOUR TOES POINT UP AND YOU CAN SEE THEM. CEILING SPOT. LOOK OVER YOUR EYEBROWS. CEILING SPOT. LOOK AT YOUR TOES (Getman, 1964).

4. ATTENTION POSITION. EYES ON YOUR CEILING SPOT. SWEEP THE FLOOR WITH YOUR ARMS UNTIL YOUR HANDS ARE WAY UP OVER YOUR HEAD. CLAP THEM THERE. SWEEP THE FLOOR AND HIT YOUR SIDES. SWEEP YOUR ARMS UP AND CLAP. FEEL THE FLOOR UNDER YOUR ARMS. SWEEP YOUR ARMS DOWN AND HIT YOUR SIDES. UP! DOWN! NOW YOUR EYES ARE GOING TO WORK WITH YOUR ARMS. WHEN YOUR ARMS SWEEP UP, YOUR EYES LOOK OVER YOUR EYEBROWS. WHEN YOUR ARMS SWEEP DOWN, YOU LIFT YOUR HEAD, PUT YOUR CHIN ON YOUR CHEST AND LOOK AT YOUR TOES. UP AND CLAP AND LOOK OVER YOUR EYEBROWS. DOWN AND HIT YOUR SIDES AND LOOK AT YOUR TOES (Getman, 1964). TRY IT A FEW TIMES TO SEE IF YOU CAN DO IT. Let them experiment on their own. Handing out candy or cereal treats encourages concentration. Be sure the child has his head straight and looks directly up and not off to one side. If necessary, remind him of his ceiling spot and hold his head still while only his eyes move up. This is plenty for the first session. They tire easily. A change of position and more action helps.

5. *Rocking Horse* (Getman, 1962): ROLL OVER ONTO YOUR STOMACH AND SEE IF YOU CAN BE A ROCKING HORSE. PULL YOUR HEAD AND CHEST WAY UP OFF THE FLOOR. NOW LIFT YOUR LEGS AND KNEES UP OFF THE FLOOR. ROCK BACK AND FORTH. SUSAN CAN DO IT. WATCH HER. NOW SEE IF YOU CAN DO IT. DON'T HOLD YOUR FEET. THAT KEEPS YOU FROM ROCKING. CAN YOU DO IT WITH YOUR ARMS WAY BACK BEHIND YOU? Remember A. Jean Ayres "inhibiting the tonic neck reflex"? Some children need extra help to do this. Try using a cushion under the child's abdomen.

6. SIT UP NOW. PUT YOUR HANDS ON THE FLOOR BEHIND YOU AND RAISE YOUR BODY OFF THE FLOOR. WAY UP! LEAN BACKWARD. NOW RELAX AND SIT DOWN. TRY IT AGAIN. PUSH YOUR BODY UP OFF THE FLOOR, LEAN BACKWARD. FREEZE. NOW SEE IF YOU CAN LIFT YOUR RIGHT FOOT OFF THE FLOOR. Another time try the left foot, then alternate.

7. LIE DOWN ON YOUR BACK. HOLD YOUR ARMS WAY OUT IN FRONT OF YOU AND PULL YOURSELF UP UNTIL YOU ARE SITTING. DOWN AND TRY IT AGAIN. Some children need help. Stand over them, holding their ankles with your foot, reaching for their hands to encourage them to pull up. Give assistance only as essential. Be sure the child's back does the pulling, not your hands. Some children need this extra help with their hands because they are totally unaware of how to move their backs without arm support. They tend to use their elbows on the floor to push themselves up. Sometimes you can have children hold each other's ankles while they do sit-ups. Still, watch that the elbows are off the floor. The sit-up position of hands clasped behind the neck is much too difficult for these children.

8. End the session with a crawling exercise: NOW PRETEND THAT YOUR WRISTS ARE HANDCUFFED TOGETHER AND YOUR KNEES CAN ONLY MOVE TOGETHER. CAN YOU CRAWL LIKE A PUPPY DOG, HANDS TOGETHER, KNEES TOGETHER? TOMMY CAN DO IT. WATCH HIM. SEE IF YOU CAN DO IT. NOW PUPPY-DOG-CRAWL OVER TO YOUR SHOES AND COATS AND PUT THEM ON.

Developing More Complex Coordinations

In subsequent sessions quickly review the first lessons, adding more complex coordinations little by little. Use a variety of movements each session so that the children don't overtire of one routine. If a movement is difficult, leave it, but come back to it each session, strengthening it little by little until they can accomplish it. Keep them on task, thinking of what they are doing. We are working for cognitive control.

1. ATTENTION POSITION. EYES ON YOUR CEILING SPOT. THIS TIME, ROBOT, ONLY YOUR LEGS CAN MOVE. YOUR LEGS OPEN AND SWEEP THE FLOOR. NOT TOO FAR! KEEP YOUR KNEES STRAIGHT. KEEP YOUR

BODY STILL, YOUR HANDS TOUCHING YOUR SIDES. NOW CLOSE YOUR LEGS (Getman, 1964). OPEN AND FREEZE. CLOSE AND FREEZE. YOU ARE THE ROBOT, SO LISTEN CAREFULLY—I MIGHT SAY IT FAST OR SLOW. OPEN! CLOSE! (vary the tempo so that they have to concentrate on what you are saying. Some children have difficulty keeping the hands at the sides, without moving them also. You might have to hold their arms still until they understand and have control. Make a game of it. TOMMY IS REALLY THINKING. I CAN'T CATCH HIM.

2. Next have arms and legs work together: LEGS GO OPEN AND ARMS SWEEP THE FLOOR AND CLAP. ARMS AND LEGS DOWN AND CLOSED. ARMS AND LEGS OPEN AND UP. DOWN AND CLOSED.

3. NOW THIS IS A HARD ONE. YOU WILL HAVE TO THINK HARD, ROBOTS. NOW YOU HAVE TO MOVE YOUR ARMS, LEGS AND EYES ALL TOGETHER. ARMS AND LEGS OPEN AND UP, AND EYES LOOK OVER YOUR EYEBROWS. ARMS AND LEGS DOWN AND CLOSED AND EYES LOOK AT YOUR TOES (Getman, 1964). I prefer using the fully worded directions rather than *counting off*, "one, two!" It seems to help the child to concentrate and stay with me.

4. THIS TIME YOU ARE GOING TO MOVE ONLY YOUR RIGHT SIDE, ROBOTS. RIGHT ARM AND LEG OPEN AND UP. MAKE YOUR HAND GO ALL THE WAY UP OVER YOUR HEAD. WAY UP! RIGHT ARM AND LEG DOWN AND CLOSED. OPEN AND UP, DOWN AND CLOSED. Repeat several times. You might need to hold a child's left arm and leg still until he feels and understands the lack of movement in that side. NOW ONLY YOUR LEFT SIDE WILL MOVE. LEFT ARM AND LEG OPEN AND UP, DOWN AND CLOSED. Repeat several times. NOW, WE ARE GOING TO GET REALLY TRICKY. YOU WILL HAVE TO THINK HARD. RIGHT ARM AND LEG OPEN AND UP, DOWN AND CLOSED. LEFT ARM AND LEG OPEN AND UP, DOWN AND CLOSED. Repeat several times.

5. ROLL OVER ONTO YOUR STOMACHS. PULL YOUR ARMS WAY BACK LIKE A THUNDER JET, AND LIFT YOUR CHEST OFF THE FLOOR! SEE IF YOU CAN HOLD IT THERE WHILE WE COUNT, ONE THUNDER JET, TWO THUNDER JETS, THREE THUNDER JETS, FOUR THUNDER JETS, FIVE THUNDER JETS. OH, THAT WAS HARD! RELAX. GET ALL SOFT AND LOOSE. NOW YOU HAVE NO BONES. Help the children learn to relax. Go around lifting arms and hands and letting them just fall back

onto the floor. Move a leg. MAKE IT ALL SOFT. PRETEND YOU ARE DEAD.

NOW SEE IF YOU CAN LIFT JUST YOUR LEGS. KEEP YOUR FACE DOWN ON THE FLOOR. CAN YOU LIFT YOUR KNEES OFF THE FLOOR, TOO? DROP THEM. RELAX. NOW TRY IT AGAIN. KNEES OFF THE FLOOR, ONE LEG, TWO LEGS, THREE LEGS! DOWN AGAIN. This is very difficult. Give them plenty of rest between leg lifts.

6. The children love this Bottle-Capping Machine (Getman, 1964). ATTENTION POSITION. ARMS SWEEP OUT TO THE SIDE LIKE ANGEL WINGS. NOW LIFT YOUR ARMS UP OFF THE FLOOR AND CLAP THEM IN FRONT OF YOUR NOSE. ARMS BACK DOWN TO ANGEL POSITION, DOWN TO YOUR SIDES. Repeat. NOW THIS TIME WHEN YOU CLAP IN FRONT OF YOUR NOSE, YOUR RIGHT LEG WILL COME UP AND KICK. ARMS, ANGEL POSITION, CLAP AND KICK YOUR RIGHT LEG. ANGEL POSITION FEET TOGETHER. ATTENTION POSITION. TRY IT AGAIN. ANGEL, RIGHT FOOT KICK AND CLAP, ANGEL, DOWN. After repeating several times with only right and only left feet, try alternating the two. ANGEL, RIGHT FOOT KICK AND CLAP, ANGEL, DOWN. ANGEL, LEFT FOOT, KICK AND CLAP, ANGEL, DOWN.

7. *Chimpanzees* (Getman, 1962): ATTENTION POSITION. LIFT YOUR LEGS OFF THE FLOOR. NOT TOO FAR, JUST A LITTLE WAYS. About six inches or a foot. NOW, TRY TO HOLD IT WHILE WE COUNT TO TEN CHIMPANZEES: ONE CHIMPANZEE, TWO CHIMPANZEES. . . .

8. ROLL INTO A TIGHT BALL. TIGHTER, TIGHTER! WHEN I SAY "THREE," YOU PUSH OUT OF THE BALL AND STRAIGHTEN YOUR BODY. ONE, TWO, THREE!

9. ATTENTION POSITION. PUT YOUR RIGHT ARM UP. NOW ROLL OVER TO YOUR RIGHT SIDE. CAN YOU BALANCE THERE WHILE I COUNT TO TEN? ROLL ONTO YOUR BACK AGAIN. NOW PUT YOUR LEFT ARM UP AND ROLL TO THE LEFT. HOLD IT WHILE I COUNT. All of the routines where the body rolls on the floor give a big impetus to body awareness.

10. *Balancing on hands and knees:* HANDS AND KNEES POSITION. LIFT UP YOUR RIGHT HAND AND KNEE. CAN YOU BALANCE WHILE I COUNT TO TEN? LIFT UP YOUR LEFT KNEE AND HAND. BALANCE WHILE I COUNT. NOW SEE IF YOU CAN BALANCE ON YOUR RIGHT HAND AND LEFT KNEE. LEFT HAND AND RIGHT KNEE. CAN YOU BALANCE ON

YOUR RIGHT KNEE WITH YOUR LEFT FOOT FLAT ON THE FLOOR? NOW
HANDS TOUCHING THE FLOOR. NOW BALANCE ON YOUR LEFT KNEE
WITH YOUR RIGHT FOOT FLAT ON THE FLOOR.

11. *Bear crawl:* NOW YOU ARE A BIG BEAR, VERY BIG AND VERY
HEAVY. YOU ROLL FROM SIDE TO SIDE AS YOU CRAWL. USE FIRST YOUR
RIGHT HAND AND KNEE, THEN YOUR LEFT HAND AND KNEE.

12. Have each child wear a weighted red wristband on his
right wrist, or cotton gloves could be dyed red to designate the
right hand. Tie a length of red roving or yarn around his thigh
above his left knee: ON YOUR HANDS AND KNEES. PUT YOUR RED
HAND AND KNEE FORWARD AND BACK, FORWARD AND BACK. NOW PUT
YOUR OTHER HAND AND KNEE FORWARD AND BACK. WE WILL CALL
THAT THE WHITE HAND AND KNEE. RED HAND AND KNEE FORWARD,
BACK. WHITE HAND AND KNEE FORWARD, BACK. NOW WE ARE GOING
TO START TO MOVE. RED HAND AND KNEE FORWARD, WHITE HAND
AND KNEE FORWARD, RED HAND AND KNEE, WHITE HAND AND KNEE.
KEEP GOING. USE THE RED, THEN THE WHITE. WATCH WHAT YOU ARE
DOING! GO VERY SLOWLY.

13. *Sleep position:* ON YOUR STOMACHS. TURN YOUR HEAD TO THE
RIGHT AND LOOK AT YOUR RIGHT THUMB. CAN YOU SEE THAT LITTLE
CRESCENT MOON ON YOUR THUMB? NOW BEND YOUR RIGHT KNEE UP
A LITTLE TO THE SIDE. TURN YOUR HEAD TO THE LEFT, AND LOOK
AT YOUR LEFT THUMB. CHANGE LEGS, TOO. YOUR LEFT LEG IS BENT
AT THE KNEE NOW. THE OTHER LEG IS STRAIGHT. LOOK AT YOUR
RIGHT THUMB. DID YOU CHANGE YOUR ARM AND LEG? CHANGE AND
LOOK AT YOUR LEFT THUMB.

14. *Alternate arm and leg movements* (Getman, 1964). AT-
TENTION POSITION. PUT YOUR RIGHT ARM UP ABOVE YOUR HEAD.
OPEN YOUR LEFT LEG. NOW YOU ARE USING OPPOSITE SIDES OF YOUR
BODY. CLOSE THEM, OPEN THEM. NOW WHEN YOU CLOSE THAT RIGHT
ARM AND LEFT LEG, TRY OPENING THE LEFT ARM AND RIGHT LEG.
Using the red wristbands and roving helps, except that now they
cannot see the leg. They can feel the weight of the wristband,
however. LET'S TRY IT AGAIN. RIGHT ARM AND LEFT LEG OPEN. NOW
SWITCH ARMS AND LEGS. SWITCH AGAIN. SWITCH.

Getman (1964 and 1970) has developed a number of more complex coordinations. There are other alternate movements such as

the Windmill, and several rolling exercises such as the Rolling Sit-up, The Hands and Feet, and the Hands and Knees Roll. These help the child to comprehend how, when he turns over, his left-right orientation changes.

By the time the child is able to do all of these routines with precision on command, he has made giant steps in listening, concentrating and cognitive control of his body.

REFERENCES

Andrews, Gladys: *Creative Rhythmic Movement for Children.* Englewood Cliffs, New Jersey, Prentice-Hall, 1954.

Bartelt, Jeanne: Movement Exploration Language for Action. Sacramento, California, San Juan Unified School District, Carmichael, California.

Diem, Liselott: *Who Can . . .* Frankfort, Germany, Wilhelm Limpert, 1962.

Ferraiuolo: *First Fitness.* Palo Alto, California, Products of the Behavioral Sciences, 1968.

Getman, G. N.: *How to Develop Your Child's Intelligence.* Luverne, Minnesota, Getman, 1962.

Getman, G. N., and Kane, Elmer R.: The Physiology of Readiness. Minneapolis, PASS, 1964.

——— et al.: *Developing Learning Readiness, Teacher's Manual.* Manchester, Missouri, McGraw-Hill, 1970.

Hackett, Layne C., and Jenson, Robert G.: *A Guide to Movement Exploration.* Palo Alto, California, Peek, 1966.

Hap Palmer Record Library. Educational Activities, Inc., Freeport, New York, 11520.

Irving, Robert, and Murtha, Jack: *The Physical Fitness Part of a Physical Education Program.* Sutter County Printer, Yuba City, California, 1964.

Lind Climber. Lind Climber Company, 807 Reba Place, Evanston, Ill., 60202.

Mosston, Muska: *Developmental Movement.* Columbus, Ohio, Merrill, 1965.

County of Sacramento, Superintendent of Schools, Quiet and Semi-active Games; County Schools Office, Sacramento, California, 1960.

San Juan Unified School District: Exploration of Movement, Teacher's Physical Education Guide. San Juan School District, Carmichael, California, 1962.

Stegel: (Plans for construction of the Stegel) Orinda Union School District, 8 Altarinda Road, Orinda, California 94563.

Stein, Joe: Head Over Heels. Enrichment Materials Company, Campbell, California, 1963.

MOVEMENT EXPLORATION FILMS

Anyone Can. (30 min. color), CANHC Movie Distribution, P O Box 1526, Vista, California, 92083.

Fun With Parachutes. (11 min. color), Documentary Films, 3217 Trout Gulch Road, Aptos, California 95003.

Movement Exploration. (22 min. color) (A Hacket and Jenson film), Peck Publications, 4067 Transport Street, Palo Alto, California 94303.

Thinking, Moving, Learning. (20 min. color), Bradley Wright Films, 309 North Duane Avenue, San Gabriel, California 91775.

Up and Over—Exploring on the Stegel. (20 min. color) Bradley Wright Films, 309 North Duane Avenue, San Grabriel, California 91775.

Chapter Nine

Reading and Writing

READING
Children and Reading

SOME CHILDREN LEARN to read very well with any method used. The teacher simply tells them a word once or twice (sight reading) and because they have excellent visual and auditory memories they are able to recall the word at each future exposure. These children learn the first one hundred words very quickly. Thereafter, words become too similar, so that they need to know the consonant sounds to differentiate the words. Some word, phrase, and sentence drills are used to augment this method of teaching reading. Expression in reading is emphasized and considerable time is spent in discussing the meaning of the text.

These bright children use the context clues and visual memory of small words or word parts to unlock new words. Thus they learn to read at least to the first basal reader level without needing to know the vowel sounds or any other word analysis skills. They learn the consonant sounds incidentally. However, they are still dependent on the teacher to tell them many of the new words. Take away the pictures and/or the context and they usually are unable to analyze any new words independently. This group of children finishes the first basal reader and probably a couple of *enrichment* books by the end of first grade. They may test from 1.7 to 3.5 grade level on a test such as the Metropolitan Reading Test, in June. A fourth to a half of a class may be in this category of learners. The above approach is basically the method of the basal readers used by most of the teachers in this and other English-speaking countries and is often referred to as the reading-for-meaning method, or the whole-word or sight method. The amount of phonics used and the many techniques vary from teacher to teacher even within the same school.

The middle reading group of children start out gamely with the pre-primers (with almost any method) but usually slow down in about the third pre-primer of basal readers where the words are too similar. They have trouble with *what* and *want, chickens* and *children, surprise* and *something.* They might do phonics dittos well, but have difficulty *applying* phonetic analysis to recall even *learned* words. They are unable to blend sounds into words. But again, with the picture and context clues and often good auditory memories (if not visual) they, too, succeed, though on a smaller scale. The teacher uses more repetition and drill with them and they memorize whole stories. Flash words without context or picture clues may be difficult.

Teachers become exasperated with these middle children because they seem capable, yet are not doing well; it is surmised they are not applying themselves. They just don't concentrate as well as the top group. They need a marker to keep their place in the book. They appear less motivated. It is often said, "They could do it if they would only try a little harder." Parents are often counseled to put more pressure on their children. Thus begins a tug-of-war, with the child in the middle. A resentment of school may start here. By June they may be in the first basal reader and score between 1.5 and 2.0 grade level on the Metropolitan Reading Test. We scold them for lack of drive and pass them on to second grade.

The low reading group of children in our classrooms is the principal subject of this manuscript. They may learn the first twenty words (or only four or five) before they become bogged in a mire of frustration. Those with good auditory memories may appear to be reading, especially if the sentences have been repeated frequently. But with independent flash words they are lost. One little Mike read three pre-primers with only a few errors, but could not read even the names of the primary characters in these books when they were presented on flash cards.

The children in this low group seem to discriminate gross differences only or grasp at single clues. Thus they might use only the word shape and confuse *said* and *and, come* and *can.* They reverse words and call *was, saw;* and *on, no.* A single clue gives them *Tom* for *Tip.* Again they use context and picture clues and come up with *dog* for *Flip, house* for *cabin.*

These children might recognize a word in one sentence or type of print or size, but not in another. They have difficulty finding one certain word on a page. They have more visual-acuity problems than the rest of the class, especially astigmatism and far-sightedness. Their eye movements may be spastic or jerky. They may be unable to follow a sentence across the page without being confused. The teacher may need to isolate a word in a sentence to get the child to focus on it. Some of these children read well from charts and flash cards made with a broad felt pen, but are lost in the small, tight print in books. They may score low with gross distortions and rotations and reversals in tests of visual perception such as the Winter Haven, Bender, Frostig, and Beery, discussed in Chapter Four.

These struggling children are often unable to hear the sounds adequately, since their auditory perception of the sound is distorted. Being unable to discriminate sounds accurately, they have difficulty learning letter sounds. Phonics worksheets and workbooks are usually hit-and-miss or badly mutilated. They sometimes score dramatically low on the Wepman, a test of auditory discrimination. That is, *pet* and *pat* might sound the same. So might *chip* and *ship,* or *tot* and *top.* Children whose gross articulation problems require the services of speech therapists are most often in this group of slow readers.

Another major problem with these slow learners is their inability to make associations. They try to remember what you tell them about a word. They really want to learn, but they are unable to associate those crooked marks with anything at all. The main association they make is that the story you have told them is there. But they lack the skills with which to unlock the words. They do not relate a sound heard to a symbol seen, thus letter-sound association is often nil. Auditory memory and sequence are often lacking. Sequence of letters in words and sequence of words in sentences are badly scrambled. Incorrect sequence of sounds in a word result in *spas-kete* for *spaghetti*. Sequence of events in the telling of a story is often jumbled so that the tale makes no sense. These children do not know their addresses, phone numbers, or even their parents' names or occupations.

These problem learners are really nonreaders. By chance and guess they obtain scores on most standardized reading tests from 1.0 to 1.8 grade level. Here, then, is our bottom reading group, an eighth to a third of our class, ten to thirty percent of our population, our behavior problems, our dropouts, our juvenile delinquents, our drug addicts, the misfits of our society. Test these children, and their IQ scores fall within the normal range, some quite high verbally, but often with marked highs and lows in subtests.

The Great Debate

Education has had more debate in the field of reading (and more research) than in any other subject. In this century the pendulum has swung from the somewhat linguistic approach of the McGuffy Readers to forty or fifty years of whole-word and reading-for-meaning (discussed earlier), and now back again to linguistics and phonics. Thousands of research studies have been done on the subject. The list is staggering and would be even difficult to computerize because of the lack of details on many of the studies. The conclusions of many of the investigators may not agree with the findings of their own studies. Proponents of differing theories often find opposite conclusions in the findings of the same study (Chall, 1967). There are enough variables and multiplicity of educational research to support almost any theory. Many educators choose from the volumes on the subject to find and quote just those studies which appear to support their opinions.

On the teacher's side, she is usually tied to the basal series that is supplied by her state or her school district. Library books are limited in number and too few are easy readers for beginners. The teacher can't possibly buy enough books for her whole class, so she is bound to the basal series. Since these do not do the job, she is continually searching for better materials. She makes piles of charts and spends hours creating stories on dittos to supplement the readers.

The teachers' colleges across the country seem to have clung to the reading-for-meaning method of the basal series in spite of ample evidence of the superiority of other methods. They seem to be somehow threatened by all the newer techniques and often lash out vehemently against them even though their knowledge of these is sometimes only hearsay. It is apparently easier to label all children who do not learn to read with the basal readers as slow learners, than to acknowledge the failure of the method used. We seem to prefer failing our children rather than ourselves and our teaching methods. It is really a travesty on education to have our idealistic young people coming out of colleges so thoroughly indoctrinated with one reading method that they are automatically biased against all other methods. This has built a barrier against the newer findings and methods which has probably cost educators at least twenty-five years of progress in reading and brought unnecessary reading failure to thousands of our children.

Teachers, concerned with the failure of an eighth to a third of their children, were overjoyed with the resurgence of interest in the teaching of reading in the sixties, and with the addition of special reading teachers and workshops on reading. "Maybe we will get some new materials!" echoed through the teachers' rooms. However, in meeting teachers from New York to California during our summer forays, we found them bitterly disappointed when those anticipated workshops turned into echoes of the same reading-for-meaning tunes they had heard in their early college years. Those teachers were often frustrated because they lacked better materials and methods and did not know where to turn for help. Then some of those special reading teachers too often simply canceled off the problem learners as being incapable of learning, and spent their time trying to up the scores of the middle children. Some even told the classroom teachers, "Don't bother to send me problem children like that. Send me children I can teach!"

Now since the purse strings were loosened and some Federal monies were available, many dedicated educators took the bull by the horns and initiated studies on a wide variety of newer methods. With teachers severely disenchanted with their state-supplied basal readers to which they have always felt handcuffed, there was eagerness to try anything. Heretofore, most of the studies on reading methods were initiated to fulfill master's thesis requirements for psychologists and administrators. Now it was more the determination of the teacher, a principal, a psychologist, or a special reading teacher to find a way to teach problem learners. The object was to improve reading ability in children, not just carry on a study. This classroom research for methods we shall call action research. Results were often unpublished, usually only copied for in-district consumption. Through seminars and the professional grapevine, word of these studies spread and visitors from other schools and districts beat a path to the doors of the classrooms of innovative teachers.

Katrina deHirsch researched symptoms of children with reading problems and early identification in her *Predicting Reading Failure* (deHirsch, 1966) and thus opened the door to teachers to recognize and diagnose potential reading failures. She recommended that we then endeavor to find methods with which we might reach and teach these children according to their disabilities, their modality strengths and weaknesses.

We have heard many discussions recently on auditory versus visual learners. Some remediation teachers test a child's modalities to see which is stronger and thus choose an appropriate method by which to teach him. Generally, it is felt that the child with poor visual perception and good auditory perception desperately needs to have very thorough reading instruction in phonics with remedial training in visual perception to strengthen that modality. With the reverse perceptual problem, the child will learn better with a reading method that utilizes a multiple repetition of the visual reading process, with additional training in auditory discrimination and decoding. The child with problems in both auditory and visual areas (Katrina deHirsch found most problem learners to be in this category) must have perceptual training in both areas and very detailed training in letter-sound association in a step-by-step progression that takes no learning for granted.

Code-Emphasis Methods

As we flail about searching for methods and experimenting with a variety of them, Jeanne Chall (1967) comes to our rescue with a dispassionate look at the maze of materials and methods and research in teaching reading. The results of her three-year study are fully described in her book in which she comes up with some conclusions and recommendations for beginning reading programs.

The main conclusion, of greatest significance to us teachers who have been so deluged with the reading-for-meaning basal readers and their advocates, is that an initial code-emphasis method of teaching beginning reading is superior, at least through the third grade. Further longitudinal studies beyond the third grade are not available. In fact, most reading studies culminate with end of first or second grade scores.

By code-emphasis we mean that the focus of the reading method is on deciphering the code of the printed word. We call this decoding. It might be comparable to the method of learning the Morse code. Thus the skills of letter-sound association, phonics, and blending sounds into words are taught. In initial instruction, sight reading is discouraged, expression in reading is ignored, meaning of words is secondary. It is felt that understanding of the meaning of a story is due to language facility not reading ability per se. Most children's stories are easy enough for them to understand. If you read a story to a child and he does not understand it, it is a deficiency in language ability, not reading ability. Since language is an important and sorely neglected skill, we shall devote a later chapter to this subject.

The crucial skills needed for beginning reading are those which help the child to decode or analyze a word. If he cannot do this, he cannot read. Guessing, context and picture clues, and word configuration are crutches, not skills. In fact, since these often prevent a child from learning to decode a word, they are eliminated from the code-emphasis method. The newer linguistic books have colorful pages, but the pictures are usually unrelated to the words and stories. When the child uses the above crutches to read, the greatest danger is that he will deceive the teacher into believing that he can read. Therefore, she will not take it upon herself to teach him. Later, in second or even third grade, it is discovered that he is a nonreader.

Jeanne Chall found that a code-emphasis method is especially needed for children of average and lower ability, with those from disadvantaged backgrounds, and with those whose predictability of reading failure is high. Thus if we are responsible for teaching these children, we must initiate a decoding method in our classrooms. The next problem then is Which one? or What combination of methods and materials will do the job most effectively? There are new alphabet systems, such as I.T.A., and phonetic systems as Words in Color, Phona-visual, and Phonetic Keys. Then there are the Fernald kinesthetic approach, and the Slingerland and Gillingham methods.

Readers

For books, there are several new series of programmed and linguistic readers available. The latter usually have phonetic words introduced in rhyming sets (*hat, cat, sat, mat*) and add the essential sight words (*said, was, to, do*) at varying speeds. However, some of these series move much too rapidly for the slower children and deluge them with too many words the first weeks. Also, many of them begin with teaching the letter names instead of the letter sounds and fail to teach blending of the sounds.

The linguistic and phonetic and code-cracking reading programs teach first graders many more words (1,000 to 2,000) than the basal reading-for-meaning books. The basal series usually contain between 325 to 400 words in the first grade. The words used most often in these books include the Dolch words which are too often sight words, impossible to decode, and not words which the children use verbally or for writing. Actually, the basal readers contain an artificial language. Who says: "See something!" "See something funny!"? Training in the basal series can warp children's ability to express themselves in writing. Their resultant stories consist of "See Bobby" and "See me run." Whereas, with a decoding method, a child can write in the same manner that he talks, using his natural vocabulary which is much more refreshing and creative.

Books vary in their use of picture clues. The SRA Linguistic Series and the Merrill Series use completely irrelevant pictures merely to brighten up the pages, not to supply clues. Others, such as the Sullivan Programmed Readers, have a profusion of pictures to help the child identify the words in a self-teaching process.

The amount of testing varies, also. Some programs provide no tests at all to ascertain the acquisition of the skills. Thus it is easy to get the children too far along in the program before the teacher finally realizes that the child is completely lost and she has to go back to the beginning again. Sullivan Programmed Readers have four tests in every book. The programmed Distar materials ask for individual child responses after every group response, and then test every few lessons to determine if the child has assimilated all the material presented up to that lesson and is ready to progress further.

Reading Programs

According to Chall's investigation of methods for children with special reading problems, we must be sure to use a method which teaches letter-sound association, the blending of these sounds into words, and then augment this process with the use of lower-order responses, such as tracing, writing, and pointing at the sounds and words read. She quotes Orton as saying that the teaching of the blending of sounds is a problem greater than that of letter confusions. Yet very few methods of teaching reading, even phonetic and linguistic systems, teach this blending as a separate skill.

The slower children are often overwhelmed with some of the concentrated phonetic systems, such as Phonetic Keys, which mature middle class children take in stride. The Lippincott pre-primer introduces twenty-four sounds in thirty pages. Besides being much too rapid for problem learners, auditory and visual perceptual problems are ignored, in that the first sounds include those which are both auditorily and visually similar. All the short vowels are taught, plus *m, n, h, d, p,* and *g.*

We find that children with auditory-discrimination and articulation problems become especially frustrated with a massive phonetic approach. They have enough trouble learning sounds without having so many thrown at them all at once. Therefore, we need a method which teaches the sounds slowly, systematically, beginning with sounds and letters that are easily discriminated.

Some phonetic and linguistic methods add words too rapidly and add sight words before the child is secure with the phonetic words. This confuses the child who has visual-memory problems. Now he can't depend on his visual discrimination of the words. He can't trust his own senses or his own judgment. He becomes discouraged and frustration replaces eagerness to learn.

Some reading series require smooth reading without the use of the finger. It has been found that if the child is allowed to use his finger when first learning, that his attention is focused and his learning more assured. As he thus becomes more fluent he will relinquish the use of the finger and gain the speed of the *normal* reader. As Fernald says:

> . . . the suppression of adaptive movements in the initial stages of learning leads to the continuance of these movements in the more advanced stages and slows down the entire reaction. (Fernald, 1943, p. 169)

When the child learns the sounds first, then blends those sounds into words, his first reading is slow and arduous and finger-guided. This serves to keep him on task and eliminates his guessing. However, this might be rather frightening to teachers who have been instilled with the importance of reading with expression. If there are never any exceptions at first to his use of the code (e.g. *e* is always *eeee*) and the same words are repeated frequently, he very quickly develops a sight vocabulary of the often repeated words. Thus, the words are read more quickly as the year progresses and the finger use drops away. By the end of the first-grade year, these children who labored to read a single word the first months of school are as fluent or even more so than children taught in whole words, phrases, and sentences from the start. By the time the child has a reading vocabulary of about one hundred words, he is ready for those essential sight words, such as *said, was,* and *to,* and takes them in stride with just a bit more practice.

The Reading Teacher

Another prerequisite of a reading program which will teach the children about whom we are concerned is an interesting and rewarding reading session. Mature children can sit for long periods and concentrate on involved instructions and dry routine. The problem learner needs a session that is stimulating and exciting, even dramatic. The ham-actor teacher does an excellent job with these children. She can become enthusiastic about their smallest responses. They feel that she really cares and that they are smart and are succeeding.

Often-overlooked prerequisites to teaching reading to problem learners are attitude and personality of the teacher. Since this can rarely be changed, it predisposes the failure or lack of progress of the children. Problem learners need a teacher who really *cares,* who believes in them, and has not prejudged their lack of ability.

In a study in South San Francisco, California, (Rosenthal, 1966) children were given a group test described by the examiners as one that would predict "intellectual blooming." The teacher was told that the results showed that these specific children (actually chosen at random from this low socioeconomic school area) would make outstanding gains during the next eight months. They did! In fact, the average gain in reasoning IQ was seven points more than their peers. At the end of the year, the teachers described the bloomers as "more interesting, curious, happier, more appealing, better adjusted, and more affectionate, with less need for social approval." Why was this? Because the teacher believed in them and, believing, gave them the extra consideration, encouragement, and attention that inspire any child to greater efforts with his renewed self-confidence.

Probably the greatest roadblock to finding a method that will teach our seemingly slower children to read is the firm belief of many teachers in the sanctity of IQ scores. Having always heard that there is a high correlation between intelligence and reading ability, between socioeconomic group and reading ability, and between the ability of siblings, it is easy to quickly label the whole bottom reading group, and children of certain families. This, then, gives the teacher an excuse for not teaching them.

Lack of sibling progress and a deprived home background are often the basis for such statements as: "Well, what more can you expect of him?" "Oh, he's a dumb-dumb, I had his brother last year. He was the same." "Well, if you would just meet his parents!" "He just barely scored in the 90's. He won't do much." Such attitudes on the part of educators is unprofessional and detrimental to the welfare and learning of the children. In fact, as long as the teacher really *believes* that the child is incapable of learning, she will not be able to teach him. The number one prerequisite for a reading teacher must be the belief that the child can learn, and that she can teach him. Only if she feels this way will she put forth the necessary effort to do so.

The teacher who stimulates the children to respond vocally and enthusiastically will be better able to teach them. We have seen ample evidence of this. Our vocal, noisy groups progress faster. We found this to be especially true in teaching sounds, blending, and rhyming. The children learn these best vocally, saying them distinctly and firmly. Probably, this is true because a positive, loud, vocal response of the child stimulates him auditorily and kinesthetically, and perhaps has positive emotional overtones as well. Remember also that the potential problem learner must be stimulated by several of his receptive senses for each new learning, in order to form new and multiple connections between neurons.

We made the error once of giving a quiet, nonexpressive group of children to a reserved, soft-spoken teacher's aide because they would be easier for her to handle. When we realized that this group of potentially average readers was about ten days behind a hyperactive, inattentive, immature group, we switched reading groups with her. Those quiet children were giving the responses so softly, briefly, and with so little effort that they were failing to learn. Remember that the hypoactive child needs the figure to which he is to attend to be heightened, to be dramatized (Chapter Five, *Figure-Ground Perception*). In this case, the figure is the sound or blending which you are teaching.

We have found that the negative teacher who does not believe in the ability of potential problem learners looks for the children's errors rather than their successes. They may even tally the errors, retreating the instruction backward each time the child errs. Even the child's corrections of his own errors are ignored. Thus the old sounds, words, and concepts are repeated so frequently that the sessions are deadly, the children discouraged, having lost faith in their own abilities. Even kindergarteners and first graders are reluctant to go to reading sessions with these instructors. "Do we have to?" "She's crabby!" "We just work on old words!"

Siegfried Engelmann tells of a Distar project in East St. Louis, Missouri, where the children had a mean reading score of 2.9 at the end of the year. He compared this group with another in Dayton, Ohio, taught with the same methods and comparable teachers, whose mean score was 1.4 on the same measure. He found only one variable as the cause of this discrepancy in scores: The East St. Louis group had simply covered more lessons, had progressed further in the program. Thus positive teaching, well paced lessons, forty to sixty days more lessons, made one grade-level difference in end-of-year reading scores.

Children should not be carried through programmed material without passing certain criteria or steps along the way. However, in judging the children's ability it is best to always give them the benefit of the doubt and not tighten up standards to make the program an obstacle course. For example, in testing sounds in the Distar program, the child gets more than one chance to identify a sound. And the criterion is that more than two children (in a group of four to eight) must each miss one sound before you take the group back to repeat old lessons.

The instruction should always be positive. Encourage each response. Be enthusiastic over the most simple, the smallest responses and the children will respond in turn by learning so well that your amazement about their progress will be genuine.

It is a revolving turbine that can take them only upward. YOU ARE SO SMART! THAT WAS TOO EASY FOR YOU! WOW! HOW DID YOU DO THAT SO FAST?

They like to compete with each other and with you. Rather than being discouraging, this can be most stimulating for them. LET'S SEE HOW FAST YOU CAN SAY THESE SOUNDS! or WHO CAN SAY ALL THESE WORDS THE FASTEST? TOMMY, YOU READ THAT WHOLE STORY SO SMOOTHLY! THAT WAS BEAUTIFUL! LET ME SHAKE YOUR HAND. THAT'S HARD TO DO, BUT HE DID IT! CAN ANYONE ELSE DO THAT? Or, LISTEN TO ME. I'M SMART! I CAN READ ALL THE WORDS ON THIS PAGE FAST: SAT, HAT, CAT. WHO CAN DO THAT? Challenge them with an easy task. YOU WON'T BE ABLE TO DO THIS. THIS IS TOO HARD! Or, I'LL BET YON CAN'T DO THIS. When they prove you wrong, their egos are strengthened tenfold. Or deliberately challenge them by erring. Say the words or sounds wrong and let them catch you. At early stages of "hooking" them on learning with these techniques, give them a cereal treat when they beat you, and give yourself a treat when you beat them. Of course, they always win the contest but you win in the end.

EXPERIMENTATIONS WITH READING METHODS

Our reading program has taken at least six years to develop and is still being changed. It began with action research in 1964. This was classroom pretesting and posttesting and experimentation with methods for the sole purpose of improving instruction. We have learned with the children and we still have much to learn. Perhaps, if I take you with me through the development of our program you will be able to find yourself and your children somewhere along this continuum. Perhaps our experiences can save you time and give you guidance in progressing from your present methodology.

In my first years of teaching first grade I used the state basal series. Feeling as frustrated as that bottom group of children, I spent hours making parallel story charts with matching sentence strips to augment the state readers. These were used with a variety of games wherein the child tried to FIND THE SENTENCE THAT SAYS . . . Thus there was multiple-repetition of the words, phrases, and sentences. Still, too many children were failing. My first clues to their dilemma were perceptual-motor problems. Therefore, I chose to take all the probable first grade failures or low achievers into one class. I called this a maturity-training class. The main goals were to prevent initial failure of slow and immature children, to provide specific instruction to prevent future reading disabilities of the perceptually handicapped, to work out techniques of applying perceptual, gross motor, and language training to a class of twenty-five to thirty children, and to develop a delayed reading program aimed toward the success of these children.

Organic Method

Thus I delayed beginning formal reading six weeks or more for the slower children. I began with Sylvia Ashton Warner's organic method (Warner, 1963), using the children's own words. Each child searched for his own words on cards scattered on a table or the floor. He read them to the teacher independently and was then given a new word daily. He traced the word with his finger and said it five times. From these we made up experience stories, then parallel stories to introduce the words of the state basal series. In February the top group bypassed the repulsive pre-primers and went right into the primer. The middle group began with the pre-primers and the bottom group were taught games of memory, sequence, and language. By the end of the year, the top group was reading the first reader, the middle group a second series of third pre-primers, and the low group was just beginning the first pre-primer.

The September Metropolitan reading-readiness scores for this experimental class were almost five points lower than the control group (Fig. 32). The May scores of the Metropolitan Achievement Tests in Reading grade level was just two months ahead of the control group. On these children's second school year, they gained five months over the control group in reading. The control group's mean IQ on the Kuhlmann Anderson had risen from 82 in October to 87.8 in May, while the experimental mean IQ went from 88 in October to 103 in May. We had some rather

KUHLMANN ANDERSON
Mean Deviation IQ

	October '64	May '65	Mean grain:
Control:	82	87.8	5.8
Experimental:	88	103.0	15.0

METROPOLITAN READINESS Mean Scores:			METROPOLITAN ACHIEVEMENT Mean Grade Levels:			

| | October '64 | | May '65 | | May '66 | |
	Reading:	Arithmetic:	Reading:	Arith:	Reading:	Arith:
Control	53.6	13.5	1.3	1.3	1.7	2.1
Experimental	48.8	13.7	1.5	1.8	2.2	2.3

Figure 32. Experimental Study, 1964–66.

dramatic gains with certain children who had severe perceptual problems in September and were a year behind in mental age.

Visual-perceptual training certainly did *not* teach the children to read, but it positively did train skills needed for reading and for all other academic work. The children now had cognitive awareness and better control of themselves. The changes in behavior were striking. We had raised all of the children's basic abilities as measured by the Kuhlmann-Anderson, the Frostig Test, and the Winter Haven Perceptual Forms Test. The children were happy. They had not yet known frustration from inability to learn, and they were at least ready for first grade, half were ready for second grade. But the reading problem was still there, so the search for better reading methods continued. With a mean IQ of 103 now, lack of innate ability could not be an excuse for lack of reading skill. There had to be a method. The children had not failed, I had.

Language Approaches

In subsequent years, with my co-worker, Joan Fields, we tried a variety of other methods. After the children had learned about twenty words through the organic method, we taught the key words (basal words) at the rate of one a day. These were *I, can, like, the,* and *and.* We made up sentences using these words in conjunction with the children's own words, which were usually nouns and verbs. Thus, this was more of a language approach. Since the children could generate no more enthusiasm for *See Susan* than we could, we tried using the children's interests and their key words in high interest topics from *Flipper* and *Batman.* We copied coloring book pictures, made up texts of the basal words, and stapled these pages into books. The dialogue, using repetition of the basal words made *See Batman* as uninspiring as *See Susan.*

We also tried labeling techniques of matching words and pictures according to Frostig (1964). We worked on speech articulation and phonics with ideas from Louise Binder Scott's *Talking Time,* and materials from Houghton Mifflin's *Phonics R* and *Letter Sounds* programs. We also opaqued story pages onto a screen to focus the children's attention on the reading task.

Slingerland Techniques

Still the bottom group made no more progress and simply could not learn the letter sounds and could not do phonics seatwork. Since the top readers were learning the sounds well, we felt that the clue to teaching the problem children lay somewhere in the realm of letter-sound association and memory. We began visual-memory exercises which we found quiet successful, and will explain later in this chapter. We had to find a better way to teach the sounds! So we then tried Beth Slingerland's method of teaching the letter sound, name, and clue word along with repeatedly tracing over the letter, first on paper, then in the air. This method helped considerably. Now two thirds of the children learned all the letter sounds. Still, the better readers in the slower class had a limited total sight vocabulary of only about one hundred words by the end of the year.

In reading, these children would not stop to analyze a word but reverted instead to guessing. They knew the sounds but could not blend them into words. Guessing was the easy way out. The Slingerland method of analyzing a word sound-by-sound required deep concentration and attention of the class while one child performed. Our immature children were too distractable for this. However, the Slingerland method of retracing the very large letter and saying the sound did help with learning to discriminate the letters and especially with learning to write. The kinesthetic impulses set up by the large muscle movements contributed to their learning. Since we still incorporate these techniques into our writing program, we will go into more detail about this later.

On our state reading test, the Stanford Reading Test, the children would look at a picture, decide on its name and then mark the word that began and ended with the correct sounds. For example, on a picture intended to be labeled *cabin,* they marked *horse,* believing it was *house.* For a picture of a board breaking, the answer was *break;* they marked *bread* thinking it to be *board.* Thus they *were* using *some* consonant-sound clues and applying the skills which we had taught them. But with insufficient clues and the inability to analyze all the words, they were still guessing.

ENGELMANN-BRUNER TECHNIQUES

We still needed sound-blending and word analysis, and a better system of teaching that bottom, hard-core third of the class the sounds (some were still lacking up to twelve sounds by the end of the year). Into this gap strode the dynamic methods of Siegfried Engelmann and Elaine Bruner. Having sent to the University of Illinois Press for a book on kindergarten language training, as fate would have it we received instead a description of the new programmed reading methods as outlined by Elaine Bruner (1968). We were jubilant! Here, for the first time, was the reading task analyzed into its component skills. We had to learn how to teach these skills of blending and rhyming and letter-sound association! These were the deficits in our program!

Then Siegfried Engelmann came to our area for a workshop and a whole new approach to education was before us. His techniques gave us a dynamic method of keeping the interest of the very slowest learners while using specific methods of teaching sounds, rhyming, sequencing and blending. As the materials had not yet been published, we spent hours every week making up almost all the lessons ourselves using the sequence outline of Elaine Bruner. We had no aides to help, just two teachers for sixty children, fifteen children in a reading group.

The results were spectacular! Our school's reading scores had always been among the lowest in the district, along with those of the other schools in our compensatory area. Now, even on a very difficult state reading test (Stanford Reading Test), our children doubled the raw scores of the year before. They were excited about reading as they had never been! They were reading everything they could find! Every word was a challenge to them! Excited parents told us that the children read road signs, labels on cans, television ads, titles of books, and neon signs. We could not find enough library books for them. By the middle of their second-grade year, many of them were reading at a third-grade level. In May 1971 on The Cooperative Primary Test our mean reading-grade-level score for first grade was 2.1.

Our very lowest group of three handicapped children had learned all the sounds and could blend them into words. They could read very short stories of large print. They could blend the sounds to read a thousand words (by count). Their remaining problem was attention. Although they could read, they were still too distractable to stay with a story independently and read it through. They required considerable reinforcement for every concentrated effort. Their second year, we purchased the newly published Distar materials (Engelmann, 1969). These slowest children had regressed over the summer, and we had to take them back to about the middle of the Distar program. Still this was far ahead of where our slow children had been in previous years. The second year, their progress was steadier, more constant. So far, even our most pronounced visual and auditory perceptual problem children, are progressing with this method but simply at a slower rate than the others. It may take them two years to gain the fluency and skills of their classmates, but to date we have *no* failures, *no* nonreaders. In previous years children with the same initial symptoms as these, remained two to four years behind grade level in reading all through school.

A Total School Program

Experimentation with reading methods by many of our teachers finally evolved into a total school program. Now we start all our beginning readers, kindergarten, first, second, and educationally mentally retarded, in the published Distar program. The fastest first and second grade children go through the program quickly in about one hundred days. The lowest first grade group may reach day 100 of the 159-day program by the end of the year. The top kindergarteners finish the program while the very slowest kindergarten group reaches about the middle of the program by the end of the year.

When the children are reading quite well (day 130 on) we begin encouraging them to read simple library books such as the Beginner Reader Series. When a reading group finishes Distar Reading I, it is moved right into the Distar Reading II program. Distar II teaches the comprehension of the written language and zeros in on the child's ability to do convergent thinking and analysis of the reading material. We have been using the S.R.A. Linguistic Series in the second and third grades to tie the Distar programs into the state textbooks of the middle grades.

When the children have finished the Distar programs and the linguistic series, they can read almost all the words that they will ever encounter. The emphasis can now be put on expanding the children's language vocabularies to include the monstrous words which they can now decode. Now science and social studies can be explored to much greater depths than ever before.

We are able to adapt this program to the needs of all of our children. Our bright students learn faster than before. New children transferring to our school must be fitted into the program. Even top readers from other school programs must usually be started in our slower groups in order to learn the decoding skills. With quick children, it may take only two or three weeks to teach them the sounds they lack (usually the vowels) and the blending. They then may be transferred to a faster moving group. We keep the program flexible, moving children up or down levels according to their progress. We expect to have even more noticeable gains in reading in the future, since the Distar Language *and* the Reading are now being used in both kindergarten and first grade. These kindergarten programs will better prepare the children for greater progress in first grade.

Distar Reading

We feel that the careful programming of the reading skills in the Distar program in a step-by-step progression, demanding proficiency of the child in order to progress through the levels, has brought about a spectacular gain in the reading ability of our compensatory children. The Distar program teaches the basic reading skills in several strands. In one strand the child learns an auditory-motor sequence. The teacher performs a two-or-three-sequence clapping or slapping routine which the children imitate. She then tests them by changing the sequence of the routine. Lessons go into; WHAT DID WE DO FIRST? THEN WHAT DID WE DO? to synthesize the idea of sequence in time. Later the sequence is presented through pictures of children doing certain motions. We follow the arrow with the children on it from left to right and imitate what they are doing.

The second strand teaches the letter sounds. The Distar I program does not teach the letter names. Nor does it use an identifying word or picture as do most of the phonetic programs. The first visual and auditory discriminations are gross, between *m, a,* and *s,* an ice cream cone, and a Christmas tree. Each sound is repeated over and over many times every day until the child has instant recall of the sound when he is shown the letter. The children become very proficient. Difficult to discriminate sounds and letters, such as *b* and *p,* do not appear until the children are well along in reading. They are also taught *sh, ch, th, wh,* and *ing.* Both long and short vowels are taught, the diacritical marks are used on the long vowels. It has been our experience that after the children have learned the sounds of the small letters, the capitals and the letter names are learned incidentally, or are very easily taught in about two weeks.

Rhyming is taught through auditory-vocal association also, beginning with long words. *Hamburger* is rhymed with *sam-*

burger, mamburger, and *lamburger.* Then they rhyme smaller words such as *sam,* with *mam* and *ram,* until the children can rhyme with any word, given just the beginning sound with which to start.

The fourth strand is the blending taught by the teacher breaking words into syllables with a few second's pause between syllables. At first the teacher uses large words such as MOTOR . . . CYCLE. SAY IT FAST! The children say: "Motorcycle!" In just a week or two the children are able to blend three single sounds into words, (S . . . A . . . M . . . SAY IT FAST! SAM!) The next process is to teach the children to take words apart into their separate sounds, a say-it-slow process of pulling the word apart, elongating it, and then pushing the word together to SAY IT FAST! Thus they spell by sounds and say: "Man, Mmmmmaaannn! SAY IT FAST! MAN! They are first taught blending of sounds that can be held easily and that slide smoothly together such as *m, s, r, l, n.* The stop sounds (*t, d, c, h*) are taught first at the ends of words: "mmmaaat." Later they learn to quickly slide the beginning stop sounds: *heee* and *taaannnn.* Remember that all of this is done with an auditory-vocal process until the children are proficient.

The final strand introduced later when the aforementioned skills are solid is the word-sliding or word-reading, wherein all the previously well-learned skills are utilized to analyze a word. Thus the word, *sam,* appears on an arrow, left to right. The teacher points to the *s* and the children say it, stretching the sound out until she points to *a,* and then slides slowly on to the *m.* The process is repeated and the sounds are blended a little more quickly the second time. The teacher then says: SAY IT FAST! and the children say the whole word quickly. They become very excited with this process. They are delighted to show you how they can slide the sounds together to form words. They often become very exhuberant and are no doubt the noisiest and happiest reading groups in the school. Their enthusiasm is largely due to the elation they get from their independence and the feeling that they taught themselves. They are no longer dependent on the teacher to tell them if a word is right or wrong.

They know they are right! They know they are smart! They beam!

Silent letters (as on the end of the word *like*) are made very small for the first hundred encounters and then are increased in size gradually. Sight words are added to the program very slowly after the children have confidence in their abilities. At first they are taught to slide out the sight words as they are spelled and then the SAY IT FAST as it is locally pronounced. The sound-sliding exercises are often done with rhyming patterns, so that the children soon gain a sight recognition of these patterns such as *ake, am,* and *ill.* Since the children are exposed to three or four times the vocabulary of the basal series, they also learn the meaning and use of a larger language vocabulary. Thus although comprehension as such is not stressed in the Distar I program, the children are really receiving a richer base. The take-home stories are amusing with fat rats and kissing cows, accompanied by novel cartoon pictures. The lessons are interesting and fast-moving with but a few minutes spent on each strand daily.

The children have very few problems making the transition from the Distar stories to linguistic books. At first they may carefully slide out each word, but this soon passes and they gain visual memory of words, and become fluent readers. By about day 130 of Distar I, the children are excitedly reading library books.

ELEMENTS OF A SUCCESSFUL READING PROGRAM

From our experience, then, with all these different reading programs over the years and from the excitement and success of our children today, certain elements of a successful program become evident. First, a reading program must teach letter-sound association beginning with dissimilar letters and sounds. The program must include the main vowel sounds. Training must be auditory-vocal so that the child hears, says, and feels the sounds as he looks at the letter. There must be multiple repetition of each sound, reviewing and repeating all the previous sounds learned every day. The practice of having the child MARK THE PICTURE THAT STARTS WITH . . . should be recognized as an uneconomical task. It does not teach the child letter-sound association or blending of sounds into words. The Distar method of practice on sounds for about two to five minutes a day, every day, all year, provides the repetition and reinforcement required by children with learning problems. There should be a programmed sequence to the teaching of blends, digraphs, and word endings, so that there is a step-by-step progression and no learning is incidental.

The next most important skill which children must be specifically taught is the blending of sounds into words. This the Distar program does better than any other at present. From the onset the teacher must never tell a child a word and the children should never be allowed to guess words. They must learn to rely on their decoding skills.

Today's children are conditioned by modern television to passive participation and little mental exercise and do not receive the challenge to their conceptual abilities at home. The old home customs of reading to children and playing games of skill with them was much better training of cognitive skills. The children were challenged by things that had to be thought out. Now they would just rather not bother thinking at all. Thus, one of our most important tasks in the schools is to teach children to concentrate and to think. When they rely on word memory and configuration and picture and context clues for reading, they are taking the passive route. Word analysis calls for convergent thinking and takes more effort, more concentration. Our poorest readers tend to guess rather than make the mental effort to sound out a word. When they stop guessing and sound words consistently, they begin to progress quickly and we are able to move them up to faster groups. Children make rapid progress in a concentrated decoding program. However, if they return to classroom reading of basal series and guessing, they fail to make further progress and often regress. Thus our special reading teachers in California have found that they must keep a child in a good decoding program until he has learned all the skills of the total program and can read everything. Only then will he be able to return to classroom reading and succeed there, too. This is a real eye-opener to the fact that our classroom teachers are actually failing to teach. They are simply dragging the children through those basal series without teaching the skills essential to reading.

Reading Texts

The reading program's stories or books must be linguistic (containing phonetic words) so that sight words are avoided as much as possible and the guessing is eliminated. The first stories need not be meaningful. The children are so engrossed in decoding the words that they don't mind or care that the stories are tongue twisters and nonsense. They know that they are reading and they feel successful. This is enough for them! At this stage, they don't have to be reading stories that make a great deal of sense.

The first two books of the S.R.A. and Merrill linguistic series are such tongue twisters, but still the children enjoy the challenge of being able to read through them. However, since the stories are nonsensical, these books can become dull. Therein lies the danger. These books should be read quickly and for fun, with all the sounds and sound-blending skills having been taught before the child begins to read the book. If a group reads five to seven pages a session, the children enjoy these books and gain confidence in themselves and in their abilities. If, on the contrary, the pages and stories are frequently repeated, and progress is slow and the children come to hate it as a millstone about their necks. Reading *Pig Can Jig* again becomes a punishment, a sentence for having failed.

If a child is struggling with the first books of the S.R.A. series, it may be due to the small tight print rather than inability to decode the words. Try a larger-print book, such as Merrill, before you judge his reading ability. Books for visually handicapped children are excellent for problem learners. Children with problems in convergence, binocular coordination, subnormal vision, ocular motility, or ambliopia (lazy eye) read more easily with larger print. Some children with eye problems who are not usually in a program for the visually handicapped and often, in our experience, not even under ocular care must strain so hard to see the print that they are unable to blend words, follow a line of print, or read smoothly. Or they might not know what they have read after they have finished the arduous process. In some cases, the latter has occurred because the ocular muscles were under too great a strain. Thus even though the child supposedly has normal vision or better, he may still need larger print. Children demonstrating eyestrain in reading, or difficulty tracking or following a line of print, should be referred to special optometrists who have been specifically trained to aid children with learning problems.

If textbooks have very small print, sometimes a copy of the text with a large-print primary typewriter helps. Textbooks should be printed with the similar letters different in some way. The *d* could be taller and more football-shaped with a slightly longer *stick* even protruding slightly below the bottom line. The *t* would be more easily distinguishable from the *f* if it did not have the lower curve, but were entirely straight as in the Distar program. The capital *I* should never be simply a straight line. This is too confusing for them as it resembles *l*.

If a child cannot read the first linguistic books easily, then go back to the basic skills, direct teaching with auditory-vocal methods and short fun stories which you may have dittoed yourself.

Remedial Reading

The Distar program provides a firm base for reading words. This program is used with older children by starting with the first days' basic skills, but by progressing much more rapidly through the material, especially with the addition of sounds. The program is designed for children who know no sounds at all, and these older remedial children often know at least ten or twelve of the sounds. Elaine Bruner says that all concepts in this program are taught with the *rule of three,* repeating each new concept at least three days. Thus for eight- or nine-year-olds who already know some sounds, after the first lessons, you might skip and do only every third day's lesson, according to the progress of the children. They should instantly recognize all the old sounds, except perhaps for the last one introduced before a new-sound lesson is attempted. Thus it is much more profitable to use the Distar program with six- to ten-year-old nonreaders, rather than drag them through linguistic books for which they lack the decoding skills. After they have finished the Distar program, they will be able to read these books easily.

In the third books of these linguistic series, the vocabularies have been increased to such an extent that the stories are more real and the children see their meaning and enjoy them. By this time they are reading fluently and quickly. Comprehension and meaning of the written word is better taught through workbook-type exercises and a good strong language program. Since this is an area which has been neglected by our schools, we will go into this more in Chapter Eleven.

Reading Instruction

The reading lesson should be fast moving and interesting. Using unison responses involves all the children and they reinforce each other and get more repetition. Whether teaching sounds, words, or reading sentences, have the children first respond in unison, then individually. The first is teaching and practice, the latter is testing. For example, you are flashing words for visual memory and speed. First see: WHO CAN SAY IT FIRST? and the whole group gets into the act. If one child is responding particularly well while the others lack interest, say: JIMMY IS FAST! WHO CAN BEAT JIMMY? The second time through the same group of words, call on individuals to respond. I'M GOING TO SEE IF I CAN CATCH SOMEONE! or I AM GOING TO SEE HOW SMART YOU ARE NOW!

Unison reading of stories is excellent practice. This is actually practice in the *neurological impress* method. In unison reading, all the children are working; all learning. No one is sitting it out, waiting for his turn. Nonparticipating is not permitted. Every child must attend and participate every minute of the instruction. The teacher may first read right along with the children, pulling their reading along, keeping a rhythm going. She might beat a steady rhythm by slapping her thigh or the table, or by tapping her foot. Then they reread the sentence or passage in unison while she just beats out the rhythm to keep them together. If one child tends to race ahead of the others, to beat them, tap the rhythm on his thigh or arm while he is reading.

When reading individually, have each child read just one or two lines moving quickly around the group. Each child must keep his finger on the word being read. With immature children who have difficulty attending, use cereal rewards for children who have a finger on the word. This will help to keep them all on task. When a child is reading independently do not allow the children to supply a word on which he hesitates. TOMMY CAN FIGURE IT OUT HIMSELF. HE'S SMART! YOU DON'T WANT HIM TO TAKE YOUR TURN AWAY FROM YOU! or IT IS NICE TO HAVE YOUR OWN TURN, ISN'T IT?

Reading should be fun, exciting, rewarding to both teacher and children. If it isn't, something is wrong with the method or techniques used. Don't overlearn a book or story or reading will become dull drudgery. If the child finishes a book and is not ready for the next level, find another book at the *same* reading level.

In the reading group keep the children on task! Teach! Don't socialize! Make every minute count! WE ARE WORKING HARD! Don't let the children get in over their heads. Be sure they are at an instructional level, achieving successfully, or they are not learning at all. Don't go on to the new skill until they have learned the old thoroughly. Teach in unison, but test individually before you go on. Children must be continually reinforced that they are smart and are doing well.

Leisure Reading

When children are reading well, we encourage them to do as much outside reading as possible. The first Distar "take homes" we send home daily. Then, about day 40, when the stories begin, we save them daily and staple them together into weekly books. We designate each reading group's books by color—green group, green books. At the end of the week, we staple each child's pages together into a construction paper book, along with a note that says: . . . HAS READ DAYS . . . (40–50) TO ME . . . TIMES. The teacher fills in the child's name and the correct *day* numbers. The parents or older siblings fill in the number of *times,* sign it and return it to school. The child gets a treat and a star on a chart for each book that he has read and for which he has a book note. We have noticed marked progress in visual memory of words in children who read to their parents frequently. Some parents are wonderful and make sure that their children read the books often. Other parents are apathetic and rarely find time to have their children read to them. So we had to jog these parents to return book notes. We will not let a new book go home until the child has returned all but the last book note. Thus when a note is not forthcoming, we have a second message we send home: . . . IS . . . BOOKS BEHIND HIS READING GROUP. PLEASE LISTEN TO HIM READ DAYS . . . TO YOU AND RETURN THE BOOK NOTE TO SCHOOL. We will fill in the *day* numbers to designate the missing book. The word *behind* sends the parents into action. Thus few children *get behind.*

We scrounge for easy-reading pleasure books such as the *Just Beginning to Read* books and the *Beginner Books* series. We keep these on a special shelf and check them out to children daily from about February on. The child takes a book note home with each library book for the same reward procedure as above. State supplied basal readers might also be used as library books, after the children have finished Distar I. Some children become avid readers with a book a day and are reading at third-grade level by the end of the year.

GROUPING FOR READING

An essential element of a good reading program is the small reading group of from six to ten children for a half-hour session. Beyond this number the teacher is unable to keep a clear understanding of each child's skills and give enough individual practice and attention. The top groups should be the largest. Slow-moving groups with children who have more problems should be kept as small as possible. Unless there are a number of reading groups at different levels, children are not adequately placed according to their ability and their skill levels.

Each reading group deserves the teacher's full attention. Preferably, there will be no other children in the room who need supervision at this time. Although many teachers of reading advocate various types of seatwork to keep the rest of the class occupied, we have never found this successful or reasonable with immature children. To us, all that seatwork is, is *busywork*, or as Engelmann so aptly puts it, *slop-time*. Nothing is learned unless the children are attending to the reading group that is in session. The teacher is too often distracted from her instruction when there are other children present.

Three teachers of first and second grade classes have solved the problem by their own version of team teaching. We are very pleased by the results after three years. In September we test every child for his knowledge of the sounds and ability to read, and make out a card on his reading level. These we sort into about eight groups according to the levels and the number of teachers and aides we have. Each group is designated by a color. We use lengths of colored plastic surveyor's ribbon, tied around the children's waists the first week of the program to identify the different groups. Thus we can easily check to see if the children are in the right places. Each reading teacher has a list of the children to be in her group. Each classroom teacher has a total list of all the children in all the groups.

One teacher, who is exceptional in social studies and has had training in the Taba techniques, heads our social studies and science program. She teaches about forty to sixty children the first half hour (Fig. 33). The other two teachers take reading groups in the empty rooms. The second half-hour period I take a large group of children (forty to sixty) out to physical eudcation,

FIRST PERIOD: 30 minutes	SOCIAL STUDIES Groups 3, 4, 5	READING Group 1	READING Group 2
SECOND PERIOD: 30 minutes	PHYSICAL EDUCATION Groups 1, 2, 5	READING Group 3	READING Group 4
THIRD PERIOD: 30 minutes	PHYSICAL EDUCATION Groups 3, 4	SOCIAL STUDIES Groups 1, 2	READING Group 5

(For smaller reading groups add aides, reading teachers, and other school personnel to the schedule.)

Figure 33. Team-Teaching Schedule.

while the other two teachers have reading groups. The third half-hour, I take a second group to physical education (those who were in reading during the previous session). One teacher takes a second group into social studies, and the remaining teacher takes another reading group. The two social studies groups are coordinated or taught by the same teacher.

With this cooperative program, we are able to have much more flexibility in the grouping of children into reading levels. In this way, also, the child is more accurately placed at his own level and this alone enhances his chances of learning. Occasionally, we even take second graders or EMR's from other classrooms into our reading groups when these children can better receive instruction at these levels.

We keep one group as the low-low one, continually shuffling the slower readers down. Thus, one slower child does not drag a faster group down. Conversely, the top two of the lower groups are often given a boost into a higher group to be certain that they are progressing at their own rates.

During each reading session the teacher's complete attention is on the group she is teaching, and thus the children receive the full benefit of her skill. The children do not have to be bored with piles of tedious busywork. By the end of the hour and a half, the children have had excellent training in reading, social studies, science, and physical education. Not a minute has been wasted.

Our two remedial reading teachers each take a reading group, as does our teacher of the visually handicapped, who must work with our children who are registered in his V.H. program. When we have compensatory money, we have paid aides who take extra reading groups, giving us more levels and keeping the number of children per group small. Thus we may have eight or nine first grade reading groups instead of the usual three. We also have high school aides who come daily at specific periods to help us group social studies children into story and discussion groups, and into physical education skill groups. They receive a grade for their work and have been a tremendous help to us.

Some schools that operate a team-teaching approach also use

their school psychologists, vice-principals, and speech therapists to take reading groups. Some high school and college students and parents are trained in the methods desired, and they also instruct reading groups. Possibilities for grouping are only as limited as your determination.

When untrained personnel, such as students and parents and paid aides, are teaching reading groups, we find it best to alternate teachers to keep careful control of the instruction. Thus if an aide teaches a group at one reading session, she switches groups so that a certificated teacher has them the next session.

EVALUATING THE READING PROGRAM

Evaluation of reading progress is most difficult because there is actually no adequate standardized reading test available. We need a good diagnostic test which will measure the children's skill and mastery of the code (letter-sound association and blending), and will also test word recognition and finally comprehension. It is also important that the mechanics of the test are not the cause nor the occasion of errors on the test. On the Stanford Reading Test it is very difficult for the children to follow the lines of minute print and to figure out which answer boxes are to be used. They can hardly see the tiny red print identifying the boxes. Thus the test directions must be simple, easy to follow, and the print large and clear. The comprehension should be at six to eight year levels. Hopefully, someone will author such a sound diagnostic reading test in the near future.

The Distar II program begins with a simple word-reading test which is individually administered in September and which indicates and provides any recycling necessary before the child is ready for Distar II.

As mentioned before, we also use the WRAT test on children finishing the program, or at certain stages of our program. We feel that testing at the end of a program gives us a good indication of the effectiveness of our program. We can use these scores to evaluate and compare individual child progress.

Our present state first grade reading test, the Cooperative Primary, has sharp print and clear mechanics, but measures divergent thinking more than reading and decoding. Even our teachers had difficulty determining the correct answers for the test. Since the choice of answers is only one of three, the chance factor is high. For example, a nonreader may score 1.8, and a good reader only 1.3. Thus individual children's scores are invalid. This end-of-year state testing gives us only a very general measure and average or mean of total scores of all children in our school as compared to other schools. It does not measure the children's progress. The first year that we used Distar, our mean raw score on the state test was double that of the previous years! It was difficult to compare the mean scores from our second year Distar program because the state test changed; however, the mean grade levels between the two tests were just a month different.

Our teachers don't need a standardized test score to tell them that our children are making excellent progress. We see it in their amazing ability to read much more difficult texts than our children were ever able to read in previous years. Another measure of increased ability is evident in their avid reading of library books. We have had to double our purchase of books and still don't have enough to fill the need. Our librarian is amazed at the high level of the books our second and third graders read. Teachers have had to back their children in their choices of books, and convince the librarian that the child is capable of reading his choice.

Our parents are very enthusiastic about our program. They are impressed with the eagerness of their children to read everything. The only parental complaint we have is that we did not have this program years ago when their other children started school! Many of our primary children outshine their older siblings in reading.

We are often asked about the value of teaching our brightest children with this method since they learn easily with other methods. Our answer now is the story of Michelle and Michael, who are siblings from a middle-class home. Michelle, the elder and the typical mature girl, attended our school and easily learned to read through the sight method. She has been in the top reading group all five years of her schooling. Everything has been easy for her. Then along came little brother, two years behind her. He was a typical immature boy, poorly coordinated, inattentive, with visual-perceptual and visual-motor problems. He plugged along in one of our lower Distar reading groups. In second grade he "took off," finishing Distar and the linguistic series soon after. Now, in third grade, Michael can read anything. Fifth-grade Michelle is still in all the top groups, but she relies on context clues and pictures to decode new words. So to add insult to injury, while she is struggling to figure out a new word, along comes that pesky little brother with "Oh that's . . . .", and beats big sister.

VISUAL-MEMORY TRAINING

After children have learned to blend sounds into words and have had many exposures to a large vocabulary, visual memory of those words should be trained. This can be done first with a variety of subjects or pictures, and with the use of several different audiovisual machines. Visual-memory training can be started with just the basic shapes, with letters, with simple outline pictures, or with arrows, or tic-tac-toe exercises. In the latter, the child must recall the position of the ○'s or ✕'s. It is best to start with the flashing of at least one of these types of objects before beginning word-flashing. Remember that we must always work from the simple to the more complex.

Flashing can be done very simply by having the subjects on cards to flash quickly before the children. Or put these same cards in an opaque projector. Flash them on a screen by opening and closing the lens cap quickly. Or put the subjects on acetate and use the overhead projector, turning the switch on and off again quickly. Filmstrip on which things can be drawn, written, or typed is now available (*U Film,* 1968). Coloring every other frame with black flow pen enables you to turn to the desired frame and then quickly on to the darkened frame. Or turn to the desired frame and prop against the lens a book which can be removed and replaced quickly.

Timed speed does not appear to be as important as the

flashing itself and the immediate closing of the eyes to retain an image on the retina. Have the children look at a diamond of red paper, then close their eyes to see the retinal image of the diamond. You might do this several times with different bright shapes. Be in front of the class so that you can see which children are unable to close their eyes. Some children have great difficulty doing so. You might have to hold your hands over a child's eyes, or have him hold his eyelids closed with his fingers.

Most children are unaware of their ability to hold a visual memory of an object or picture. Tell them: YOUR EYES ARE LIKE A CAMERA. TAKE A PICTURE WITH YOUR EYES. CLOSE THEM TIGHTLY. SEE THE PICTURE IN YOUR HEAD? The child will remember best the object which he last saw before closing his eyes. If he looks around at something else after the flashing, your face for example, he loses the image. Try it yourself and you will see how this works. Look at one object, then a second. Close your eyes and see which image is on the retina. It will always be the last one.

Cut ditto masters of the different sets of subjects which you flash. Each child then has a ditto on which he identifies the subject flashed. If you wish to flash letters, make a ditto of nine to twelve letters widely spaced in three rows (Fig. 34). Or have a ditto of nine different shapes or pictures. Each child then needs a copy of the ditto, and a dark crayon. When using audio-visual equipment, darken the front of the room, but leave the curtains open a few feet in the back of the room so that the children will be able to see the items on the ditto easily.

Have the crayon (or pencil) placed away from the child's hand, either on the floor at his side or in a groove at the top of his desk. He must not be holding it in his hand or he will be too tempted to use it before he has closed his eyes.

The lesson might go like this: CRAYONS ON THE FLOOR. EYES ON THE BOARD. ONE, TWO, THREE! Flash the subject. CLOSE YOUR EYES! SEE IT IN YOUR HEAD! NOW OPEN YOUR EYES, FIND IT ON YOUR PAPER AND PUT A BOX AROUND IT. PUT YOUR HAND OVER IT SO NO ONE SEES WHAT YOU MARKED.

Check to see who was unable to identify the correct object. Reassure these children that it is all right if they didn't. Tell

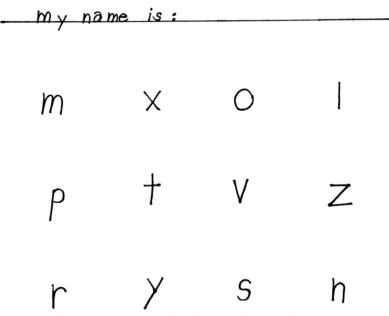

Figure 34. Letters for Visual-Memory Flashing Exercises.

them that you will flash it again, that they are not to copy some-
one else's. I WANT YOU TO LEARN TO TAKE A PICTURE IN YOUR OWN
HEAD. YOU CAN DO IT. I WILL HELP YOU. I WILL FLASH EACH PICTURE
THREE TIMES OVER FOR YOU. NOW THIS IS THE SECOND TIME. I'M
FLASHING IT FOR TOMMY, MIKE, AND SUSAN, SO THEY CAN FIND IT ON
THEIR PAPER. THE REST OF YOU CAN SEE IF YOU HAVE IT RIGHT.
Repeat the flashing.

Check to be sure that your children having problems are closing
their eyes. This is their most common error and their reason for
lack of retention of the visual image. They just don't close their
eyes to see it. This may be why these children can look at things
without learning. Their perceptions are unstable and they have
no memory of them. This is a debilitating handicap. You must
teach the child to overcome it.

If a child still does not identify the object after three exposures,
uncover the subject completely and help him find it and mark
it. Help this child in subsequent flashings by placing him near

you and physically covering his eyes after each flashing as necessary.

When you first begin these exercises with problem first graders, it is not easy for them. They will need much reassurance and repeated practice. Use visual flashing exercises about twice a week, beginning in the spring after training in visual perception. It might seem hectic at first with so many children having difficulty (sometimes as many as six or seven children are unable to identify the first flashing). After only a few days practice you might have just one or two still erring. With practice, they will all soon be making the correct responses after only one flashing. When the shapes, arrows, and letters are easily identified on the first flashing, go on to flashing words which they have learned.

A little more complex flashing exercise is to flash a tic-tac-toe graph (Fig. 35) with three ◯'s or three ✕'s. Begin with a definite order such as three circles in a row, perhaps vertical, then horizontal, then diagonal, then in three corners, then in more random placements. Then use three ✕'s in the same manner. A more complex exercise would be using two ◯'s and two ✕'s in the same graph. Put only about nine graphs on a ditto and number them. The flashing of six separate figures may be enough for one session. The children see the graph flashed, close their eyes, and then draw in the ✕'s or ◯'s in the proper spaces on their dittoed graphs. After flashing circles and the children have closed their eyes, you might say: OPEN YOUR EYES AND DRAW THE CIRCLES IN NUMBER . . . . If children err, have them erase what they have done, and flash the image again.

This visual-imagery skill can be taught right in the reading group to enhance the children's recognition of difficult words. For example, there is a sight word or a word which a child has to carefully blend each time he sees it. You want him to obtain a visual memory of that word. LET'S ALL TAKE A GOOD PICTURE OF THAT WORD. EYES ON THE WORD. CLOSE YOUR EYES. SEE IT IN YOUR HEAD. WHAT IS IT? OPEN YOUR EYES AND LOOK AT IT AGAIN. CLOSE YOUR EYES AND SEE IT IN YOUR HEAD AGAIN. WHAT IS IT? NOW SEE IF YOU WILL KNOW IT FAST THE NEXT TIME YOU SEE IT. A minute later, return to the same word to see how fast they can say it. Call

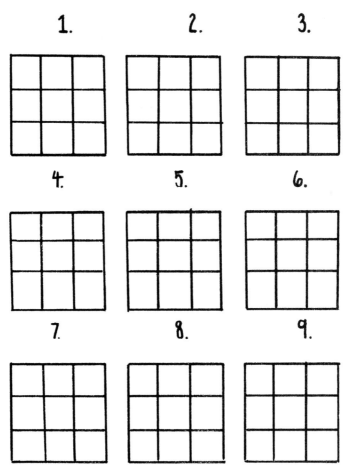

Figure 35. Graphs for Flashing *X's* and *O's*.

their attention to this word each time they encounter it. TOMMY SAID THAT WORD FAST! HE TOOK A GOOD PICTURE OF IT! For children who still err the next day or so, repeat the picture-taking. The next time the word comes up in a lesson, have a race with the children. THIS WORD I AM HIDING IS THE WORD WE TOOK A PICTURE OF YESTERDAY. LET'S HAVE A RACE TO SEE WHO CAN SAY IT FIRST. Uncover it and give a treat to the child who says it first . . . TOMMY BEAT US AGAIN! BUT SUSAN WAS PRETTY FAST, TOO! I'LL BET SHE WILL BEAT US NEXT TIME!

TRAINING IN VISUAL-MOTOR CONTROL

Before the child is ready to learn the intricacies of writing between lines, he needs training in visual-motor control. He gets much of this through puzzles and the Montessori-type materials (Chapter Six), the template training, pegboards (Chapter Seven), ball and beanbag skills (Chapter Eight), and art projects. Drawing, cutting, and pasting are excellent activities for training the various coordinations needed for writing.

Teaching Cutting

The first week of school would be a good time for the first cutting lesson, the object of which is to teach the handling of scissors. The easiest material to learn to cut is plasticine clay. Have the children pat it out into flat cakes and cut at will. Demonstrate how to hold the clay with one hand with the thumb on top, and the scissors with the other hand. The thumb is in the top hole, two fingers under the lower blade and two in the bottom hole. The tips of the fingers curl around the scissors. Children often extend their fingers and therefore don't have control. Show how the scissors must be held so that the blades are in a vertical position to each other. Let them try cutting with the scissors held at an angle to see the difference. Show how they are not to cut just with the tips or points of the scissors, but that the best cutting edge is far inside. In controlled cutting, the scissors never close all the way to the points. Thus the children must open the scissors up wide in order to get the clay into the inside part. Talk about squeezing firmly to make the scissors cut.

The second cutting exercise would be with a heavy paper such as tagboard. This puts up more resistance to the scissors so that the children can better learn the correct holding and cutting positions. The project could just be to fringe the tagboard all the way around, or on just two sides. Demonstrate with your large teachers' shears, holding the paper in a downward position so that the children can see the direction the scissors are pointing. SEE HOW I HOLD THE SCISSORS STRAIGHT UP AND DOWN. I HOLD THE PAPER IN MY OTHER HAND WITH MY THUMB ON TOP. I PUT THE PAPER WAY INSIDE THE SCISSORS AND POINT THE SCISSORS WHERE I

WANT TO CUT. WATCH! IF I POINT THE SCISSORS TO THE RIGHT, THEY CUT TO THE RIGHT. Exaggerate the position. IF I POINT THE SCISSORS TO THE LEFT, THEY CUT TO THE LEFT! IF I POINT THE SCISSORS STRAIGHT AHEAD, THEY CUT STRAIGHT AHEAD. NOW WATCH HOW I POINT THE SCISSORS STRAIGHT AHEAD AND SQUEEZE THE SCISSORS. OPEN THEM UP AND SQUEEZE, OPEN THEM UP AGAIN AND SQUEEZE AGAIN. SEE HOW WIDE I OPENED THE SCISSORS EACH TIME BEFORE I SQUEEZED THEM? NOW I WILL DO IT AGAIN, AND SEE IF I CAN MAKE ANOTHER STRAIGHT CUT JUST A FINGER SIZE AWAY FROM THE LAST CUT. I WILL POINT THE SCISSORS STRAIGHT DOWN. IF I POINT THEM SIDEWAYS, LOOK WHAT HAPPENS? Cut off a strip of fringe. NOW I KEEP CUTTING STRAIGHT DOWN AND I CAN MAKE A FRINGE ON BOTH ENDS OF THE PAPER.

Do the demonstrating very close to the children so that they can see your every move. While you are demonstrating, you must have their full attention. They should have nothing in their hands. Ask questions to solidify the instructions: HOW DO I HOLD THE SCISSORS? DO I HOLD THEM SIDEWAYS? USE YOUR FINGERS LIKE SCISSORS TO SHOW ME. WHAT HAPPENS IF YOU HOLD THE SCISSORS SIDEWAYS, LIKE THIS? HOW FAR DO YOU OPEN UP THE SCISSORS TO CUT? SHOW ME. SHOW ME HOW TO POINT THE SCISSORS TO CUT OVER THIS WAY. NOW THIS OTHER WAY. NOW STRAIGHT AHEAD. Hand out the scissors and paper. Help children as needed with your hand on top of theirs.

Try construction paper now. A simple ditto of a house with thick straight sides would be a good subject. Perhaps let them color and decorate it themselves to their own tastes first. Demonstrate how to point the scissors right on top of the line in order to cut in that direction. Show them how, when they get to a corner, the holding hand has to shift the paper and they have to re-aim the scissors. Demonstrate thoroughly; ask questions for feedback on their comprehension of the task. From this exercise go to curved shapes with broad lines which they may cut out. Designate which line to cut either with very broad lines or with a double line.

Now go to the free cutting of shapes. Halloween is a good time to integrate their learning on form perception and their cutting.

Make an oval (pumpkin) out of a rectangle (paper). A cat is easily made by folding a 9″ x 12″ piece of construction paper in half, across the width. Then cut a half circle out of the middle of the open side. That makes the opening between the cat's legs. The paper removed becomes the head of the cat and is pasted up on one of the top folded corners. A Japanese lantern is a good cutting exercise, too. Use inexpensive newsprint to teach free cutting of folded Christmas trees, hearts, and bells. Then go to the more expensive construction paper. Poster paper is a medium-weight paper which is easier for young children to cut than construction. The latter tears too easily.

In demonstrating each cutting activity, be very sure that you emphasize the spatial concepts and clarify each word of your vocabulary. I HOLD THE FOLDED SIDE IN MY LEFT HAND. IS THIS THE FOLDED SIDE? OR IS THIS? AM I DOING IT RIGHT NOW? WHAT IS WRONG?

Chalkboard Routines

The use of the chalkboard is one of the best training devices for use with children with learning problems. Here they come to grips with the midline problem, learn eye-hand control, develop peripheral vision and full smooth arm movements. The child receives many more stimuli—auditory, visual, tactile, and kines-thetic—from the rubbing of the chalk across the board than from paper, pencil, crayon, or paints. Since his work can be easily erased and changed, the child feels less stress with his perform-ance. Also, the standing position is more comfortable, more natural for him than a chair or desk. Finally, at the chalkboard he is able to see the results of such larger movements of his arms. The chalk leaves a trace in space of the actions he per-formed in time. Thus he can move his arms vertically, horizon-tally, or in a circle and actually see the results of his movements. This is vitally important to the child who is unaware of what his limbs are doing.

Experimentation

It is important for the child to be able to experiment freely at the chalkboard. The one-half inch jumbo chalk is preferable for all chalkboard work. The child should be allowed and encouraged to draw and write on the board. Let every child have at least one turn drawing freely at the board before starting the more formal chalkboard patterns. If the child's first tracings at the board are small and cramped, show him how he can use big, flowing arm movements in a large scribble. Children can draw to music, one time a smooth, flowing tune, and another a sharp staccato. Observe the differences in the tracings. The child might like to sing or hum his own tune, and draw to that rhythm.

Circles

Have the child make large and small circles on the board. Kephart (Radler and Kephart, 1960) says not to hold a child's hand to show him how, but if his circle is too flattened, to make a wide circle with the side of the chalk and have the child trace it. He also suggests that the child with the midline problem stand to the side of his tracings, away from his preferred hand, until he has learned to make the circles. Later, move the child over until he is working directly in front of his body and must cross the midline to make a large circle. To keep him from moving side-to-side as he draws a large circle, make an X on the floor on which he must stand to perform all the chalkboard routines. Have him draw large and small circles, experimenting with the use of either hand, and both hands together.

Racetracks

The child touches his nose to the chalkboard and makes an X on that spot for a target. He then uses large chalk in each hand to make two circles at the same time. He continues tracing around on his initial circles, JUST LIKE CARS GOING AROUND AND AROUND A RACETRACK. He must keep his eyes on his target, and learn to use his peripheral vision to keep the chalks on the *tracks.* He then steps back and judges his own work. So as not to discourage him with the first effort, be concerned only that he sees one element that needs work. First he needs the bilateral control. ARE THE RACE TRACKS EMPTY IN THE MIDDLE LIKE HOLES IN DOUGHNUTS? THIS TIME, KEEP YOUR EYES ON YOUR TARGET, BUT WATCH CAREFULLY OUT OF THE CORNERS OF YOUR EYES TO SEE

THAT YOUR CHALK STAYS ON THE TRACK.

As the child works say: KEEP YOUR EYES ON YOUR TARGET. Gently run your fingers up and down on the lateral sides of his eyes. WATCH YOUR HANDS OUT OF THE CORNERS OF YOUR EYES. When he has learned some control, then you can have him judge his tracing according to other elements: ARE BOTH RACETRACKS ABOUT THE SAME SIZE? ARE THEY CIRCLES OR OVALS? ARE THEY BOTH JUST AS HIGH ON THE BOARD? If the circles are too big: FEEL YOUR SHOULDERS RIGHT HERE. Have him touch his shoulders with his hands. CAN YOU MAKE YOUR RACETRACKS AGAIN IN FRONT OF YOUR SHOULDERS?

When these skills are accomplished, try changing direction. CAN YOU STOP, AND GO THE OTHER WAY WHEN I SAY "STOP"? STOP! REVERSE! GOOD! After reversing several times: SEE HOW YOUR HANDS ARE GOING IN TOWARD YOUR BODY. REVERSE! NOW THEY ARE GOING OUT AND AWAY FROM YOUR BODY. Still later: NOW CAN YOU START AT THE TOPS OF YOUR RACETRACKS AND MAKE BOTH HANDS GO TO THE RIGHT, TOWARD JERRY OVER HERE ON YOUR RIGHT? Use your hands to give his hands a little push and keep him from choosing the wrong direction. Help him get started, and then leave him alone to experiment to see if he can control his hands to go all the directions at will. When he can stay on the tracks, reverse, and go in and out, right and left, then this is really an accomplishment. He now has good eye-hand control and is ready to learn to write. Make a big deal out of this accomplishment and have a special reward for each child when he has achieved it. These routines can be taught to all first grade children, as well as kindergarteners, and second graders. When the child has successfully accomplished this task, then the chalkboard exercises are no longer necessary and the child is free to go to other activities.

Other Chalkboard Routines

There are several other routines which can be used intermittently with the racetracks to keep the activity interesting and stimulating. A number may be found in Getman (1964), Kephart (1960), and Radler and Kephart (1960). These include vertical lines which the children make like fence posts, horizontal lines like two fathers mowing their lawns, one single circle made with both hands together, and lazy eight (Fig. 36). The children especially like the latter. While they are doing it, emphasize the movement which crosses the midline by saying: DOWN THE HILL, DOWN THE HILL. NOW REVERSE, GO THE OTHER WAY. UP THE HILL, UP THE HILL. This seems to help them to continue the pattern instead of being distracted to the other intersecting line.

You can also teach the children to make different kinds of lines and shapes on demand. MAKE A SHORT, VERTICAL LINE; A LONG HORIZONTAL LINE; A WAVY, VERTICAL LINE; A SMALL CIRCLE WITH THE LEFT HAND; A DIAGONAL LINE FROM TOP RIGHT TO BOTTOM LEFT. The child with more severe problems can be taught to make straight lines between two X's placed in different positions. Children enjoy the dot game (Radler, 1960, Getman, 1964, and Kephart, 1960). This game helps to teach the child *stopping*. You simply make a dot on the board on which the child places

Figure 36. Lazy Eight.

his chalk. Then make another dot and the child must take his chalk directly to it and stop. Teach him to use his eyes and look at the new dot before he moves the chalk. If he has trouble stopping at the dot, use an eraser just above the dot to help him stop. Use short lines at first. Later use longer lines and quicken the pace.

Clock Game

The clock game (Kephart, 1960) contributes to eye-hand control and peripheral vision. It consists of a somewhat clocklike arrangement of numerals on the board with a large dot for the center. The child is instructed to move his two chalks simultaneously to and from specific numerals. Some movements are toward the center, some away from the center, and some are parallel movements.

Pattern Cards

After the children have learned some bilateral coordinations with the *racetracks,* introduce pattern cards. Klasen's (1969) training with them is excellent. The program includes a paperback book of background information on sensorimotor training (especially bilateral) and instructions for using the forty pattern cards included. These latter are intriguing designs which the child can make on the chalkboard with the simultaneous use of two pieces of chalk as with the *racetracks.* The patterns include sixteen with round movements derived from the movements of the arms in clockwise and counterclockwise directions, sixteen with angular movements, and eight with left-to-right movement of both hands in unison. The children enjoy reproducing these designs when they are presented to them in the sequence of increasing degrees of difficulty. The designs are not to be rigidly followed; in fact, the children enjoy making up their own variations.

WRITING

It is a mistake in teaching writing to first graders to begin with making letters that are too small and thus lack spatial direction and placement. The greatest waste of time in our schools is that given to overabundant copying of material which the teacher has written on the blackboard. The child looks back and forth from the board to his paper, trying to shrink what he sees in his distant vision into the correct size and place it on his paper with his near convergence. He is unable to keep his place as his eyes dart up and down, so the words and sentences all run together. Being so involved in the copying, he errs in the formation of the letters, placement, and spacing. For children with any visual-acuity or perceptual problems, the board-to-paper copying is an impossible task. Yet they are forced to try to do it and thus are forced to fail. What a way to keep children from learning! Worse yet, they are given this task first thing in the morning and this ruins their whole day because their opinions of their own abilities are so crushed.

In board-to-paper copying, the child actually reinforces and learns his errors so thoroughly that it is then more difficult to teach him correct letter formation and smooth writing.

Spatial Concepts in Writing

Teach the writing of each letter as it is introduced in the reading. The secret to the correct formation of the letters is in the position of the letter in space. To dramatize this it is necessary to demonstrate the letter in an exaggerated size. Use the whole size of the blackboard. The *m* begins on the left and at the top. So start at the top left-hand side of the blackboard. I START UP HERE AT THE TOP AND GO DOWN, RIGHT BACK UP ON THE SAME LINE, MAKE A HUMP AND DOWN, BACK UP AND MAKE ANOTHER HUMP AND DOWN TO THE BOTTOM. WATCH! I'LL DO IT AGAIN! Repeat. NOW LET'S SEE IF WE CAN DO IT IN THE AIR. TAKE YOUR WRITING HAND. POINT YOUR TWO FINGERS UP LIKE THIS. NOW LOOK STRAIGHT AT ME, BUT CROSS YOUR ARM ACROSS YOUR BODY UNTIL IT IS ON YOUR LEFT SIDE. This is for right-handed children. Give different directions for lefties. SEE HOW MY ARM CROSSES MY BODY? In demonstrating for right-handed children use your left hand, crossing over to your right side. SHOW ME HOW YOUR ARM CROSSES YOUR BODY.

NOW WE ARE GOING TO MAKE THIS "M" IN THE AIR. SIT BIG! FEET

FLAT ON THE FLOOR. NOW START UP HIGH BY THE LEFT SIDE OF YOUR HEAD. GO DOWN, BACK UP IN A HUMP, BACK UP IN A HUMP AND DOWN. LET'S DO IT AGAIN. Repeat several times. This is best done with the children sitting erect at their seats. Be sure that they are sitting straight though, or all their direcions will be confused. Some children are unable to cross their bodies and simply turn the whole body to get the right arm over on the left side. Hold this child at the waist to keep him from turning. For this child, doing the air-writing at his desk helps to orient him toward the front of the room. Be sure that the child's hand is in front of his body where he can see it. These children often put their arms up and on their left side but often going *over* their heads and pointing behind them. They do this to keep from crossing the midline of their bodies in front of their eyes where the confusion lies in orientation. Also have them follow their hand movements with their eyes. IS YOUR ARM CROSSED IN FRONT OF YOUR BODY? ARE YOUR FINGERS POINTED UPWARD? NOW WATCH YOUR FINGERS! FOLLOW THEM ALL THE WAY. KEEP YOUR EYES ON THEM.

Cluster left-handed children on the left side of the room and give them special help with direction. They have to tilt their papers to the right. They must learn to cross their bodies to make the letters starting on the right. They usually cross their *t*'s and *f*'s from right to left because they can then see the trace of their pencils more easily. Since they usually have so many fine motor and perceptual problems, there is no reason to make an issue of the direction a *t* is crossed.

Another way to dramatize the position of the letters in space is to form it with your whole body, and then have the children imitate you. This is especially good for children with up-down confusions. However, when standing with no desk to help orient them, left and right are not stabilized. STAND TALL. CLASP YOUR HANDS TOGETHER LIKE THIS. NOW REACH WAY UP HERE TO THE TOP LEFT. You are demonstrating as above, clasping your hands on the right side of your head. NOW WE GO STRAIGHT DOWN TO THE FLOOR. BEND YOUR KNEES. IT HAS TO GO ALL THE WAY DOWN. NOW BACK UP IN A HUMP. ALL THE WAY DOWN TO THE FLOOR AGAIN.

BACK UP IN A HUMP. AND NOW ALL THE WAY DOWN TO THE FLOOR ON YOUR RIGHT SIDE AND STOP!

A third process is to have children demonstrate their understanding of the spatial concepts of the letter on the blackboard. This is a testing device to show how well they learned by their movements, where their learning is deficient, and clue you as to how you can help them to clarify their problems. LET'S LET EVERYONE IN ROW ONE COME UP AND SHOW HOW YOU CAN MAKE IT VERY LARGE ON THE BLACKBOARD. ON WHICH SIDE WILL YOU START? If a child is unable to form the letter, try to analyze what understanding he lacks. For example, if he doesn't start on the correct side then hold his body straight at the waist, help him to cross his arm over and start at the very edge of the board. After showing him, erase it and have him repeat it several times. If the strokes do not go all the way down to a solid baseline, take him back to tracing the letter with his whole body as above, making sure he bends his knees and goes all the way down. Then take him back to the board to repeat the letter several times.

If, with all of this instruction, the child is still unable to reproduce the letter, hold your left hand over his eyes, your right hand on his right hand (if he is right-handed) and help him trace the shape very large on the board, over and over. Do it in a smooth rhythm. Gradually let his arm take over the movement. NOW I AM GOING TO LET GO AND YOU ARE GOING TO DO IT ALL BY YOURSELF. FEEL THE RHYTHM OF YOUR ARM. NOW DO IT BY YOURSELF. His eyes are still covered. You might need to touch his wrist lightly to guide him on certain parts of the letter on which he has difficulty. When his rhythm of forming the letter is constant, uncover his eyes and let him continue to retrace the letter over and over. Then erase the whole thing and let him make it all by himself. The child with gross visual perceptual problems is confused by his vision so that taking the instruction to the kinesthetic without the vision gives him a kinesthetic perception on which he can stabilize his visual perception.

Rainbow Tracing

For the first writing on paper I prefer Beth Slingerland's method (1968). Use a 12″ x 18″ manila drawing paper (it is heavier and stays put) on which to crayon a large letter covering the whole paper in the vertical position. The *m* would start about the middle of the paper so that later you can dramatize the tall letters like the *h,* starting at the very top of the paper. Put a red crayoned *X* at the point where the child is to start tracing the letter. Also make a red arrow showing the direction in which the child is to make the first stroke. This is especially important with letters like the *d* and *g* (Fig. 37).

When the child has demonstrated his ability to make the letter on the board, give him this paper on which he retraces the letter many times. Frostig calls this *rainbow tracing* (1964), and the children use their different colors to trace the letter. Since the multiple repetition and rhythm of making the letter are most important encourage them to use the same crayon over and over in a rhythm. I don't make a fuss if the child does use several colors unless he is not getting enough practice in the process. DO IT QUICKLY. SWEEP AROUND IT. Check to be sure they are using a whole-arm movement and a smooth rhythm. Being exactly on

Figure 37. Rainbow Tracing.

the model is not as desirable as the free sweeping movement.

Teach them to make the letters and numerals in one continuous movement, e.g. the *a* starts on the right and goes around the circle and connects, then straight up and straight down, without lifting the crayon. Children with perceptual-motor problems are more able to learn this continuous movement than two separate strokes. This is why they are so often taught cursive writing in private schools instead of printing. Also, using this continuous movement, it is easier to connect the letters to form cursive writing later.

The *8* is not two separate balls, but starts on the right as an *S* does, and then goes back up to the top. Be sure you teach the *S* before the *8*. I START MAKING AN "S" AND THEN I CHANGE MY MIND AND TURN IT INTO AN 8.

The *b* begins up high, goes down to the bottom, half-way back up the post and then the ball rolls out to the right and down to the bottom of the post. The *p* stroke goes down to the bottom, all the way back up to the top and circles around to the right.

The *9* is made by starting like the *0* and *a* on the right except that it starts higher on the right. Make the ball, connect it, and then the stick goes down to the bottom. Teach the straight stick so they don't confuse it with the *6*. The *6, 8,* and *9* begin on the top right. Practice them together. THE 6 STARTS OUT AS A CIRCLE, TO THE LEFT ALL THE WAY DOWN TO THE BOTTOM AND BACK UP HALF WAY. THEN THE 6 CHANGES HIS MIND AND DECIDES TO MAKE A LITTLE CIRCLE AT THE BOTTOM, SO HE GOES BACK DOWN. The children seem to enjoy this type of patter and learn the numeral *6* more easily. If a child is clutching the crayon to laboriously stay on the model during the rainbow tracing, hold his wrist and help him make the large rhythmic movement quickly. It should not take longer than three seconds to trace any letter. Be sure he is using his whole arm. Stress the bending of the elbow. If he is using wrist movement only, put your hand on the inside of his elbow, pulling it back with each downward stroke until he gets the idea. BEND YOUR ELBOW! DON'T GLUE YOUR ARM TO THE DESK. YOUR LITTLE FINGER MUST SLIDE OVER THE DESK. If you can't get that arm unglued, have him stand or kneel in his seat to make the letter. In writing sitting in their seats, teach them to use the subdominant arm to hold the paper. SPREAD OUT YOUR FINGERS TO HOLD THE PAPER. YOU CAN'T WRITE IF THE PAPER IS MOVING. IT TAKES TWO HANDS TO WRITE. GET THAT LAZY ARM UP THERE!

The children say the sound of the letter or the name of the numeral as they trace it. Or they might verbalize the movement, and say the sound after the letter is traced: "Down, hump, hump, m." If they are verbalizing the movement instead of the sound, several times while they are working ask individuals or the class: WHAT ARE YOU MAKING? After the letter has been traced repeatedly, say: NOW SEE IF YOU CAN MAKE SOME SMALL *m*'S ANYWHERE YOU HAVE ROOM ON YOUR PAPER. BE SURE YOU START ON THE LEFT!

Some children have difficulty stopping at the base of the letters; therefore, their strokes do not stop at the same spot each time. Some continue on until they are off the paper entirely and writing on the desk or are stopped by the metal edging on the desk. For these children, put a straight red line about two inches up from the bottom of the paper for the base. The child must stop when he hits the line. If this does not stop him, place a ruler there that he can bump. While they are tracing, praise sweeping movements and stopping. Be sure they are starting on the X, and going the right direction.

Name Writing

Use 12″ x 18″ manila drawing paper to crayon each child's first name about six inches high. Put a red X at the point he is to start each letter. Use a red arrow to show the direction to go from the starting point. Each child then traces his own name many times with his crayons. Go around, helping each child. When they have finished, have them write their names all by themselves on the top and bottom left of the paper. From the latter you can determine how much more practice each child will need. After this has been done several days, many of the children will be ready for smaller letters and paper with large three-inch lines (described later in this chapter). Again, write each child's name on the lines and have him trace it many times. Individualize this instruction so that in one class period some children will be still using the drawing paper to trace their names, some the three-inch lined paper, and perhaps some the smaller-lined paper in standard school supply.

Pencil Techniques

One of the main goals of writing is to teach the use of the whole arm for writing instead of the cramped hand position. When writing in the air and tracing, emphasize the fact that the fingers (or pencil) are pointed upward and the whole arm moves. BEND YOUR ELBOW. PULL WITH YOUR ELBOW. When writing on paper, again have the pencil pointed upward, the point extended so that they can see it. Be sure the whole arm is moving. Sometimes just pulling gently on the child's elbow while he writes helps to show him what you mean. If he is bending his wrist when writing, place your hand on his with your thumb and little finger under his wrist to keep it straight. Or put a tongue depressor under his wrist up into his palm, holding it with a piece of elastic. Talk about the arm sweeping the desk when writing. PULL WITH YOUR ELBOW. SWEEP THE DESK WITH YOUR ARM. If these skills are taught with the tracing exercises, the resultant writing will be smoother and freer, and you will have fewer bad habits to break later.

Use the lead-weighted wristband (described in Chapter Seven) on the child's writing wrist to help give him more kinesthetic feeling for his dominant hand.

Do this finger exercise daily: HOLD YOUR CRAYON (or pencil) UPRIGHT IN YOUR FIST. NOW FLIP YOUR CRAYON UP AND PUT THREE FINGERS UNDER IT (the correct pencil-holding position). FIST, THREE FINGERS UNDER. Have children repeat the exercise daily until they can all do it quickly and easily. When you are holding the pencil correctly (three fingers under) say: SEE HOW LOOSELY I AM HOLDING IT? I CAN PULL THE PENCIL IN AND OUT WITH MY OTHER HAND. CAN YOU DO THAT? LET'S SEE IF I CAN PULL THE PENCIL OUT OF YOUR HAND EASILY. When they are writing on paper, or the board, emphasize the position of the medium as pointing upward just like the fingers do when tracing in the air. BE SURE YOU

CAN SEE THE END OF YOUR CRAYON UP THERE. Otherwise, they clutch it with their fist and are unable to see where the point is making its trace. The point of the medium must always be visible to them, pointed upward. If not, it causes a poor head and eye position. The child has to put his head down to the left and close to his hand in order to see what he is doing. Thus it becomes difficult to focus and his whole perception is distorted by his head and eye position.

Another clue to a good writing and focusing position is a pencil hold which is about an inch and a half from the point. Have them always hold the pencil on the painted part. Or use a hunk of clay or a doubled rubber band to designate the finger position on the pencil. The child holds the pencil behind the rubber band or behind the clay. There are vinyl triangular grips that slip over the pencil (Posture Pencil Grips) which help this problem.

Box Writing

For practice on forming letters in the correct positions, and as preparation for writing between lines, teach box writing. After the child has learned the sound, tracing the letter in the air, writing on the board and on the paper with the rainbow tracing, the next step is box writing. This idea came from Marianne Frostig (1964). Make a ditto for the letter, with one-inch square boxes and with a dotted line across the middle of each box for the center line. Leave a one-half-inch aisle between rows of boxes for a clearer perception. Into the first row of boxes make the letter with the X and arrow for the starting stroke. In succeeding rows of boxes, place only the X and arrow (Fig. 38). The child traces the first row for practice, saying the sound each time he makes it. Then he starts on the X, follows the arrow, and makes the letter in all the boxes on the page. The X must be placed on the far side of the square so that the child cannot reverse the letter. Thus he never practices the letter in the wrong direction. This is one of the main faults of board-to-paper copying. Then the child diligently reverses all the letters and thereby learns the reversals.

Before you hand out the box-writing papers, demonstrate

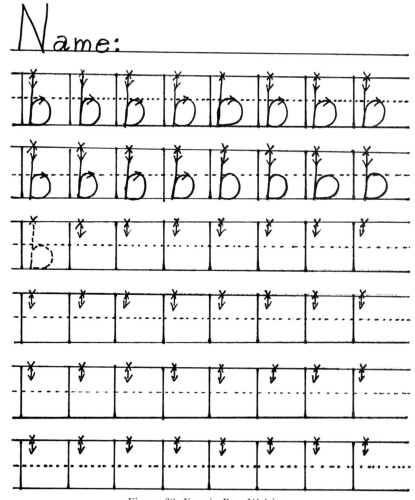

Figure 38. Frostig Box Writing.

with a very large box on the board how the children are to form
the letters in the boxes. WE START ON THE "X," FOLLOW THE ARROW,
GO DOWN TO THE LINE, STOP, GO BACK UP TO THE DOTTED LINE AND
HUMP, DOWN TO THE LINE AND STOP, BACK UP TO THE DOTS IN A
HUMP, DOWN AND STOP. SEE HOW I STOPPED RIGHT ON THE LINE?
AND SEE HOW THE HUMPS HAVE TO TOUCH THE DOTS? WATCH! I WILL
DO IT AGAIN. NOW POINT YOUR TWO FINGERS UP AND LET'S ALL MAKE

IT IN THE AIR! Pass out the dittos. While the children are working, go around making sure they are pointing the pencil up, holding it back from the point, moving the whole arm, sliding the little finger across the desk, making the small letters touch the dots, and stopping on the line. These are a lot of separate problems and some children have all of them. So don't expect perfect papers or they probably don't need the practice. Encourage them to do a little better each time. Find something good about even the worst paper because this is a multiple of difficult coordinations. If a child has difficulty stopping, find the one time when he did stop and put a star by that letter. I REALLY LIKE THE WAY YOU REMEMBERED TO STOP ON THIS ONE. Or I AM GOING TO PUT A STAR HERE BECAUSE YOU MADE THE HUMPS TOUCH THE DOTS SO NICELY ON THIS ONE. Or, YOU FIND THE BEST "M" ON YOUR PAPER AND WE WILL PUT A STAR ON IT. OH, YES, THAT IS A GOOD ONE! They can see the difference between their successes and failures. This is why some of them are so easily discouraged by their poor coordinations. So pile on the encouragement. LOOK AT THIS GOOD PAPER! TOMMY HAS A TERRIBLE TIME MAKING HIS LETTERS. IT'S HARD FOR HIM! HIS HAND JUST WON'T DO WHAT HE WANTS IT TO DO, BUT TODAY HE DID THIS WHOLE ROW BEAUTIFULLY! They can accept each other's problems if you accept theirs, too. Then they will encourage each other, and all that peer support is worth its weight in children.

Large-Lined Paper

For the first lined paper for children with perceptual and coordination problems, I prefer another idea from Beth Slingerland's program. Ditto or mimeograph two rows of three-inch-wide writing lines horizontally on legal-sized paper. Use solid top and bottom lines and dotted center lines. On one of these masters write the straight letters and those which start on the left (including *b* and *p*). On another put the letters which start on the right: *o, a, d, g, c, s, e, 6, 8, 9* (Fig. 39). A third master could have just the lines, and a fourth, just capital and small *O*'s. Begin with tracing the *O*'s over and over in an easy rhythm. Be sure the hand and arms are moving. Allow no separate finger action. Then use

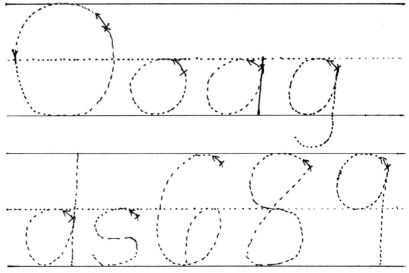

Figure 39. Writing Practice; Three-Inch Lines.

the first two papers with the letters. Tracing the letters on these pages can be done in unison, saying the sound as they retrace each one several times.

After the children can trace these all correctly and easily, then go on to the paper that has just the lines. This time, demonstrate each letter on the board before the child attempts to make it on his paper. The spatial concepts are clearer if you use blue chalk for the top line, brown for the bottom, and green dots for the center line. Space the lines about four or five inches apart on the board. WATCH! THE *h* STARTS WAY UP HERE IN THE BLUE SKY. Put an X at the starting point. IT GOES WAY DOWN TO THE GROUND, STOPS, BACK UP TO THE GREEN GRASS IN THE MIDDLE, HUMPS AND DOWN AGAIN TO THE GROUND. WATCH WHILE I DO IT AGAIN. Repeat. Next have them write it in the air and then on the lined paper, retracing it over and over. It is important that this be a teaching exercise, not independent seatwork, or they may just learn their errors. So don't just write it and have them copy it. They have to learn the placement of each letter on the lines and they must be free to concentrate on just the one letter they are making. Check each child's letter to be sure he is making it correctly. If not, *you* form the letter for him to trace correctly, and if necessary, hold his wrist while he traces it. *Never let him fail! Never let him practice error!*

Teach the line writing of similarly formed letters together, e.g., *h, m, n,* and *r.* Begin the circle letters with the *o,* then the *a,* then the *d,* and last the *g.* Delay teaching the *b* and *P* until the *e, a, d,* and *g* are solid.

Use this same wide-lined paper to write words, simple sentences, and their names (Fig. 40). When writing sentences, demonstrate each letter on the board as above, then have the children write it. Do one letter at a time. Don't get ahead of them or they become upset and frustrated and may quit altogether. Show them how you use two fingers of the left hand to hold a space between words. Help them to do it.

Writing Stories

When all the letters are well formed and easily made (probably in the spring) go on to your regular school supplies—five-eighths-inch lined paper. Still use the process of demonstrating each letter before they make it. Now they are also blending sounds into words, so let them help you make up and spell the stories. LET'S WRITE A STORY ABOUT TODAY. WHAT IS IT LIKE TODAY? WHAT CAN WE SAY? Susan says: "It is hot outside." YES IT IS! LET'S SEE! HOW DO WE SPELL "IT"? SPELL "IT" BY SOUNDS: *iiiit.* RIGHT, EXCEPT WE ARE JUST STARTING TO TALK SO WE MAKE IT INTO A BIG CAPITAL "I." SO IT STARTS WAY UP HERE ON THE BLUE LINE. IT STILL SAYS *i,* THOUGH! WRITE IT. NOW, WHAT SOUND DO WE MAKE? YES, "T." IT STARTS UP HERE IN THE SKY, TOO. WRITE IT. NOW THAT IS THE END OF THE WORD "IT," SO WE PUT TWO FINGERS HERE TO HOLD THE SPACE. NOW, *iiisss.* THIS TIME THE *i* IS LITTLE AND STARTS ON THE GREEN DOTS AND THE DOT GOES UP HERE IN THE SKY. The children watch you write the letter and then do it on their papers. Some children won't even have to watch your execution but can write much of the story themselves. Still, you might have to go slowly for the others.

Next, try a partial story that they complete: "I am. . . ." "I can. . . ." "I like. . . ." "I wish I were. . . ." "I want to be. . . ."

Figure 40. Name Tracing on Lines.

Help them to spell by sounds (Distar technique) the words they choose to complete the sentences. If the words they want are not phonetic and they can't sound-spell them, you can write these on the board. You will need just one unfinished sentence for a day's lesson. The child can write several sentences using "I like. . . ." After this background in writing, the children will be able to completely create their own stories. When so doing they will spell many words phonetically, as the words sound when the child sound-spells them. These stories should be accepted as they are without teacher-correction of the spelling. The goal of a creative writing lesson is *creative writing, not* correct spelling. If you insist that the child erase his errors in spelling at this stage of learning, you are deprecating his work, often crushing the very creativity you were endeavoring to teach.

Teach spelling as a separate skill at a different time. We find our first grade program leaves little time for spelling. The other skills are more important at this time, so we leave the spelling for the second grade teachers.

With a background in a decoding method, it is easy to teach these children the rules for spelling. When you do teach spelling, group words into rhyming families and rule groups. Teach pure phonetic words first, grouping them together (*cat, hat, sat*). Teach the long-vowel-with-silent-*e* words together (*like, make*). Teach TWO VOWELS GO WALKING, THE FIRST ONE DOES THE TALKING, and group these words into one lesson (*seat, meat,* and *sail, fail*).

Writing should be enjoyable, not drudgery. Everyday practice in writing is unnecessary and undesirable. Two or three times a week is sufficient. The first of the year alternate between the large letter-tracing, the box-writing, templates, body-image activities, and Frostig worksheets in perceptual constancy, visual-motor, and position in space. Later, vary between tracing on the large lines, copying your felt designs, Frostig figure-ground, and spatial-relations worksheets. In the spring the children should be writing on the large- and later the small-lined paper, alternating this writing with the visual-memory exercises, reading workbooks, and pegboards.

Other Seatwork

There are few reading seatwork papers that have any real value. They were invented just for busywork. The usual phonics dittos are valueless. The child is to circle all the pictures whose names start with the given sound. If he already knows the sound thoroughly, he does the paper in about thirty seconds. If he doesn't know the sound, he guesses, sometimes right, sometimes wrong. He learns nothing in the process. Sounds can be learned only by hearing them said and repeating them under supervision so that they are learned correctly.

Reading Workbooks

Good reading workbooks are valuable reinforcers of learned words. Workbooks should be done on an independent seatwork basis. That is, they should be slightly below the present reading level so that they are easy for the child to do. We find it best not to start workbooks until winter or spring when the children are reading easily. Children then progress through them at their own speeds. When one level workbook is completely correct, then the child is given the one on the next level. Have some kind of chart on the bulletin board showing where each child is working in his book. Being able to see where they are going gives them a feeling of accomplishment and incentive to do more work.

The good workbook needs no small print instructions. But if some direction is necessary, it should use the words from the child's vocabulary at that level. A good workbook will use only about four different types of exercises, and thus has fewer mechanics of operation to confuse the child. Basically, they should be CROSS OUT WHAT DOES NOT BELONG; CIRCLE THE RIGHT WORD OR SENTENCE; DRAW A LINE TO THE RIGHT WORD OR PICTURE; or PUT THE RIGHT NUMERAL IN THE BOX. Linguistic series often have better workbooks. The Distar Reading I program includes workbooks, the latter sections of which are good. We also like the S.R.A. linguistic workbooks.

REFERENCES

Ayres, A. Jean: *Perceptual-Motor Dysfunction in Children.* Monograph from the Greater Cincinnati District, Ohio Occupational Therapy Association Conference, 1964.

Bruner, Elaine C.: The Distar Reading Program. Submitted for publication in the Proceedings of the College Reading Association, April 5, 1968.

Chall, Jeanne: *Learning to Read, The Great Debate.* New York, McGraw-Hill, 1967.

Cooperative Primary Tests, Reading. Palo Alto, California, Educational Testing Service, 1965.

deHirsch, Katrina, *et al.: Predicting Reading Failure.* New York, Harper & Row, 1966.

Engelmann, Siegfried, and Bruner, Elaine C.: *Distar Reading Program.* Chicago, Sci Res, 1969.

Fernald, G. N.: *Remedial Techniques in Basic School Subjects.* New York, McGraw-Hill, 1943.

Frostig, Marianne: University Extension lecture, May, 1965.

————: The Education and Guidance of Children with Learning Difficulties. Davis, California, University of California Extension, 1964.

Gattegno, C.: *Words in Color—Background and Principles,* revised edition of the Morphologico-Algebrac Approach to Reading and Writing. New York. Learning Materials Incorporated, Xerox Education Division, 1962.

Getman, G. N., and Kane, Elmer: *The Physiology of Readiness.* Minneapolis, PASS, 1964.

Kephart, Newell C.: *The Slow Learner in the Classroom.* Columbus, Ohio, Merrill, 1960.

Klasen, Edith: Audio-Visuo Motor Training with Pattern Cards. Palo Alto, California, Peek, 1969.

Kuhlmann-Anderson Test, 7th Ed. Princeton, New Jersey, Personnel Press, 1964.

Metropolitan Achievement Tests: Primary I Battery. Chicago, World Books, 1961.

Metropolitan Readiness Tests. New York, Harcourt, Brace & World, 1949.

Posture Pencil Grips. Creative Associates, P. O. Box 281, Aptos, California, 95003.

Radler, D. H., and Kephart, Newell C.: *Success Through Play.* New York, 1960.

Rasmussen, Donald, and Goldberg, Lenina: *S.R.A. Basic Reading Series.* Chicago, Sci Res, 1965.

Rosenthal, R.: Self-fulfilling prophecy. *Psychology Today,* Sept. 1966.

Scott, Louise Binder: *Talking Time.* Great Britain, Webster, 1951.

Slingerland, Beth: Lecture in Sacramento, California, March 1968.

Stanford Achievement Test, Primary I Reading Tests. New York, Harcourt, Brace and World, 1964.

Stern, Catherine: *Structural Arithmetic.* Boston, Houghton-Mifflin.

U. Film. Irving-on-Hudson, New York. Hudson Photographic Industries, Incorporated, 1968. Also available from: Educational Progress Corporation.

Warner, Sylvia Ashton: *Teacher.* New York, Bantam, 1963.

CHILDREN'S PLEASURE READING SERIES

And I Can Read Book. New York, Harper & Row.

Beginner Books. New York, Division of Random House, published by Beginner Books.

Just Beginning to Read Books. Chicago, Follett.

Chapter Ten

ᴀ*rithmetic*

THE TRADITIONAL AND DISCOVERY METHODS
OF TEACHING MATH

CHILDREN WITH LEARNING problems are often unable to comprehend mathematical relationships with traditional teaching methods. They do not learn with the discovery method because they lack the basic skills required. They have no foundation, no concepts through which to discover, or base any relationships. They cannot understand what $4+2$ is, because they do not really understand what 4 is. They don't know which is more, 4 or 2. *Plus* and *equals* are obscure words often unrelated to their symbols. These children often write and say: $4+=2$.

Many times the children cannot recognize and name numerals or count accurately. Yet we have not usually taught this. We took for granted that beginning first graders had these concepts, and began our instruction at too high a level. Children who do not progress in this program are dubbed *slow*, and often their heritage is blamed. "He's doing as well as you might expect." Or, "He just does not have it!" It is so easy to blame these children for our failures. But if we call ourselves teachers, we must be willing to take the responsibility of teaching them. We must begin instruction where the children are, not where we think they should be. We must take no learning for granted. We must teach them every step!

In September only half of our sixty first-graders can recognize and name numerals through ten and count past thirty. A fourth of our children might know only four numerals, or even none at all, and be unable to count to ten. We must begin instruction on at least three different levels: (1) numeral recognition of 1 to 4 and basic counting, (2) numeral recognition of 5 to 10 and counting *to* and *from* a number, (3) reading numerals over 10, joining of sets, and computation symbols of $+$, $-$, and $=$. As the year proceeds, the gap widens and more instructional groups are needed.

Children with learning problems have difficulty integrating ideas. They can be taught to solve an equation without really understanding the concept. Change the numerals or the sign and they are lost. Their act is mechanical, rather than conceptual. The New Math instruction, teaching the relationships between the numerals, is unclear to them. They can solve $4+2=6$, and $6-4=2$, without seeing that the sum of the addition equation becomes the first digit of the subtraction equation, or that the answer for the subtraction problem is one of the addends. They might count out both problems on their fingers. Or they see where another child got the answer and copy it down without understanding the concept. At any rate, the relationships are nonexistent to them.

Using Concrete Objects

It does help to use objects, counters, colored number rods, such as the Cuisenaire Rods, to teach quantitative relationships such as *more than, larger, greater than, the same as,* and *less than.* However, in our experience with extensive use of the rods, the children with letter and numeral recognition and association problems still cannot transfer their understanding of the rods to the symbols and the written equation. So with math as with reading, it is crucial to teach the child to *crack the code,* as Engelmann puts it. After the child has a firm foundation in counting, in the meaning of the numerals and those all important signs, $+$, $-$, and $=$, then he is ready to discover relationships between numbers and to solve equations. Not before!

Classroom Demonstrations

With the New Math demonstration methods, the teacher may often give an excellent demonstration of a number concept and have three or four eager children come to the board and make all the right moves. Responding as a class of thirty, they might appear to be making all the right sounds, too. Then the teacher hands them a page of examples of the concept, and very few children are able to proceed confidently. There is too great a gap between the demonstration and the independent solution of an equation. The children do not see the relationships; they are unable to integrate the concepts. Also, how many of the children were actually "with" the whole demonstration? Attention of six-year-olds strays so very easily—they can be looking at you, but not be thinking with you. Small group instruction and active participation are essential to teaching math to problem learners.

Individual Differences

One of the most blatant errors we make in teaching math is to parrot that trite and very misused phrase, *individual differences,* and then hand out the same math page to thirty children. Five complete it before the rest of the class receive their papers. Five more are done in three to five minutes. We then give them coloring, or other busywork to keep them out of our hair. The instruction and worksheet were probably unnecessary for them. These faster pupils already knew the concept. We taught them nothing. We then have time to work with about ten middle children individually during the period. They seem to profit from our extra help. These we teach!

That bottom five to ten frustrate us as only teachers can be frustrated. We try to help them but they just do not respond consistently. They look for the answer on the teacher's face. They want to succeed, but their papers reflect complete failure to master the concept. They often put down any numerals at random and by chance get one to five, out of twenty, problems correct. The period often is over before we have time to help them. The next day we go on to a higher concept and we have lost that bottom group for the rest of the year. Oh, well, we will retain them next year. But with the same instruction they will fail again.

Fact Learning

Traditional math programs emphasize the memorization of the addition facts and often do not allow for other concepts to be introduced until the facts are memorized. This causes an unnecessary delay in math instruction. Children with learning problems often have great difficulty memorizing anything, particularly number facts. Through detailed programmed instruction they can understand number concepts long before they are able to memorize number facts.

In studies of deprived children it has been found that they are extremely impulsive. The difference between middle-class children and the deprived is less a factor of intelligence than of impulse control (Hallahan, 1970). Thus, if these children are not given a solid foundation in number meaning, they take the line of least resistance and impulsively guess answers. With faulty memories from which to extract the data, their papers are often fifty percent incorrect. Instruction must, therefore, emphasize the meaning of the equation, and problem solving. Only after the children have a thorough basis in these should the memorization of the facts be started. When understanding of the relationships of numbers is solid, the child memorizes the facts easily and quickly. He should not be allowed to rely on memorization of facts alone until the concepts are solid, or he will resort to guessing.

Whenever a child makes even one error, he should correct it, not by guessing, but by problem solving. Whenever he makes more than three errors, he should be required to use some method of demonstrating the number quantities in every equation he works. We insist that this child use tally marks under each numeral to show the quantity of the numeral. Thus he can see the equality factors of the equation easily, the solution is more obvious to him, and he will be less likely to randomly guess. All instruction must use concrete objects and/or tally marks to solidify the concept and to be sure every child understands.

PROGRAMMED MATH INSTRUCTION: THE ENGELMANN PROGRAMS
The "Preventing Failure" Program

There are two excellent programs for basic math instruction, both by Siegfried Engelmann. One is the Distar program, co-authored by Doug Carnine, which includes the teachers' instructional books and worksheets for the children. The other program is in Engelmann's book *Preventing Failure in the Primary Grades*. Chapter VI describes step-by-step just how to teach each math concept from beginning numeral recognition through multiplication. Chapter VII goes on into carrying, borrowing, etc. As independent practice is needed, there are examples of worksheets for which the teacher may cut dittos. In using the program in this book, we found it best to go through the whole program before school started, cut the dittos for each concept and file a hundred copies of each one for use as needed for our classes.

Chapter VI is a whole year's first grade program in math, and more. Our children finish this program with really solid concepts well into second-grade level. Some of our younger middle-group children were happily bringing to school pages of multiplication (through five) that they had done at home. They had been taught the concepts at school and so enjoyed the challenge that they found pleasure in working these equations in play situations at home. With this math program the children gain the basic mathematic ability to reason, a foundation for all future math work. For the first time our children really understand math. This is in sharp contrast to the ability of our children in past years with instruction in traditional math, in the New Math (Greater Cleveland Program), and in the use of the number rods.

There are two drawbacks to this program, however. It neglects the basic counting skills which the teacher must then supplement. Second, there is the danger of the teacher giving practice in only one or two skills a day, neglecting the essential repetition of basic skills and old concepts. If the children are taught one mathematical concept at a time without replay of the old concepts as well, they get into a set way of operating equations. For example, if the current emphasis is on subtraction, the child seems to forget his addition skills, ignores the symbols of the equation, and resorts to subtracting everything. Thus $6+2 = 4$.

The Distar Math Programs I and II

The Distar I program contains programmed lessons for 220 days. It begins with very basic counting and numeral recognition skills for preschoolers and kindergartners. The program includes a pretest to place kindergarten children in the program at their skill levels. Since most first graders pass this test too easily, it does not aid their placement into the program. Thus we use our own battery of tests (Classroom Tests, Math Concepts, Chapter Four) to determine the children's placement into groups for Distar instruction. Small instruction groups with children with similar deficits or abilities are really essential to the success of both Engelmann programs. Each math group must be carefully started in the program, so that no basic skill is neglected. Take no previous learnings for granted.

Our bottom first-grade group began this program about day 60 and proceeded by learning the skills they were missing from two or three lessons a day. About the ninetieth day of the program, the children were at a good instructional level and one day's instruction was then sufficient for each thirty-minute session. This group will probably nearly finish the program by the end of the year. The other three first-grade-math groups began the program around days 70 or 80, and were able to skip more lessons. They should complete the Distar I program in the spring and make some progress into Distar II Math.

The Distar programs include worksheets called *take-homes,* to follow each day's instruction. These give individual practice on the mechanics and skills which have been done on the blackboard in unison with the teacher's guidance. Now the child reveals his understanding of the instruction by his ability to do the independent worksheets. These require only a very few minutes. Actually, they are more a testing device and reinforcement than instruction, because they simply contain samples of the instruction which was done as a group.

The Distar program is extremely thorough, programming every minute preskill needed to establish each mathematical concept. No learning is taken for granted. A major emphasis of this program is on the counting skills.

There are several differences in these two Engelmann programs. The Preventing Failure program is a lifesaver to the teacher who is unable to talk her administration into purchasing the more expensive Distar program. She can at least afford to buy the one book herself, and this program will be much more effective than any basic text with which she has been provided. However, the Distar program is much more thorough, more complete, and contains more basic preskills, such as the grouping and counting concepts. The Distar program gives daily lessons, telling the teacher every word to say in each lesson, so that the essential repetition of each concept is built-in. Some techniques are used in both programs.

Program Structure

Engelmann organizes the basic concepts in strands as separate skills, as with the reading program. As the skills are attained, the strands converge to the equation, much as the naming and blending of the sounds in the Distar reading program converge into the printed word. You teach some skills of each strand in every lesson. Thus in one lesson you might teach numeral recognition for two minutes, rote counting for two minutes, number meaning, the *plus* concept, *equals,* and *zero,* for the rest of a twenty-to-twenty-five-minute instructional period. When all of these concepts are solid—anywhere from two weeks to two months, depending on where you must start the program—the equation is presented. Since children have thoroughly learned each part of it previously, the equation is no problem to them. Children who come without any number concepts at all may take two or three months' instruction in the basics before they are ready for the equation. But then they do understand and progress well. We have had no failures with either of the Engelmann programs. Even our children who test in the 70 and 80 IQs proceed slowly but surely. Tiny, immature Fernando, fresh up from Mexico, who did not know any numerals or any counting in September, was doing missing addends independently by June.

Symbols

As with the reading program, the math symbols and numerals are taught independently of equations. There might be a page of large numerals. The teacher says: THIS IS A 2. SHE POINTS TO AN-

OTHER. THIS IS A 2. THIS LITTLE THING OVER THERE IS A 2. She points at an *1* or a picture. IS THIS A 2? You can play various games with this page: SEE HOW FAST YOU CAN NAME THESE. Or: I'LL BET YOU DON'T KNOW THIS HARD ONE! Or: I AM GOING TO RACE YOU WITH THESE NUMERALS! I'LL BET I CAN SAY THEM FIRST!

The blackboard can be used for teaching the numerals and symbols, +, −, and =. The teacher simply writes the numeral or symbol on the board. When the children name it correctly, she erases it and writes another. The children's favorite numeral game, of which they never seem to tire, is Engelmann's *Race* (Engelmann, 1969, p. 261). The teacher writes the numeral on the board and then races with the children to see who can name it first. Scores are tallied right there on the board so the children can see who is winning. The children always win, of course, or you are using too many unknown numerals at once. Use mostly known numerals with one or two new numerals. It is a great way to begin an instructional session because it focuses the group's attention on the board on which you will be teaching them.

First, *race* with the whole group, then individuals: OH, YOU ARE ALL BEATING ME. I KNOW WHOM I CAN BEAT. TOMMY! NO ONE HELP HIM NOW. At first use numerals for individuals that you are sure they know, so that they gain confidence in speaking out alone. Keep track of the numerals which each child needs to learn, crossing the numerals off your list as they are learned. Later, when only a few children have individual numerals they lack, make a big play on these. I KNOW THE NUMERAL ON WHICH I CAN CATCH TOMMY. HE DOESN'T KNOW THIS ONE. Don't rush him or try to *beat* him to his answer. Give him some time to recall, but don't drag it out until he feels self-conscious and inadequate. Remember the principle of *forced recall*. If he can possibly pry it out of his brain just once, he is on the road to learning it. If he gets it, no matter how slowly, give him a tangible reward, a cereal or candy. If he cannot recall it, have the children tell him and then give each of them a cereal treat for knowing it. Use a flow pen to write it large on the palm of his subdominant hand. Have him trace it with two fingers of his other hand and say it. LET US ALL HELP TOMMY LEARN 5. EACH TIME YOU SEE HIM TODAY

ASK HIM WHAT IS ON HIS HAND! IF HE DOES NOT KNOW, TELL HIM.
Make a big deal at your next session out of seeing if Tommy knows his numeral. Another aid is to have the child behind him write the numeral on his back several times while Tommy says it. The children love to help each other learn and will root wildly when "Tommy knows 5!" Also, make the numeral on large drawing paper for him to rainbow trace (Chapter Nine) for extra practice. He should say its name while he traces it.

Counting

Rote counting and counting objects are done in rhythm. Engelmann believes that children unable to count one-to-one are lacking the fundamental rhythm and sequence more than the ability to match one-to-one. Thus the children learn to count in rhythm with a hand signal from the teacher. Or they clap with a flourish, accenting each number dramatically.

CLAP SIX TIMES! HOW MANY TIMES ARE WE GOING TO CLAP? YES, SIX! EVERYONE GET READY TO START. HOLD YOUR HANDS WAY OUT. HOW MANY ARE WE GOING TO CLAP? YES, SIX! HERE WE GO! COUNT WITH ME! ONE, TWO, THREE, FOUR, FIVE, SIX! HOW MANY DID WE CLAP? YES, SIX! Here the child learns the important concept that the last number stated is the total name of the group. Therefore, you always ask a HOW MANY? question at the end of each task.

Use a similar procedure for counting without clapping. HERE IS A HARD ONE FOR YOU. LISTEN BIG! COUNT TO SIXTEEN. WHAT ARE YOU GOING TO COUNT TO? YES, SIXTEEN! GET IT GOING, ONE, TWO. . . . Bring your hand down as a signal for them to count in unison. The Distar program includes correction procedures for each task. If the children err, you demonstrate. I CAN DO IT. I AM GOING TO COUNT TO SIXTEEN. ONE, TWO. . . . I DID IT! I COUNTED TO SIXTEEN! DO IT WITH ME! ONE, TWO. . . . GOOD COUNTING! YOU CAN DO IT! When the children have some confidence in their ability to do the task, then they do it without you. Finally, you call on each child to do the task individually. First, you teach to the whole group, then you test individually. The individual response is not teaching, just testing. The bulk of learning with the multiple repetition (which is so very essential) is done via the group response.

The children learn to count *from* and *to* specified numerals given vocally by the teacher. WE ARE GOING TO COUNT FROM SIX TO TEN. WHAT ARE WE GOING TO COUNT TO? YES, TEN! Get it going. SIX (use the hand signal as above), SEVEN, EIGHT, NINE, TEN! WE DID IT! WE COUNTED FROM SIX TO TEN! Gradually, this leads to counting *from* a numeral written on the board *to* a number given by the teacher. And later from the board numeral to the making of the correct number of sticks, lines, or tallies to arrive at a total specified by the teacher. This is a very important preskill needed for the child to understand counting *from* the first numeral of an addition equation *to* the total on that side of the equals, to determine the sum. It also helps to clarify the missing addend concept (or algebra addition, as Engelmann calls it). Teaching these basic skills gives the children a more solid background for all mathematical equations.

Engelmann teaches the counting of an encircled set of pictures of objects. Later he draws two separate sets within the circle. He teaches the children to FIND THE FIRST GROUP (the one on the left) AND COUNT THE OBJECTS. Or: FIND THE SECOND GROUP (the one on the right) AND COUNT THE OBJECTS. HOW MANY ARE IN THE FIRST GROUP? HOW MANY ARE IN THE SECOND GROUP? HOW MANY ARE IN THE CIRCLE?

They learn to count two, then three, groups of lines within a circle. Later, a numeral is substituted for the first group of lines. HOW MANY ARE IN THIS GROUP? WHAT NUMERAL IS THIS? YES, SIX! GET IT GOING. . . . SIX (then tap the three lines in the second group), SEVEN, EIGHT, NINE. HOW MANY ARE IN THE CIRCLE? YES, NINE! This prepares the children for later adding two numerals to find the sum. Using the numeral at the first addend and counting *from* it eliminates the need for the child to count out the first digit of an equation on his fingers as many immature children do.

Teach children to count objects and pictures like this: LET'S COUNT ALL THE BOYS IN THIS ROW. COUNT BIG! Touch each one with a flourish as you accent the number. ONE, TWO, THREE! HOW MANY BOYS ARE THERE? YES, THREE!

Vary the counting order: THIS TIME LET US START ON THE LEFT SIDE TO SEE HOW MANY BOYS THERE ARE. ONE, TWO, THREE! HOW

MANY? YES, THREE. THIS TIME LET US START WITH JERRY HERE IN THE MIDDLE. I BET THERE WILL NOT BE THREE THIS TIME! Mix them up and count them again to show that the sum is always the same regardless of the order. Practice counting many different objects. Count sets of objects, using the term *set*. THIS IS A SET OF TOYS. COUNT THEM. Or: EVERYTHING IN THIS BOX IS PART OF THIS SET! LET US SEE HOW MANY ARE IN THIS SET!

Make long tally marks on the board as the children count. Again, have them COUNT BIG! making the marks dramatically as they say each number. When you stop, ask: HOW MANY LINES ARE THERE? Ask a child to come up and make a specified number of lines or tallies on the board. Before he starts, ask him how many he is going to make. When he finishes, ask him how many he made.

Engelmann uses the tally marks to aid the teaching of the meaning of the terms *plus* and *minus* (Engelmann, 1969, p. 255). I HAVE ONE STICK ON THE BOARD, AND IF I PLUS ONE MORE I WILL HAVE . . . . Give the children time to come up with the answer before you make the second stick. YES, TWO. I HAVE TWO STICKS AND IF I PLUS ONE MORE I WILL HAVE . . . . Continue to ten. NOW I AM GOING TO MINUS STICKS! TEN, MINUS ONE (erase one) IS NINE. NINE MINUS ONE (erase one) IS EIGHT. Continue to zero. At first the children will be just listening and then will gradually join in with you as they catch on. Encourage this. TOMMY CAN SAY IT WITH ME! HE IS SMART! When you first begin the *minusing*, they may not be able to join in until you get down to only four or five. Gradually they will learn the pattern until they can say the whole thing with you. Then you hesitate on each number, allowing them to say it first.

Equals

First you teach the naming of the symbol $=$ along with the numerals, as above. Then you simply write the sign on the blackboard and make the statement: THIS IS "EQUALS." WHAT IS IT? YES, EQUALS! IT TELLS YOU THAT AS MANY AS YOU CAN COUNT TO ON THIS SIDE OF THE EQUALS, YOU HAVE TO COUNT TO ON THE OTHER SIDE (Engelmann, 1969). LET US ALL SAY THAT. Repeat statement with them several times while pointing to the side of the equals. IF I PUT TWO LINES ON THIS SIDE, HOW MANY DO I HAVE TO PUT ON THIS OTHER SIDE? YES, TWO. HOW DO YOU KNOW? YES! AS MANY AS YOU. . . . TWO EQUALS TWO. WHAT DOES TWO EQUAL? YES, TWO! IF I PUT THREE LINES ON THIS SIDE, WHAT DO I HAVE TO PUT ON THIS OTHER SIDE? YES, THREE! WHY? YES. LET US ALL SAY IT! AS MANY AS YOU. . . . WHAT DOES THREE EQUAL? YES, THREE. NOW I AM GOING TO PUT FIVE LINES ON THIS SIDE. WHO KNOWS WHAT TO DO? CAN YOU FIX IT? Call on one child. WHAT DID YOU DO? WHY? WHAT DOES FIVE EQUAL? NOW I WILL SEE HOW SMART YOU ARE. I WILL PUT A THREE HERE AND A FIVE HERE. HOW IS THAT? NO? WHAT IS WRONG WITH IT? ISN'T IT EQUAL? WHAT DOES THE EQUAL MARK TELL YOU? With each concept you show several examples and then you challenge the children, first requiring group responses, then individual. They must be thoroughly versed in the concept to be able to apply it with no help from the teacher. If not, then you go back and reteach until every child understands the concept. You always teach to the slowest child in the group. The child also learns that "if there are five lines on this side," he can group those five lines on the other side in several *different* ways $(3 + 2, 4 + 1, 5 + 0)$. He does exercises in this concept on his take-homes every day for weeks. Thus he is learning the meaning of 5 in a very concrete way.

In another step, the child must count the lines on one side (12) and then since there are only seven lines on the other side he must plus some more lines to make the equation equal. This is tied into the counting *from* a number (7) *to* a number (12). All of this makes the concept of equivalency so crystal clear to the children that they do not confuse the various types of problems: addition, subtraction, or missing addend.

Computations

The Engelmann method utilizes two major techniques toward the computation of equations, the *hand operation* and the use of *lines* drawn on the board like tally marks. Both techniques are taught, often using both with the same problem. We have so often heard arguments against the use of the fingers for counting for fear this will become a crutch and slow the child down. This is not true. Once the concept is solid the child no longer uses fingers, but memorizes the facts and is very fast. The child's continuing the second year or so to use his fingers for every equation is indicative of the absence of a solid understanding of number concepts. He should be taken back to basic concepts and given a firmer foundation. Using the fingers and lines interchangeably gives the child a more solid foundation which is irrevocable, the facts are really meaningful, and thus easier to memorize.

When first doing a written equation you indicate the quantity of each numeral with tally marks. HOW MANY DOES IT TELL US TO MAKE HERE? YES, TWO. So you make two lines under the numeral. AND HOW MANY DOES IT TELL US TO MAKE HERE? YES, THREE. Make three lines under the numeral. WHAT DOES THE EQUAL MARK TELL US? YES, AS MANY AS YOU CAN COUNT TO. . . . SO LET US SEE HOW MANY ARE ON THIS SIDE. Count the lines with the children as you trace each line precisely. ONE, TWO, THREE, FOUR, FIVE. HOW MANY ARE ON THIS SIDE? SO HOW MANY GO ON THIS OTHER SIDE? YES, FIVE! HELP ME COUNT THEM OUT. Make the lines on the other side as they count with you. HOW MANY ARE THERE? YES, FIVE. WHO CAN WRITE 5 HERE? You very soon eliminate the need for making the lines on the sum side of the equation, and thereafter simply write the numeral.

After much practice to be sure the concept of equals is solid, you eliminate the tally marks for the first addend. I AM SMART. I CAN REMEMBER THERE ARE TWO HERE. I DO NOT HAVE TO MAKE THESE STICKS. I CAN COUNT FROM TWO. I WILL JUST MAKE THE STICKS FOR THIS OTHER NUMERAL, THREE. NOW I WILL COUNT THE FAST WAY (Engelmann, 1969). HOW MANY DO I START WITH? YES, TWO. TWO. . . . GET IT GOING . . . (Retrace the first stick in the second group.) THREE, FOUR, FIVE. CAN YOU COUNT IT THE FAST WAY?

In the Distar program hand operation, the child counts *from* the first addend of the equation. He holds up fingers to represent the second addend. HOW MANY DO WE START WITH? YES, FOUR! AND HOW MANY DO WE PLUS? YES, TWO! DO YOU HAVE TWO FINGERS UP? GOOD! GET IT GOING! FOUR . . . FIVE, SIX! He touches each finger.

HOW MANY ARE ON THIS SIDE OF THE EQUALS? YES, SIX! SO HOW MANY
DO WE PUT ON THE OTHER SIDE? YES, SIX! LET US READ IT! FOUR PLUS
TWO EQUALS SIX! GOOD WORK! If the child errs on an addition
equation, he is asked: HOW MANY DOES IT TELL YOU TO MAKE HERE?
HOW MANY HERE? WHAT DOES THE EQUAL MARK TELL YOU? HOW
MANY DID YOU COUNT TO ON THIS SIDE? SO HOW MANY DO YOU HAVE
TO COUNT TO ON THIS SIDE?

Word Problems

Another very important part of the Engelmann programs is the
use of word problems. Each concept is taught in simple word
problems, preferably using the children in the group as subjects. I AM GOING TO TELL YOU A STORY ABOUT SUSAN. SUSAN HAD
FOUR SCHOOL DRESSES. YESTERDAY SHE WAS RUNNING FAST AND SHE
TORE ONE OF HER DRESSES ALL THE WAY DOWN THE BACK! HOW MANY
SCHOOL DRESSES DOES SHE END UP WITH NOW? Many more word
problems are used in the Engelmann programs than in other
programs. They are all verbal stories told by the teacher, until
well into Distar II, when the child must read the story. At first in
Distar I, the teacher tells the story and the children might figure
it out with a hand operation, or they might dictate to the teacher
how to write the necessary equation on the board, and then
solve it with lines. Later in the program, after the teacher tells the
story, the children have to figure out how to write it on their
take-homes. SHE BOUGHT FOUR MORE! SO WHAT DO YOU DO? PLUS
OR MINUS?

Synopsis of the Programs

Thus in both Engelmann math programs in his book, and in
the Distar Program, you teach the counting, the numeral recognition, the number meaning with objects, the meaning of the symbols, all in separate strands, intertwining them in each lesson
until together they form the basis, the building stones of the
equation. You begin each lesson with a good starter, an attention-
getter, then perhaps go to a new or harder concept, finish off with
easier practice and then have them do a simple page of four to
six computations. The latter is for practice and as a testing device

to see how well individual children perform. When counting, numeral and symbol recognition, and the meaning of equals are solid, the addition equation is taught, then the missing addend or algebra addition equation, and lastly subtraction and algebra subtraction. Distar II goes into multiplication, fractions, money, and negative numbers.

Each concept is taught through multiple repetition. In one lesson a principle or a process might be repreated five to ten times. The trick then is to keep coming back to that principle day after day for a long time to really cement-in the concept. *Do not make the mistake of teaching until the concept appears solid and then leaving it for the rest of the semester.* You do not want to isolate a concept to such an extent that the child can operate only one concept at a time. Children too often get into a set pattern such as addition, and then simply add all the digits in a problem regardless of the sign. The Distar program is so precise that it eliminates this danger; however, if you are using the book, be sure that you teach examples of several types of problems every day. Thus the day you are teaching subtraction with a missing addend, be sure you also present review problems in addition, addition-missing-addend, and subtraction. If you teach just one concept at a time, the child gets in a rut, forgets past concepts. He is unable to restructure his thinking to do another type of equation. Thus if you give him a paper with a mixture of different kinds of problems on it, he would ignore the various signs and simply add them all.

Instruction is done next to a low chalkboard, or with a 2′ x 3′ board on the teacher's lap. The major technique used in the Engelmann programs calls for an auditory-vocal response. The children listen, and then they respond by speaking or by doing something. The children are actively involved every minute of the lesson. There is no passive child-listening while the teacher puts on a twenty-minute demonstration. After every couple of sentences the teacher requires a child response. No tuning-out is allowed.

Every child participates every minute. If you do not have every child's attention, you liven up your lesson to get it. There are many ways to do this, by changing your approach, using a different tactic, making an obvious error, using an attention-getter, moving to an easier concept that has already been learned, or by challenging them to a demonstration of their prowess. One way you do this is by saying: I AM GOING TO CATCH YOU THIS TIME. Or call on individual children for responses, giving a desirable reward for correct answers. Be sure the poor listener responds and is rewarded for his good behavior. We will talk more about behavior modification in the last chapter.

The child learns to think each question through and apply the concept without having to rely on the teacher's judgment of right or wrong. He knows he is right! He cannot be shaken. In the whole program you never tell him the answer to an equation, but you ask him the leading questions to make him use the basic principles to reason-out the problem himself. Thus the aim of the program is to teach convergent thinking and mathematical reasoning rather than memorization of number processes and facts.

In this section we have described some of the initial techniques used to teach the preskills. The methods used to teach the more advanced concepts are very unique and amazingly simple, too. Even the teacher's understanding of math concepts is enhanced by Engelmann's techniques of teaching such things as negative numbers and fractions.

The progress of our children in both the Engelmann programs is amazing. With the discovery techniques of our state texts, only our top ten children could confidently compute equations through sums of ten. The middle children struggled, made many errors, and had no confidence in their own abilities to comprehend math. Few could comprehend missing addends at all. They relied on incomplete memorization of facts, the fingers of both hands, the look on the teacher's face, or copying others. They might be doing sums through six by the end of the year. Our bottom children were completely lost. They could only be sure of failing, day after day.

Now even our slowest children have complete confidence in themselves. They know they can do it. By June they are all successfully completing missing addends with sums in the twenty's, thirty's, and forty's ($42 + \square = 48$). They can take dictation of word problems, decide whether to plus or minus, and compute the equation. The look of triumph on their faces with daily 100's on their take-homes is positive proof of the success of the program.

GROUPING CHILDREN FOR MATH INSTRUCTION
Testing

We used a series of simple tests to place all of our first graders in math groups (Classroom Tests, Math Concepts, Chapter Four). These tests give us a comprehensive picture of the math background of each child. We have an accurate picture of where the child is mathematically, and thus know where to start him in the Engelmann programs, and in which math group to place him. Actually, for placement into Engelmann math instruction groups, the numeral recognition test and identification of the name of a set, or the relating of a numeral to the number of objects, is all that is needed. We divide our sixty children into instruction groups which are as equal in size as possible, leaving the lowest group as the smallest.

Independent Math Packets

To teach these problem learners, small instructional groups are imperative and require the full, undivided attention of the teacher. To manage this, we had to have good independent work for our children to free us to instruct another group in math. Our state-supplied workbooks jump from one concept to another, and require separate instructions for each page. Sometimes even one page may include two or three different types of exercises. Therefore, our primary teachers pooled their dittos and math worksheets. We then designed packets, or bundles, of ten to twelve worksheets on each concept. We limited the number of types of exercises to be included. Thus it requires a minimum amount of instruction for a child to complete all the worksheets independently. These worksheets were deliberately easy for the child to do, far behind the concepts being taught in his instructional group, and hopefully, interesting. We included fun sheets like dot-to-dots and coloring-by-number dittos.

The purpose of all of this was to allow for independent seat-work without the teacher's supervision. She could then give her full attention to her instructional group. Thus Group A might go to their seats to work on their packets perhaps with the super-vision and encouragement of willing sixth graders. Group B would gather for about twenty minutes of instruction. Then they would go to their seats to do their packets and Group A would come to instruction.

We arranged a sequence of concepts according to Engelmann's instruction which we were following and including desirable

1. NUMBER MEANING:
   A. 1–4.
   B. 5–7.
   C. 8–10.

2. ADDITION (Horizontal):
   A. Sums 1–6.
   B. Sums 6–10.
   C. Algebra Addition (Missing Addend).

3. SUBTRACTION (Horizontal):
   A. 6–10.
   B. Algebra Subtraction (Missing Addend).

4. CONSOLIDATION (of Distar I concepts and State text):
   A. Column Addition of Single Numerals.
   B. Column Subtraction of Single Numerals.
   C. Associative Property (adding three single numerals).
   D. Horizontal Addition and Subtraction of Larger Numerals: More-less; Missing Sign; Making Sides Equal.
   (End of Distar I)

5. MULTIPLICATION: (Begins in Distar II):
   A. By 2's, 5's, and 10's.
   B. By 9's and 4's.
   C. By 8's and 3's (plus review of all previous concepts).

6. NEGATIVE NUMBERS AND ANALOGIES (Sequential number patterns).

7. FRACTIONS:

8. COLUMN ADDITION:
   A. Numerals over ten, no carrying
   B. Numerals over ten, carrying

9. MONEY:
   Nickels, dimes, quarters, dollars.
   Story problems included.
   (End of Distar II)

10. TENS CONCEPT
    A. Numerals to 40.
    B. Numerals to 100.

Figure 41. Sequence of Math Packets.

parts of our State programs (Fig. 41). For each concept and/or packet we made a sample page of twenty equations as pretests and posttests. The child must do the test in a limited time and with three or fewer errors. If he fails the test, then this is the concept on which he needs instruction and practice. The first packet he is given in September is on the step of the last test which he passed. Thus he begins with an easy packet, gains confidence in himself, while he is given the necessary instructions for the concepts in the next packet. When he has completed the packet with all errors corrected, he is given the next packet in the sequence. On the completion of all future packets, he takes a posttest which he must pass before he is given the next packet. Failing it, he repeats the packet for more practice and, of course, receives more instruction in that area. A child might be on Packet 1c, or 2a, for independent work, while he is learning addition and algebra addition (missing addend) in his instruction group. He might complete a packet in a day or so, or take over a month to finish it, depending on his motivation level for independent work. A few of our top students work so quickly with their packets that they catch up with the instruction in their groups. Then we have to provide extra seatwork for them to do. Often we just staple together extra pages from our state texts, or give them the state workbook.

We make no attempt to correct packets in class. At the end of the period the children place their packets in the IN box and we correct them after school. If we find that a child has a particular problem, a repeated error, we take some time the next day to help him. Repeated errors and misconceptions are rare when using the Distar Math I program.

Children really seem to enjoy working the packets. They even choose to work on them during free periods. They often skip the fun pages to do the equations. Thus in our new revision of the packets we will eliminate most of the nonmath type papers.

We keep 3" x 5" cards on each child with records of the tests he has taken, packets completed, test scores, and dates when work was accomplished. We also make pertinent comments. This gives us accurate records of each child's progress. We also have a chart on the wall wherein the child's "rocket" with his name on it moves up toward the "moon" with every packet completed (Fig. 42). This individualizing of progress according to effort is extremely stimulating to the children. It encourages responsibility and independence. The child feels that he has some control of his education. "I finished my packet!" says Tommy with a glowing face. Or we hear: "I did three pages today!" Or: "I have only two pages to go!"

CONCEPT OF PLACE VALUE

In the Distar Math Program the numeral ten is made with a tall one and a small zero placed on the top right side of the one: $1°$. It appears more as if it would read "one degree." Then eleven is written, $1°1$, and twelve is $1°2$. This begins back in the numeral recognition strands and forms a basis for understanding the tens concept later in the program. The children learn to read these numerals easily. The teacher writes "ten" on the board: $1°$. I HAVE TEN . . AND IF I PLUS FIVE, (add a "5") IT IS . . YES, FIFTEEN. Erase the five. I HAVE TEN AND I PLUS SEVEN. Write $1°7$.

Figure 42. Rockets to the Moon.

YES, IT IS SEVENTEEN. TELL ME HOW TO WRITE NINETEEN. The children say: "Ten on the left and nine." Thus the place-value concept is built into the program step-by-step.

One way to begin instruction of the tens concept (without the Distar materials) is from Engelmann's description of *carrying* (Engelmann, 1969, p. 333). You write a column of single numerals one to five and then draw a vertical line to the right of these numerals. You then state the rule: WHEN YOU SEE A ONE ON THIS SIDE OF THE LINE IT IS NOT A ONE. IT IS A TEN. Point to the 2. WHEN YOU SEE A TWO ON THIS SIDE OF THE LINE, IT IS NOT A TWO. IT IS A TWENTY. The demonstration continues by first placing 0's on the right side of the line beside each numeral, then 1's, then 2's. Later, you use a mixture of two digit numerals using the 1 in different positions in each column of numerals to give extra practice. These columns are read slowly by the children; e.g., 21. WHEN IT IS ON THIS SIDE IT IS NOT A TWO, IT IS TWENTY. TWENTY PLUS ONE IS TWENTY-ONE.

Except for exercises such as the above, there is no instruction in the *tens concept* or *place value* in Distar I or II. Perhaps they will cover this concept in a future Distar III program when hundreds are taught. In the meantime, since our state program does include these concepts, we feel that we must teach place value with our own methods.

Place-Value Cards

The place-value cards help the children to gain a visual picture of the numerals and to form a connection between the auditory sound of the number and the written symbol. Cut thirty tag strips about 5" x 14". Make a lengthwise line with a felt pen down the middle of the card. With the strip in a vertical position, write the numerals 0 to 9, evenly placed on the right of the line. The numerals should be spaced so as to allow a child to place a milk bottle cap on the left of the line, directly beside each numeral. With a card for each child, have the children count to nine as they touch each numeral. WHAT COMES AFTER NINE? YES, TEN. THIS BOTTLE CAP I AM GIVING EACH OF YOU WITH THE 1 ON IT IS ONE TEN. PUT IT TO THE LEFT OF THE LINE BY THE ZERO. NOW

WHAT DOES IT SAY? YES, TEN! MOVE THE BOTTLE CAP DOWN UNTIL
IT IS BESIDE THE ONE. TEN PLUS ONE IS. . . . YES, ELEVEN. MOVE IT
DOWN TO THE TWO. WHAT IS IT NOW? Continue in this manner
counting to nineteen. NOW WHAT DO YOU NEED? YES, TWENTY! HERE
IS A BOTTLE-CAP WITH A TWO ON IT. IT IS TWENTY. PUT IT ON THE
LEFT OF THE ZERO AND LET US COUNT IT OUT. Continue in this
manner using bottle caps with 3's and 4's and 5's (Fig. 43). NOW
LET US GO BACK AND SEE IF WE CAN MAKE THE NUMERALS ALL THE
WAY TO FIFTY-NINE. GET YOUR FINGER READY TO START. LET ALL OF
US SAY IT! ZERO, ONE, TWO, THREE, FOUR, FIVE, SIX, SEVEN, EIGHT,
NINE. NOW QUICKLY GET YOUR TEN UP THERE. READY? HERE WE GO.
TEN, ELEVEN, TWELVE. . . .

The forties are easier for the children than are the teens, the
twenties, the thirties, and the fifties, because *forty* actually names
the first digit of the numeral. *Twenty* does not sound much like
a two to them, and *thirty* does not sound like a three. So start
this exercise with forty.

NOW LET US SEE WHAT YOU CAN DO. TAKE YOUR FORTY AND SEE

Figure 43. Place-Value Cards.

HOW FAST YOU CAN MAKE THE NUMBER THAT I SAY. I AM GOING TO SKIP ALL AROUND, SO WATCH IT. FORTY-SIX! MAKE IT. GOOD! TOMMY WAS FAST! FORTY-TWO! After you have thus practiced with the forties, work with the twenties and thirties and fifties, and lastly, the teens. When working with the teens, do fourteen and over first, as these numerals are easier. When they have more confidence, go on to eleven, twelve and thirteen. Do these slowly, giving them ample help.

When the children are competent at making the numerals with each of the tens, twenties, etc., mix them all up. LINE UP YOUR BOTTLE CAPS SO THAT YOU CAN SEE THEM EASILY. NOW I AM GOING TO SAY ANY NUMERAL FROM TEN TO FIFTY-NINE. YOU SEE IF YOU CAN MAKE IT. READY? THIRTY-FOUR! DID YOU GET YOUR THIRTY UP THERE? GOOD! FORTY-SIX! GOOD! HERE IS A HARD ONE! FOURTEEN! WHAT DO THE TEENS HAVE TO HAVE ON THE LEFT? YES, A TEN! TEN PLUS FOUR IS FOURTEEN.

To keep all the children on task all of the time when working with these place-value cards, use a cereal reward. Just move around the group and leave a Cocoa-Puff with each child who is participating. You need not reward each child each time he performs. Make it more casual so that you reward each child about every three numbers. Accompany the cereal with a simultaneous verbal reward, complimenting children for desirable behaviors. MARY ANN IS FAST! SUSAN GETS THEM ALL RIGHT! Encourage the child who has difficulty by possibly giving him more help and time to perform, and perhaps by rewarding him more frequently, or after every one that he does.

For practice on writing two-place numerals, put a vertical line on the blackboard to divide the *tens* and *ones*. Make a game of it by having the child who is one of the first to make the numeral on his card, to be the one to go to the board and write the numeral. MIKE MADE IT FAST! MIKE, CAN YOU WRITE IT ON THE BOARD? WHAT WILL YOU PUT ON THE LEFT OF THE LINE? Give each child a turn. You will have to especially emphasize the teens.

Vary this game by having the child who writes the numeral on the board choose the next number for the children to make on their cards and then choose the child who will go to the board to make it.

Bundles of Sticks

Cut quarter-inch doweling into five-inch lengths. Make a three-sided wooden bench of one-half-inch plywood about 6″ x 12.″ Drill nine holes in the top of the bench which will accommodate the doweling. Make a second bench for tens, about 18″ x 10″, with nine large holes, each of which will hold a bundle of ten sticks of doweling. Place the benches on their sides, the tens bench on the left. Place a small blackboard directly behind the benches, and make a vertical line down the middle of it. On the left write *tens* and on the right write *ones*. Give a child one stick. HOW MANY IS THIS? The children all respond: "One." The child puts the stick in the *ones* bench. CAN SOMEONE WRITE IT ON THE RIGHT SIDE OF THE LINE? Call on a second child. THERE, NOW, WE HAVE ONE STICK AND ON THE BOARD IT SAYS ONE! HERE IS ANOTHER STICK. The first child places it in a hole. HOW MANY ARE THERE NOW? YES, TWO. CAN YOU WRITE TWO? Have the second child do all the writing. Continue through nine. When you hand the first child the tenth stick he cannot find a hole for it. WHOOPS! THERE IS NO ROOM FOR TEN! BESIDES, TEN HAS TO GO ON THE LEFT SIDE OF THE LINE. LET US BUNDLE UP THESE STICKS WITH A RUBBER BAND AND PUT IT INTO THE "TEN'S" BENCH! Turn to the second child. HOW WILL YOU WRITE THAT? HOW MANY TENS? HOW MANY ONES? Continue this process counting in sequence. Another day, choose two different children and repeat the process.

Later, place any number of sticks, bundles and ones in the benches. HOW MANY STICKS ARE THERE NOW? WHO CAN WRITE IT CORRECTLY ON THE BLACKBOARD? If the child has difficulty, ask him leading questions to help him succeed. HOW MANY TENS ARE THERE? WHERE DO YOU WRITE IT? HOW MANY ONES? When they are familiar with this game, have the child who writes the numeral correctly on the board also change the sticks in the benches and then call on another child to write the correct numeral.

Vary the procedure by writing the numeral on the board and calling on a child to put the correct number of bundles and

Figure 44. Tens and Ones Benches.

sticks in the benches (Fig. 44). He, in turn, writes a numeral for another child to place the sticks.

Say a number and have one child place the correct number of sticks and another write the numeral on the board. Have the child at the board say the next number and then call on two children to place the sticks and write the numeral. He must verify the correctness of their work.

Writing Numerals in Color

Write numerals 0 to 9 horizontally, about four inches high on about a ten- or twelve-foot-long blackboard. Space the numerals well. Have the children say the number as you write it. TEN. HOW DO I WRITE TEN? YES! LET US PUT IT WAY OVER HERE ON THE LEFT UNDER THE ZERO. ONE TEN AND ZERO ONES. JUST FOR FUN, LET'S MAKE THE ONE TEN WITH RED CHALK. For eleven, put one red 1 and one white 1 right under the 1 in the first row. ONE TEN AND ONE, ONE. For twelve, put one red 1, and one white 2 right under the 2 of the first row. ONE TEN AND TWO ONES. Continue to 19.

NOW WE HAVE TWO TENS, OR TWENTY. LET'S MAKE THE TWENTIES ALL PURPLE. Write a purple 2 and a white 0 under the zeros on the left of the board. As you make each numeral, say: TWO TENS AND A ONE, TWO TENS AND TWO ONES. Or say: TWENTY AND WE BRING THIS "ONE" DOWN HERE, TWENTY-ONE. TWENTY, AND WE BRING THIS "TWO" DOWN HERE, TWENTY-TWO. TWENTY, AND WHAT SHOULD I PUT IN THIS ROW? Designate the vertical row of 3's.

Continue the process, making the thirties one color, the forties another. Then have the children all count in unison while you point at the numerals in sequence. NOW I AM GOING TO SKIP AROUND. WHAT IS THIS NUMBER? THIS ONE? YOU KNOW, I SEE A PATTERN ON THIS BOARD. I SEE A WHOLE HORIZONTAL ROW OF RED TENS. LOOK! THERE IS A RED TEN IN FRONT OF EVERY NUMERAL IN THIS ROW. CAN YOU FIND ANOTHER PATTERN ANYWHERE ON THE BOARD? Tommy finds a vertical row of 5's. You draw a chalk line through the row. Continue while children identify all the vertical and horizontal patterns.

Writing Numerals in Sequence

Cut a ditto with ten vertical and ten horizontal one-inch squares. Write the numerals 0 to 49 in the top half of the paper. Begin the bottom half with 0. It might help to have the children retrace some of the numerals with small crayons, as you have done on the board. This makes the patterns more pronounced. Or all the children can retrace all the numerals while saying them in unison. Then have them write 0 to 49 in the squares on the bottom half of the paper using your board numerals and the top half of the paper to guide them. Call attention to the patterns to help the child who errs. WHAT ARE YOU MAKING? TWENTIES? THEN WHAT HAS TO BE ON THE LEFT OF EVERY NUMERAL IN THIS ROW? YES, A TWENTY. Or: WHAT IS IN THIS COLUMN? SO WHAT DO YOU HAVE TO PUT ON THE RIGHT OF EVERY NUMERAL IN THIS COLUMN?

One of the biggest problems children have with writing numerals is reversals of the two digits. Have these children use weighted wrist bands while writing numerals. With all but the teens, have the child say the number and then ask him what he

said first; e.g., FIFTY-TWO! WHAT DID I SAY FIRST? YES, FIFTY. SO
WHAT SHOULD YOU WRITE FIRST ON THE LEFT? THEN WHAT DID
YOU SAY? YES, TWO. SO WRITE THE TWO NEXT, ON THE RIGHT. When
a child is having difficulty, it also helps to go back to the zero
and have him say the numbers while you point to them. Continue until you come to his error. Stay with him for the next
few numbers, having him say it first, and then write it.

To successfully teach place value, begin after the children can
rote count to 100. We find it best to delay this instruction until
after the children have had both the addition and subtraction
(perhaps in the spring of the year), or after Distar I has been
completed. Use the above sequence of activities from the place-
value cards to the sticks to the numerals in color and the writing
of numerals. Yet vary the games and activities which you use to
keep interest high. The children get tired of any one activity
repeated too frequently. Be sure that the children succeed every
step of the way. Tie the concept into the daily routine as much
as possible. WHAT IS TODAY? THE TWENTY-SIXTH! WHO CAN WRITE IT
ON THE BOARD? HOW MANY TENS? HOW MANY ONES? Or in reading:
WE ARE ON PAGE FORTY-FIVE. WHAT MUST BE ON THE LEFT? HOW
MANY TENS? ONES?

Individual Seatwork

Learning the concept of place value requires considerable
practice. Besides the writing of the numerals in squares, there
are other practice sheets that can be used. The children love
dot-to-dots. These we copy from dime-store books. Be sure that
the numerals are clear and precise. Choose subjects which require lines to move in a random order on the page because
children quickly learn to simply connect all the numerals around
the periphery without counting at all. Use more complex pictures wherein the child will have to read and count carefully.
The subject should not be recognizable until it is correctly finished, but then the picture should be clear.

Make dittos of rows of bundles of sticks whereon the child must
identify the number of sticks present by writing the correct numeral in the answer box. It makes it easier for the child if you put

a vertical dotted line through the answer box and write *tens* and *ones* at the top of each vertical row of answer boxes.

Counting Money

Reinforce the tens concept with the counting of cardboard or real money. At this time, use pennies and dimes only. Count ten dimes in sequence. Rote count by tens. Present a number of dimes and pennies and have the children count up the total, beginning with the dimes. Make dittos of dimes and pennies on which the children can count out the total and then write it in a square.

CLASS GAMES WITH NUMBERS
Individual Bingo Cards

Make Bingo cards of 4″ x 5″ tag for every child. Covers for the numerals can be larger cereals which don't roll around. We use Fruit Loops or Honey Combs. Write the letters *B, I, N, G, O* widely spaced at the top of the blackboard. As you call out a number, say what letter it is under, and write it under that letter on the board. You might also further identify it by saying: TWENTY-SIX. TWO TENS AND SIX ONES. Give winners who cover a whole row correctly a candy treat. Continue the game without removing the old numbers. This way you will have more winners. It is very frustrating to the children to have to remove all the covers when just one person has Bingo.

Blackboard Bingo

Blackboard Bingo is a much more flexible game. You can use it with numeral recognition as above, or with sums of addition problems or remainders of subtraction equations. Make two identical Bingo charts on the blackboard, with five rows each way and using the desired numerals. Just put the equations on cards with the answers on the backs, and then place these answers at random on the two Bingo charts. The two charts should be identical. One Bingo chart is for children on the right side of the room, the Pirates; the other is for the team on the left, the Giants.

Begin with the first child on one team, the Pirates. Uncover an equation. If the child correctly solves it, he may go to the blackboard and cross that numeral out on his team's Bingo card. If he cannot, the turn goes to the first child on the other team, the Giants. If that child fails, the turn then returns to the Pirates and to the second child on that team. Turns pass back and forth between teams until one team has crossed out all the numerals on a horizontal, vertical or diagonal line. Even after a *Bingo,* continue the turns around the room in the same order so that every child has equal turns.

If the correct answer has already been crossed out on that team's Bingo, then simply uncover another card which the child can use and give him another turn. The winnings can be easily spaced between teams with a little discreet card shuffling. The children become so excited with this game that it is necessary to end it with a recess to let off steam.

Baseball

Again, divide the class into two teams, the Pirates and the Giants. Divide your slowest children evenly between teams. Use tag cards with either two-digit numerals to be read, or with addition or subtraction equations to be solved. Designate three bases in the room. Home base is the front blackboard where the "runner" who makes it "home" makes a tally mark for his run. The Pirates are at bat. Uncover an equation. The first Pirate solves it and moves to first base. If he fails it, mark an "out" for his team on the blackboard. Now it is the turn of the second Pirate. If he succeeds, he goes to first base and the first runner goes to second base. They cannot sneak bases, but change only when one of their teammates has a correct answer. When there are three outs, the Pirates on bases take their seats, and the Giants are up. We use this game toward the end of the year to help with the memorization of the number facts. It moves very quickly, and the children become very excited. Again, a recess right afterward is desirable.

OTHER TECHNIQUES
"What Makes Four?"

In the spring, when the children are quite competent with the various addition and subtraction equations, they have a solid basis for discovery techniques. Since they understand the equation thoroughly, they are now able to discover special relationships between numbers. Draw a solid line across the middle of paper plates. Give each child a plate and four pieces of candy corn. WHAT MAKES FOUR? HOW CAN YOU SEPARATE THESE FOUR CANDY CORN INTO TWO SETS, ONE ON EACH SIDE OF YOUR PLATE? SHOW ME! CINDY DID IT! WHAT DID YOU MAKE, CINDY? RIGHT! TWO AND TWO! TWO PLUS TWO IS . . . YES, FOUR. LET'S ALL SAY IT. WATCH! I CAN WRITE IT ON THE BOARD! WHAT ELSE MAKES FOUR? WHAT DO YOU HAVE, MIKE? YES, ONE PLUS THREE! I CAN SAY THE WHOLE THING! ONE PLUS THREE EQUALS FOUR! LET'S ALL SAY IT! CAN YOU WRITE IT ON THE BOARD, MIKE? Be sure they find four plus zero, and also reverse all equations.

Write the equation $3 + \square = 4$ on the board. SEE IF YOU CAN FIGURE IT OUT WITH YOUR CANDY CORN! LET'S READ IT FIRST: THREE PLUS HOW MANY EQUALS FOUR. PUT THREE ON ONE SIDE OF YOUR PLATE! HOW MANY MORE DO YOU NEED FOR THE OTHER SET TO MAKE FOUR? YES, ONE. ANN, YOU WRITE IT IN THE BOX. Make the reverse equation: $1 + \square = 4$. NOW LET US SEE WHAT HAPPENS WHEN WE TAKE SOME AWAY! YOU HAVE FOUR. NOW COVER UP THE SET OF THREE WITH YOUR HAND. FOUR MINUS THREE IS. . . . YES, ONE! LET'S ALL SAY IT. THIS TIME LET US TAKE AWAY THE ONE. FOUR MINUS ONE IS . . . YES, THREE! SAY IT. SEE IF YOU CAN FIGURE OUT THIS ONE. Write $4 - \square = 3$ on the board. LET'S READ IT! NOW LOOK AT YOUR PLATE. YOU HAVE FOUR AND YOU WANT TO END UP WITH THREE. HOW MANY DO YOU HAVE TO MINUS? YES, ONE! Write: $4 - \square = 1$. Help them to solve it and see the relationships. Now give them one more piece of candy corn, and a piece of wide-lined paper. WHAT MAKES FIVE? HOW MANY DIFFERENT WAYS CAN YOU DO IT? SEE IF YOU CAN FIGURE IT OUT AND WRITE THE EQUATIONS ON YOUR PAPER. WOW! JERRY WROTE DOWN TEN WAYS TO MAKE FIVE! At the end of the period they get to eat their candies.

Quantitative Relations with Number Rods

The number rods such as the Stern blocks and the Cuisenaire rods are excellent for teaching size comparison and other relationships. We have tried using the blocks the first part of the year, but out children are so lacking in basic number concepts that they have no basis for understanding the blocks and then interpreting them with the written equation. The four block does not seem to represent *fourness* to them as does a group of four separate objects. The children get a better foundation with the Engelmann techniques. After they have a good understanding of numbers (perhaps in the spring) or when Distar I is completed, the number rods help them to see the relationships between the addends and the sum of an equation, and between the various number quantities.

Every child must have a set of blocks. We made our own with a half-inch square for the base one. You ask the children such questions as: WHICH IS THE LONGEST BLOCK? WHICH IS THE SHORTEST? WHICH IS THE BIGGEST? WHICH IS THE SMALLEST? SORT THEM OUT SO THAT YOU HAVE ALL THE SAME-COLORED ONES IN ONE PILE. MIX THEM ALL UP AGAIN. NOW SORT THEM OUT AGAIN, THIS TIME PUTTING THEM IN SETS ACCORDING TO THEIR SIZES. WHAT DID YOU FIND OUT?

SEE IF YOU CAN MAKE A STAIRWAY BEGINNING WITH THE SMALLEST BLOCK. NOW, TAKE ANOTHER SMALL BLOCK AND WALK IT UP THE STAIRS. WHAT DID YOU DISCOVER? IF WE CALL THE SMALLEST BLOCK A ONE, WHAT WOULD THE NEXT ONE BE? THE NEXT? NOW, LET'S WALK THAT SMALL BLOCK UP THE STAIRS. FIRST PUT IT ON THE ONE. ONE PLUS ONE MORE IS . . YES, TWO. NOW PUT IT ON THE TWO. TWO PLUS ONE MORE IS . . . YES, THREE! Continue to ten. NOW LET'S TAKE THE SMALL BLOCK DOWN THE STAIRS. PUT IT ON THE NINE BLOCK. NOW IT MAKES TEN. TEN TAKE AWAY ONE IS . . . NINE. NOW PUT IT ON THE EIGHT BLOCK. NINE, TAKE AWAY ONE IS . . . YES, EIGHT.

Another day: TAKE A FOUR BLOCK! NOW IT IS A TRAIN. SEE HOW MANY TRAINS YOU CAN MAKE THAT ARE THE SAME SIZE AS THE FOUR BLOCK. SUSAN HAS A THREE AND A ONE. SEE, SHE PUTS IT RIGHT BESIDE THE FOUR AND THEY ARE THE SAME SIZE. I CAN SAY

WHAT SHE HAS MADE: THREE PLUS ONE IS FOUR. CAN YOU SAY IT? WHAT ELSE CAN YOU FIND? After the children have found all the different arrangements which make *four,* go on to another number block. When they discover an arrangement, help them to verbalize it into an equation and even go write it on the board.

TAKE A FOUR AND PUT A THREE ON TOP OF IT LIKE THIS. THREE PLUS HOW MANY MORE WOULD MAKE FOUR? WHAT DO YOU NEED? YES, A ONE! GOOD! Repeat this exercise with different numbers.

Hold up something like a three-plus-one block on top of a four block. LET'S SEE WHAT HAPPENS WHEN YOU MINUS THE ONE. WE HAVE FOUR AND WE MINUS THE ONE. Take off the one block. WHAT DO WE END UP WITH? YES, THE THREE! Do this with each different combination.

These ideas for the manipulation of number blocks are just a random few. You will find many more uses for the blocks and suggestions for challenges for the children in Gattegno's book (Gattegno, 1966).

Instant Recognition of Small Quantities

Slow children seem to have difficulty recognizing the number of objects in a group without counting them out each time. You give them even four Cocoa-Puffs and they have to count them to tell you how many they have. So they need practice in identifying sets of objects. Use about 4″ x 6″ size tagboard cards. On them draw or paste clearly outlined objects to form familiar sets. Old Animal Rummy cards usually have bright-colored pictures that are good for this.

Use the groupings as on dominos and playing cards, plus other arrangements. Three objects could be placed in a vertical row on one card, a horizontal row on another, and in a triangle on a third card. SEE HOW FAST YOU CAN TELL ME HOW MANY THERE ARE ON THE CARD. Uncover a card. YES, THREE! TOMMY WAS FAST. SEE IF YOU CAN BEAT HIM THIS TIME! Uncover another one. You could also give the card to the child who identifies the number first, or give some reward. Encourage the parents of children who have problems recognizing number groups to play cards and dominos with them at home.

Teaching Sequence

Sequence is an integral part of math and an excellent tool for learning mathematical concepts. In counting forward and backward and making tallies, you are teaching number sequence. In teaching the natural order of whole numbers and the plus concept, frequently repeat this sequential routine: ONE PLUS ONE IS TWO. TWO PLUS ONE IS THREE. THREE PLUS ONE IS FOUR. It helps to clap for each number in a rhythm while saying it. Repeat this routine frequently until the children are able to say it alone. Then say: ONE PLUS ONE IS . . . . and let them supply the answer. This routine is a good opener to an instruction session.

When concepts are clear and you want to teach them to memorize addition facts, begin with like addends in sequence. Again, clap to the numbers in a rhythm. ONE PLUS ONE IS TWO. TWO PLUS TWO IS FOUR. THREE PLUS THREE IS SIX. FOUR PLUS FOUR IS EIGHT. Continue up to twenty. When you teach multiplication, teach counting by 2's, 3's, 4's, and 5's.

There are other ways of teaching sequence outside of math. We shall be discussing some of these under Language (Chapter Eleven).

REFERENCES

Cuisenaire Rods. Cuisenaire Company of America, Inc., 12 Church Street, New Rochelle, New York, 10805.

Engelmann, Siegfried: *Preventing Failure in the Primary Grades.* Chicago, Sci Res, 1969.

Engelmann, Siegfried, and Carnine, Doug: *Distar Math Program, I and II.* Chicago, Sci Res, 1969.

Gattegno, C.: *Mathematics, with Numbers in Color, Book A.* Mount Vernon, New York, Cuisenaire, 1966.

Hallahan, Daniel P.: Cognitive styles—preschool implications for the disadvantaged. *J Learning Disabilities, 3* (No. 1): 7–10, Jan. 1970.

Chapter Eleven

ℒanguage

TRADITIONAL LANGUAGE INSTRUCTION

ONE OF THE BASIC goals of kindergarten and first-grade programs during the last two or three decades has been language development, but the emphasis has been mainly on listening to and enjoying language. A traditional kindergarten language program usually consisted of songs, poems, and stories—mostly the presentation of auditory language to be received by the child. There has been some emphasis on vocal language in that the children were to repeat the songs and poems and usually also participated in some kind of share-and-tell time. Since children can listen without hearing, or appear to listen, without understanding the words spoken, they can go through several years of this type of training without an accurate reception, without really learning any language. Since the teacher has presented the lessons, and the child did not receive or integrate the language, he was simply thought to be dull, perhaps even retarded.

Since the share-and-tell was usually done only by children who were willing to participate, the children who most needed the practice in vocalizing, were thus passively eliminated from the experience. The child who was unable to discriminate auditorily, who had poor reception of language, who lacked the language background to understand and integrate the spoken word, or who was unable to verbalize adequately was lost in this traditional environment and was not taught. He was frustrated by his inability to understand language, to follow auditory and written directions, to comprehend stories and jokes.

SYMPTOMS OF LANGUAGE DISABILITY
Receptive Problems

The child who does not seem to listen to stories may be handicapped in auditory reception. This may be because of poor auditory discrimination or due to an inadequate vocabulary. He does not understand what the other children find so funny, so why pretend to listen? He does not follow the directions of an assignment because he cannot understand those directions. He may confuse prepositions, pronouns, verb forms, adjectives. His ability to do the task may not be deficient at all, only his ability to understand what he is expected to do. If he does not laugh at jokes, maybe it is due to his inability to receive the message. I have tried reading Beginning Reader's *Riddles* to classes wherein not one child understood.

Errors in reading comprehension are a lack of *language* ability, not necessarily of *reading* ability. The child who is unable to discriminate sounds, the basis of words, has great difficulty learning to read, or to spell phonetically. Again, failure in other subjects such as history, science, and social studies may be due to lack of an adequate vocabulary and background on which to base new learnings.

Expressive Problems

The child with expressive language problems might understand spoken language but lack the ability to put ideas into words and sentences. He may speak only in short phrases, getting others to supply the words he lacks by pointing, gesturing, saying "that there," or "you know." He might be quiet, reticent to speak, even withdrawn. You might think him dull because he does not participate in classroom discussions or answer questions vocally. Maybe he does not understand and has receptive language problems, too. However, he may be receiving every word which transpires in the classroom and months later may still be able to remember details. Little Billy, whose sentences consisted mainly of "my gots," could report the details of a once-told story (with no pictures) a year later.

Delayed Speech

Delayed speech in the young child may be an early warning of future learning problems. We have often thought this child to be simply slow developing and often expected that he would outgrow his difficulties in a couple of years. However, Zedler (1966) has found this to be a very serious mistake. The child's crucial language-learning period may be lost to him and in a year or so he may become so frustrated by his disability that he is hardly amiable to instruction. He may build up a defensive wall of resistance and feel: "They think I am stupid, but I do not care! I do not want to do that stuff anyway! And I hate teachers!"

Aphasia

Impairment or loss of the faculty for the use of language is known as *aphasia*. A person with problems in receptive language is often labeled as *receptive aphasic*. These terms usually refer to those who have had language function which is subsequently impaired by some type of brain insult. However, there are sometimes children who have not developed language. These are referred to in various terms such as aphasic-like or *childhood aphasia*. A child who does not develop language may really be suffering from a number of things, including hearing problems or autism. It is very difficult to diagnose some of these children. They may receive different diagnoses from different clinicians.

Autism

A complex condition related to language disability is *infantile autism*. The autistic child has difficulty relating to his environment. His ability to relate new stimuli to remembered experience is impaired. He is often obsessively interested in the mechanical, more particularly *one* mechanical object. In infancy he may do crib-rocking and head-banging incessantly. When he is picked up or carried, he does not cooperate, may stiffen and be difficult to hold. He is fearful of strangers. The autistic child may do some kind of repetitive or ritualistic play and become furious if anything is changed. He may stare off into space, looking right through people. He may have peculiar feeding problems such as eating very little or excessively, or craving one thing only. He often has excellent memory and musical ability and spatial ability. He may compose a puzzle upside down as well as right side up. He may have strange speech traits, high-pitched voice or monotone, or never use *I* or *yes*. Some autistic children rarely speak, or they repeat set phrases over and over in a delayed echolalia. The autistic child may have poor perception of stimuli, and be insensitive to peripheral pain and lack perception of danger. He cannot learn from experience.

In David Horne's film *The World Outside* children with severe autism are portrayed. One boy, for example, just squats hour after hour curled in a fetal position. Another film, *Infantile Autism, The Invisible Wall,* shows several children with different symptoms and peculiar traits. One boy is intrigued by circular movements and sits spinning an ash tray repeatedly. Another rocks back and forth, while another endlessly paces. It is very difficult to get these children to attend to stimuli outside themselves. Some never talk, and yet some enjoy listening to stories but cannot attend for very long. Some have marked advanced abilities in specific skills, such as the four-year-old who can draw detailed pictures.

Bernard Rimland, Director of the Institute for Child Behavior Research, San Diego, California, has researched this malady extensively and submits the hypothesis that the difficulty might be due to impairment of the function of the reticular system (1964). We spoke of the sorting and alerting function of this system earlier under Figure-Ground Perception (Chapter Five). It is very interesting to note that Bender (1961) also mentions reticular formation as a possible site of impairment in childhood schizophrenia. Somehow these children are not receiving and sorting stimuli normally. Although the authorities in each field (autism, schizophrenia, learning disabilities) carefully outline symptoms of their maladies as completely separate, there is great controversy and division of opinion on diagnosis of these children. Some children have been diagnosed several times and given several different labels. A child could be diagnosed by two or three clinicians as autistic, yet not be considered autistic by Rimland's criteria. Some day we may find all of these labels to be excessive and invalid or unnecessary, and simply look for the physical cause of the disability—inaction of hypoaction of the reticular system, or overaction of the system, so the child over-concentrates on one thing. Hopefully, then, our researchers will come up with the chemicals necessary to bring about a balanced function of the reticular system and desirable behavior. Today a hypothesis, tomorrow a reality!

Although in our classrooms we may never have a child who is diagnosed autistic, schizophrenia, or aphasic, we should still be aware of these conditions and alert to the symptoms. We do have children who stare right through us, who do not seem to relate to people, who seldom speak, who seem to be in a world of their own. Perhaps someday, advances in the areas of the severe behavior problems above may bring help to the children who operate on the periphery of our classrooms and of life.

THE NATURE OF LANGUAGE

Language is the tool of cognition. Language is the vehicle for social interaction, communication. Language is the means of behavior control.

The cooing infant has no language. As he becomes aware of touching, hearing, and seeing, his family gives him the language, the names of his perceptions, *Daddy, bottle, dolly.* Then comes the more descriptive language of *too hot, hurts, hungry, cold, pretty,* etc. These he stores for future use. If the child makes the right connections and remembers that the stove is *hot,* and dolly is *pretty,* we conclude that he is learning to *order* his environment, and that he is able to connect ideas, that he is intelligent.

This then is the basis of his development in language and cognition. Without language he is unable to organize incoming information, to integrate concepts. They tell him that the iron is hot. He knows from his experience with the hot stove, that heat will burn him, so he does not have to touch the iron to understand that *it* will burn him, too. He is learning.

As his vocabulary increases, incoming information is multitudinous. He must have more ways of organizing that data or it is simply a confusing mass of babble. So his parents or his teachers help him to classify, to sequence, to organize or schedule this human computer. These are *vehicles,* you ride in them. These are *foods,* you eat them. These are *plants,* they grow. These are made of *glass,* they break. He learns sequence: "First you plant the seed, then it grows into a carrot. Then you can eat it." Or, "First it is morning, then it is afternoon, then night." "First you unscrew the nuts, then you take the top off, then you can see the wheels inside." "Spring follows winter." "Punishment follows crime." "If you tear sister's dress, you will be spanked." "If you get an *A,* Father will be proud!" Now that he has the classifying and sequencing skills, he is able to store a multitude of separate bits of information in his brain for future use.

Reception

We receive information from our senses. If we understand that which we receive, we say that we *decoded* it. A child screams and we run to the rescue. We auditorily received (decoded) his screaming. We understood that he needed help. We see a deer and recognize it from our stored past information; we visually received (decoded) the deer. We feel a hot pan and we understand that it is too hot to pick up without a hotpad; we used tactile-kinesthetic reception (decoding).

An inaccurate perception feeds distorted information into the language system, and the perceptions are misunderstood. Most pronounced of these misperceptions is that due to poor auditory discrimination. You say *stop,* and the child thinks you said *shop.* You say *team,* and the child hears *Tim.* You say *Tab,* and he hears *tag.* Since the sounds are distorted, the words are misunderstood and the directions are not followed. As Myklebust (1967) has found, a deficiency in auditory perception or reception is a debilitating handicap in acquiring language.

We tested sixty kindergarten children with twelve sets of words which differed either in blend, digraph, beginning or ending consonant or vowel. Ten children could not discriminate six to nine of the word sets. When retested by a different examiner, the same children missed exactly the same sets of words, verifying the diagnosis that the children had poor auditory discrimination ability.

Expression

Language expression is through vocal and motor channels. To respond by vocalizing is *verbal expression* (vocal encoding). Any time you are talking, you are verbally expressing yourself (vocally encoding). When you are in action, moving in response to language, you are expressing yourself through manual expression (motor encoding). Someone tells you to pick up a pencil. When you do so, you are manually expressing. You think that it is too hot, so you take off your sweater. Again, you are manually expressing. You tell a child to write his name at the top of his paper. If he does so, he is successfully manually expressing your directions.

Integration

The receptive acts of auditory, visual, and tactile-kinesthetic reception (decoding) and the expressive acts of vocal and motor expression (encoding) operate reciprocally. You auditorily receive the sound of a child screaming and your manual expression is the act of dashing to the rescue. This is auditory-motor association. You visually receive the picture of a child picking up a rock, and you verbally express the command for him to drop it. This is a visual-vocal association. The connections, the associations made in your mind, told you from stored past experience and training that a screaming child could be a child in mortal danger. And that a stone in a child's hand is an accident looking for a place to happen. Thus your brain integrated the perceptions and signaled the appropriate responses to you. The person unable to integrate perceptions is severely handicapped, often mentally retarded. He is able to receive and perhaps store information, but he is unable to make the proper connections in his brain to use the information. Thus he might see something falling toward him and just stand there and let it fall on him. He has seen things fall before, has had things hit him, but is not able to make the connections to realize that he must move to avoid being hurt.

When we talk about integration of data and association, we are discussing the inner language, as Myklebust (1967) defines it. An inner language deficiency, an inability to integrate incoming data and therefore to act intelligently, is the basis for what we know as intelligence. It is this ability to reason, to intellectualize, to make association, to draw conclusions, that is the gross difference between the Einsteins and the mentally retarded.

Intelligence is not usually something which everyone does or does not have. It is all a matter of degree of ability, and more particularly of variety of ability. One person may find mathematical associations easy to manipulate. Another may have excellent word storage and retrieval and be a writer or a public speaker. Some have exceptional visual memories, read almost as quickly as they can turn the pages. Others have excellent long-term memories and can remember intricate details of incidents, stories, dates, statistics. Some people can clearly see relationships in the use of machinery, and have exceptional mechanical talent. Some have great insight into the words spoken or written by others and can easily see through such elusive things as evasion, false premises, innuendo. Others take every word spoken at face value only. Most of us have some degree of ability in all of these areas with some strengths and some deficits.

A multitude of auditory and visual data is coming at you constantly. You are sitting outside—the birds are singing, flying, eating, tending their young. The trees, flowers, and plants are all around you. Insects crawl up stems and fly or jump from plant to plant. All of this is happening. What do you perceive? Do you make only a general conclusion that it is a lovely day and the birds are singing? Or do you perceive the details and store this knowledge and make associations that inform you about the flora and fauna? That is the song of a chipping sparrow. That tapping sound is from the flicker up in that tree. This is a spruce with new needles on the tips of the branches. Those birds flying in circles up there are swallows gathering insects. That is a golden-mantled ground squirrel dashing across the lawn. Some people can observe all of this and *see* nothing, gather no new information. Others can learn so well from simply observing nature that they can be proficient naturalists without ever attending formal schools. This is the talent of the self-educated man. You often hear of highly trained professors going to visit a particular woodsman who has gathered fantastic knowledge from his environment. Again, the ability to receive the perceptual data might be there, but the number of associations made with that data determines the organism's alertness, his degree of what our society defines as intelligence and education. None of this could be accomplished without accurate reception, integration, and expression of language. Thus language is the basis for that intelligence which we rate so highly in our present society.

When we teach language skills, we are increasing intelligence. Our measure of intelligence, IQ tests, includes large percentages of language ability. Some IQ tests are totally language tests. Yet, it is ironical that although we esteem intelligence and value IQ tests much beyond their worth, we have not attempted to train our children in the very factors found relevant in those tests. We have excused ourselves with the incredible cliché "we must not teach a test." We would not think of testing a child in multiplication before he is taught the concept, but we fail to teach language, classifying, sequence, and reasoning before labeling a child with results of IQ tests.

The Highest Forms of Language

Of greatest importance in language development is the ability to make associations. Next is the reception of language perceptions, and lastly is the expression of language. Written language is the highest form of expressive language and, according to Vgyotsky (1962), is the most difficult to learn. In order to write, one must have a full score of vocabulary and information. He must be able to form sentences and to sequence ideas. He must be *taught* these language abilities.

Reading, according to Tompkins (1963), is "the last skill acquired." It requires integration of auditory and visual channels for the perception of the written word. After the words are analyzed, the sentence still may mean very little to a child unless he has an adequate language background. Lack of comprehension in reading is not lack of ability to unlock the words, the symbols, but inability to understand the language itself. Children are poor in reading comprehension because they are poor in language. If the child can read: "The kitten scrambled across the road," but cannot answer the question, "What did the kitten do?" or "Where did the kitten go?" it does not indicate an inability to read. The child simply does not understand the language, the words.

Thus receptive, associative, and expressive language are the *basis* for those two most highly esteemed *R*'s, reading and writing. Reason enough to set aside a specific period daily to teach this most important, basic, and neglected *R*.

Can Language Be Taught?

Helen Keller was taught to comprehend language, even though she could neither hear nor speak, but it took a dedicated teacher to do it. Kastein (1966) tells how an uncontrollable child of four who had a gross language deficiency and no speech, received language instruction which helped her to make average progress by sixth grade. For years speech therapists have been successfully training children in the articulation and discrimination of sounds and words. Back in the classroom these children often make dramatic gains not only in oral language ability, but also in reading, spelling, and social studies.

Especially since the development of the Illinois Test of Psycho-Linguistic Ability, children have been tested, trained in language deficits and then retested. Studies have been made with a wide variety of subjects. One study by Outridge (1964) consisted of nine weeks of language training for a heterogeneous group of children from receptive aphasic, to mentally retarded, and diagnosed dyslexic. Gains in language age ranged from eleven to thirty-three months.

A study by Hart (1966) was with visually handicapped children who were two years retarded in oral language and reading. After a seven-week language program, posttesting showed a one-year, eleven-months mean gain in language, and one-year, six-months gain in reading. A previous study by Hart (1963) with cerebral palsied children gave training in specific language deficits. In seven weeks there was a 12.3 months gain in language against the control group's 1.1 month gain. It is significant that these studies often show gains in reading comprehension and word recognition, even though the children received no additional instruction in reading. Again, this shows us that language training is basic to reading.

LANGUAGE TESTS
The ITPA

The Illinois Test of Psycholinguistic Abilities (the ITPA) is a diagnostic test designed to pinpoint language abilities and deficiencies. With this information, language instruction may be concentrated in the weak areas to help the child overcome his handicaps. Often his strong areas may be used as the channel of the instruction. The subtests are (1) *Auditory Reception,* (2) *Visual Reception,* (3) *Visual Sequential Memory,* (4) *Auditory Association,* (5) *Auditory Sequential Memory,* (6) *Visual Association,* (7) *Visual Closure,* (8) *Verbal Expression,* (9) *Gramatic Closure,* (10) *Manual Expression,* (11) *Auditory Closure,* and (12) *Sound Blending.* The Closure Sequential Subtests are related to the ability to respond automatically without conscious effort and to repeat or reproduce a sequence of symbols heard or seen.

Using these test results as a basis for instruction, teachers can tailor instruction to individual children. This is an excellent practice, but often teachers are unable to make use of it because of the length of time required for the testing and the need for trained personnel to administer it. There is also the factor of feasibility of the individual prescriptive instruction. We might be able to form small groups for instruction, but for a regular classroom teacher, individual instruction is almost impossible. ITPA's contribution to the classroom teacher is the classification and analysis of language factors which give us a framework for planning a language curriculum. The second half of this chapter will contain suggestions for language training in the receptive, expressive, and sequential factors of the ITPA. Even though we are unable to test our children individually, we can train all of our children in these important language factors.

Wepman

The Wepman Test of Auditory Discrimination contains like pairs of words and also pairs which differ in beginning or ending consonant, or in vowel. The child is asked to listen to the two words with his back turned to the examiner and determine whether the words are the same or different. If the child scores low in this test, he needs training in auditory discrimination. This is an individual test, but is easy to administer and requires only a few minutes.

Peabody

The Peabody Picture Vocabulary Test is used with children with limited oral speech ability. It is especially used with younger children with speech difficulty who need only point to a picture to indicate the answer.

Engelmann Test

The Basic Concept Inventory Test developed by Siegfried Engelmann (1967) takes an entirely different approach to language diagnosis than does the ITPA. Here Engelmann asks specific questions of the child to determine the actual words and concepts missing, rather than the deficient language channel. We shall discuss the language traits in this test later in this chapter.

Other Diagnostic and Intelligence Tests

Since intelligence tests contain language subtests, these are often used to help identify language problems. Zedler (1966) used the language portions of the WISC to identify children with language learning problems. Valett's test, A Psychoeducational Survey of Basic Learning Abilities, contains several language factors. The deHirsch Predictive Index has language sections. There are Digit Span and Memory for Sentences tests referred to in

Chapter Four of this book. Also, under Suggested Battery of In-formal Tests (Chapter Four) there are some simple measuring devices for *auditory perception, discrimination* and *recall, expressive language* and *conceptual development, sequence* and *classifying.* These are more practical for the regular classroom teacher to utilize.

Classroom Clues

With a background knowledge of receptive, associative, and expressive language, even responses to seemingly casual questions can be enlightening. Children with language problems have dif-ficulty answering WHAT IS YOUR ADDRESS? They often do not know house numbers or phone numbers, parent's names or place of business. Even their siblings' names and their own middle and last names are elusive.

Children with language problems often give incomplete or ir-relevant responses to questions in classroom discussions. Watch for children who are unable to express themselves, to describe some-thing familiar. Once the children saw the truck from the dog pound in front of the school. Knowing the custodian had cor-ralled a stray dog, they knew the purpose of the truck. They made incomplete sentences about "the pon man" even though they had not seen him. Yet when I opened the matter up for class discussion, not one child was able to make a clear statement that: "The pound truck is out front. The man from the pound must be here to get the dog." They understood, but could not express.

Children have naming problems. They often point instead of naming objects or peers. Even toward the end of the school year, they have difficulty naming their classmates. They will say "that boy" and be unable to name the culprit.

THE LANGUAGE OF THE DISADVANTAGED

The speech of the disadvantaged child differs from that of the middle-class child. The deprived child speaks in phrases and in chopped and incomplete sentences. His language is not adapt-able to the sharing of ideas, giving of opinions, or making complex analysis. The vocabulary is sparse, often full of incorrect grammar sequences such as double negatives and improper verb forms. Final consonants are often eliminated. In our school, this latter is particularly a trait of Spanish-speaking children.

The Bereiter-Engelmann Project of the Institute for Research on Exceptional Children at the University of Illinois, researched the speech of the disadvantaged child.

1. He omits articles, prepositions, conjunctions, and short verbs from statements.
2. He does not understand the function of *not* in a sentence.
3. He cannot produce plural statements correctly, and cannot perform the actions implied by plural statements.
4. He cannot use simple tenses to describe past, present, and future action.
5. He cannot use the pronoun *it* to refer to an inanimate object.
6. He does not understand many of the common prepositions and conjunctions.
7. He can often perform a direction, but is not able to describe what he has done.
8. He does not realize that two or more words can describe one object. (Osborn, 1968, pp. 2–4)

Thus (1) instead of whole sentences like: "This is my truck," the disadvantaged child might say: "My truck," or "Dis truck." If you ask him to show you something that is *not* red (2), he will point out something red. For "These are trucks" (3) he may say: "D'ese truck," or "These is trucks." If you show the child sequence pictures of before, during, and after an action (4), he is unable to identify the picture to go with the statement which you make; e.g., FIND THE PICTURE OF THE BOY WHO IS GOING TO BLOW UP THE BALLOON. Or: FIND THE PICTURE OF THE BOY WHO IS BLOWING UP THE BALLOON. He might refer to his truck (5): "Him busted." He also misuses object pronouns: "Her goed." "Him stold!" "Mine truck." "My gots."

The disadvantaged child cannot stand (6) *in front of* his desk, or *next to* Susan, or understand *between four and six*. If you ask him to give you a red *or* green crayon, he will give you both. You say: PUT THE CRAYON ON MY DESK (7), he does so. But then ask: WHERE DID YOU PUT THE CRAYON? he will say: "Desk," or "Crayon on desk." He is unable to classify things (8), to call them more than just their name, or to describe things. If you ask him to describe a table, he cannot say that it is *furniture,* or *big,* or *made of wood.* At share-and-tell time he will hold up a toy, and in spite of prompting by the teacher, will say little more than its name. If you say: WHAT DO YOU DO WITH IT? his reply will be: "Play." If you say: WHERE DID YOU GET IT? he will say "Home."

The Language of Instruction

Remembering now that disadvantaged children have such difficulties with words, try examining your classroom instructions to them. Take a common phonics exercise: SAY THE NAMES OF THE OBJECTS IN THE FIRST ROW. WHICH ONES START THE SAME? DRAW A LINE UNDER THE PICTURES THAT START WITH THE SAME SOUND. Easy? Not for disadvantaged children. Because of their deficiencies with language, they may not understand: *say, objects, in, row, first, which, start, same, draw, line, under, with, sound.* Thus, auditory discrimination of the sounds might be *excellent,* yet the child could be totally unable to follow the instructions and therefore might fail the assignment.

If the child is to perform well in school, he must be able to understand the words used in classroom instruction. For this reason, and as a result of the findings of the Bereiter-Engelmann project, work was begun on instructing teachers on the techniques of teaching the language of instruction to disadvantaged children. Although the teachers were rigorously trained in the separate techniques, it took hours of time for the teacher to collect the pictures and objects for her instruction. The chalkboard was used extensively, but some teachers had difficulty drawing quickly. Then there was the problem of remembering to program in that essential repetition. There was also a lack of consistency between teachers in the program. It was finally decided to construct a printed program for the teachers to follow. The result was the Distar Language I Program (Englemann, 1969).

Distar Language is a rigorous, carefully programmed series of highly structured lessons in direct instruction of language. You read aloud the print in green, and do the instructions that are in black. You ask the questions as you point at the pictures. You correct the incorrect or incomplete answers by demonstration. Then you have the children repeat the correct statements. Sometimes you ask for one-word answers, and sometimes for whole sentences with the clue: SAY THE WHOLE THING. This is a thorough, precise program. The same patterns of instruction are used throughout the whole program so that the child moves gradually from the simple whole statement: "This is a tree," to much more complex statements: "After I touched the flower, I touched the book and then I touched the lamp," or "All of the containers have flowers in them." Or: "These pencils are white and do not have erasers."

Thus as the structure of the language becomes more complex, the language statements involve the children in higher cognitive processes, classifying, sequencing, and problem-solving. This highly structured program is essential to overcome the children's deficiencies and to provide two year's growth in one, to bring disadvantaged children up to the level of their middle-class counterparts.

This whole language program is dramatically different from the traditional programs of early childhood education that emphasize the social and expressive use of language. As Jean Osborn says:

> We do not believe, given the short number of hours the child spends in school, that the traditional nursery school approach of experience and exposure is sufficient to meet the very particular and desperate needs of disadvantaged children.
>
> It is our thesis, however, that proper and precise understanding and use of instructional language will not result from a program which concentrates only on social and expressive use of language, whereas the direct teaching of an instructional language will in a very short time produce a richer social and expressive language. This thesis is borne out by the scores of our children on the vocal-encoding section of the Illinois Test of Psycholinguistic Abilities. Although our language sessions demand highly perscribed and verbatim responses from the children, significant gains on this subtest, which requires the child to freely describe an object, were made. When the first year's subjects were tested after six weeks of school, which is when they were tested for the first time, they averaged one year below normal. Three months later, they averaged at the normal level, and three months later yet,

they averaged four and one-half months above normal. (Osborn, 1968, pp. 6–9)

The Engelmann-Osborn Distar Language Program has been carefully researched and revised several times before printing. These programmed daily lessons eliminate the possibility of teacher error and lack of planning and consistency. Even the most competent teacher, working long hours, has great difficulty planning the lessons, collecting the materials (pictures, objects) for daily sequential language lessons. This is probably the reason language instruction has been so badly neglected. Teachers spend all their extra energies preparing reading and math lessons. The Distar Language program does all the preparation work for her, providing the near-perfect program. It is almost foolproof, baring negativity or resistance on the part of the teacher. The programmed lessons are so efficient and effective that once you have taught with them, you will find that your own planned lessons are sadly lacking and will incorporate the direct-teaching techniques in the rest of your curriculum.

The teacher's major problem with obtaining the Distar program is financial. Our materials are usually selected and purchased by administrators far from us. In our educational system we teachers have too little control over the choice of the materials that we use in our classroom. Our tools are too often mediocre. A plumbing or electrical contractor would never expect to hire his men at several thousand a year and then fail to provide the most efficient tools for them. It simply is not good economics. Yet our shelves are lined with state-supplied books which are useless to us. Therefore, if we want to do a better teaching job with our children we must often purchase our own materials or make them ourselves. Our greatest boon consists of Federal funds and available study and research grants.

The language disorders of children with MCD are often more striking, more pronounced, or more unusual, with distorted perception, confused associations, or inadequate expression. The Distar program concentrates on clear and precise auditory and visual reception, and on making the correct associations according to reliable data, and on precision responses. Thus, although it was primarily designed for the disadvantaged, children with neurological language impairment often make excellent progress with this program.

DEVELOPING YOUR LANGUAGE PROGRAM

Language is the foundation, the organizer, the tool of intelligence, of higher cognitive function. The same foundation is required for growth in reading and writing skills. Language can be trained. The child's measurable intelligence can be raised. This training can in turn enhance reading and writing.

First, you must understand the language system—how the child receives, associates, and expresses language. Then try to become more aware of the language deficiencies of the children in your classroom. Listen for auditory-discrimination problems and Osborn's eight language traits. You probably will not be able to prescribe and tutor individually; however, you can group your children with the most pronounced language problems and have just two language groups to instruct. Have a sixth grader read a story to one group while you instruct the other for fifteen minutes. Then change groups. In this way you are better able to keep the attention and obtain the participation of every child.

Teach a concept, such as *behind*. Use direct teaching methods, have the group respond in unison until the concept appears solid. WHERE IS THE CUP? YES, THE CUP IS BEHIND THE CHAIR. Put the cup behind different objects and children so that the exercise is repeated perhaps ten times. Then call on individual children to respond to be sure that every child progresses with you. If a child has difficulty, reteach the concept and retest him. Place these children who err close to you, keep their attention, and call on them most often. The children understand when you tell them: THIS IS HARD FOR TOMMY. LET US SEE IF HE CAN DO IT NOW. When Tommy finally gets a concept, the children often applaud and compliment him.

There are three moderately priced books available from the University of Illinois Press at Urbana. They are *Learning Language I, II,* and *III.* One is the *parts* book. It contains in a spiral binder large outline pictures easily visible to the children. We colored the pictures with flow pens for more contrast between the parts. With each picture is a series of suggested questions for the development of the concept. With these pictures you teach the name of the object and its parts, the use of each part, and the material from which each part has been made. For example: WHAT IS THIS? A shovel. YES, THIS IS A SHOVEL! SAY THE WHOLE THING! (Engelman 1969). THIS IS A SHOVEL. IS THIS A SAW? No. SAY THE WHOLE THING. This is *not* a saw. I AM GOING TO TELL YOU THE PARTS OF A SHOVEL. THIS IS A HANDLE. A SHOVEL HAS A HANDLE. SAY IT! A shovel has a handle. THIS PART IS A SCOOP. A SHOVEL HAS A SCOOP. SAY IT! A shovel has a scoop. NOW TELL ME ALL THE PARTS OF THE SHOVEL. SAY THE WHOLE THING. (Point at the handle.) A shovel has a handle. (Point at the scoop.) A shovel has a scoop. WHAT IS THE HANDLE FOR? To hold it. RIGHT! WHAT IS THE SCOOP FOR? To pick up dirt. RIGHT. WHAT IS THE SCOOP MADE OF? Metal. WHAT IS THE HANDLE MADE OF? Wood.

With the above type of dialogue used with each object you are teaching an identity statement, a *not* statement, names of parts, uses and names of materials. You can also add the classification of each object: THIS IS A TOOL. YOU CAN WORK WITH IT (Engelmann, 1969). IS THIS A TOOL? CAN YOU WORK WITH IT? YES. IF YOU CAN WORK WITH IT, IT IS A TOOL. WHAT KIND OF TOOL IS THIS? A shovel. YES, THIS TOOL IS A SHOVEL. SAY THE WHOLE THING. This tool is a shovel. (Then go to the other tools in the book, using the same type of dialogue.)

Learning Language II is concerned with the understanding of action concepts. Again, large outline pictures are used to depict a story using the desired verb over several times. As you read the story to the children, you emphasize the verb used, ask questions about it, and have the children repeat the correct sentence structure using the verb.

You can also teach verbs by collecting a set of action pictures. WHAT IS THIS? A boy. YES, THIS IS A BOY. SAY THE WHOLE THING. This is a boy. WHAT IS THE BOY DOING? Running. YES, THE BOY IS RUNNING! SAY THE WHOLE THING. The boy is running. IS THE BOY WALKING? No. SAY THE WHOLE THING. The boy is *not* walking (Engelmann, 1969).

Learning Language III is a book of songs mostly derived from familiar repetitive melodies. The songs teach diverse language concepts such as parts, body schema, verbs, and pronouns. The children enjoy the songs and it is easy to learn them and to alter them many ways to teach different concepts. For example, the words to the song "He's with Her and She's with Him" are altered to "They're with Him and He's with Them."

Pronouns can also be taught with a collection of magazine pictures. LOOK AT THIS PICTURE. WHO COULD SAY, "I AM EATING"? A child points at a girl eating. EVERYONE! WHAT COULD THE GIRL SAY? "YES! I AM EATING!" WHO COULD SAY, "YOU ARE EATING"? The dog. Yes! EVERYONE, WHAT COULD THE DOG SAY? You are eating (Engelmann, 1969).

Show groups of objects and pictures to teach plurals. WHAT ARE ALL OF THESE? Animals. SAY THE WHOLE THING. These are animals.

Use objects to teach opposites. Have three blocks: THIS BLOCK IS LONG. THIS BLOCK IS LONG. THIS BLOCK IS NOT LONG. IS THIS BLOCK LONG? Etc. Later: THIS BLOCK IS SHORT. THIS BLOCK IS SHORT. THIS BLOCK IS NOT SHORT. Also teach: *hot-cold, hard-soft, big-little, rough-smooth, full-empty,* and *loud-soft.*

Bereiter-Engelmann's book, *Teaching Disadvantaged Children in the Preschool,* also contains many language exercises which can be used through second grade.

The conscientious teacher must develop an intensive, comprehensive, daily language program using a good twenty to thirty minutes of each classroom day. It must be carefully structured to efficient use of the time, no casual, haphazard program. If you do not have the complete Distar Language program, make up a program of your own with whatever materials you do have.

Make a picture file of categories such as animals, plants, foods, buildings, fish, insects, vehicles, tools, toys, and people. Use these pictures for teaching classifying, pronouns, family relationships and occupations. Collect objects such as tools and foods, to teach classifying and prepositions. Place objects and children in various relationships to teach prepositions: WHERE IS THE ERASER? In the wastebasket. NOW WHERE IS THE ERASER? Under the wastebasket. SAY THE WHOLE THING (Engelmann, 1969). The eraser is under the wastebasket. NOW WHERE IS THE ERASER? Over Susan. WHERE

IS THE ERASER NOW? Under Tommy. SAY THE WHOLE THING. The eraser is under Tommy.

The amount of time spent on each concept depends on the ability of your certain group of children. With two groups you will find that one can move quickly on to new concepts, while the slower group will need to spend considerable time on building basic vocabulary. Teach a concept until it is solid, but continually retest and review. Keep the program interesting by using a variety of topics in each lesson. Don't run a subject to the ground until the children groan at the thought of it, but keep coming back to it until it is learned.

It is important to organize your program well so that you cover all the required skills. You might draw up a detailed list of all the skills your children need, or all of the language topics you want to cover. Include all the materials available to you. Then check off the skills as you teach them, but continually sweep back over the old skills to reinforce them. If you are following a list of topics or ideas, use a red check mark to indicate what you have taught the low group, and a blue pencil mark for the top group. Or, if you are using a book such as *Learning Language,* clip a piece of red paper to the page on which you wish to start the low group the next day, and a piece of blue paper to mark the place of the top group.

Begin your lessons with basic vocabulary, parts of things, singulars to plurals, prepositions, verbs, and then go on to opposites, similarities, comparisons, classifying, sequencing, and reasoning.

Jean Osborn, the master teacher of the Bereiter-Engelmann Preschool and co-author of the Distar Language program, offers these tips to successful teaching of language to a small group:

The teacher should:

1. Diagnose and evaluate what the child knows that is relevant to what she is going to teach.
2. Decide on the learning tasks of a period and teach them, not letting the children distract her with chance remarks from the intended program.
3. Speak quickly and distinctly, changing tasks frequently.
4. Restructure and reorganize presentation when children are not learning.
5. Present learning tasks in the most simple and logical way possible,

adding only one new concept at a time.

6. Give instant feedback to children, correct wrong responses, praise correct responses.
7. Intercept wrong responses, when possible, before or while they are being made.
8. Give the answer to a child who seems about to make a mistake, or who is silent.
9. Get the attention of misbehaving or distracted children by patting or touching them on the shoulder or the knees instead of interrupting the lesson with verbal admonishments.
10. Move on to new tasks when children have mastered a task and not spend time drilling on material the children already know.

Corrections are made quickly and without rancor. Wrong responses are interrupted for two reasons: The child should not practice an incorrect response, and the other children in the group should not hear wrong responses. Since almost instant responses are necessary, a long pause almost always indicates that the child does not know the answer. Allowing him to sit silently on the premise that he might think of the answer is more likely to result in wild guessing and in feelings of shame about being wrong. It must be remembered that one of the more difficult concepts for disadvantaged children to learn is "I don't know." (Osborn, 1968, pp. 15–16)

METHODS IN TRAINING AUDITORY RECEPTION

Getting Attention and Giving Directions

Don't be sure that inattention is always willful or the result of a lack of home training. Check medical histories for neurological causes (Chapter Three). Refer highly distractable children for medical checkups. (Chapter Three, Referrals to Doctors.) The child may be unable to screen out or to select incoming auditory and visual stimuli (Chapter Five, Figure-Ground Perception). Try to eliminate unnecessary distracting stimuli (Chapter Five, Planning the Environment).

Set the scene for listening. Be sure you have their full attention before beginning instruction. With immature, distractable children, have desks clear and hands empty. Never pass out the materials to be used before giving the instructions.

Demonstrate how to do a task. Use actions more than words. When possible, put three or four exact examples of the paper exercises on the chalkboard. Present the problem. Ask the questions needed to solve the problem. Have several children (those with the most difficulties) do the examples on the board. Never call on your best children for this. They can do anything! You want to be sure that your slowest children can perform, then you know that the rest of the class can do it. Then pass out the papers and let the children get out their pencils and get to work.

When demonstrating an art project, first show finished product. Then show how to do it, using actions more than words. Repeat demonstration again, this time verbalizing the instructions more into steps. FIRST I FOLD IT INTO A TRIANGLE, MAKING SURE THE POINT IS SHARP. THEN I HOLD IT ON THIS LEFT SIDE AND CUT THESE LOOSE EDGES HERE. Perhaps demonstrate again, this time pausing to let the children supply the key steps. FIRST I FOLD IT INTO A . . . YES, TRIANGLE, MAKING SURE THAT THE . . . YES, POINT IS SHARP. SHOULD IT BE LIKE THIS? (show it in error) NO. THAT ISN'T SHARP, IS IT? THEN I HOLD IT . . . ON WHICH SIDE? YES, THE LEFT SIDE. IS THIS THE LEFT SIDE? NO. IS THIS? YES. THEN WHAT DO I DO? YES, CUT IT. WHERE DO I CUT IT? RIGHT. Put the work down and have the children recite in unison the steps necessary. NOW WHAT DO YOU DO FIRST? YES. TOMMY KNOWS. HE IS READY FOR THE PAPER. Sometimes it helps to have each child tell you what he will do first before you give him the paper. Or have the materials lined up on a counter. Have a row of children recite the steps, and then come up to get the materials, while the second row recites the steps. Very careful instructions will eliminate frustration for both you and for the children.

Now the children are starting the task, but Jerry still says: "I don't know what to do." Instead of repeating the instructions to him, ask him the leading questions to solve his problem himself. If he cannot answer the questions, call on peers. JERRY DOESN'T KNOW WHAT TO DO FIRST. WHO CAN TELL HIM? RIGHT! NOW HOW DO YOU DO THAT, JERRY? Don't do it for him. He must do it himself, then he will remember how to do it. Guide his hands if necessary. Be sure he succeeds. Reinforce him with ample praise for each correct move he makes. Then he will have the confidence to continue.

Be extremely aware of your vocabulary in giving instructions. Ask questions to be sure that every word is understood. Use synonyms extensively to clarify meaning. If instructions are misunderstood by more than one child, it is your fault, not the children's. Examine their errors to find where you erred. With new insights into their problems, reinstruct the lesson. Admit your "goof." It reassures the children so that they are more willing to accept their mistakes. Problem learners are often highly critical of themselves. Thus if you make a big to-do about your errors, I DID IT AGAIN! I GOOFED! I AM ALWAYS MAKING MISTAKES!, then you can gradually get them to admit an error without being devastated by it.

Enlarging Vocabulary

The Engelmann-Osborn techniques of direct teaching enrich the vocabulary with nouns, parts of things, classifying, and the language of instruction. But you must be aware of the need to clarify vocabulary in every classroom activity. Be certain that all the children understand every word in every story, song, and lesson. Because a few children respond does not mean that the whole class understands. When telling a story, pause to ascertain understanding, to clarify concepts. For example: THE COTTAGE BY THE STREAM. WHAT IS A COTTAGE? WHAT ARE SOME OTHER WORDS FOR IT? IS IT VERY BIG? WHAT IS A STREAM? IS THE COTTAGE IN THE STREAM?

When you don't want to interrupt the story, use many synonyms interwoven into the narrated story to clarify meaning: COTTAGE, CABIN, SMALL HOUSE. STREAM, CREEK, SMALL RIVER. Or: HE WAS GAY, HAPPY, LAUGHING.

Use motions to clarify meaning of words. Children with problems in auditory reception are often dependent on visible movement to interpret meaning from words. They especially watch your expressions to clue them in. HE TUGGED AND TUGGED, PULLED AND PULLED. Make pulling motions showing the strain of the action. PRETEND YOU ARE THE BOY. SHOW ME HOW YOU WOULD TUG AND TUG. HE WAS STARTLED. (demonstrate) CAN YOU PRETEND YOU ARE STARTLED? HOW WOULD YOU LOOK IF YOU SAW A BEAR ON THE OTHER SIDE OF THE BUSH?

Use kinesthesis to clarify meaning of words and to increase

vocabulary. Let each child have a scrap of satin to feel and rub on his face, hands, arms, and neck. Help them describe the feeling. HOW DOES IT FEEL? DO YOU LIKE THE FEELING? DO YOU KNOW ANYTHING ELSE THAT FEELS LIKE SATIN? WHAT WOULD YOU EAT THAT WOULD FEEL AS SMOOTH AS SATIN IN YOUR MOUTH? Reuse the word frequently on later dates. Have them feel many types of fabrics and other objects that are rough, bumpy, smooth, scratchy, and sticky.

Listening Exercises and Sound Discrimination

Make up a feltboard story about an elf who listened. He used small ears for loud sounds, middle-sized ears for conversation, and very large ears to catch the tiny, faint sounds in the woods. IF HE WERE RIGHT HERE IN OUR ROOM TODAY, I WONDER WHAT HE WOULD HEAR AND WHICH EARS HE WOULD USE? WHAT EARS WOULD HE USE TO HEAR THOSE CHILDREN YELLING ON THE PLAYGROUND? WHAT EARS WOULD HE USE TO HEAR US TALKING HERE? NOW CLOSE YOUR EYES AND LISTEN VERY CAREFULLY. DO YOU HEAR ANY OTHER NOISES? WHAT EARS WOULD THE ELF USE TO HEAR THAT CAR WAY OUT THERE ON THE STREET? CAN YOU HEAR ANY NOISES FROM THE OFFICE? FROM THE KITCHEN? LISTEN TO THAT TRUCK. IS IT COMING CLOSER OR GOING AWAY FROM US?

1. LISTEN VERY CAREFULLY. I AM GOING TO MAKE SOME KIND OF SOUND BEHIND THE FELTBOARD. SEE IF YOU CAN FIGURE OUT WHAT IT IS. Ring a bell, or use any rhythm instrument. Drop a pin. Hit two sticks together. Turn a page. Fold a paper.

2. With the children's backs to you and eyes closed: Hit the counter. Put a chair down. Open a drawer. Clear your throat. Pour water. Sweep the floor. They try to identify what you did.

3. Choose a child to move across the back of the room in some manner. The children guess if he hopped, skipped, ran, walked, tiptoed, or jumped. Or the child makes a noise like an animal and the others try to guess what animal he represents.

4. With all heads down and eyes closed, choose a secret child to go into the closet or behind the door and say something. The children try to guess who it is.

5. Teach *loud* and *soft* by demonstrating on the various in-

struments. Then strike an instrument and have the children tell whether it was loud or soft.

6. Tape familiar noises and have children identify them verbally or by selecting appropriate pictures. Use door slamming, mixer going, pots and pans rattling, baby crying, dog barking, lawn mower running.

7. Use similar instruments such as a bell and finger cymbals. CLOSE YOUR EYES AND LISTEN CAREFULLY. I AM GOING TO MAKE TWO SOUNDS. YOUR EARS MUST DECIDE IF THEY ARE THE SAME OR TWO DIFFERENT SOUNDS. Alternate between like and different sounds. Use two wooden instruments, two metal shakers with different contents.

8. Use different tonal patterns on a xylophone or piano. ARE THESE THE SAME OR DIFFERENT? Use keys c, e, g, and f, a, c; c, e, g, and c, e, a.

9. As ability to discriminate sounds increases use two tones of the same instrument; e.g, two Melody Bells, or two *tone bells,* or two brass bells, or two notes on a pitch pipe, piano, or a xylophone. First, use tones widely spaced, perhaps more than an octave apart. CLOSE YOUR EYES AND LISTEN CAREFULLY. I WILL PLAY TWO TONES. ARE THEY THE SAME OR DIFFERENT? Work on both high and low tones and on the middle tones, too. Make the discriminations more acute by using nearer tones; e.g. c and g, then c and e, then c and c#.

10. Place objects producing varying tones into identical cans. Use 35 mm film cans. The child shakes a can and places it into sequence of soft to loud tones. Cans may contain sand, beans, pebbles, sticks, or tones of jingle bells. Make a second identical set perhaps with different colored lids and the child matches the cans with the like tones.

11. Have two sets of musical tones such as from Melody Bells, or the tones from Child Guidance's Railroad or Tower of Chimes. Lacquer spray each set one color. The child sounds a bell and tries to find its component sound in the other set. At first just use three tones; e.g. c, e, g. When these are readily matched, add more tones until the child can match all eight tones.

12. Again, beginning with just three tones of one set of bells,

have a child line them up in order of low to high tones. Add more tones until the child can line up all eight tones in sequence low to high.

13. NOW YOU ARE ROBOTS AND YOU CAN MOVE ONLY AS THE DRUM SAYS. LISTEN TO THE DRUM AND MOVE ONLY THE WAY IT TELLS YOU. IF THE DRUM STOPS, YOU MUST STOP, TOO. Begin with a 4/4 walking rhythm. When the drum stops, they freeze in place. Use a broken rhythm for skipping and galloping, a loud distinctive rhythm for jumping, a soft rhythm for tiptoe, and a fast rhythm for running. Intersperse rhythms with pauses to keep them alert and listening.

14. Teach child to discriminate *high* and *low* tones by their own production of various tones. They can imitate the voices of the three bears, talk like a giant, like the *Three Billy Goats Gruff, The Little Red Hen*. To teach high pitches, it is best to relate them to very small things. CAN YOU BE A LITTLE TINY GNAT AND MAKE YOUR VOICE GO WAY UP HERE LIKE THIS? Make high and low tones and have them match them. Match piano tones with their voices. Sound a tone and have them say if it is high or low. Then have them stand tall for high tones and crouch low for low tones.

Auditory-Motor Association

The child hears, and responds to show he understood by performing a motor act. If a child is very quiet and either does not wish to or is not able to express himself orally, you can ascertain his understanding of the spoken word by asking him to do something. A child with severe speech articulation problems could thus be tested. Children slow to respond in the classroom might have inadequate ability in auditory reception. Be sure your speech is clear and distinct. Enunciate carefully. Teach the words you are going to use in the class through the direct teaching techniques. Be sure that the children understand every word. Then present the following exercises as practice in using this language:

1. First, teach body parts and the spatial directions of their desks: on top of, inside, under, the right side, etc. Then have the class close their eyes. Give commands they can do without seeing: TAP YOUR HEAD. TOUCH THE TOP OF YOUR DESK. PUT YOUR RIGHT HAND ON YOUR LEFT KNEE.

2. Dramatize verbs that you have taught: SHOW ME HOW YOU WOULD DRINK A COKE, MOW THE LAWN, EAT AN ICE CREAM CONE, ROLL COOKIE DOUGH.

3. Read *Ann Can Fly,* by Fred Phleger, Beginner Books, Random House. Have children act out flying the airplane. PUSH THE STICK FORWARD. NOW WE ARE DIVING DOWN, DOWN.

4. HOW WOULD YOU STEP OVER A BIG BRANCH? HANG THE TOWELS ON THE CLOTHES LINE? CLIMB UP A TREE? Then: THIS IS A LITTLE CREEK. RUN AND JUMP OVER IT. DON'T GET YOUR FEET WET.

5. Give directions for placing figures on the flannel board: PUT AN APPLE ON THE RIGHT SIDE OF THE FLANNEL BOARD. PUT A MOON ON THE LEFT SIDE. PUT TWO BLUE CIRCLES AT THE TOP. PUT A DOG AT THE BOTTOM.

6. On paper at their seats: MAKE A RED BALL ON THE RIGHT SIDE OF YOUR PAPER. MAKE A BLUE BALL ON THE LEFT SIDE. MAKE A BLACK BALL AT THE TOP OF YOUR PAPER. MAKE A YELLOW BALL AT THE BOTTOM OF YOUR PAPER. MAKE A PURPLE "X" IN THE MIDDLE OF YOUR PAPER.

7. STAND BESIDE YOUR DESK. I AM GOING TO NAME DIFFERENT THINGS AND SAY THAT THEY FLY. IF THEY REALLY DO FLY, YOU FLY LIKE THIS WITH YOUR ARMS. IF THEN DON'T FLY, KEEP YOUR HANDS AT YOUR SIDES. BIRDS FLY. Wave your arms out horizontally. AIRPLANES FLY. CARS FLY. Keep waving your arms. Children have to think to make the right responses.

8. First teach the ordinals. MARY ANN, YOU MAY LINE UP HERE FIRST. TOMMY MAY BE SECOND. GINNY MAY BE THIRD. Line up five to ten children in this manner. Then: NOW I HAVE CHANGED MY MIND. CINDY MAY BE FIRST IF SHE CAN SEND THE FIRST CHILD TO HIS SEAT. BILLY MAY BE THIRD IF HE CAN SEND THE THIRD CHILD TO HIS SEAT.

9. Have dittoed sheets with five numbered rows of circles. Give directions orally, or on tape for use with the listening post. IN THE FIRST ROW, COLOR THE THIRD BALL RED. COLOR THE LAST BALL BLUE. IN THE SECOND ROW, PUT A RED STAR IN THE FIRST BALL. PUT AN ORANGE "X" IN THE FOURTH BALL.

10. THIS IS THE FIRST ROW (Indicate a row of desks in your classroom) . WHO IS THE FIRST CHILD IN THIS ROW? WHO IS THE THIRD

CHILD? THIS IS THE FOURTH ROW. WHO IS THE FIFTH CHILD IN THIS ROW? When this is solid, make more of a game of it: NOW WE WILL SEE HOW SMART YOU ARE! WILL THE FIRST BOY IN THE SECOND ROW STAND UP? WILL THE LAST CHILD IN THE THIRD ROW CLAP HIS HANDS? WILL THE SECOND CHILD IN THE FOURTH ROW COME GET A JELLY BEAN? KANDY, YOU MAY TAKE THE FIFTH SEAT IN THE SIXTH ROW.

11. Creative rhythmic movement to music: I WAVE MY MAGIC WAND AND I TURN YOU ALL INTO KANGAROOS. YOUR HIND LEGS ARE BIG AND STRONG, AND YOU CAN JUMP HIGH INTO THE AIR.

12. Clap a set rhythm pattern like: ONE, TWO, THREE, FOUR. Point at the children. YOUR TURN. They repeat the same rhythm. Don't change rhythms until they can match the first one correctly. WATCH ME AGAIN. Vary the rhythms: One, Two, Three, Four, and; One, and, Two, Three, Four.

Auditory-Vocal Association

The child listens, understands, and/or verbalizes a response. Build the child's confidence in himself so that he has the right answers and believes in his abilities to respond. The following techniques reinforce not only auditory-vocal association but also cognitive thinking.

1. Conceal your arm and tap several times. The children tell how many times you tapped. Begin with a simple, slow, easy-to-count rhythm that every child can comprehend. Then gradually vary the taps in loudness, speed, and rhythm.

2. After every child knows all the colors, have them use their visual imagery by asking: WHAT COLOR IS THE SKY? A FIRE TRUCK? AN ORANGE? A BANANA? YOUR HOUSE?

3. FOR WHAT DO YOU USE A BEATER? A DRILL? A VACUUM CLEANER? A BARN?

4. HOW COULD YOU USE A ROPE? EACH ONE IN THE GROUP MUST THINK OF A DIFFERENT WAY.

5. After you have taught classifying, choose two items that are in a common category: HOW ARE A SAUCEPAN AND A TEAKETTLE ALIKE? HOW ARE BEARS AND DEER ALIKE? HOW ARE SHOES AND COATS ALIKE?

6. WHAT BELONGS TOGETHER? WHAT DOES NOT BELONG? WHY?

Name three objects that move alike, are made of the same material, or are used together, or are in the same category; and one object which is foreign to them; e.g., HORSE, SADDLE, BOAT, REINS. DOG, CAT, BANANA, HORSE. NAIL, SCREW, SCISSORS, DRESS, PAN.

7. Describe an object or an action, and the child identifies it. THE BOAT WAS GOING VERY FAST. THERE WAS A LONG ROPE FROM THE BOAT TO THE MAN, AND HE WAS STANDING ON A BOARD IN THE WATER. WHAT WAS HE DOING? Or: IT GROWS IN THE GARDEN. IT HAS THORNS. IT IS BEAUTIFUL AND HAS A WONDERFUL SMELL. WHAT IS IT? Or: HE WEARS A BLUE-GREY UNIFORM AND LEAVES SOMETHING AT YOUR HOUSE ALMOST EVERY DAY. WHO IS HE?

8. WHAT IS THE DIFFERENCE BETWEEN A COW AND A HORSE? A BRIDGE AND A TUNNEL? A TRACTOR AND A CAR? A PIECE OF SANDPAPER AND A PIECE OF SATIN? A ROCKET AND A BOAT?

Whenever you ask questions and ask children to respond, you are training them in auditory-vocal association. Thus a word problem in math, a discussion question in social studies, a comprehension question in reading, are all exercises in auditory-vocal association. Always discuss every film after the showing. Not only ask questions about what they saw, or what happened, but have them do convergent thinking and draw conclusions. HOW IS THE DEER PROTECTED. WHY DIDN'T THE DOG CHASE THE SKUNK? WOULD A RACOON EAT A TURTLE?

Auditory-Vocal Automatic

We learn some responses so well that they become automatic. The direct teaching methods of Engelmann use this automatic response factor. A large part of our grammar we learn through automatic repetition without referring to a rule of speech. This is called grammatic closure.

1. Singular and plurals: ONE IS A MOUSE, TWO ARE. . . . ONE IS A DEER, TWO ARE. . . . ONE IS A CHILD, TWO ARE. . . . ONE IS A CAT, TWO ARE. . . . When you find one that they don't know, teach it through direct teaching methods, and multiple repetition.

2. Past tenses: TONIGHT I AM GOING TO BED, LAST NIGHT I . . . (went) TO BED. TONIGHT I AM GOING TO SLEEP. LAST NIGHT I . . . TO SLEEP. I HAVE AN APPLE TODAY, YESTERDAY I . . . AN APPLE. I WILL

SEE THE STARS TONIGHT, LAST NIGHT I . . . THE STARS. I SING TODAY, YESTERDAY I . . . I SWIM TODAY, YESTERDAY I . . .

3. Opposites: SEE HOW FAST YOU CAN SAY THE OPPOSITE OF WHAT I SAY: HOT . . . IN . . . SWEET . . . HARD . . . ROUGH . . . ON . . . BAD . . .

4. Pairs of words or ideas: HOW FAST CAN YOU SAY WHAT GOES WITH WHAT I SAY? BACON . . . SALT . . . BREAD . . . TABLE . . .

5. Teach children to respond quickly. Begin with something they know very well, like their own names. WHEN I CLAP MY HANDS AND POINT AT YOU, SEE HOW FAST YOU CAN TELL ME YOUR NAME. THIS TIME WE WILL BE TRICKIER—SAY YOUR MOTHER'S NAME. NOW WHEN I CLAP MY HANDS AND POINT AT YOU, NAME A BREAKFAST CEREAL.

SEE HOW FAST YOU CAN THINK OF ANIMALS. I'LL CLAP MY HANDS AND POINT AT YOU AND YOU MUST NAME SOME KIND OF ANIMAL. YOU CAN'T USE ANY ANIMAL THAT ANYONE ELSE SAYS. THE ANSWER MUST COME OUT OF YOUR OWN HEAD. I'LL ASK YOU TO NAME A BIRD, A BEAST, OR A FISH. The same exercise can be done with *toys, tools,* and *vehicles.* Or use *food* or *clothing.*

METHODS IN VISUAL RECEPTION

When you see something and understand what you see, you are visually receiving the message. You visually receive objects, pictures, graphs, and the written word. The quiet child who does not verbalize may be tested in his ability to understand language and concepts by having him point at pictures and objects. You can simply say: SHOW ME THE BALL and the child points to it. Or give him pictures to sequence or group in categories.

Training in visual reception is training in visual perception. The child learns to sort things according to sizes, colors, shapes, etc. Many methods are described in Chapters Five, Six, and Seven.

Visual-Motor Association

The child sees pictures, objects, etc., understands their meaning, and responds by some motor act. He might dramatize. Show an object or tool or picture of one. HOW WOULD YOU USE THIS? SHOW ME. Puzzles of various kinds are practice in visual-motor association. Many of the visual perceptual exercises in the earlier chapters are methods in visual-motor association.

Visual-Vocal Association

The child sees something, understands it, and then makes a vocal response. We have trained the child in visual perception, and now we want him to learn to express himself through speech.

1. Put several objects or pictures in the chalkrack. Describe one. I AM GOING TO GIVE YOU THREE CLUES TO SOMETHING. IT IS BLUE, HARD, AND SMALL. WHAT IS IT? — WHAT ARE YOU LOOKING FOR? SOMETHING THAT IS . . . Get them to repeat the two or three clues which you gave, then call on one child to name it.

2. Place objects or pictures in the chalkrack. WHICH BELONG TOGETHER? WHY? Or: WHICH GOES WITH THE ONE I AM HOLDING? WHY? Sets of phonics cards are often of a good size and variety of subjects to use for the two above exercises.

3. Show a complex or amusing picture and have children describe all that they see. Also, let them draw inferences from the scene. WHAT TIME OF DAY IS IT? WHAT SEASON? WHAT DO YOU THINK HAPPENED JUST BEFORE (or just after) THIS PICTURE?

4. A child performs something or acts something out and another child describes what he did.

5. Use a simple set of pictures, felt shapes, or drawings on the chalkboard. The child must describe what he sees in full sentences. "There are two dogs and one cat." "There are a yellow circle and a blue triangle." "There are two big rectangles and one small one."

6. Hold up any two objects. They could be items brought to school for share-and-tell. HOW ARE THESE TWO THE SAME? They might both be toys. HOW ARE THEY DIFFERENT? One might be made of wood, the other of metal. Or one large and the other small. Or one smooth and the other rough.

METHODS IN VERBAL EXPRESSION

Verbalizing, describing, showing you understand by speaking is verbal expression. Vocabulary and sentence structure are best taught through Engelmann's direct teaching methods. Children learn to talk through modeling. They model their parent's speech. If the children have not had good models from whom to learn, then their speech and their sentence structure are inadequate. Thus the teacher must model the speech which she wishes the children to use. She need not mock or ridicule the speech of the home to do this. Just make a matter-of-fact statement: YES, WE TALK LIKE THAT AT HOME, BUT AT SCHOOL WE LEARN TO SAY. . . . I HAVE A DOLL. LET'S ALL SAY IT. I HAVE A DOLL! Don't be critical of a child's speech when he is trying to tell you something. Just listen to him, then make a note of his grammatical error and incorporate it into your language lesson.

1. A child says: "I gots a magnet." Just say YOU HAVE? and let him tell you about it. No immediate correction is necessary. Later at a language session: I HAVE A NOSE. DO YOU HAVE A NOSE? YES! SAY THE WHOLE THING. I HAVE A NOSE. DO YOU HAVE EARS? SAY THE WHOLE THING. (Use body parts and clothing that the children have in common. Then for checking individuals, ask about other items of clothing.) DO YOU HAVE A SKIRT, SUSAN?

2. When *have* is solid, work on eliminating "I don't gots." LET'S TALK ABOUT OUR PETS. I HAVE A DOG. DO YOU HAVE A DOG? SAY THE WHOLE THING. I have a dog. DO YOU HAVE A CAT? SAY THE WHOLE THING. I have a cat. DO YOU HAVE A KANGAROO? No! I DON'T HAVE A KANGAROO. SAY THE WHOLE THING! (Name other impossible pets to reinforce the "don't have" statement. Then check individuals for both *have* and *don't have*.) DO YOU HAVE A LION, TOMMY? SAY THE WHOLE THING. I don't have a lion. DO YOU HAVE A HORSE, KANDY? SAY THE WHOLE THING. Yes, I have a horse.

3. The child chooses something in the room and whispers it to the teacher. He then describes it through color, size, and perhaps one more attribute. Help the children to repeat his clues: HE SAID IT IS. . . . (hold up one finger) YES, RED. AND . . . YES, SMALL, AND . . . YES, ROUND. NOW FIND SOMETHING IN THIS ROOM THAT IS THESE THREE THINGS. WHAT DOES IT HAVE TO BE? Have them name the three clues again. Let the child then call on peers to guess his secret. If a child gives a logical answer, say THAT WAS GOOD THINKING. IT IS RED AND SMALL AND ROUND, ALL RIGHT. If a child

gives a nonsensical answer, ask him to repeat the three necessary clues and ask him if his choice has those qualities.

4. Animal, vegetable, or mineral: I KNOW A SECRET OBJECT SOMEWHERE IN THE WORLD. TO FIND WHAT IT IS YOU WILL WANT TO KNOW WHETHER IT IS AN ANIMAL, A VEGETABLE, OR A MINERAL FIRST. Be sure they understand these three categories. Describe if necessary. THEN YOU WILL WANT TO KNOW ITS SIZE, COLOR, HOW IT MOVES, OR HOW IT IS USED. YOU CAN ASK ANY QUESTIONS, BUT I CAN ANSWER ONLY, "YES" OR "NO." Guide the questions. YOU HAVEN'T ASKED ME ABOUT ITS SIZE. Or: YOU DON'T KNOW WHERE IT IS IN THE WORLD. When a child guesses the answer, he gets to choose a secret about which the children will ask him. He whispers his secret to you so that he won't change it in the middle of the game and so that you can help the children with the questions.

5. Make up a story: ONCE UPON A TIME THERE WAS A LITTLE GIRL. HER NAME WAS SUSAN. SUSAN WENT WALKING IN THE WOODS. SHE . . . TOMMY, YOUR TURN. WHAT HAPPENED? WHAT DID SHE DO? He adds a thought, description, or action, and then it is the next child's turn to do likewise. Let them use their vivid imaginations. The story can be fantastic!

6. When a child misbehaves, or is idle in class, ask him: WHERE SHOULD YOU BE, JERRY? WHAT SHOULD YOU BE DOING? Or: WHAT TIME IS IT NOW? Or: WHY AREN'T THE OTHER CHILDREN DOING THAT? Or: HOW DO THINK YOU MADE TOMMY FEEL ABOUT YOU?

7. Have *tasting parties* to increase the children's abilities to perceive and to describe those perceptions. Begin with well-known items such as crackers. Have the children close their eyes and put their hands behind their backs. Put a cracker in each child's hand. The children feel it and describe it (rough, smooth, bumpy, etc.) They feel its shape: round, square, rectangular. They break or move it to see if it makes any noise. They smell it. They taste it with their eyes closed and describe it: sweet, salty, sour, vanilla flavored. Then they open their eyes and note its color and any other characteristics which they had not known before. Use different kinds of breakfast cereals and teach them the difference between flavors of corn, wheat, and rice. Taste and describe flavors of cookies and candies, then branch out and introduce

more exotic foods such as Japanese crackers, Chinese cookies, avocados, guavas, fresh pineapple, coconuts, and all kinds of nuts, fruits, and vegetables. Let them bring anything they want to school for tasting parties. One child brought a cucumber he grew in his garden.

METHODS IN SEQUENCING

As we have said before, it is necessary to learn to sequence time and space, to be able to organize the multitude of data which is perceived. Many things have no meaning without sequence. *Two* means nothing unless you know that it is more than one and less than three, and comes between the one and three. Without sequence of numbers, there could be no sequence in time. Two o'clock is an hour after one o'clock, and an hour before three o'clock. Things happen in a particular sequence. It is morning, then afternoon, then evening. You put on your socks *before* your shoes. You brush your teeth *after* eating. The words *before, after, then, until, when, if,* and the ordinals, all denote a specific sequence of action or time. A frequent deficiency of problem learners, disadvantaged or MCD children is a lack of understanding of sequence. Misunderstanding sequence is the cause of a lot of confusion, especially in following directions.

Auditory Sequential Memory

One of the most efficient methods of teaching sequencing is through the auditory-vocal channels. As described in Chapter Ten, counting is taught through rhythmic clapping while chanting the numbers. Counting forward, backward, and by 2's, 5's, and 10's is taught by the teacher chanting it rhythmically. The children chime in as they are able until they can do it alone. The exercise is repeated day after day until it is learned.

Teaching The Days

Again, it helps to clap rhythmically while you say it. Announce what you are going to do first. I AM GOING TO SAY THE DAYS OF THE WEEK. WHAT AM I GOING TO SAY? YES, THE DAYS OF THE WEEK. SUNDAY, MONDAY, TUESDAY, WEDNESDAY, THURSDAY, FRI-

DAY, AND SATURDAY. WHAT DID I SAY? The days of the week. NOW, LET'S ALL SAY THE DAYS OF THE WEEK. WHAT ARE WE GOING TO SAY? The days of the week. SUNDAY . . . WHAT DID WE SAY? The days of the week.

To learn the days of the week it helps (if you have five rows of children) to name each row by a weekday. Begin on the children's left, because that is the direction of the names of the days on the calendar, in the front of the room. The children in Monday's row share-and-tell on Monday, Tuesday's row shares on Tuesday, etc. Daily, then, recite the days of the week by pointing at the correct row. THE FIRST DAY OF THE WEEK WAS SUNDAY. WHAT DID WE DO? Stayed home. YES, WE STAYED HOME AND WENT TO CHURCH. THEN IT WAS . . . (point at the first row) MONDAY, THEN TUESDAY (point at the second row), TODAY IS WEDNESDAY (point at the third row). SO WHOSE TURN IS IT TO SHARE? (Also, use this pointing method to note: TODAY IS WEDNESDAY, YESTER-DAY WAS TUESDAY WHEN THIS ROW SHARED, AND TOMORROW WILL BE . . . YES, THURSDAY. WHO WILL SHARE ON THURSDAY? (Say the days of the week while pointing at them on the calendar, and also note *today* is . . . *yesterday* was . . . and *tomorrow* will be. . . .

Children with Time Confusions

Some children are always asking, "Is it lunch time?" (Maybe they are hungry, too.) Or "Is it time to go home?" or "Is it time for reading?" Keep a strict sequence of daily program until the children are secure in school. They are more secure at home because they know what to expect. Make a sequence on the board of your main daily activities: reading, recess, language, physical education, recess, etc. Rebus or stick figures might help to picture the activities better. Go over the sequence with the children. Help them to learn the sequence. Then when a child asks "Is it time for P.E.?" you have a sequence to take him through to orient him. He really needs orienting in time or he would not be asking the question. He must have the security of knowing what to expect and what you expect of him.

Teaching "Before" and "After."

Teach *after* first. *Before* is more difficult to learn. It is the first weeks of school and the children are going out to recess.

WHAT DO WE DO AFTER RECESS? The children are finishing math and someone asks if it is time for recess. WE FINISHED OUR MATH. NOW WHAT DO WE DO AFTER MATH? Language. YES, LANGUAGE. THEN WHAT DO WE DO AFTER LANGUAGE? Go to recess. YES, AFTER LANGUAGE IS RECESS!

Going for a walk: Draw an arrow across the blackboard from left to right. THE OTHER DAY I WENT FOR A WALK. I WALKED ALONG UNTIL I CAME TO A BIG TREE. Draw a tree on the left of the line. THEN I WALKED ON UNTIL I SAW A BIRD. Draw a bird to the right of the tree. THEN I WALKED ON UNTIL I CAME TO A HOUSE. Draw a house to the right of the bird. THEN I WALKED ON UNTIL I CAME TO A FLOWER. Draw a flower to the right of the house. WHAT DID I SEE FIRST? (Point at the tree.) The tree. WHAT DID I SEE AFTER I SAW THE TREE? (Point.) The bird. WHAT DID I SEE AFTER I SAW THE BIRD? (Point.) The house. WHAT DID I SEE AFTER THE HOUSE? (Point.) The flower. (Ask the same questions again in random order.) Check children individually. If they understand this, then proceed with teaching *before*. If not, save it for another day and another walk, on which they tell you what they saw when going for a walk.

Teaching *before*. WHAT DID I SEE BEFORE I SAW THE BIRD? (Point first at the bird, then at the tree.) The tree. WHAT DID I SEE BEFORE I SAW THE HOUSE? (Point first at the house and then the bird.) When you have used this exercise several times, you can eliminate the pointing at the answer. Remember that these first exercises are *teaching*, so you must point to be sure the children all say the correct answer.

When lining up children for some school exercise, make a language game of it to teach *after*. JERRY, YOU MAY GET YOUR SCISSORS FIRST BECAUSE YOU ARE READY. SUSAN MAY GET HER SCISSORS AFTER JERRY. TOMMY, YOU ARE AFTER SUSAN; KANDY IS AFTER TOMMY.

You have taught the days of the week for some time, and you have been teaching *after*. Point either at the days on the calendar or at the rows of children. FIRST COMES SUNDAY. THEN AFTER SUNDAY COMES MONDAY. AFTER MONDAY COMES . . . YES, TUESDAY. AFTER TUESDAY COMES. . . . When you finish the routine, ask:

WHAT COMES AFTER SUNDAY? WHAT COMES AFTER MONDAY? (Later skip around.) WHAT COMES AFTER THURSDAY? WHAT COMES AFTER MONDAY?

You have taught *Going for a Walk* and the days of the week, and it is in the spring of the year, and the children are reading. Draw an arrow on the blackboard as for a walk. On this, write the days of the week. Point at the words as you say them with the children. LET'S READ THE DAYS OF THE WEEK. SUNDAY, MONDAY, TUESDAY. . . . AFTER SUNDAY IS . . . MONDAY. AFTER MONDAY IS . . . TUESDAY. The children supply the word as you point. Eliminate the pointing as they are able to do it alone. Test individually. Then skip around asking the days out of sequence. When this is solid, go to teaching *before*. BEFORE SATURDAY IS . . . (Point.) YES, FRIDAY. BEFORE FRIDAY IS . . . YES, THURSDAY. Later skip around asking before and after.

Teaching the Months

The months can be much more difficult to teach. The hardest are the fall months. It is best to start with these and teach the sequence more slowly. NOVEMBER, DECEMBER. SAY IT WITH ME. NOVEMBER, DECEMBER. Enunciate carefully. These words have many confusing parts. Then go to: OCTOBER, NOVEMBER, DECEMBER. SAY IT WITH ME: OCTOBER, NOVEMBER, DECEMBER. Repeat a few times daily. After this has been learned, expand it to include September. When these four are learned, then go to teaching all of the months. WE ARE GOING TO SAY THE MONTHS OF THE YEAR. WHAT ARE WE GOING TO SAY? YES, THE MONTHS OF THE YEAR! JANUARY, FEBRUARY. . . . Again, say them in a rhythm. You might want to clap or to tap your foot, as an accent. When you have finished: WHAT DID WE SAY? YES, THE MONTHS OF THE YEAR! Repeat daily until they can recite them individually.

Teaching the Seasons

During the year, discuss the present season frequently. Then in the spring: REMEMBER WHEN IT WAS SO VERY COLD AND WE ALL HAD TO WEAR OUR COATS OUTSIDE? THAT WAS WINTERTIME. THEN THE DAYS BECAME WARMER AND THE BLOSSOMS AND THE LEAVES

STARTED TO COME OUT ON THE TREES. THAT WAS SPRINGTIME. NOW IT IS GETTING HOTTER AND HOTTER, AND IT WILL SOON BE SUMMERTIME. AFTER THE SUMMER, WHEN IT STARTS TO GET COLD AGAIN AND THE LEAVES FALL OFF THE TREES, THEN IT WILL BE FALL. SOON THE LEAVES ARE ALL GONE AND IT IS COLD AND IT IS WINTER AGAIN. Repeat the story again, letting the children supply the name of the season. Then: LET'S NAME THE SEASONS! WHAT ARE WE GOING TO NAME? YES, THE SEASONS: WINTER, SPRING, SUMMER, FALL. WHAT DID WE NAME? YES, THE SEASONS! LET'S DO IT AGAIN. You might use motions to help the children recall the season and say the sequence. Hug yourself for winter, wave your arms for summer's heat, etc.

What Is Missing?

STOP ME IF I LEAVE SOMETHING OUT, AND TELL ME WHAT IS MISSING! ONE, TWO, THREE, FIVE. Stop! WHY DID YOU STOP ME? I LEFT OUT FOUR? HOW DID I DO THAT? I'LL TRY AGAIN! NINE, TEN, ELEVEN, THIRTEEN. WHAT'S WRONG NOW? Do this with counting by twos, fives, and tens, days of week, months, and seasons. Also teach *o'clock*. ONE O'CLOCK, TWO O'CLOCK, THREE O'CLOCK, FIVE O'CLOCK. Stop! WHAT'S WRONG? I LEFT OUT FOUR O'CLOCK?

Memorizing Number Sequences

Teach the children their addresses and phone numbers. In order not to confuse the two, teach them entirely separately. Write each child's number on a piece of paper and give it to him. The next day, give a prize to each child who can recite his number correctly. Pair off your sharper students with the children having problems, and give them the number to practice. Give a prize to both *teachers* and *students* who succeed. It is surprising how much they can teach each other, even in a short recess.

Story Sequence

Sometimes tell a story in parts and have the children recall the previous day's sequence before continuing the story. Do the same with a story in a reader. Have the children tell a story of a sequence of his own actions. WHAT IS THE FIRST THING YOU DO WHEN

YOU GET HOME FROM SCHOOL? KANDY? I change my clothes. THEN
WHAT DO YOU DO. Then I eat something. THEN WHAT?

WHAT IS THE FIRST THING YOU DO WHEN YOU ARE GOING TO
GET READY FOR BED? . . . THEN WHAT? . . . FOR SCHOOL? . . . IF YOU
WERE GOING TO GO SWIMMING, WHAT WOULD YOU DO FIRST? . . . IF
YOU WERE GOING TO CROSS THE STREET, WHAT DO YOU DO FIRST?

Behavior Sequences

Johnny comes into the room after recess and goes over and
looks out the window. JOHNNY, WHAT SHOULD YOU DO WHEN YOU
COME INTO OUR ROOM? WHAT DO YOU DO FIRST? THEN WHAT DO
YOU DO? Give the problem child specific instructions. FIRST WE
WALK INTO THE ROOM. THEN WE HANG UP OUR COATS. THEN WE GO
RIGHT TO OUR SEATS. Have him repeat it after you. Then have him
go back to the door and try it again. Keep the same simple instructions all year so that he can recite it to remind himself to
control his own behavior.

Recalling a Sequence of Items

I AM GOING ON A PICNIC AND I AM GOING TO TAKE AN APPLE.
Jerry: "I'm going on a picnic and I am going to take an apple
and a sandwich." Each succeeding child adds one item to the
menu until someone goofs. It helps to have each child who participates come up to the front of the group as it is his turn and
stand in a row. Thus it is easier for the children to see and
remember the sequence.

Sequences in Songs and Stories

Teach songs, poems, nursery rhymes, and fingerplays that are
catchy and easy for the children to memorize. Repeat them over
and over until they know them well. Say parts of rhymes and let
the children supply the missing words or lines: LITTLE MISS
MUFFET SAT IN A . . . EATING HER . . . ; ALONG CAME A . . . AND SAT
DOWN . . . , AND FRIGHTENED . . . Retell the stories: "The Indian
Boy and The Bear," "Strange Company," "The Old Woman
And Her Pig," and "This is The House That Jack Built."

BINGO. (With this song, it helps to write the letters *B I N G O* on the board, and then cross out each *letter* as it is substituted with a clap.

Old MacDonald had a dog, and Bingo was his name, oh.
BE, EYE, EN, GEE, OH. (Repeat twice.) And Bingo was his name, oh.

(The second time the song is sung, a clap is substituted for the *O*. The third time, two claps are substituted for the *GO*, etc., until there are five claps instead of the letters BINGO.

OLD MCDONALD HAD A FARM

Old McDonald had a farm, ee, yi, ee, yi, oh.
And on his farm he had a pig, ee, yi, ee, yi, oh.
With an 'oink, 'oink here, and an oink, oink there,
Here an oink, there an oink, everywhere an oink, oink.
Old McDonald had a farm, ee, yi, ee, yi, oh.
Second Verse:
And on his farm he had a duck, ee, yi, ee, yi, oh.
With a quack, quack here, and a quack, quack there.
Here a quack there a quack, everywhere a quack, quack.
An oink, oink there and an oink, oink there,
Here an oink, there an oink, everywhere an oink, oink.
Old McDonald had a farm, ee, yi, ee, yi, oh.

Add other animals, each time going back over the sounds of the previous animals.

UNDER THE SPREADING CHESTNUT TREE

Under the spreading chestnut tree,
With my sweety on my knee.
Oh, how happy I would be,
Under the spreading chestnut tree.

For *spreading*, use arms outspread. For *chest,* hands on chest; for *nut,* hands on head; for *tree,* hands above the head. The second time you sing the song, eliminate the word *tree,* substituting the motion for it. The third time, use motions only for *nut* and *tree;* the fourth time, motions only for *chest, nut,* and *tree;* the fifth time, motions only for *spreading, chest, nut, tree,* and the last time, motions only for *under the spreading chestnut tree.*

COMIN' ROUND THE MOUNTAIN

1. She'll be comin' round the mountain when she comes, toot-toot!
   (Repeat four more times.)
2. Oh, we'll all go down to meet her when she comes. Hi! There!
   (On the last repeat, also add *Toot-toot.*)

3. She'll be driving six white horses when she comes. Whoa, Babe!
   (On the last repeat, also add *Hi there,* and *Toot-toot*)
4. She'll have to sleep with grandpa when she comes, snore, snore!
   (Again on last repeat, also add *Whoa, Babe, Hi there! Toot-toot.*)
5. Oh, we'll kill the old red rooster when she comes, Kuh, kuh!
   (On the last repeat, add *Snore, snore! Whoa, Babe! Hi, there! Toot-toot!*)
6. We'll all have chicken and dumplings when she comes, Yum! Yum!
   (Add all the former motions.)

THERE WAS AN OLD WOMAN

1. There was an old woman, she swallowed a fly
   Chorus: I don't know why, she swallowed a fly. Perhaps she'll die.
2. There was an old woman she swallowed a spider.
   It wiggled and tickled and giggled inside her.
   She swallowed the spider to catch the fly.
   (*Chorus*)
3. There was an old woman she swallowed a bird.
   Oh, my word! She swallowed a bird!
   She swallowed the bird to catch the spider
   That wiggled and tickled and giggled inside her.
   She swallowed the spider to catch the fly.
   (*Chorus*)
4. There was an old woman who swallowed a cat.
   Think of that! She swallowed a cat!
   She swallowed the cat to catch the bird,
   She swallowed the bird to catch the spider, etc.
5. There was an old woman, who swallowed a dog.
   What a hog! She swallowed a dog!
   She swallowed the dog to catch the cat., etc.
6. There was an old woman, she swallowed a goat.
   She just opened her throat and swallowed a goat.
   She swallowed the goat to catch the dog, etc.
7. There was an old woman, she swallowed a horse.
   She's dead, of course! (*The end*)

GREEN GRASS GREW ALL AROUND

In the woods there was a tree,
The prettiest little tree that you ever did see,

And the tree was in the ground,
Chorus: And the green grass grew all around;
All around, and the green grass grew all around.
2. And on that tree there was a branch,
   The prettiest little branch that you ever did see,
   The branch was on the tree, the tree was in the ground
   (*Chorus*)
3. And on that branch there was a twig, etc.
4. And on that twig there was a nest, etc.
5. And in that nest there was an egg, etc.
6. And in that egg there was a bird, etc.
7. And on that bird there was a feather, etc.
8. And on that feather there was a flea, etc.
9. And on that flea there was a germ, etc.

IN THE BOTTOM OF THE SEA

1. There's a hole in the bottom of the sea (Repeat.)
   There's a hole! There's a hole!
   There's a hole in the bottom of the sea.
2. There's a log in the hole in the bottom of the sea (Repeat.)
   There's a log! There's a log!
   There's a log in the hole in the bottom of the sea.
3. There's a bump on the log in the hole on the bottom of the sea
   (Repeat.)
4. There's a frog, etc.
5. There's a wart, etc.
6. There's a hair, etc.
7. There's a flea, etc.
8. There's a nit, etc.
9. There's a germ, etc.

THERE WAS A LITTLE FORD

1. There was a little Ford, the prettiest little Ford,
   The cutest little Ford that you ever did see.
   The Ford was on the wheels, the wheels were on the ground,
   And the engine in the Ford made the wheels go 'round.
   Match in the gas tank, Blam! blam!
2. There was a little seat, the prettiest little seat,
   The cutest little seat that you ever did see.
   The seat was in the Ford, the Ford was on the wheels,
   The wheels were on the ground,
   And the engine in the Ford made the wheels go 'round.

Match in the gas tank, Blam! blam!
3. There was a little girl, etc.
4. There was a little hat, etc.
5. There was a little flower, etc.
6. There was a little bee, etc.

Visual Sequential Memory

We have discussed mostly sequence in time. The child must also learn sequence in space. But it is the *language* used in reciting the sequence that helps the child to learn.

1. Draw a sequence on the board: HERE IS A CIRCLE, THEN A SQUARE, AND THEN A CIRCLE, AND THEN A SQUARE AGAIN. NOW, WHAT COMES NEXT? WHO CAN FIGURE IT OUT? A child comes up and draws a circle next. GOOD! WHAT COMES NEXT? WHO CAN DO IT? Call on a different child to make each shape. If a child has difficulty, have him repeat the sequence verbally with you. Continue the sequence across the board. Use simple shapes that the children can reproduce easily. Be sure that this is not a test on their drawing ability. As long as they know what shape is next in sequence, you can help a child to make it.

2. Use large plastic pop-beads. WATCH! I PUT A RED BEAD HERE, THEN A BLUE ONE, THEN A GREEN ONE, AND THEN A RED ONE AGAIN. LET'S SAY IT. This reinforces the visual sequence. RED, BLUE, GREEN, RED. . . . NOW WHAT COMES NEXT? WHO CAN PUT IT ON?

3. Use a sequence of floor blocks in the chalkrack. WATCH! FIRST I PUT A LONG BLOCK, THEN A SQUARE, THEN A MIDDLE-SIZED BLOCK, AND THEN A LONG BLOCK AGAIN. I AM BUILDING A FENCE. I WANT IT TO BE THE SAME ALL THE WAY ACROSS MY PROPERTY. WHAT SHOULD BE NEXT? LONG, SQUARE, MIDDLE-SIZED, LONG. . . .

4. Color large square blocks three or four distinctive colors. Make enough small blocks (one-inch square) of all three or four colors so that each child has a set to manipulate. Make a sequence of the colored blocks in the chalkrack. The children all copy your sequence at their desks. Or use the colored number rods or Cuisenaire rods to form a sequence for the children to copy.

5. Obtain beads of different colors and shapes. Make up a sequence of these beads on a shoelace and insert into heavy cardboard. Insert an extra shoelace just below this sequence. Let

the child try to reproduce your sequence with extra beads from an assortment in a box.

6. In the chalkrack, place a red book, a blue book, a green book, and then another red book. WHO CAN FIND THE BOOK THAT SHOULD BE NEXT? WHAT COLOR SHOULD IT BE? Or use different sizes.

7. Use a series of pictures which show a sequence of action. Put them into a pocket chart in random order. WHAT DO YOU THINK HAPPENED FIRST? WHAT PICTURE SHOULD BE FIRST? WHO CAN DO IT? When a child places a picture, ask him: WHY DO YOU THINK THAT PICTURE SHOULD BE FIRST? WHAT IS HAPPENING?

Auditory-Sequential Memory

The child listens to directions in sequence and then he performs. This is a daily occurance in every classroom, but it is just taken for granted that the child can remember the sequence. (Be sure the children understand prepositions before you do these exercises.)

1. Group directions; the children act individually, but in unison. I AM GOING TO TELL YOU TWO THINGS TO DO. DON'T DO ANYTHING UNTIL I SAY, GO. FIRST, I WANT YOU TO STAND ON THE RIGHT SIDE OF YOUR DESK AND THEN SIT DOWN. NOW, GO. THIS TIME I WANT YOU TO CRAWL UNDER YOUR DESK AND THEN SIT DOWN. GO. As the children succeed in this, use three items, then four, if possible. Use prepositions *over, under, in front of,* and *behind.* Also, add items such as clapping the hands a stated number of times, jumping, and hopping. Observe the child who merely watches others and imitates. Try to get him to think for himself. Do some games with the eyes closed. FIRST TAP YOUR HEADS, THEN RUB YOUR TUMMIES, AND THEN CLAP YOUR HANDS TWICE. GO!

2. One child performs: This game is not as efficient as the above because not enough children are responding but it does offer a change of pace and they watch quite carefully. LISTEN CAREFULLY. I'M GOING TO ASK SOMEONE TO DO SOMETHING. I WANT SOMEONE TO WALK AROUND THE EASEL ONE TIME AND BACK TO HIS SEAT. KANDY, CAN YOU DO IT? GOOD. NOW THIS TIME I WANT SOMEONE TO WALK AROUND THE EASEL ONE TIME, SIT ON THE PIANO STOOL, AND GO BACK TO HIS SEAT. MARY ANN! EVERYONE KEEP VERY QUIET.

DON'T TELL HER WHAT TO DO. IF SHE GOOFS, THEN IT WILL BE SOMEONE ELSE'S TURN. GOOD! NOW, I WANT SOMEONE TO WALK AROUND THE EASEL ONE TIME, SIT ON THE PIANO STOOL, GET A BOOK AND TAKE IT TO HIS SEAT AND SIT DOWN. MIKE! Keep adding one new item until a child goofs. Then call on someone else to do it correctly. If it is too difficult for anyone to do, begin again with one new item.

SUMMARY

In this chapter we have described how language develops in the child, how to recognize and diagnose language problems, and how we receive and express language. We then discussed the language of the disadvantaged and the teaching of the language of instruction through the Distar Language program. This program is quite complete in itself, and far superior to all other language programs. However, lacking funds for this program, the classroom teacher needs to plan daily language instruction to overcome her children's deficiencies. To fill this gap are the books, *Learning Language I, II, and III,* and suggestions for the use of pictures and objects to teach basic language, sentence structure, and vocabulary. Methods in language reception and expression are grouped according to topics which closely parallel the subtests of the ITPA. These can be used with small groups of children with deficiencies in these specific areas, or they can be used with a whole class, endeavoring to employ some methods from each category in order to provide a well-rounded language program. This latter program would be aimed at prevention of language confusions or disabilities.

REFERENCES

Bender, Lauretta: The brain and child behavior. *Arch Gen Psychiat,* 4:531–547, 1961.

Bereiter, Carl, and Engelmann, Siegfried: *Teaching Disadvantaged Children in the Preschool.* Engelwood Cliffs, New Jersey, Prentice Hall, 1966.

Engelmann, Siegfried: *The Basic Concept Inventory.* Chicago, Follett, 1967.

———. *Preventing Failure in the Primary Grades.* Chicago, Sci Res, 1969.

———, et al.: *Learning Language, I* and *II.* Urbana, Ill Pr.

———, et al.: *Distar Language I.* Chicago, Sci Res, 1969.

Hart, N. W. M.: The Differential Diagnosis of the Psycholinguistic Abilities of the Cerebral Palsied Child and Effective Remedial Procedures. *Special*

Schools Bulletin, Queensland, Vol. V. (No. 2), 1963.

Hart, N. W. M.; Phillips, B., and Searle, E.: The Use of ITPA and An Associated Language Program With Partially Sighted Children. Special Schools Bulletin, Queensland, Vol. VIII (No. 2), 1966.

Kastein, Shulamith: *The Birth of Language.* Springfield, Thomas, 1966.

Kirk, Samuel A., and McCarthy, James P.: *Illinois Test for Psycholinguistic Abilities.* Urbana, U Ill Pr, 1961; rev. ed., 1968.

McCormick, Molly, and Osborn, Jean: *Learning Language, III.* Urbana, U Ill Pr.

Myklebust, Helmer: *Learning Disabilities.* New York. Grune & Stratton, 1967.

Osborn, Jean: *Teaching a Teaching Language to Disadvantaged Children.* Urbana, U Ill Pr, 1968.

Outridge, M.: Psycholinguistic Abilities of Five Children Attending a Brisbane Opportunity School. Special Schools Bulletin, Queensland, Vol. VI (No. 1), 1964.

Peabody Picture Vocabulary Test. Nashville, PPVT American Guidance Service, 1959.

Rimland, Bernard: *Infantile Autism.* New York, Appleton-Century-Crofts, 1964.

Tomkins, Calvin: Children's neurological development program, the last skill acquired. *New Yorker,* Sept. 24, 1963.

Vygotsky, L. S.: *Thought and Language.* New York, Wiley, 1962.

Wepman, Joseph M.: *Wepman Test of Auditory Discrimination.* Chicago, Sci Res, 1958.

Zedler, E. Y.: *Screening Scale for Children with High Risk of Neurological Impairment. International Approach to Learning Disabilities of Children and Youth.* Tulsa, Oklahoma, Association for Children with Learning Disabilities, 1966.

FILMS

A Time for Georgia. (15 min.) Pre-Schoolers Workshop, 38 Old County Road, Garden City, New York, 11530.

Infantile Autism, The Invisible Wall. Behavioral Sciences A.V. Laboratory. 800 Northeast 13th Street, Oklahoma City, Oklahoma, 73104.

Oral Language a Breakthrough to Reading. (24 min.) Ohio State University Department of Photography, 156 West 12th Avenue, Columbus, Ohio, 43210.

Perception and Communication. (32 min.) Ohio State University, Department of Photography, 156 West 12th Avenue, Columbus, Ohio, 43210.

Revised Illinois Test of Psycholinguistic Abilities. (43 min.) University of Illinois, Visual Aids Service, 1325 South Oak, Champaign, Illinois, 61820.

Techniques of Non-Verbal Psychological Testing. (20 min.) International Film Bureau, 332 S. Michigan Avenue, Chicago, Illinois, 60604.

The World Outside. David Horne and Gerald Schiller. S. L. Productions, 5126 Hartwick Street, Los Angeles, California, 90041.

$\mathcal{M}$odifying $\mathcal{B}$ehavior

DEFINING TERMS

BEHAVIOR IS THE ACTION, the conscious or unconscious response of the individual. Every observable behavior or response, whether it is social, emotional, physical, or intellectual, is a behavior. The function of the schools is to elicit the responses from the students which will enhance their learning. We want them to attend, to respond, and to learn the subject matter which we present to them. However, if they are not motivated to receive the material or interested in the manner in which we present it, they will not make the desired responses and will not gain the knowledge. A large part of the student's responsiveness to the materials which we present lies in his own feelings about himself, and his abilities, and in his reaction to, or acceptance of, us as teachers. We cannot motivate children. Motivation comes from within the child. It is the old trite adage: "You can lead a horse to water, but you can't make him drink." What, then, can we do? How can we get them to "drink"?

By *modifying*, we mean to change in some degree, to alter, to teach. To elicit the desired responses from our students we must understand their relationships to us as adult figures, figures of authority or even as a potential threat to their well-being or freedom. The child must accept us or he probably will not accept our teaching. He may learn exactly the opposite things from those which we want him to learn. We may be teaching our children to rebel, to become aggressive, or to withdraw, without really being conscious of it. If the child accepts us completely and we do nothing to shake his initial trust of us, then the only behavior we need modify in him is his academic learning behavior. We want to keep him busy, interested, eager to learn, making the right learning responses. However, if the child comes to us as the overindulged child who has never had to do anything he did not feel like doing at the moment, then our effect as a teacher of academic material is at stake. The disadvantaged child who roams at will from the moment he rolls out of bed in the morning to the time when he collapses from exhaustion on a bare mattress is as overindulged as the coddled child of highly protective parents. Then, of course, there are the overly aggressive children lashing out at the whole world, and the withdrawn children who have no faith in themselves or their own abilities, who find it easier to simply withdraw from life than to accept themselves in it. The child who has neurological deficiencies has a more distorted, confused world with which to deal. We must clarify the distortions and somehow modify, or change, the undesirable behaviors.

TRADITIONAL CLASSROOM CONTROL

The old image of the classroom teacher is that of the authoritarian who rules with an iron hand. He passes out facts, which must be unquestionably accepted. He allows no speech which is not in direct reply to his questions or commands. Rebellion is dealt with swiftly, as it threatens his authority and he cannot tolerate this. Because he feels that his own security, his own position as a teacher, is at stake, he may react emotionally, vindictively. He has more classroom control than teacher self-control.

We like to think that this old teacher-image is gone, a thing of the past. But it is not. It is still here today in one form or another. One teacher said that she never smiled at her class for the first two or three months of school in order to stabilize her position. In some primary classrooms child-language is extremely limited. The teacher might speak in a soft voice, but rules with an iron hand. Other teachers harangue the children or resort to ridicule or to shaming. The children might be talked to or yelled at, but are not allowed any part in the altering of the curriculum. They do not learn responsibility for their own actions.

Such classrooms are usually curriculum-centered, rather than child-centered. Previous learnings are taken for granted. The child who is unable to perform is dubbed stupid, inept, a product of his inferior environment or inheritance. His needs are ignored. The curriculum marches on. He is expected to attend class, go through the motions by at least conforming to classroom discipline, but is not really expected to succeed.

There are classrooms where there is never anything out of place. No problems for any custodian. No activity is tolerated which will cause any litter. No project will ever be started which will not be completed within the one period, with no telltale signs left. These teachers often beat the children out of the room at the end of the day. No teaching is done the last half-hour so that all is in preparedness for the bell. Before the bell rings, the whole class has been dismissed and is waiting at the bus or in front of other classrooms.

Many of these situations are the fault of the system, rather than exclusively that of the teacher. The administrator visits the classroom and writes detailed derogatory comments about the messy bookshelves, the clutter on the science table, the esthetically disordered bulletin board where the children have proudly put up their own work. He notes how quiet and busy the children appear to be, though *busy* may be only idly turning the pages of a book, coloring a ditto, laboriously copying from the blackboard, or doing some worksheet a year below the children's level. In some schools and districts the teacher is required to follow a set curriculum precisely and is not allowed any deviations from it. Since all of this negative information goes on the teacher's record and usually determines her employability for the next year—and longer—any classroom noise or apparent confusion is a threat to her job. Thus, often a potentially good teacher is forced to compromise her own principles of education, her own feelings for the children in order to keep her job. This is often the frustrating, heart-rendering position of the probationary teacher. Sometimes the principal is well-meaning and does not intend to be a threat to the teacher. Still, because her future is at stake and evaluation is undefined, incomplete and erratic, she feels threatened. Until and unless a teacher is considered a professional person, free to teach her children according to adequately defined measures and ethical and moral considerations only, the children and the educational system will suffer and we shall still have the headmaster with the stick and the duncecap.

In teacher-training institutions, often the only mention of the process of contacting and motivating the children is under the heading of "classroom control." This is frequently simply a list of "do's" and "don'ts" in the classroom, with no solid theoretical background. Thus the teacher has difficulty applying the ideas or evaluating their effectiveness. It is like having the pieces of a puzzle but never the whole picture. Having a solid basis in learning and reinforcement theory enables us to evaluate our results and reorder our procedures accordingly.

College methods courses often emphasize arts-and-crafts type projects as a means to gain children's interest and teach concepts in an intriguing manner. However, these might be an inefficient use of classroom time. We should be aware at all times of the direct objectives of our teaching, the time allotted to that concept, and the efficiency of our teaching methods. Too often projects take the place of concentrated teaching because the former are easier on the teacher and guarantee a positive response from the students. The teacher may know no other way to keep her students interest and attention and to gain rapport as a "fun" teacher.

It is more difficult to settle children down to a concentrated study or learning period. It takes more skill and a knowledge of reinforcement theory. Engelmann recognizes that deprived children are a year or so behind their classmates already. Thus instruction must be more concentrated, not less, to teach two years of learning in one.

Beginning teachers are usually told to *start strict* and keep *tight control,* that they can loosen control later when they have established rapport with their children. The problem is that they are never taught *how* to achieve this rapport, and every act that children commit that is in any way undesirable appears then to be a reflection of the teachers' *lack of control. This,* therefore, is a threat to the teacher and she tightens controls more. Punishment is satisfying to her because she then feels that she has *done* something, she has *proven* her control. She does not realize that punishment has taught the child nothing. That the behavior is suppressed only temporarily, and that it has committed her to further punishment.

The public and the government have stressed knowledge of subject matter to such an extent that we have teachers coming out of colleges and universities steeped in subjects, knowledgeable in curriculum, but completely inept when it comes to handling the children. Their first days and year of teaching are often a nightmare to them. Many resign in despair. They are unable to teach the children because they cannot get their attention and cooperation.

We are going to have to bring pressure to bear on our teacher-training institutions, perhaps through our legislatures, to see that all teachers have a deeper background in psychology and child development with a minimum of one required course in behavior modification and one on normal children with learning problems.

With an increase of mental health problems in our country (especially among school children) has come the determination of dedicated men to find more positive ways of modifying children's behavior. William Glasser (1965) has come up with reality therapy; Eric Berne, with transactional analysis; B. F. Skinner, with operant conditioning and schedules of reinforcement; and Frank Hewett (1964), with the engineered classroom. Add to these the teaching techniques of Hilda Taba, Edmund Amidon (interaction analysis), and J. Richard Suchman (inquiry training). We need to study the work, teaching methods, and findings of all of these therapies to better understand the teachers' role in the classroom. For the purposes of this book, we will take just a quick look at a few of these.

REALITY THERAPY

William Glasser explains some of the basic tenets of this theory so beautifully, I can but quote him:

> We start with the idea that everybody has basic needs. These are the two needs which seem to apply most: *the need for love* and *the need to feel worthwhile;* the idea we are worth something to ourselves and to the world seems to be built in. These are two-way needs:

to love and to be loved implies someone who loves us. If we don't have this we suffer. For some children the form of this suffering is not learning to read and they won't learn to read until they get the idea that someone is able to care for them and they *can* learn. We need to feel we are worthwhile to at least one other person, who thinks we are worthwhile. Even without this you still have to maintain a modicum of care about yourself. The child who has given up on believing in himself and becomes apathetic is the most difficult. He doesn't think there is anything in the world for him.

Assuming these two needs are important—if they are not fulfilled people suffer. Suffering is the only way they can see to meet needs. It is the best they can do at the moment. Children suffer by not learning, or they get tired of suffering and cause others to suffer. . . .

The teacher's first job is to make contact with these children—as a person who cares—a person interested in them—not as a teacher, but as a person. The child needs to feel "This is a good person who likes me, who talks to me, and I have a good time with him—and—he does teach reading." Everyone is doing the best he can do—at the time. If he could do better, he would. You can't convince them they can do better until they relate to you and begin to meet their needs. . . .

The teacher says "I can't teach these kids—they are not motivated." *Motivation is equivalent to involvement.* The teacher doesn't understand what motivation is who says she can't teach children who are not motivated. Teaching is motivation. Once children are involved they automatically become motivated. . . .

. . . You must be personal and get emotionally involved. Not getting emotionally involved is like not giving a hungry man bread. (Glasser, 1966, pp. 1–2)

In this last statement we have the main break between the traditional authoritarian teacher and the teacher who really cares about her children. She is less concerned about what her peers and her administrators think of her and more concerned with her relationship to the child. She is not made of stone. She is human. She cares and she must show it. She laughs with her children and she may come near to crying with them. When little Susan's puppy was run over, the child felt alone in the crowded classroom. The teacher took the child into her arms and just held her. It required no explanation to the rest of the class. They understood. Susan was given the same work as usual, encouraged with a hug or a pat, but no demands were made on her academic performance that day. This did not result in endless tears as some stern disciplinarians are likely to think. Instead, her teacher's and peers' concern for her sustained her so that she then had the strength to continue with her work in spite of her loss. With no concern from others, she may have sat and mourned all day.

William Glasser would no doubt agree with Leo Bascaglia (1969), who said, "The most important thing the classroom teacher can give a child is a big, warm, loving body." Glasser's therapy begins with love and involvement and the child's need for a feeling of self-worth. The child must then be able to evaluate his behavior and choose a direction or goal more helpful to himself and others. After making a value judgment, he must commit himself to his choice. After his commitment to change his behavior, no excuse is acceptable for not following through. Glasser feels that the teacher who cares, accepts no excuses. If she accepts his excuses and does not make him follow through, she proves to him that she does not really care (Glasser, 1968). In *Schools Without Failure*, Glasser proposes eliminating grades as not being reinforcing, teaching thinking skills, and holding class meetings to discuss social problems and stimulate thinking. These meetings also help the children to feel that their ideas are worthwhile and that they have some control over their own destiny. There is hope and a future.

TRANSACTIONAL ANALYSIS

Here again is another therapy which is difficult to summarize in a few paragraphs, but which has marked implications for modifying classroom behavior. Tom Harris's book *I'm O.K.— You're O.K.* (Harris, 1967) is excellent reading for the teacher.

The individual is seen as having three states existing in him at one time, the Parent, the Adult, and the Child. The recordings from his parents, their rules, admonitions, laws, external events, imposed ideas, constitute the Parent state. This would also include the religion and the example of his parents. Parent data kept him from harm as a small child. "Don't go out in the street." "Don't play with knives." This data can be valid, reasonable or not, according to his parents. "Don't touch toads, you will get warts" would be unreliable data. "Never mind that teacher. You can do that if you want to." This is data which might bring the child into conflict with himself and the adults he contacts.

The Child state is more a recording of internal events, of feelings, desires, tantrums, and self indulgence. The child is unreasoning, "I don't want to. I don't care! I wish . . ."

The Adult is logical, reasoning, mature, able to solve problems, to make adjustments, to accept situations. The Adult computes the data from his Parent (rules) and his Child (feelings) and can make decisions. He asks logical questions in order to find answers. He can accept a lack of certainty. He is realistic. He accepts and gives opinions.

The Parent is static, cannot change. Neither can the Child accept changes. Only the Adult can change. Only in the Adult in us can we overcome our problems, learn to live with ourselves. Even the very young child has some reasoning Adult in him. Thus, only as we are able to support the Adult in the problem child, to get him to think things out and to make decisions, can we ever hope to change his attitude toward life, toward school, and his feelings for himself and his worth.

The well-adjusted adult feels secure about himself and accepting of others: *I'm O.K.—You're O.K.* The young infant's first feelings are *I'm Not O.K.—You're O.K.* (Harris, 1967). The parents' care of the child, their dependability, the validity of the sensory data the child receives, the faith of the child in himself and his own worth give him the Adult reasoning ability and the success experiences which help him to feel *"I'm O.K.—You're O.K."* However, this position is thought to be at least uncommon, if not rare. Therefore, we must accept the fact that most of the children sitting in our classrooms lack this warm security in themselves and feel that either they are not O.K., or that you are not O.K. Children probably have a general feeling of inferiority. In order to reach these children, in order to teach them, you must give them confidence in themselves, help them to make decisions, to feel successful, to use some measure of Adult reasoning. To feel, *I'm O.K.,* the child needs "strokes" in the form of lots of praise, support, success, and things to make him feel good.

Tactile stimulation of the infant is essential to his physical survival and to his feeling of *I'm O.K.* Orphans often died in the foundling homes where they did not receive this early stroking from being cared for and fondled. In Chapter Five we discussed the protective system in the child and how some children are oversensitive to stimuli and repulse your touch of them. E. Schopler (1965) feels that the child who receives stroking, but who for a physiological reason of a high stimulus barrier is deprived of the sensation of the stroking, may become an autistic child, unable to relate to others. The infant does not respond to the stroking and does not like to be held. The parents then often withhold their handling of the child. Perhaps if this child were given additional vigorous tactile and kinesthetic stimulation he would overcome the barrier. This appears to tie in with A. Jean Ayres' hypothesis (Chapter Five).

We have long heard the debate of which environment produces the creative child, the controlled, or the undisciplined. Tom Harris, psychiatrist, believes that many valid parent directives become so automatic that the person is thus freed to be creative:

> . . . Were we to start from scratch in every decision or operate entirely without the data that was supplied by our parents, our computer would rarely have time for the creative process.
>
> Some people contend that the undisciplined child, unhampered by limits, is more creative than the child whose parents set limits. I do not believe this is true. A youngster has more time to be creative—to explore, invent, take apart, and put together—if he is not wasting time in futile decision making for which he has inadequate data. . . . The most creative individual is the one who discovers that a large part of the content of the Parent squares with reality. He can then file away this validated information in the Adult, trust it, forget about it, and get on with other things—like how to make a kite fly, how to build a sand castle, or how to do differential calculus. (Harris, 1967, p. 35)

The child comes to us in school with all his past fears, frustrations, hangups. He may come with pent-up aggressive feelings about adults, school, authority. He might have immature parents who do not adequately supply his needs. He may be in the turmoil of rejection or sibling rivalry. He may never have had to listen to anyone or to do anything he did not care to do. So where does this leave us, the classroom teachers? We must accept him the way he is, right now, today. We cannot change his home, his environment. We cannot erase his past experiences. But we can accept him, show him honest concern, love, become involved with him. We can build up his own feelings for himself, give him success and confidence in large doses. When he feels more like he's O.K., then he will be more accepting of us and our teachings. If we are stable and logical and reasonable in our dealings with him so that he knows that he can trust us, then he can trust the data that we give him. With the correct data, we can then guide him into making decisions, coming to logical conclusions, hooking his Adult. The child will change his behavior when he finds that he is capable of change.

REINFORCEMENT THERAPY

Reality therapy and transactional analysis have important implications for our attitudes in our classrooms. Through these we learn to love, accept, respect, and become involved with our children. We try to get them to accept responsibility, to think things through, to make decisions and commitments. However, with thirty children reacting to us in different ways, and all at the same time, we are often overwhelmed with the confusion they create. Long-range goals, class discussions, individual talks are great! And certainly desirable in our classrooms! But when we are trying to get the attention of those thirty children to impart some valuable information, we need a bag of tricks. For instant help we turn to reinforcement therapy and positive reinforcement.

Extinguishing Undesirable Behavior

We have two major goals for the immediate behavior of our children. We want to extinguish the unacceptable behavior and to reinforce the desirable behavior. To extinguish a behavior, we take away all reinforcers of that behavior, all the things which make the child behave the overt way he does. The biggest single step is ignoring the undesirable behavior (unless he is hurting others). We don't look at the child or show him any attention for his act. This can be done in several ways, according to the causes and cumulative effects of the misbehavior. If the child is merely bidding for attention, give attention to the other good performers: MY! YOU CHILDREN ARE SUCH GOOD WORKERS! THAT IS VERY GOOD, JERRY! KANDY GOT TO WORK RIGHT AWAY! SUSAN KNOWS WHAT TO DO! A pocketful of candy or cereal treats is a handy reinforcer for the first of the year when you are trying to shape good behavior. Just drop one quickly on the desk of each child who is working. Say nothing about the nonworkers or give them hope of soon receiving a reward, too. OH, YOU ARE STARTING, TOO! I'LL BET YOU ARE GOING TO DO A GOOD JOB, TOO! Wait a minute or so, and then reward the errant children to encourage their work. Hyperactive children, or more uncontrolled children, will have to be reinforced sooner and more frequently. We will talk later about this scheduling.

We must also remove the environmental reinforcers which promote this overt behavior. We spoke in Chapter Five about eliminating the stimulations which distract the child. We pull the curtains if passing children are distracting. We cut down on room clutter and displays and bulletin boards in the instruction center of the classroom. We also find it best to tell children to leave their toys at home. If they come with little cars, dolls, etc., these are set aside until it is time to go home. Otherwise, the child's attention is constantly drawn to the compelling interest in his hand. He does not attend to instruction. He does not learn.

We also remove the peer reinforcer. Tommy loves to tease Jody, so we separate them. Or Kenny plays with Susan's hair. We move him. For instruction, we put the inattentive children directly in front of us and close to us so that we can reinforce them more readily. In instruction groups, some children play with hair barrettes, jewelry, strings, their shoes, coats, etc. Collect all these, too. These are environmental reinforcers. Especially in hot weather when shoes are a heavy distraction to children, several pair are often tossed behind the teacher to get them out of sight and mind.

Positive Reinforcement

Now we have tried to extinguish the inattentive behavior, but Tommy still is not listening or participating. Now comes the magic of positive reinforcement. We must find something that he desires or needs to which he will respond.

A positive reinforcer can be anything that is desired or needed by the student. A positive reinforcer will strengthen the response it follows and make that response more likely to reoccur. (Hunter, 1967, p. 1)

A reinforcer can be intrinsic or extrinsic, coming from within the child or from without. Success in accomplishing a task and achievement are intrinsic rewards. If the child is usually successful with his endeavors, he is exhilarated by these intrinsic rewards. If, however, he has had few successes in his short life, he has never had these wonderful kinds of feelings. Thus the reinforcement must come from outside of him, from extrinsic rewards. These might be stars, any foods, candies, toys, tally marks, pennies, or sugared cereals. We find these latter desirable to the child, and most readily available and inexpensive (not nutritious). They are more easily replaced with praise or social reinforcement than candy.

Our problem children crave attention, so this becomes a powerful reinforcer, too. We praise them, call the other children's attention to them, shake a hand, pat a back, give lots of hugs, or just listen to them.

The child also responds to stars, having GOOD written on his paper, seeing his "rocket" go up, getting a fun thing to do, or the privilege of doing some special task for the teacher.

Other reinforcers are built right into the lesson. Things like dramatic pauses in instruction just before the vital words, or presenting a challenge, or pretending to *catch* or *beat* the child to an answer. If you instruct at a level low enough so that the child is sure to achieve success, you can praise or otherwise reward him more often, and his attention and responses will improve as he gains confidence in himself. Keep the lesson moving, interesting. Learning should always be exciting! Be enthusiastic! Sell your product! The children then love it and learn. When you pass out reinforcers, cereals or praise, make a big show of it. You are much more likely to extend too little praise than too much. Can there ever be too much praise? Don't you revel in praise, even when you are a little embarrassed by it?

Punishment

Punishment is used to suppress undesirable behaviors. This could be anything unpleasant, or *not* desired by the child.

Johnny is jumping up and down in his seat. You forcibly push him down. This is punishment (unless he enjoyed the attention). It does not have to be physical contact. It could be isolation or elimination of an immediate privilege, no recess, no treat, no participation in some desired project. It should be immediate and not prolonged. A sharp command is punishment. STOP THAT! This latter could be somewhat of a shock technique. Another would be loud clapping of the hands in front of his face. Or if the child is sitting near you, a resounding slap on the thigh. These must be sudden and immediate. You use them only when there is absolutely no chance to positively reinforce, or if the child hurts another or does something socially unacceptable (spits on a child). Use the smallest amount of punishment necessary to accomplish the response you must have immediately. The goal of the punishment is not to hurt the child, but to stop the overt act.

If the misbehavior is mild or new, you probably will be able to ignore it to cause its extinction. If it is too distracting, obnoxious, or too constant, you may have to punish. However, you have shown the child only what *not* to do, and unless you follow it very soon with what *to* do, you will just have some kind of undesirable behavior recurring.

Punishment usually suppresses the behavior only temporarily. It does not train the child to control his own behavior. It does not teach him anything. It does not give him an alternate choice of behavior. Punishment commits a teacher to further punishment. Schaefer and Martin say:

> Under a procedure of punishment, a response is neither weakened nor removed. Instead it emerges in unchanged form under different conditions or under the same conditions if the punishing event no longer follows. (Schaefer, 1969, p. 35)

When children are misbehaving, we try to ignore it to extinguish it. But then we must look for some way to reinforce good behavior and thus show the child what *to* do. The class has come in from recess. Jerry is standing over by the window. Susan has her hand in the fishbowl. Others are in groups talking. You want them in their seats and ready for work. What is the fastest way to accomplish this? If you start scolding the misbehavers, you may be *reinforcing* the misbehavior and irritating yourself because you are seeing only the bad. Scolding the misbehavers would also take considerable time and they would still dawdle their way to their seats or look for some other mischief to do. Thus you are certainly not attaining your goal of in-seat behavior. Punishment gains nothing in this situation. It only compounds the situation.

Look for the *one* child who is behaving well. There are no doubt more than one. You simply have not noticed them. BILLY WENT RIGHT TO HIS SEAT! I LIKE THAT! HE KNOWS WHAT TO DO! THAT REALLY HELPS! You might give Billy a pat, a smile, or even a treat. Then, as quickly as other children go to their seats, begin to reinforce their good behavior too. You don't have to reward every single one. Let the last few get to their seats without reward, but remember that this then is punishment for them, a desire withheld. Don't begrudge these children their former poor behavior. Forget it. Just see how well they are performing now. Your goal is to elicit favorable responses which you can then reinforce. So catch these errant children behaving well soon, and reward them.

Everything you say or do to a child is either reinforcing, or extinguishing a behavior. Basically, any attention given the child is reinforcing that behavior. Removing all attention extinguishes the behavior. Little Tommy scribbles on his desk. Since he probably craves attention, you reinforce this behavior when you respond by shocked looks or by saying: TOMMY! WHAT DID YOU DO THAT FOR? YOU SHOULDN'T. . . . IF YOU DON'T. . . . YOU MAKE ME SO MAD! NOW LOOK WHAT YOU HAVE DONE! You may think of this as punishment, but is it? With negative attention such as this, you may have really reinforced this behavior. He cannot get attention for anything good because, as yet, he never does anything good. So why not get attention this stimulating way? With negative attention as with punishment, you have only told the child what not to do. Only positive reinforcement tells the child what to do.

Punishment not canceled with successive positive reinforcement commits the teacher to constant negative punishment. Thus the teacher is on a nerve-racking treadmill from which she cannot escape. If you punish a child, as soon as possible find something which you can positively reinforce. Say you have used a shock technique of slapping a child's thigh to get his attention to your instruction. As soon as he attends for a moment, even while he is still in shock, reinforce him with a treat, and give him a very simple task that he can hardly refuse. This could be just repeating something you say. TWO PLUS TWO EQUALS FOUR. I CAN SAY IT! CAN YOU SAY IT? GOOD! YOU DID IT! Reinforce with a treat, too.

Your whole class is unruly and you have just used some statement, hopefully positive, to get the class to their seats and ready for instruction. It is then essential that you immediately find some way of reinforcing the in-seat behavior with positive reinforcement, or you will not have taught them good behavior, but only temporarily suspended the bad. You must, therefore, get good responses from the group and reinforce immediately: THIS ROW IS LISTENING ALREADY! YOU KNOW HOW TO LISTEN! I REALLY APPRECIATE THAT! THAT HELPS. You can pair this with treats if necessary, to the first children ready. Begin instruction with something they like to do and can do easily. Thus they respond well and can be positively reinforced immediately. With young children this can be done with a poem, a fingerplay, a song, or an easy repetitious exercise: LET US ALL SAY THE DAYS OF THE VEEK! Or in math: ONE PLUS ONE IS TWO. TWO PLUS TWO IS FOUR. Or use challenging statements: LOOK WHAT I CAN DO! YOU CAN'T DO THIS! Or: WATCH HOW I CAN BEAT YOU! When they have done it, reinforce them. You might pretend you are disappointed. YOU ARE TOO SMART FOR ME! I DIDN'T THINK YOU COULD DO IT! THAT WAS TOO EASY FOR YOU! LET US TRY SOMETHING HARDER. Then go into your lesson or directions.

If a teacher fails to elicit good reinforceable responses from his students after a punishment, as Schaefer and Martin say:

> . . . He will either have to continue to punish or else resign himself to an unruly group of students. Punishment does not and cannot teach anything. Punishment suppresses responding.
>
> . . . Punishment is widely used for the simple reason that it is instantly reinforcing to its user. The person who uses punishment typically wants to stop some ongoing behavior. He wants a quick change in behavior—and, of course, he gets it. At that time—that is, at the time when he gets the change he wanted, when he stops whatever behavior he wanted to stop—it is not evident that the change he produced is merely temporary. (Schaefer, 1969, p. 36)

You can change a punishment to good reinforceable behavior quickly by forcing the child into the same stance you desire, and then rewarding him for being there. Say there is obnoxious behavior. You force a child down into his seat with pressure on his shoulder. If he stays there for an instant after you remove pressure, reward him for being seated. Or you force a screaming child in a tantrum to put his head down on his desk, hold it there, and go on with your class as best you can, praising other children loudly for good behavior. When he stops screaming or resisting, reward him! YOU CAN HOLD YOUR HEAD ON THE DESK ALL BY YOURSELF! GOOD FOR YOU! A treat helps here. A minute later. YOU KNOW HOW TO SIT QUIETLY NOW, SO YOU MAY SIT UP. A minute later reinforce his good sitting. This way you are not giving the child a chance to behave any other way. You are ensuring his correct response.

There are many magic tricks to eliciting good responses. You will discover some of your own. Use preventive measures to keep bad behaviors from occuring. Be prepared with lessons and materials. Don't keep the children waiting. Foresee difficult situations and forestall problems. Give hyperactive children extra jobs to do to keep them busy. Tony can't remain in a cross-legged position on the floor. He continually gets up on his heels to see more closely and blocks the view of the storybook from the others. A heavy dictionary in his lap keeps him down. Mike sits absorbed in his stockings, pulling the elastic thread out. Put something large and bland in his lap (a large folder).

Use surprises! Change your reinforcers, their kind and frequency. You are teaching a lesson and suddenly you have the attention of only one child. MARY ANN IS WATCHING. SHE KNOWS WHAT TO DO! Give her a whole handful of treats. Or only one child is responding: MIKE KNOWS! LISTEN TO HIM! HE IS SMART! HE IS THE ONLY ONE HERE WHO CAN DO IT! SHOW THEM, MIKE! SEE, ISN'T HE SMART? Or: MIKE AND I ARE THE ONLY ONES HERE WHO CAN DO THIS! IT IS HARD, BUT WE CAN DO IT! Reward him and yourself, too, with a treat. Or beat the group to an answer when they are slow responding and give only yourself the treat. Make a big show of enjoying the treat: BOY, THIS IS REALLY GOOD! YUM!

Negative Reinforcement

A more difficult concept to explain is *negative reinforcement.* This is a negative aspect of punishment. You punish a child or threaten him with consequences if he does not finish his work. He cannot do it, or just does not want to, so he finds an easy way out. He copies someone else's work. The ruse succeeds. He avoids the punishment. He has found a devious route around it. He is thus reinforced by his copying and therefore will resort to this subterfuge more quickly another time.

A child may also lie to prevent punishment. You gave him some homework which he must return signed by his parents. He loses it or throws it away to avoid doing it. He tells you that his baby sister tore it up or that Mother said he didn't have to do it. If this excuse is accepted and there is no follow-through (a reassignment of the same task or a phone call home to Mother), the false excuses will come more easily next time. Our over-indulged and irresponsible children often neglect completing papers and handing them in. Therefore we keep a careful check on all seatwork. Each child must complete all work or he must repeat it. No work is complete until all errors have been corrected. It takes time and bookwork to follow through with assignments, but if you don't you are reinforcing the lying, the cheating, the avoidance of the work. As Glasser says, the teacher who cares accepts no excuses for the child not carrying through his commitment. If you don't insist that all papers be complete and corrected, the child feels that it is not important, that you don't care.

Shaping and Schedules of Reinforcement

To reach your goal of desirable behavior, you must positively reinforce. But first you must elicit some response from the child which you can reinforce. In other words, you achieve good behavior by getting the child to behave that way and then reinforcing it. The most important factor here is determining what behavior you desire, and then breaking that down into the very smallest or shortest goal or steps you can achieve immediately. To do this, you don't wait for a miracle of that final desired behavior. You make it happen by rewarding those very small steps toward that goal. For example: You want Tommy to do a page of addition. He goofs off, wanders around the room, and does nothing. Shorten the goal. The first could be to get him in his seat. Even if he only perches there once, use that instant to give him a treat and praise. Always pair the treats or extrinsic rewards with praise. YOU KNOW HOW TO GO TO YOUR SEAT! THAT'S WONDERFUL! I WONDER IF YOU KNOW WHAT ELSE TO DO? Here you are giving him a clue as to his next move that will be rewarded. As soon as he gets out his paper or picks up his pencil: OH, YOU ARE STARTING TO WORK ALREADY! THAT'S GREAT! (He has made another step toward your goal for him.) Another treat. Don't ignore his good behavior now. As soon as he has one row or even one problem done, come up with another treat. WOW! YOU HAVE THAT ONE RIGHT! WONDERFUL! What you are doing here is shaping the behavior you desire in a planned step-by-step manner. The plan you have used is your schedule of reinforcement. A highly distractable child will require many more rapid, more constant reinforcements.

Maybe the first day his total accomplishment is only that one row. Make a big fuss over it and next time he may do two rows. Keep the reinforcement coming and soon he will be finishing the whole page. Now you have shaped the behavior you desired.

Your schedule is the relationship of frequency of the behavior to the frequency of reinforcement. If you reinforce every time the child performs the desired behavior, you are on a regular schedule of reinforcement. A regular schedule of reinforcement makes for fast learning. Thus, when you are trying to shape a new behavior, you must use a regular schedule. You must reward every time the child performs. The difficulty is that a teacher so often reinforces irregularly, unconsciously according to her mood and her irritability level. These decisions must be made at a conscious level, or you have no schedule of reinforcement, the new response will not be learned rapidly, and the child will revert to his old behavior.

You have reinforced regularly and the learning is solid, but the child is dependent on you for the continued reinforcement. If you tire of this game and withdraw the reinforcement suddenly, the child reverts to his old behavior and the new is forgotten. If the expected is withdrawn, the child feels cheated and will not perform again. We can draw a parallel with your expectancy of a candy machine. You expect a candy bar when you put your dime into the machine. If you don't get one, you probably will not put in another dime, at least not more than once again. You complain loudly to the manager. You have been cheated. You demand that your money be refunded. This is the child's reaction to your sudden withdrawal of regular reinforcement. He regresses.

After a new behavior has been shaped with regular reinforcement, as soon as possible change to an intermittent schedule. Now you do not reinforce every time, but only intermittently on a declining rate. You have shaped the behavior of Tommy doing his page of math. Even in shaping this behavior you have spread out the reinforcement, so that by the time he is doing a whole page of math, you are no longer rewarding him for simply sitting in his seat or picking up his pencil. Now you are just rewarding him for finishing the whole page, but you want to get away from this regular reinforcement. First, you do not continue the regular reinforcement any longer than absolutely necessary. Maybe you have rewarded a whole page finished two or three times. You have been using a candy-treat reward and praise. Now you reward one day with the praise only, and the next with the treat and praise. The third day, praise only, and maybe some statement like: YOU REALLY KNOW HOW TO WORK NOW! YOU DON'T NEED ME TO REMIND YOU! This time go two days without a treat, but keep the praise coming. Gradually eliminate the treat entirely, or return to it only for extra special behavior, like the day he does two pages or an especially difficult page, or because he really persevered in spite of noisy peers near him or other distractions. This intermittent schedule will develop resistance to forgetting.

A parallel to this intermittent reinforcement with children is the adult's reaction to gambling. The first time you play the slot machines, putting a dime in here and there, and receiving no reinforcement, you stop. After all, you want a candy bar for your dime and you aren't getting it. But if you put in the first dime and get three back, you joyfully put more in. Nothing for a while, and then suddenly you get ten dimes. Now you are hooked! You may continue putting in dimes and as long as you get some returned now and then you continue to play, even though you may have several dollars invested by now. There is also the intermittent reinforcement of bells ringing, red lights flashing, and jackpots of ten and twenty-five dollars being paid the other patrons. Now you don't mind not getting those small three and ten dime rewards. You are continuing to feed that machine in hopes of a larger reward. An intermittent schedule hooks the subject on the desired behavior.

Changing Behavior

You must first identify the behavior which you want to change. If you are working with the gross problems of just one child, you may want to take him aside and have him recognize his problem also. Don't rant and rave about a whole list of behaviors. Find the basic problem, such as inability to get along with peers, not learning, not completing work, or not participating. If the behavior is too strong, decide on the negative to suppress it. Discuss this with the child so that he knows what the consequences of his bad behavior will be. It might be an immediate revocation of a privilege, calling the parent to come take the child home for the day, or complete isolation (this is rarely possible in our over-crowded schools). If he is hurting others and is not subject to spankings at home, sometimes the punishment can be having the principal spank him. Be sure that this is applicable to him. Some children receive nothing but such punishment at home, and more of the same just confirms the child's negative opinion of himself and of the world.

Discuss with the child the new behavior you will try to achieve. He has a problem and you want to help him. You are on his side. Tell him what the reward will be when he does this behavior. It may be treats or privileges, but for hard cases some kind of tally system makes for a more immediate and regular schedule of reinforcement and for planned phasing out to an intermittent schedule. This can be a 4″ x 6″ inch card marked off in half-inch squares. (The child is mean to his peers.) EVERY TIME I SEE YOU PLAYING HAPPILY WITH THE CHILDREN, OR DOING SOMETHING NICE FOR THEM, HELPING THEM IN SOME WAY, I WILL PUT A MARK ACROSS ONE OF THESE SQUARES. To make these tallies meaningful and desirable to him you need to discuss with the child what he would like to have when his card is full. Perhaps he will want a kite or a book. It does not matter as long as it is something he desires and you can provide.

Next, discuss the positive things he can do to earn these tally marks. WHAT CAN YOU DO TO MAKE THE OTHER CHILDREN HAPPY? HOW CAN YOU HELP THEM? He may be unable to state these. He may not know how to behave toward his peers and this is the basis of his problem. You then must give him ideas: YOU COULD SHARE SOMETHING YOU HAVE WITH THEM. YOU COULD ASK THEM TO PLAY WITH YOU. YOU COULD SAY SOMETHING NICE ABOUT THEM! "I LIKE YOU" OR "THAT IS A NICE PICTURE YOU MADE!" YOU COULD PUT YOUR ARM AROUND THE CHILD'S SHOULDER AND SAY: "COME ON, LET'S GO DOWN THE SLIDE." End the discussion on a good positive summary. NOW DO YOU KNOW SOME THINGS YOU CAN DO? WILL YOU TRY HARD TO DO THEM? ALL RIGHT! AND I WILL HELP YOU, TOO.

The next step is to get the child to do some reinforceable behavior which you can reward. Remember it may have to be a short stretch of the imagination to get this schedule going. GOOD! YOU WALKED IN BESIDE JERRY WITHOUT EVEN HITTING HIM! YOU GET YOUR FIRST TALLY MARK! or GOOD! THAT WAS NICE OF YOU THE WAY YOU FELT SORRY FOR SUSAN WHEN SHE FELL DOWN. (Even if he actually did nothing to help.) Now that you have begun to shape the behavior, you can require a little more and space the rewards more. At first, maybe a tally mark every time you see him *not* fighting on the playground. Then, a tally mark for each ten-minute recess which he can endure without getting into a fight. It won't be many days usually before all you need to do is give him a certain number of tallies for a whole day's good behavior. After the new behavior has been practiced, you can remove the punishment that you had originally discussed. You don't have to tell him you are removing it. His misdeeds are less severe and less frequent, so you can now go to a milder punishment. At this stage, when he regresses (and he will) you might say: OH, DEAR! YOU HAVE BEEN SO WONDERFUL! BUT NOW YOU HURT MARY ANN SO I WILL HAVE TO SCRATCH OUT ONE OF THESE TALLY MARKS. (This is your new punishment.) WHAT CAN YOU DO TO MAKE IT UP TO MARY ANN? Later find another good behavior for which you can reward him, to balance out the overt behavior. Now, if possible, you try to ignore his slips into poor behavior, so that they will be extinguished. The final step then, after the card has been filled with marks and his big reward received, is to taper off with intermittent reinforcement. Now it can probably just be praise and recognition. Thus you have progressed from shaping the behavior, to a regular schedule of reinforcement, and finally to an intermittent schedule.

Whole-Group Reinforcement

Some teachers misunderstand the principles of reinforcement and simply pass out a treat to every child in a group at the end of the instruction. They continue to do it on a regular schedule. The children expect it and are angry and sometimes rebellious if the teacher forgets to reward. When you reward with this regular schedule the good, the poor, and the "sometimes" performers receiving alike, this shapes the poor behavior. There is no reason for the poor performer to do any better tomorrow, since he was rewarded for poor behavior today. And why should the good performer continue his behavior, when Tommy got the same reward and Tommy was pinching him?

Reinforcement Based on Motivational Levels

The difficulty in teaching problem children then lies in finding some point at which they may be reinforced for good behavior. This point will vary between children according to their developmental levels of behavior motivation. Frank Hewett outlines these with his *Hierarchy of Educational Tasks* (Hewett, 1968). Let us look at these and attempt to tie them in with possible teacher techniques.

The lowest motivational level is *attention*. When a child is inattentive, the goal is to get him to attend to *anything,* not necessarily educational. Thus, if you say, LOOK AT ME! and he looks, he has attended. You want to encourage this behavior so you give him a reward. At this level, the reward must be extrinsic, a food, a candy, a sugared cereal. He should eat it immediately to solidify the reinforcement. This child is likely to be unable to respond to any less concrete type of reinforcement. Even stars and tally marks may have no effect. The best route to this child's head is through his stomach.

The next level is *response.* When a child is unresponsive, has no desire to learn, doesn't care to do anything, you must give him easy tasks which he likes. These tasks may be much below his intellectual or ability level. They may be simple physical education tasks. Many unresponsive children have been *hooked* on performing according to school criteria by receiving initial stimulus, first success at physical activities. As the child is praised for his good performance in this area he achieves the confidence in his own ability to attempt academic work. Don't underestimate the power of a good physical education program! (Chapter Eight.)

The child's reinforcement for these physical-response tasks then is the *success* which he achieves, and possibly also some extrinsic reward, and the praise he receives as a result of that success. This level requires great patience by the teacher. She is too often tempted to raise the difficulty of the task too quickly, to make demands for greater achievement before the child is ready to accept his own performance. This child might respond to stars or tally marks which are exchangeable for other rewards. But he must first succeed at a task to get these rewards.

The third level is *order.* When a child is unable to follow directions, the task is to get him to complete an assignment from beginning to end. He is rewarded for task completion with extrinsic reward and/or praise. At this stage, the reward might be stars, tally marks, or the word *good* on a paper. Again, the task given him must be simple, short, below his achievement level. It might help a child at this level to give him the task of working until the sand in the egg-timer is gone. If he stays at the task that long, he gets a reward.

The fourth level is *exploratory*. A child who perceives inaccurately needs multisensory stimulation, training in auditory, visual, tactile, olfactory, and gustatory discrimination. His reward for this is his success in the tasks and the sensory-stimulation which he receives.

The fifth level is *social*. When a child does not value social approval, we must get him to value peer and teacher approval, by pairing it with extrinsic rewards such as candy, treats, a fun assignment, tally marks, or release from undesirable assignments. Thus every time we give him a treat or a star, we praise him, pat his shoulder. We get his classmates' attention on his good traits, praising him in front of them. LOOK WHAT JERRY HAS DONE! DIDN'T HE USE NICE COLORS? As they accept him and show their approval of him, he will find approval more desirable to obtain in the future.

The sixth level is *mastery*. For a child who is deficient in achievement skills, the best therapy for the nonlearner is educational achievement. We must show him that he can succeed, that he can learn. We do this by taking him one short step at a time. He must achieve mastery at each step before he is taken on to the next. He must feel successful at all times. All of Engelmann's academic programs are based on this complete hierarchy through to the mastery level. For example, the child is not given *one* word to read until he masters all the components of the reading task, the blending, rhyming, sequence, and sounds. He achieves complete success each day or he does not progress to the next day's lesson. This child is reinforced by his success in daily lessons and by voluminous teacher praise.

The final level is *achievement*. For the child lacking self-motivation for learning, past successful achievements lead to the self-motivated learner. The treatment is to develop interest in acquiring new knowledge. His reinforcement is task success. Our educational materials have not often been very interesting or inspiring. There is nothing very exciting about *See Susan,* or about daily pages of math which have to be completed only to have to do more of the same tomorrow. Stories should be fun. Nonsense is better for children than boredom. They love the story of the fat fish who sat on the little fish, but the latter did not mind because "The fat fish was his Mom." (Engelmann, 1968). Materials should be colorful, interesting, and challenging. Subjects should be varied. Instruction can be game-oriented.

By understanding these motivational levels and recognizing and accepting our children on the levels where they are presently operating, we can begin to devise techniques and schedules of reinforcement to bring about changes in behavior. A child may be on the mastery level in math, and at an attention level in reading, according to his past experience, successes, and failures. Some children may appear to be at a low motivational level and seem to respond only to extrinsic rewards. However, as education proceeds and the child gains confidence in himself and his abilities and faith in you as a teacher he may respond quickly to social reinforcement paired with a visible short goal.

CLASSROOM TECHNIQUES
Short Goals as Reinforcement

Children are more ready to work hard, to learn, if they can see where they are going and how much they are accomplishing. Then they can make a commitment to reach a goal. To do this, we need more individualized programs, more progress according to individual achievement. We have already described a way of doing this with math (Chapter Ten). Also, arrange a sequence of reading workbooks or worksheets so that the children can do these at their own rates instead of those boring two pages a day.

Many other activities can be done in the same manner. Dittoed worksheets grouped according to similar instructions, from the Frostig (1964) masters, can be stapled together into sequential packets. When a child completes one, he is given the next packet in the sequence. If he has difficulty with a packet, he can repeat it. Working at individual rates, the child with fewer perceptual problems can do several packets of worksheets while some children are still on the first two. Begin the perception packets with Perceptual Constancy, and Position in Space. Next would be the easier Spatial Relations exercises and Visual Motor. Then the harder Spatial Relations exercises and Figure-Ground. Not all the worksheets are usab!e in this manner. You will have to pick and choose.

The child is required to practice an exercise only until he masters it. After that, only occasional review is needed. For example, he practices a template until he can successfully make the shape in several sizes, then he goes to the next, more difficult template. He has his turns doing the chalkboard routines (Chapter Nine) until he reaches a certain proficiency. Then he may choose alternate activities while you work with those who still need the practice. Or you give him more *fun* chalkboard designs to create.

In physical education the children might be doing a certain series of exercises. When they have been learned or practiced enough, these children are dismissed to free play while the teacher works with the others. The child practices the walking beam until he is able to walk forward, backward, and sideways easily without falling. He then no longer needs the practice. He can be sent off to try a pogo stick or can-stilts. Daily the children exercise and run until they are tired and their hearts are beating rapidly. Then they are dismissed to skills with balls and jumping, or to free play.

When a teacher uses practices such as these, the children can see the logic of it. They can also see an end to undesirable tasks. The teacher then is reasonable to them and they will be more likely to put forth the effort to achieve.

Children come to first grade used to choosing their own activities all the time, according to their own desires. They say matter-of-factly: "I don't want to!" Try a few of these phrases according to the situation: WELL, THAT IS TOO BAD! WE HAVE TO DO IT. Or: IT IS JUST ONE OF THOSE THINGS THAT HAVE TO BE DONE. DADDY HAS TO GO TO WORK WHETHER HE FEELS LIKE IT OR NOT. Or: YOU COME TO SCHOOL TO LEARN. I COME TO TEACH YOU. WE BOTH HAVE A JOB TO DO. LET'S GET IT DONE. Or: FIRST WE DO OUR WORK AND THEN WE HAVE OUR FUN. WORK FIRST! After comments such as these, leave the child and reward the others who are working. He will soon catch on.

Charts of various kinds showing children's progress help. For an individual math program, a paper rocket with his name that moves up toward the moon is stimulating. He loves to watch you move his rocket up when he completes a packet. Or have his name on a race car that moves across the board. Or have a large chart with a star for each book read or workbook completed, though sometimes he has a hard time finding his name on that big chart. Another device would be individual charts at each child's desk with spaces for achievement in each area. We place them inside the desk so that other children don't tear off the stars. You could mark his progress with an X and he would paste his star on it himself. This is perhaps more meaningful than having just one big classroom chart.

Further reinforcement for achievement can be obtained through the cooperation of the parents. Keep them informed of their child's progress. Be positive with them, too. Emphasize the child's gains, not faults. Be free with your good marks on the children's papers, and with grades or checks on report cards. Call parents when problem children have improved or have had a good day. Cue the parents in on your schedule of reinforcement with their child. They may initiate a similar system at home if they understand what you are trying to do. Refer parents to Patterson's *Living With Children* (1968).

The Positive Teacher

Behaviors of teachers and children have been completely changed by altering the reinforcement schedule of the teacher (Nixon, 1965). To demonstrate how a teacher's attitudes affect children, a positive teacher with a happy class was deliberately coached on the use of negative techniques. Her class was puzzled. They could not understand what had happened to their usually happy teacher. By the end of the study, the class was in turmoil and the teacher was finding her job extremely frustrating. In other studies, a negative teacher and a problem class were completely changed when the teacher was guided into seeing and rewarding only good behavior.

Teachers who constantly complain about their children are revealing their own negative attitudes. "I have a terrible class this year!" "I don't have any good kids!" "That group is so dull!" "They can't do anything right!" "He is so slow!" She's dirty!" "He smells!" In the Rosenthal study in San Francisco, teachers were told that certain randomly chosen students would make outstanding gains. They did! And the teacher's positive attitude toward them even rubbed off on other children in the class who made large gains, also. But the teacher would not accept the gains of these latter children. It was as though children who were low in her estimation were resented for their good achievement.

Even though you think you are a positive teacher, you may be perpetuating maladaptive behavior in your classroom. It may be a carry-over from your teacher training when you were told to be very strict the first of the year and not let the children get the best of you. Thus every little thing a child does that is not absolute compliance becomes a threat to you personally and to your ability to keep control of the class. If you are using any negative statements or looks, or if you are giving any attention to unacceptable behavior, you may be reinforcing it. If you are having difficulties with classroom discipline, this may well be the cause. Try tape recording a whole session with your children. Later listen to yourself and give yourself a minus every time you called attention to a misbehavior. Then set new goals for yourself. Be the see-no-evil monkey. Don't look for trouble or that is what you will find! Use praise, praise! As soon as you catch a glance of a child misbehaving, look away and praise some good behavior in another. Note the *good* behaviors of the problem children. Remember that if you ignore good behavior, you are extinguishing it.

Some teachers are afraid to disturb a child who is working well by giving him praise or attention for fear that this will distract him and he will not continue to work. The opposite is true. Be sure that you *catch* your problem children in good behavior frequently and reward them each time. With Miss Perfect Angel, you may just reward her occasionally. It is easy to play favorites and give the most rewards to those who don't really need them. At first it is important that the problem children eat the treat rewards to solidify the reinforcement. Later, however, they just like to collect them and count them to see how many they have earned. They may then even give them all away. It does not matter. The treats have achieved the purpose of being reinforcing. This is about the time to phase out the food reward, relying more on the social and the achievement reinforcers.

Generate enthusiasm for the whole class. YOU ARE THE BEST CLASS! YOU ARE ALL SUCH GOOD WORKERS TODAY! WHY DON'T WE FINISH OUR WORK AND THEN AFTER RECESS WE WILL HAVE A TASTING PARTY! Keep a supply of future taste-treats ready for use as a class reward. Be sure to *catch* the whole class performing well before they become too tired to continue good behavior.

Other Social Reinforcers

Problem children will benefit from reinforcement from other school personnel. You need to extend these children's acceptance of you to others outside the classroom. Clue in someone else on your staff on a child's problem. It might be the next grade teacher, the principal, the secretary, or last year's teacher. TOMMY! YOU FINISHED YOUR WHOLE PAPER! LET ME PUT A GOLD STAR ON IT AND TAKE IT RIGHT OVER TO THE OFFICE AND SHOW MR. JAMES! HE WILL BE SO PROUD OF YOU! This outside reinforcement is especially important for the child who is in perpetual trouble with the administration for his playground or bus behavior.

When an administrator enters your room, don't let him sit and make you nervous. Use him as a reinforcer. OH, MR. JAMES! COME SEE WHAT GOOD WORK THESE CHILDREN ARE DOING! TOMMY HAS A WHOLE ROW DONE ALREADY! Or if you are instructing a group: COME AND LISTEN TO THEM AND SEE HOW SMART THEY ARE! Start with easy tasks so that the children will be sure to succeed and be proud of themselves. If they err in front of the principal, they often become flustered and cannot correct themselves.

Isolation

Isolation has long been used as an exasperated last gesture of a teacher. She is fed up with the child's disruption of the instruction, so she sends him from the activity.

When isolation is used to try to deny the child the stimulation of his peers and his classroom for a stated period, then this is punishment. This isolation should be in a bland environment, away from all distractions. The child should not be reinforced in any way. If the isolation is in the outer school office or any spot in view of teachers and peers, then it may be positively reinforcing instead of punishing him. He enjoys watching all the activity in the office, hears all the spicy phone messages from irate or exasperating parents, and gets a smile from every adult who passes through. If the isolation is to be entirely punishment with no positive overtones, then it must be away from all activity where the child can neither see nor hear anything happening. If an outside punishment spot is used for recess violations, then teachers should be cued *not* to speak to or pay any attention to the child. These little rascals are experts at conning teachers into conversations with them: "That is a nice dress you have on, Mrs. Kost." Before you know it you have said: THANK YOU, and he beams satisfaction.

Never isolate a child from instruction! He must learn! This is why he comes to school! If you excuse him from instruction or a work period, he will probably use misbehavior to get *out* of learning or working. This is reinforcing poor behavior! It is harming the child! Level with this child! YOU ARE HERE TO LEARN! I AM HERE TO TEACH! LET'S GET TO WORK! Give him an alternative that is not acceptable to him, such as calling his parents to come take him home. (And prepare to carry it through as often as necessary to show him you mean what you say!) Make your admonition very brief and go on with your lesson, remembering to reinforce his very first good response. Use frequent reinforcement and a variety of types of reinforcement discussed earlier. Shape the behavior you desire by rewarding even small gestures toward the goal. Make good responses easy to do. The instant his attention strays, drag it back again by a surprise or unusual reinforcement to the other children, or by a change in voice or pace of the lesson or a challenge. Never do exactly the same things every day or use only the same reinforcement on a regular schedule.

If the child's behavior is very exasperating or difficult to cope with, try some shock technique or force him into some kind of response which you can then reward. As a punishment technique for a difficult child who cannot be dealt with through positive reinforcement, Siegfried Engelmann gives him a command which he physically makes the child do: STAND UP! SIT DOWN! STAND UP! SIT DOWN! YOU DID IT! YOU KNOW HOW TO LISTEN AND DO THINGS! GOOD WORK! Quickly go to a very easy task which he cannot refuse, and reward him.

If the child is acting impulsively during a free classroom period, not directing his own actions, it is often a good idea to send him to his seat, or to a designated part of the room to reassess the situation, and choose a new course of action which will be more acceptable to others. He need not stay there a specific period of time, but only until he is in cognitive control and knows what else he can do. This is not punishment, but merely redirecting the child's energies. He is then learning to take the responsibility of planning his own behavior. If the child is irresponsible again the same period, send him back to his seat. This time, before he can leave his seat he must tell you specifically *what* he is going to do. Then watch to be sure he carries through and does what he said he would do.

The Emotional Outburst

When the child has been frustrated by a task and becomes enraged, you must help him gain control. You were to blame! You misjudged the work, or you did not give clear instructions. You probably did not begin the task at the child's level. THIS IS HARD WORK. IT IS MY FAULT, TOO! I DID NOT SHOW YOU WELL ENOUGH! LET'S START ALL OVER AGAIN AND I WILL HELP YOU THIS TIME! Go on to get other materials to start again, pacing yourself to give him time to regain control. If one child is frustrated, others might be in trouble, too. So you might redemonstrate to the whole class. This also gives the child time to regain control. Then help him to do the task, holding his hand over the pencil or scissors, explaining as you go, and then following it with praise for his work: YOU DID IT! SEE, ISN'T THAT A NICE HEART?

YOU CAN DO IT! LET'S DO ANOTHER ONE! This time help only as needed to achieve success.

A violent child may have to be physically restrained from hurting himself or others. If possible you may be able to hold him, pat his back, speak reassuringly to him until he gains control. If he resists you and you have to keep him from hurting others, try just holding him down in his seat until the initial outburst is over. This is no time to reason with him or to discuss anything. Now he needs time out to cool down. Let him go outside to wash his face and get a drink of water. Don't hurry him. By the time he gets back, he will usually be calmer. Make no further demands on him for a while. Give him something at which he can succeed. Several hours later, or the next day, you should try to have a talk with him to discuss his behavior and the positive measures to prevent its happening again.

PEER RELATIONSHIPS

An important part of the child's adjustment to school is related to his feelings for his peers. When he, himself, is accepted in spite of his many faults, then he is more likely to accept his peers. He may never have learned compassion toward others at home. First, he must feel it turned toward himself, before he can feel it for others. This is why it is doubly important that the teacher make him feel worthwhile, loved. As she shows off his accomplishments to the rest of the class, thus showing her understanding of him, it usually is not too difficult to "hook" him into an act of compassion. Little Susan is crying with a tummy ache. This is an excellent time to get your most aggressive child to help take her to the office. While she is in tears and unable to express herself, he can now be the "big wheel" and tell the secretary Susan's name and difficulty. He will be elated by his experience and will begin to notice when others need help.

When you are expressing love and concern for a child, include the whole class in your statements of concern so that each child feels a part of the scene. You are then expressing love from him to his peers. This may be a new experience for him. Little David

errs. The children laugh at him before you can intervene and he
bursts into tears. OH, DAVID! WE DIDN'T MEAN TO HURT YOU. Hug
him or give him some kind of physical contact. WE AREN'T REALLY
LAUGHING AT YOU BUT JUST AT THAT SILLY . . . WE LOVE YOU. WILL
YOU FORGIVE US? By then, the childen on either side of him are
caressing him also, and for recess he has a real following of pro-
tectors and buddies.

Stabilizing Playground Behavior

The children at our school are extremely aggressive, and the
new generation coming up seems much more so than ever before. If we think we have teen problems now, the signs of the
new first graders foretell even more serious problems to come
unless we have dramatic success in dealing with them.

Our children have bus fights, and brawls in tight neighborhoods. They form gangs and beat up children on the way home.
They love to possess, perhaps they feel that little is really theirs.
They steal and trade toys and school materials so readily that it
is very frustrating to deal with the situation.

Our children were confused by sharp contrasts between demands and requirements of our different teachers. Each of us had
things we would or would not allow. The children got so that
they would look to see who was on yard duty for clues as to how
to behave. Some teachers allowed any behavior that did not
touch them directly. Some screamed directives and empty threats
at the children and did nothing. Problem children were warned
each recess by a different teacher, each one excusing the behavior.
Some teachers were run ragged trying to enforce school rules that
others ignored. All of this inconsistency kept the children on
edge. They teased and tormented others and were openly de-
fiant of teachers. The playground was bedlam. Accidents were
frequent. The teachers dreaded yard duty.

We decided that we just had to come up with a drastically new
total school plan to solve the problem. We felt that these children
needed consistency with specific boundaries for their own security.
They had to learn to take on the responsibility of their own behavior. We set up very specific rules that had to apply to *all*

pupils and teachers at *all* times. The rules and their valid reasons were thoroughly discussed in every classroom. No ignorance of these rules was then accepted. One rule which solved the problems we were having with possessions and petty thievery was that no child was allowed to bring any toys to school. After all, school is for learning.

Finally, we set up a positive set of methods of dealing with violators so that the child knew exactly what to expect as the results of his behavior. This was an important lesson. Many of our children had never been exposed to a cause-and-effect type of discipline. Here we were building-in a Parent which is dependable and would later affect the child's ability to make Adult decisions in controlling his own behavior. With the number of their siblings in trouble with the law, this was a vital lesson.

To stabilize these necessary rules and to teach the children the cause and effect of their misbehaviors, we devised a system of traffic tickets. Each teacher on yard duty carried $3'' \times 5''$ cards, mimeographed with a list of unacceptable behaviors. This aided teachers in consistency in recognizing misbehaviors. When a child broke a rule, the teacher called it to his attention, perhaps by asking him what he was doing. She then put his name, his teacher's name, the date, and the offense and her initials on the card and handed it into the office. She gave as little attention as possible to the culprit. If the offense endangered others, the child might be temporarily dealt with according to the teacher's judgment. This was mostly isolation on a line for the rest of the period, or if uncontrollable, he was accompanied to the office.

These cards were kept in a file in the office according to classrooms. When there were three cards on the same child in a month, he was called in by the principal and given a *sentence* of elimination of a certain number of recesses, wherein he had to remain alone in an isolated area while the other children played. At first these children pretended that they did not care, and engaged passing teachers and students in conversations. It was necessary to tell the teachers not to give these children any attention, to ignore them completely. The children then quickly became bored with their punishment. Severe misbehaviors could be suspended from school temporarily. Cooperation with the home was essential in these cases.

We felt that reward for good behavior was more important than the punishment for unacceptable behavior, so at the end of each month, the whole school gathered in the auditorium. Teachers had made out certificates of merit for each child in her room who had not received more than one ticket all month. This was played up big! The principal called out their names, class by class. They stood up, were applauded, and were given the certificates. Those who misbehaved were encouraged that they could perform better in the future, and their old tickets were destroyed while they applauded. They now had another chance to succeed next month. They returned to their classrooms for no further punishment, but with encouragement for better behavior. Those with certificates stayed and were served punch and cookies (treats might vary). Each teacher had purchased three dozen cookies for the occasion.

The result of this procedure was a very dramatic decrease in the number of misbehaviors (and playground accidents too) from about half of each class the first month to less than a fourth thereafter. The children knew where they stood. They knew the cause and effect of their behaviors. Yard duty became less harried, less a police assignment. Since children are very familiar with police actions in their own homes and families ("The police came and took my brother, Jeff, last night"), this learning of justice without malice, may hold them in good stead in their dealings on the streets.

Tallying the number of offenses on each item of all the cards in one month shows where our children are having the most problems. Thus we can make further plans to cut down on these particular misbehaviors, perhaps with some preventive measures. For example, we found that the majority of the children's problems were involved with the Four-Square game. Thus we developed more specific rules for the game. If there were any arguments on a play, there were positive alternatives for the children. We then made up a multiple-choice test which every child over first grade had to pass with eighty-five percent correct. We gave the teachers an instructional strategy for teaching these rules before they retested. The result has been very few arguments in our Four-Square games.

With upper grade children, we find that an instructional class in playground behavior for several days during noon recess is both punishing and constructive. Instead of a party at the end of the period, the reward for the *goodies* can then be a free play period outside with their teacher, while the culprits are in the instructional class.

With primary children, a reward-punishment session a month away might be too distant and ineffective. For first grade we found that it was better to reward ticketless children every Friday afternoon. Punishment might be carried out the next week. One class of children voted to have the punishment for offenders be one noon recess of standing by a hall pole for each ticket. In another class the offenders had to sit with heads down on their desks for a twenty-five-minute period while the rest of the class had free choice of activities. You might find that the more immediate the punishment, the more effective. Thus the previous day's offenders would have to work out their punishment the very next day.

It helps to have the children discuss the offenses and decide on the alternatives. Thus they feel that their ideas are important and that they have some control over their environment. It also eliminates rebellion against the punishments as coming from "the establishment." Instead, the children will carry out the punishment or isolation by themselves with little prompting or supervision from the teacher.

While using this whole process, remember that the reward is conducive to good behavior and the punishment merely stops the overt acts. Therefore, call more attention to and encourage the good behaviors. It's recess time and some children have received tickets for not coming in immediately after the bell: WHAT ARE YOU GOING TO DO WHEN THE BELL RINGS? ARE YOU GOING TO BE LATE? GOOD! After recess: YOU REMEMBERED! YOU ALL CAME IN RIGHT AWAY! It is Friday and this is the first week that Mike has not received a ticket. Shake his hand: CONGRATULATIONS, MIKE!

YOU DID IT! YOU DIDN'T GET A TICKET ALL WEEK! ISN'T THAT
WONDERFUL? LET'S ALL CLAP FOR MIKE! DO YOU THINK YOU CAN GO
ALL NEXT WEEK WITHOUT A TICKET? LET'S ALL HELP HIM! I'LL BET
HE CAN DO IT!

Settling Disputes

Fighting between children must be faced by all teachers. In
neighborhoods such as ours, the children are very aggressive.
They form gangs to beat up on a child for minute ills. Older
children often "pick on" little children. Asking why is a revela-
tion in itself. Many times it is simply because little brother
doesn't like Tommy following him, so big brother is enlisted to
beat up on the small culprit. Parents are quick to defend their
children's fighting, and tell them to *beat up on* anyone who mis-
treats them. Teasing is also extensive.

The cause of a fight is often so inconsequential that it is
ridiculous for the teacher to become involved in trying to solve
it. Her solution too often has to be based on WHO STARTED IT?
and this is pointless. As Alice Thompson (1969) says: "It opens
up a whole can of worms!" If the teacher attempts to mediate
the difficulty, usually nothing is solved at all. She is only playing
Parent, and the children have not made any Adult decision which
will affect their behavior in the future. The children still have
their aggressive problems and have not learned anything except
to have another fight and get some more attention. A teacher
endeavoring to settle a dispute gives out a lot of positive reinforcement.

B. F. Skinner did research with pigeons, whereby the pigeon
who pecked his cage mate was reinforced with a seed each time
he did so. Soon the poor mate was cowering in a corner, trying
to elude her aggressor. The attention you give to misbehavior is
as much a reward as the seed is to the pigeon. You might be
reinforcing aggression.

Sometimes it is a shock to a teacher after she has gone through
the throes of an agrument, getting herself emotionally involved
in the *badness* of the children, or the injustice of the situation,

to find the two culprits arm in arm a few minutes later. This is a clue for us.

To solve controversies of interactions between peers, the children must learn to deal with their own problems. They must learn to talk it over, to make some Adult conclusions. If they are very emotionally involved in the situation, a cooling-off period might be necessary before negotiations can begin. Most of the time, however, all the teacher needs to do is to temporarily remove any object which is the point of the controversy, such as a ball, and then ask the children to sit in a specified place to figure it out.

Send all bystanders away. THIS IS JUST BETWEEN TOMMY AND JERRY. IT IS THEIR BUSINESS, NO ONE ELSE'S! THEY ARE SMART! THEY KNOW HOW TO TALK IT OVER. Don't listen to their stories or excuses. Turn your back on them. WHEN YOU AGREE ON A SETTLEMENT, LET ME KNOW. Neither child can leave until a mutual agreement has been reached. The aggressor is uaually anxious to settle things quickly because he wants to go back to play. He hates sitting it out the most. He may even give in just to get out of his predicament. When the children are in agreement, they just so state to the teacher and leave. If the debate included a ball, the ball is then returned to them to dispose of as per their agreement. The matter is closed. The *children* took the responsibility for settling the dispute, not the teacher.

This talking-it-over works great for tattlers and teasers. When a child begins to complain about another child, say: DON'T TELL ME! I DIDN'T HIT YOU! GO TALK IT OVER! And be sure they do. Thus children begin to see no necessity to tattle on another, or to tease because they won't get the teacher's attention. Too, the aggressor doesn't want to have to stop playing to have a peace powwow. The teacher won't feel sorry for the victim either. He might have had it coming. She will just settle them both down to talk it over.

It isn't long before you have children start toward you with their problems, and then turn about-face, put their arms around each other and the one say: "Come on! Let's go talk it over! That is all she will say anyway!" Thus they have learned to use their

Adult to solve their problems and have made large progress toward self-responsibility and a good social adjustment to life.

One way of encouraging children to work together and to share is to make the classroom helpers or monitors work in pairs. Have two to four tasks for each two children. For example, two children share the tasks of holding the flag, counting children for lunches, putting the day on the calendar and taking notes to the office. Each day they have to decide between them who does which tasks. They usually arrange it so that each does two tasks daily. Two children can be in charge of opening and closing all the windows and curtains in the room. Two more can be paper-passers and also be in charge of the lights. Let the turn of all these helpers last for two weeks. This gives them more of a chance to perfect their sharing system and also helps us all to remember whose turn it is.

To Summarize. There is no one simple solution to the modification of the behavior of children. It is as complex as the children! The teacher must have a store of solutions available for immediate use. She should be well versed in the application of several therapies. Be sure to read Glasser's *Schools Without Failure,* Hunter's *Reinforcement Theory for Teachers,* and Harris' *I'm O.K.—You're O.K.*

PLANNING THE CURRICULUM
The Daily Schedule

Problem learners need a fixed daily schedule to give them security. A highly structured program is essential the first of the school year. Set up your time schedule in blocks which will remain the same all year. Then alternate and vary only the activities within those blocks to provide for the progress of the children. If the total school program is set up in thirty-minute blocks, it aids team teaching. We find that this is about the right amount of time for each subject. Changing subjects and often classes every thirty minutes keeps the children busy and interested. They don't have time to get bored with one teacher or subject. The day passes quickly.

Our schedule is never the same two consecutive years. Some

years we have paid aides and we have to schedule our subjects according to the time that the aides are assigned to us. We allow ourselves a fifteen-minute opening period in our own classrooms to do the necessary paper work, roll call, collecting lunch money, etc. We schedule one thirty-minute block for each subject including social studies, reading, math, physical education, language, and seatwork. There is usually a twenty- to thirty-minute block left over at the end of the day which we dub our activity period. We use physical education and social studies as the best subjects for large group instruction (thirty to sixty children). We engage high school aides to help us with the large groups. They receive an accredited grade for their work. While the bulk of our children are in one of these two subjects, the other two teachers do small group (six to fourteen children) teaching in either reading or math. Our team of teachers consists of two first-grade and one second-grade teacher. We find that we do an enormously better job with these prime difficult subjects when we have small groups with which to work and no other children to supervise at their seats at the same time. We can really concentrate on our teaching and our children achieve twice as much.

The First Grade Curriculum

The Distar reading, math, and language programs are all done with small group, intensive, direct-teaching techniques. These programs use extensive feedback from the children who must all attend and participate every minute of the instruction. No one is ever excused from participating.

We have small room-size rugs in our classrooms on which we gather our children for much of our instruction. Some children may sit on chairs—in a crescent moon—with the other children Indian style (cross-legged) in front of them. This makes for a compact group within the teacher's arm reach. Sometimes two or even three such groups are instructed in different areas of the same room.

The last ten minutes of the language period is used as a story time. This also becomes the positive reward for *good talking* (participation) in the language. As the children progress in reading, we read them the stories from the easy readers such as the *Beginner Books,* to hook them on reading library books. In the spring, the children go to the school library one day a week during this language period to check out books.

The physical education is all planned and executed by one teacher for the three classes. She conducts two sessions with thirty to sixty children each. In September the program begins with calisthenics and movement-exploration activities with the main goals being in body image, laterality, directionality, and motor planning. We try to provide vigorous physical exercise in a fun way and give the children success at the response level, and thus initiate positive reinforcement to relieve their resistance to learning. As the children progress, more difficult skills are introduced such as ball throwing and catching, jumping rope and playing Four-Square.

When a physical education group is outside, we allow for an empty classroom into which they can retreat in case of rain or severe cold. An inclement day then often gives us a chance to teach special drawing and cartooning techniques designed by one of our teachers, Sharon Pritchard. These are marvelous techniques with which even a nonartist can teach her children to draw. It is hoped that someday Mrs. Pritchard will publish her program so that it will be available to many more teachers. The Davidow book, *Let's Draw Animals,* offers some drawing techniques first graders can use.

The social studies-science for all three classes is planned and executed by one teacher, Gloria Cox, who has had extensive training and experience in this subject. She has designed a program which she feels is relevant to our children and their needs. Some of the subjects covered in this program are the economics of the American system, workers, producers, consumers, and taxes; science areas of heat, air, sound, plants, and animals; transportation; What is Man?, prehistoric man, his skills and tools, and prehistoric animals; children of the world, their basic needs for food, shelter, and clothing, and their customs; and safety and social contact skills concerned with children's feelings and responsibilities. Materials used are the Senesh program, *Our Working*

World, with supplemental books and records, Brandwein's *Concepts in Science Series,* plus a television science series; a Contra Costa County, California, social studies unit, *Workers in Our Community* (Taba, 1965) ; a proposed state framework for social studies, and a special unit on the world's children, which Mrs. Cox designed utilizing the *National Geographic Magazine,* pictures, films, folk dances, and songs. Mrs. Cox plans all her lessons and the field trips, and orders all the films and other materials used. She keeps the other teachers in the team informed on what she is doing so that we can coordinate our other programs with the social studies and science units.

Team Teaching

The third member of our team, Joan Fields, teaches three math classes and does extra work on the preparation of our math materials. Teaching has never been as exciting or as easy or as satisfying as it is with these very competent team teachers. High school teachers are never expected to be able to teach more than two subjects and in most systems, may teach only one, five times a day. Yet school personnel have been very naive to think that every elementary classroom teacher is even capable of teaching *every* subject, let alone have the time and energy to prepare for seven *different* subjects each day.

Team teaching provides for more competency in teaching and relieves the preparation load of all the teachers involved. Team teaching requires a preschool planning session in the fall to set up the schedule. After the children have all been tested, a card is made out for each child, noting his reading (or math) scores. A second meeting of the team is then held to sort the cards into reading groups and to decide who teaches which group, and where they will meet. We use colored plastic surveyor ribbon around the children's waists, or with their names around their necks, to help keep track of the children. They enjoy changing classes and help by reminding each other where to go. If a dreamer gets lost, we give him a responsible buddy or remind the whole group to keep track of Tommy and be sure he gets to class. At the end of each period the first few days, we remind the children where to go next. BLUES GO TO READING IN FIELD'S ROOM, YELLOWS TO COX'S ROOM, AND REDS, PINKS, GREENS, AND BROWNS GO TO PHYSICAL EDUCATION!

Aside from the first two team-teaching meetings in the fall, our meetings are usually casual. We don't find it necessary to have scheduled daily or weekly sessions.

With our children being taught by four teachers (two reading teachers) and sometimes three or four aides, our greatest problem is in communication. We try to keep all our groups flexible. When any of us find children having problems in our groups, we make it a point to discuss the situation among ourselves. This may often be at lunch time. Children who find the work too difficult are moved down a level. Others have sudden spurts and we need to move them up a group to give them more of a challenge. At conference or report card time, we find the easiest method of communicating is through class lists. We simply ditto off the lists of the names of the children in our classes, and give them to the teacher involved. It takes little time to write down the lesson the child is on, and his progress in the material, including any pertinent problems the child might have.

The thirty minutes we have allotted for seatwork is our only period (except for the last twenty minutes before they go home) that we have all of our children in their *home* rooms. The first week of school we use this period for testing the children (Chapter Four), to gather the data we need to place them in instruction groups and work-packets at their individual levels. The next few weeks we alternate between template training one day, tracing large letters or numerals the next, tracing their own names, box writing, and a variety of the body image, laterality, directionality, and form-perception exercises. Thus each day is a little different, and the children do not tire of one subject. As the children progress, we begin using the Distar workbooks, the Frostig perception packets, the math packets, and writing on lines. At first, we might do the workbooks one day, math packets another, and writing a third day. Later, however, this period becomes individual work time and some children are working on math, while others are working on perception packets or reading workbooks. When a child completes a packet or workbook, he places it in the IN box on the teacher's desk and works in another area. After school the teacher corrects the packets and puts them in the OUT box for the children. Thus during the period, the teacher uses her time to help individual children with their problems. Toward the end of the year, we also use this period for the flashing exercises for visual memory, and for writing sentences or short stories. Since we include so many activities during this period, we have to plan carefully to keep a balanced program.

The activity period is our catchall. The first of the year the children's attentions are short, their perceptions poor, and their experiences very limited. By this last period, they are hot and tired. Therefore, this becomes a relaxing period used to teach perceptual skills with a wide variety of games and puzzles and art media. The period is carefully structured in the fall so that each child has opportunities to learn to use each different type of media. Four children might be painting at the easels; four are doing balancing activities with a beam, can stilts, and the Scat Scoota; four are working Montessori-type puzzles, and four work with a colored dough made of salt and flour. The teacher works with four more children on the chalkboard routines. Each day we switch activities, so that at the end of six or seven days, each child has had a turn at each activity. We then vary at least one of the activities for the next few days. We bring out the simplest puzzles the first weeks, such as those for gross form discrimination. As the children perform well with these, they are replaced with more complex materials. This activity period allows much individual freedom and is a relaxing change for the young child who is not yet used to hard work in school and who tires easily. As the holidays come on, the period is used for the construction of typical art projects, with all the children working on these instead of doing the variety of activities. However, the art projects which we use are chosen for the visual-motor and spatial skills which they enhance rather than art for art's sake.

Gradually we have been eliminating those repulsive gift-making projects for Christmas, Mother's Day, etc. This evolved because we found it difficult to find a gift which the poorly coordinated children could make with enough skill to be attractive and acceptable by the parents. We always had to buy the materials ourselves, and then end up practically making or remaking the items for some of the children. These projects were thus frustrating to both children and teachers, consumed time from more important learnings, and then were often discarded by the parents. The result? No more gift-making! We just teach.

As the year progresses and children become more able to work independently and are less easily tired, the activity period becomes a free-choice program in which the children can work on their individual packets or on a puzzle, an art project, or a game. We also have tasting parties and class meetings during this period to discuss class problems. The teachers use the period to instruct children who have been absent, or need extra help. Children who have goofed-off during the seatwork period do not have free-choice, but must work. This is their punishment and puts pressure on them to work harder. It also puts the responsibility for their work on *them*. School assemblies and parties are often scheduled at this time, so it is good to have this period flexible.

THE TOTAL CHILD-CENTERED PROGRAM

In this book we have discussed separately the child's different phases of development, the training techniques to aid his maturation, and classroom methods in five areas of learning: reading, writing, arithmetic, language, and physical education. Then we have discussed the child's motivational levels and the therapies which offer us help with modifying his behavior. Now we have attempted to tie the whole program together with a summary of a daily schedule and a year's curriculum. Thus with a total child-centered program, let's attempt to summarize some of the principle ideas and add a few pertinent points that we may have missed.

1. Test children with individual measures and start instruction where the children *are*, not only academically but motivationally as well. Progress slowly, one step at a time. Use multiple repetition and strengthen teachings with the use of all the sensory channels.

2. Become involved with the children. Love them! Give them physical reinforcement, hugs, strokes. Care! Care enough to *make* them learn. Commit the children to learning and then accept no excuses for their not carrying through. The child comes to us with negative feelings about himself. "I'm not O.K. You're O.K." We must make him feel that he's *O.K.*

3. Have lessons well-planned, all materials readily available so that the children don't have to wait for you. You are ready for them.

4. Have a well-structured program. Keep it stable so that the children know what to expect and when. Yet allow flexibility, individual progress, some self-determination, and choices of action.

5. Keep them busy, interested, happy, successful. Success opens the door to more success.

6. Give extensive praise at all times, ignoring maladaptive behavior to extinguish it. But remember that if good behavior leads to nothing, it leads to extinction of that behavior.

7. When using extrinsic rewards, always combine with social reinforcement, praise. Gradually eliminate the former as the child is able to perform with the motivation from the social reinforcement and the task success, and achievement.

8. Rely more on intermittent rather than a regular schedule of reinforcement unless it is a new learning and the child is still on the attention or response motivational levels.

9. Begin with attainable goals. Reinforce any evidence of progress. Don't demand perfection or completion of work by a child on the lowest motivational levels. If he makes one good *S* on his paper, this can be rewarded. LOOK AT THIS BEAUTIFUL "S" ON TOMMY'S PAPER! THATS HARD FOR HIM, BUT HE DID IT!

10. Be positive in all your dealings with children. If you look for trouble you will find it. The more negative you are, the more maladaptive behavior you will have. Teaching negatively makes you unhappy, too. Finding fault all day is exhausting. Reinforcing is exhilarating!

11. Let the children know *where* they are going. FIRST WE HAVE TO LEARN TO MAKE THESE SHAPES! THEN WRITING WILL BE EASIER

FOR YOU! Give them reasons for the work you ask them to do. Give them no task for which you lack a reason or purpose.

12. Give them short goals to conquer so that they can see the end of a seemingly endless task. Let them progress at their own speeds. Neither hold them back with others, nor push them ahead of themselves. Individualize independent work as much as possible Don't waste their time on busywork. Their learning time is too valuable.

13. Use positive techniques with parents, too. Notify them when their children are doing well or have improved since your last contact with them. A worried parent appreciates a phone call. Give parents suggestions of ways they can help their children through toys and games. It helps to ditto lists of perception, motor, and language games as ideas for parents. For example: A list for children with visual-motor problems would have suggestions for constructive toys which parents might make or buy for him.

14. To gain the attention of the whole class get them to agree on a signal and then role-play it. The signal might just be your saying the words: BOYS AND GIRLS! The children are to look at you when you give this signal. Practice it. Praise the children who respond quickly. After asking for their attention, come in immediately with your instruction. Don't have long delays between your attention signal and your instruction.

15. When children use undesirable swear words, don't be shocked. Ignore it whenever possible. When children tattle on swearers, just tell the tattlers to go someplace else and not listen to the bad language. Later, in private, give the swearer a substitute word or words. It could be a large word which makes him feel big, or it could be a series of fun words. HOW ABOUT NAMING VEGETABLES WHEN YOU GET MAD? SPINACH! PEAS! CARROTS!

16. Let the classroom belong to the children. Let them put their own work on the boards. You can always straighten them after school if necessary. Teach the children to be responsible for the condition of their classroom.

17. Respect the children's papers. It is *their* work, part of *them!* Make only necessary corrections. A creative first grade story

should be left creative. Let them spell phonetically when they are writing their own stories.

18. When a child does not understand instructions, you erred. Either you did not teach him, or you did not get his attention and enough feedback from him, or you have him working at too high a level.

19. When you err, apologize to the child. Children are very forgiving. When even the teacher goofs, then the child can learn to accept his errors, too. He may even learn to apologize to his peers through your example. He may never have heard his parents apologize for anything.

20. Listen to your children. Look right at them so they know they have your full attention. If you don't know how to respond to their sometimes frightening stories of "father chasing mother around the house with a knife, and the police coming" just give a big hug to show you care, and make no comment. They don't need words. Just your reassurance.

21. When a child is acting impulsively, not self-directed, instead of telling him what to do, ask: WHAT SHOULD YOU BE DOING NOW? Or: WHAT CAN YOU DO NOW? CAN YOU FIND SOMETHING YOURSELF?

22. Since immature children often have the inability to delay gratification and have problems understanding time sequences, delay telling them of coming events. For example, don't announce the date of a field trip or a party until dismissal time the day before the event.

23. Aggressive acts between children are often the result of their inability to express themselves through speech. Have class discussions on what to say to aggressors and how to make friends. When necessary, give the children the words to say and have them repeat them often. "Would you play with me?" "Stop that, Tommy! I don't like that!" Procedures such as this cut down on the crying of timid children and the tattling and teasing of the more aggressive. When a child complains that he has been hurt by a peer, say: DID YOU TELL HIM THAT HE HURT YOU? GO TELL HIM HOW YOU FEEL ABOUT IT. Read: Thomas Gordon's *Parent Effectiveness.*

24. When you have impulsive children who can't resist banging on the piano, or handling fragile things, use preventive measures as you would for smaller children. Lock the piano between uses. Put tempting things away after demonstrations.

25. Try to nip any moaning about *work* in its first stages. Don't give it attention or it will multiply. Turn attention to those not complaining. I LIKE HAPPY PEOPLE! THESE CHILDREN GET RIGHT TO WORK!

26. Help the children to enjoy life, to be happy, outgoing, to contact peers. Make learning fun, exciting. When they have learned how to learn and have conquered the basic skills, show them how to reach out into other fields. Use science experiences and class discussions.

27. Believe in your children. They *can* learn, but you must *teach* them. If you don't *believe* they can learn, you will be *unable* to teach them anything. Their learning is *your* responsibility. If they don't learn, you have failed, not them.

TEACHING IS EXCITING! ENJOY IT!
REFERENCES

Amidon, Edmond, and Hunter, Elizabeth: *Improving Teaching: Analyzing Verbal Interaction in the Classroom.* New York, Holt, Rinehart & Winston, 1966.

Bascaglia, Leo: Lecture in Walnut Creek, California, September, 1969.

Beginner Books. Random House, New York.

Berne, Eric: *Games People Play.* New York, Grove, 1965.

Brandwein, Paul F., *et al.*: *Concepts in Science.* New York, Harcourt, Brace & World, 1966.

Davidow, Ann H.: *Let's Draw Animals.* New York, Grosset & Dunlap, 1960.

Engelman, Siegfried, and Bruner, Elaine: *Distar Reading Program.* Chicago, Sci Res, 1969.

Frostig, Marianne, *et al.*: *The Frostig Program for the Development of Visual Perception.* Chicago, Follett, 1964.

Glasser, William: *Reality Therapy.* New York, Harper & Row, 1965.

————: *Schools Without Failure.* New York, Harper & Row, 1969.

————: How Can We Help Young Children Face Reality and Become Responsible Human Beings? Excerpts from a speech made at the E.S.E.A. Workshop for primary reading specialists. Printed by Sacramento County Schools Office, August, 1966.

Gordon, Thomas: *Parent Effectiveness Training.* New York, Peter H. Wyden,

Inc., 1970.

Harris, Thomas A.: *I'm O.K.—You're O.K. A Practical Guide to Transactional Analysis.* New York, Harper & Row, 1967.

Hewett, Frank M.: Hierarchy of educational tasks for children with learning disorders. *Except Child, 31* (No. 4) : 207–214, Dec. 1964.

———: Educational Engineering with Emotionally Disturbed Children. Reprinted by Sacramento County Schools Office, Sacramento, California, January, 1968.

Hunter, Madeline: *Reinforcement Theory for Teachers.* El Segundo, California, Tip, 1967.

Nixon, Stewart, B.: Increasing the Frequency of Attending Responses in Hyperactive-Distractable Youngsters by Use of Operant and Modeling Procedures. Unpublished doctoral dissertation, 1965.

Patterson, Gerald R., and Gullion, M. Elizabeth: *Living with Children. New Methods for Parents and Teachers.* Champaign, Illinois, Res Press, 1968.

Rosenthal, Robert: Self-fulfilling prophecy. *Psychology Today,* Sept. 1966.

———, and Jacobson, Lenore F.: Teacher expectations for the disadvantaged. *Scientific American,* April 1968, pp. 19–23.

Schaefer, Halmuth H., and Martin, Patrick L.: *Behavior Therapy.* New York, McGraw-Hill, 1969.

Schopler, E.: Early infantile autism and receptor processes. *Arch Gen Psychiat, 13,* Oct. 1965.

Senesh, Lawrence: *Our Working World, Families at Work.* Chicago, Sci Res, 1963.

Skinner, B. F.: *Science and Human Behavior.* New York, Macmillan, 1953.

Suchman, J. Richard: Learning through inquiry. *N.E.A. Journal,* Mar. 1963.

Taba, Hilda: Thinking in Elementary School Children. Report of Cooperative Research Project #1574, San Francisco State College, San Francisco, California.

———, and Hills, James L.: Teacher Handbook for Contra Costa Social Studies, Walnut Creek, California. Contra Costa County Public Schools, 1965.

Thompson, Alice: Lecture in Sacramento, California, November 10, 1969.

———: Why teachers fail. *Saturday Review,* Oct. 16, 1965, pp. 80–102.

FILMS ON BEHAVIOR MODIFICATION

Behavior Modification: Teaching Language to Psychotic Children. (42 min.) Appleton-Century-Crofts, 440 Park Avenue S, New York, 10016.

Behavior Theory in Practice. 4 parts (20 min. each). Appleton-Century-Crofts, 440 Park Avenue S, New York, 10016.

Can I Come Back Tomorrow? (33 min.) IMCSE. 2120 West 8th Street, Los Angeles, California. 90057.

Help for Mark. (15 min.) Appleton-Century-Crofts, 440 Park Avenue S, New York, 10016.

I Can Learn Series: Directive Teaching. (30 min.) Franklin County Board of Education, 46 East Fulton Street, Columbus, Ohio, 43215.

Learning And Behavior. (26 min.) #5662, University of California, Extension Media Center, 2223 Fulton Street, Berkeley, California. 94720.

Learning Things at the Token Store. (25 min.) Jane Criver, Project Director, Theapeutic Educational Center, 1700 Newhall St., San Francisco, California, 94124.

Santa Monica Project. (30 min.) IMCSE, 2120 West 8th Street, Los Angeles, California. 90057.

Translating Theory Into Classroom Practice: Part II, Motivation Theory for Teachers. (28 min.) Part III, Reinforcement Theory for Teachers. Special Purpose Films, 26740 Latigo Shore Drive, Malibu, California

Index

A

Action games, 252-256
A Daigger & Co., ref. 197
Adler, S. J., 105, 107, 115, ref. 130
Alphabet systems, 280
Ames, L. B., 36, 38, 93, ref. 60, 95
Amidon, E., 418, ref. 472
Andrews, Gladys, 148, 191, 262, ref. 158, 197, 271
Anecdotal records, 87-88
Anyone Can, film, 252, ref. 271
Aphasia, 369
Apraxia, 134-136, 149
A Psychoeducational Survey of Basic Learning Abilities, 64, 67, 378, ref. 95
Ascorbic acid, 110
Association for Children With Learning Disabilities, 55, ref. 59
A Time For Georgia, film, 413
Attention, 122
see Hyperactivity; hypoactivity
Auditory discrimination, 24, 48, 100, ref. 96
methods, 391-393
tests, 67-68, 81
Wepman, 378, 413
Auditory memory, 24
see Digit span; sequencing
Auditory perception tests, 66, 81
Auditory reception
ITPA test, 377
training, 388-397
Auditory-sequential memory
methods, 401-410, 411-412
tests, 377, 378
Auditory-vocal association, methods, 395
Auditory-vocal automatic, methods, 396
Autism, 369
Avery, M. L., 7, ref. 15
A Visual Motor Gestalt Test And Its Clinical Use, ref. 75

see Bender Visual-Motor Gestalt
Ayres, A. Jean, 46, 47, 98, 135, 156, 163, 166, 169, 264, 266, 422, ref. 59, 130, 158, 197, 332
relationship of protective system, 106
tactile defensiveness, 133-134
tonic labrinthian reflex, 153
vestibular sense, 152, 243

B

Balance
board, 239
dynamic, 236
equipment, 239-244
methods, 234-244
static, 234
symptoms of poor, 16
tests, 78
walking beam activities, 237
Ball
bouncing, 227-228
games, 256
instant ball, 225
kicking, 230
skills, 223
throwing, 228
Barrels, 246
Barsch, R. H., 46, 98, 136, 150, 153, 167, 171-172, ref. 59, 130, 158, 197
Bartelt, J., 202, 224, 227, 232, ref. 271
Basal words, 288, 289
Bascaglia, L., 420, ref. 462
Baseball, math game, 362
Basic Concept Inventory Test, 378, ref. 412
Beat Goes On, record, 148, ref. 158, 262
Hap Palmer Record Library, 271
Beery, K. E., 64, ref. 95
Developmental Test of Visual-Motor Integration, 64, 176, 275, ref. 95
Beginner Books, 292, 301, 454, ref. 462, 333

Behavior
 changing, 433
 norms, 37
 sequences, 406
 stabilizing playground, 446
 see Reinforcement; Chapter 12
Behavior Modification; Teaching Language to Psychotic Children, film, 463
Behavior Theory in Practice, film, 463
Behind space, 172-173
Bender, L., 46, 75, 370, ref. 95, 412
Bender Visual-Motor Gestalt, 34, 64, 65, 66, 67, 78, 164, 176, 275
 figures, 72
  immature, 73
  bizarre, 74
 use of, 70-75
Bereiter, C., 380, 386, 387, ref. 412
Berne, E., 418, ref. 462
Bicycle tires, 245
Bilaterality, 161, 162
Bingo
 blackboard, 361
 cards, 361
 sequence song, 407
Biochemistry, clues for behavior from, 116
Body Image, 18, 176, 260
 definition, 139
 description of problem, 140
 identifying child lacking, 141
 problems, 141
 test, 79
 training, 143-148
 symptoms, 18
Boutons, 108
Box writing, 325
Brace, R., 123, ref. 130
Brain, 111-113
 neurons, 107-111
Brandwein, P. F., 455, ref. 462
Bright Boy, Bad Scholar, film, 60
Bruner, E. C., 124, 298, ref. 130, 298
 reading program, 290-291, 293-295
Budney, B., 190, ref. 197
Bundles of sticks, 357
Butter, C. M., 106, 110, 166, ref. 130

C

Calisthenics, 208-216
Campbell, B., 110, 111, ref. 130
C.A.N.H.C. 116, 252, ref. 291
Can I Come Back Tomorrow?, film, 463
Carnine, D., 337, ref. 366
Case Against Rubella, film, 60
Categories, 67
 classroom tests, 83
 deHirsch test, 65, 66, 67
Central nervous system dysfunction, 43
 see Minimal cerebral dysfunction
Cerebral Dysfunction in Children, film, 61
Circles
 chalkboard routines, 314
 perceptual constancy, 190
 templates, 186
Chalkboard routines, 313-317
 circles, 314
 clock game, 317
 pattern cards, 317
 racetracks, 314
 writing letters, 320
Chall, J., 276, 279, 280, 281, ref. 332
Chambers, A. J., 64, ref 95
Child Guidance toys, ref. 198
Children and Learning Disabilities, film series, 61
Children Lost in Space, film, 198
Childrens' pleasure reading series, ref. 333
Chronological age, 35, 37-38
Class games with numbers, 361-362
Class profile, 84-86
Classroom testing
 format, 75
 informal tests, 78-84, 339
 schedule, 77
Climbing wall, 248-249
Clock game, 317
Code-emphasis methods, 279
 Engelmann-Bruner, 290
 Slingerland, 289
Cognitive, 25
Cohn, R., 44, 45, ref. 59
Columbia Presbyterian Hospital, 51
Comin' Round The Mountain, song, 407

Computations, math, 345
Concepts in Science Series, 455, ref. 462
Conceptual development, 82
Concrete object, use in math, 335
Connors, C. K., 115
Cooperative Primary Test, 304, 291, ref. 332
Coordination, classroom test of, 78
Cott, A., 117
Counting
    methods, 342-344
    money, 361
Cox, G., 454, 455
Cratty, B. J., 133, ref. 158
Crawling activities, 220
Creative playthings, ref. 198
Cruickshank, R., 46, ref. 59
Cuisenaire Co. of America, ref. 198
    rods, 195, 335, 364, 366
Curriculum
    daily schedule, 452
    first grade, 453-455
    planning, 452
Cutting, teaching, 311-313
    tests, 78

D

Damerau, R., 59, ref. 59
Davidow, A. H., 454, ref. 462
Decoding, 24, 25, 372, 373
    see Reception
deHirsch, K., 6, 11, 15, 46, 57, 78, 98, 140, 278, 378, ref. 15, 32, 60, 95, 158, 332
    on hypoactivity, 28
    on maturity of achievers, 36
    on prematurity, 61
    Predictive Index, 65-76
Delayed speech, 369
Dependency, 27
Depth perception, 170
Developmental lag, 38
Developmental Learning Materials, 158, ref. 198
Diagnosis, 58, 62
    see Testing; Chapter 4
Diem, L., 147, ref. 158, 271
Digit span tests, 64, 378, ref. 95
Direction, left to right, 184-185

Directionality, 20, 80
    child with problems, 176
    description of, 168-170
    symptoms of problem, 20
    training, 180
Disadvantaged,
    see Environmentally deprived
Disassociated Movements, 259
Discovery methods of teaching math, 334
Disorganization, 23
Disputes, settling, 450
Distar Programs, 68, 281, 285, 292, 296, 330, 332, 352, 353, 354, 360, 364, 386, 387, 456
    language, 381-383
    math, 337-350
    reading, 280-291, 293-295, 298-300, 304-305
Distractability, 31
    test, 80
    see, Figare-ground
Doctor referrals, 52-54, 89, 90, 388
Dolch words, 280
Doman-Delacato, 167, 264, ref. LeWinn, 197
    We Hold These Truths, film, 199
Dominance
    description of, 165-168
    test, 79
Draw-a-House test, 80, 81
Draw-a-Man Test, 67, 76, 78, 79, 141
Drug therapy, 115-116
Dynamic balance, 162, 170, 177, 178, 236
    balancing equipment, 239-244
    walking beam activities, 237-239

E

Early Recognition of Learning Disabilities, film, 61
Ebersole, M., 157, ref. 158
Educable mental retardate (EMR) 35, 41, 88, 303
Egotism, 26
Electroencephalogram (EEG) 44, 45, 52, 53, 97
Emberly, E., 190, ref. 197
Emotional
    handicap, 55
    outburst, 444

primary & secondary problems, 57
rebellion with aggression, 55
rebellion, with withdrawal, 56
Empirical space, 103, 139
Engelmann, S., 205, 302, 351, 354, 364, 378, 396, 398, 417, 437, 438, 444, ref. 95, 158, 332, 366, 412, 462
language, 380-388
math, 337-350
reading, 290-291, 293-295
Environmentally deprived, 39-42, 46
language of disadvantaged, 379-381
Equals, 344
Exercises
figure-ground, 127
perceptual constancy, 190, 194
spatial relations, 192
see Physical education
Exercising equipment, 239
balance board, 239
barrels, 246
bicycle tires, 245
can stilts, 241
climbing wall, 248
high jump, 247
hula hoops, 250
inner tubes, 243
jumpboard, 246
ladder, 245
Lind Climber, 251, 252
Scat Scoota, 240
Scooter board, 243
Stegel, 251
stepping stones, 248
stilts, 242
twister, 243
Expression, 373
informal test, 82
language, 82
problems of, 368
Eye Gate House, Inc., 198
Eye-hand coordination, 17
see Visual motor
Eye movement control, 17, 79

F

Fact learning, 336
Faglioni, P., 112, ref. 130

Feedback, 156, 157
Fernald, G. N., 280, 282, ref. 332
Ferraiuolo, ref. 271
Fields, J., 288, 455
Figure-ground problem, 285, 370, 388
cause, 105
confusion from, 22
description of, 104
exercises for, 127-130
identifying, 113
medication for, 115
sorting exercises, 126
structuring environment, 118-121
test, 80
Films
A Time for Georgia, 413
Anyone Can, 252, ref. 271
Behavior modification; teaching language to Psychotic Children, 463
Behavior Theory in Practice, 463
Bright Boy, Bad Scholar, 60
Can I Come Back Tomorrow?, 463
Case Against Rubella, 60
Cerebral Dysfunction in Children, 61
Children and Learning Disabilities, 61
Children Lost In Space, 198
Early Recognition of Learning Disabilities, 61
Fun with Parachutes, 272
Gateways to the Mind, 198
Gesell Development and Neurological Examination in Infancy, 61
Help for Mark, 463
I Can Learn Series; Directive Teaching, 463
Infantile Autism, The Invisible Wall, 61, 413
Learning and Behavior, 464
Learning is Observing, 198
Learning Series, 61
Learning Things at the Token Store, 464
Motivation theory for Teachers, 464
Movigenic Curriculum, 198
Oral Language a Breakthrough to Reading, 413
Perception and Communication, 198, 413

Perceptual Development, I and II, 198

Perceptual Motor Training and Developing Visual Motor Skills, 198

Puzzling Children, 61

Portrait of a Disadvantaged Child, 61

Public School Programs for Learning Disabilities, 61

Revised Illinois Test of Psycholinguistic Abilities, 413

Santa Monica Project, 464

Sensoritonic Readiness Program, 198

Techniques of Non-Verbal Psychological Testing, 413

Thinking, Moving, Learning, 272

Thursday's Children, 61

Up and Over—Exploring on the Stegel, 272

Visual Perception and Failure to Learn, 198

Visual Perception Research, 198

Visual Perception Training in the Regular Classroom, 198

We Hold These Truths, 199

Why Billie Couldn't Learn, 61

World Outside, 370, 413

World We Perceive, 199

Fine and visual motor, 78

Symptoms, 17

see Visual-motor

First grade failures, 10

percentages of, 10

Forced recall, 341

Frostig, M., 6, 46, 98, 111, 113, 127, 147, 154, 289, 331, 438, 456, ref. 60, 95, 130, 197, 332, 462

box-writing, 325–327

Developmental Test of Visual Perception, 64, 176, 275, 288

figure-ground worksheets, 127, 194

rainbow tracing, 320–321

Visual Perception and Failure to Learn, film, 198

Visual Perception Training in the Regular Classroom, film, 198

Fun With Parachutes, film, 272

Functional movements, 102

G

Games

action games, 252–256

ball, 256–258

class games with numbers, 341, 361–362

indoor games, 262

outdoor games, 262

races, 258

singing games or dances, 258

Gardner, R. W., 58, ref. 60

Gates, A., 57, ref. 60

Advanced Primary Test, 65

Word Matching Test, 66

Gateways to the Mind, film, 198

Gattegno, C., 365, ref. 332, 366

Gazzaniga, M. S., 111, 112, ref. 130

Geortzel, M., ref. 60

Geortzel, V., ref. 60

Gesell Development and Neurological Examination in Infancy, film, 61

Gesell, A., 91, 169, ref. 197

Institute, 37, 38

Getman, G. N., 7, 88, 147, 185, 264, 266, 268, 269, 270–271, 315, 316, ref. 15, 130, 197, 271, 332

chalkboard routines, 313–317

gross coordination, 122

on-floor methods, 264–271

race tracks, 314–315

Gillingham, A., 6, 8, 280, ref. 15

Glasser, W., 418, 420, 430, 452, ref. 462

Goldberg, L., ref. 333

Goodenough, F. L., ref. 95

Draw-a-Man Test, 67, 76, 78, 79, 141

Gordon, T., 461, ref. 462

Gray Oral Reading Test, 65

Greater Cleveland Program, math, 338

Green Grass Grew All Around, song, 408–409

Gross motor, 16, 78, 165

see Physical Education, Chapter 8

H

Hackett, L., 147, 219, ref. 158, 271

Hallahan, D. P., 337, ref. 366

Hap Palmer Record Library, 262, 271

Harris, T. A., 420, 422, 452, ref. 463

Hart, N. W. M., 376, 377, ref. 412, 413
Hebb, D. O., 108, ref. 130
Held, R., 150, ref. 158
Help for Mark, film, 463
Hewett, F. M., 418, 435, ref. 463
  Hierarchy of Educational Tasks, 435–
  437
Higgins, A., 7, ref. 15
High jump, 247
Hills, J. L., ref. 463
Hinshelwood, J., 46, 58
Hoffer, A., 110, 117, ref. 130
Horizontal space, 160
  see Balance
Horne, D., 370, ref. 60
Horst Reversals Test, 66, 67
Hula hoops, 250
Human Neurological Organization, 167
  see Doman-Delacato
Hunt, J. M., 42, ref. 60
Hunter, M., 425, 452, ref. 463
Hyperactivity, 14, 47, 50, 133
  modifying behavior, 123
  symptoms of, 27
Hypoactivity, 53, 284
  symptoms of, 28

I

I Can Learn Series, films, 463
I.D.A. Perception Blocks, ref. 198
Ilg, F. L., 36, 38, 93, ref. 60, 95, 197
Illinois Test of Psycholinguistic Ability
  (ITPA), 34, 64, 376, 377, 378, 382,
  412
I'm O.K.—You're O.K., 452, ref. 463
Impulsivity, 29
  symptoms of, 29
Inclement weather activities, 258
  disassociated movements, 259
  isometrics, 259
  mimetics, 261
Independent math packets, 350–353
Individual differences, 336
Indoor games, 262
  see Inclement weather activities
Infantile Autism, The Invisible Wall.
  film, 61, ref. 413

Information, lack of, 25, 372
  see Reception; Language
Inner tubes, 243
Institute for Child Behavior Research,
  116, 370
Integration, 26, 373
  for perceptual motor match, 155–158
  of senses, 100
  of skills for reading, 66
Intelligence, 33
  see IQ
Interoceptors, 148
Irving, R., ref. 271
Irwin, T., 50, 51, ref. 60
Isolation, 442–444
Isometrics, 259
I.Q., 34, 35, 92
ITA, alphabet system, 280

J

Jampolsky, G. G., 59, ref. 60
Jastak, J. F., 64, ref. 95
Jenson, R. G., ref. 158
Jordon, F. L., 65, ref. 95
Jump rope skills, 231
Jumpboard, 246
Jumping skills, 232

K

Kane, E., ref. 130, 271
Kastein, S., 376, ref. 413
Keller, Helen, 376
Kephart, N. C., 6, 7, 10, 19, 46, 93, 98,
  103, 105, 107, 108, 113, 140, 147, 164,
  196, 264, ref. 15, 32, 60, 130, 158,
  332, 333
  chalkboard routines, 315–317
  clock game, 317
  feedback, 156–157
  functional movements, 102
  perceptual motor development and
  training, films, 198
  perceptual motor match, 155–158
  purposeful movements, 101
  random movements, 99
Kinesthesia, 150

Kinesthetic
  approach, 153
  discrimination, 100
  sense, 148–151
Kirk, S. A., ref. 95, 413
Klasen, 317, ref. 333
Klosovskii, Boris, 152, ref. 158
Knobs, 108, 109
Knutsen, E. J., 109, ref. 130
Koppitz, E. M., 71, 73, ref. 95
Krech, D., 109, ref. 130
Kuhlmann-Anderson Test, 7, 30, 35, 280, 287, ref. 333

L

Ladder, 245
Lakeshore Equipment Co., 198
Language, problems of,
  aphasia, 369
  approaches, 288
  autism, 369
  delayed speech, 369
  deprivation, 40–41, 379–381
  expression, 373
  instruction, 381
  integration, 373
  methods, 388–412
  nature of, 371
  program, 384–388
  reception, 368, 372
  symptoms, 24–25, 368, 379
Language Tests, ref. 412–413
  classroom tests, 81–83
  deHirsch, 66–69, 378
  Digit Span, 378
  Engelmann's, 378
  I.T.P.A., 377
  Memory For Sentences, 378
  Peabody, 378
  Valett's, 378
  Wepman, 378
  W.I.S.C., 378
Late bloomers, 37-39
Laterality, 19, 160, 161, 162, 168
  child with problems, 176
  symptoms, 19
  training, 176–180
Lawn activities, 219

Learning and Behavior, film, 464
Learning Language I, II, III, 384, 385, 387, ref. 412
Learning is Observing, film, 198
Learning Series, films, 61
Learning Things at the Token Store, film, 464
Lehtinen, L. E., 46, 98, ref. 60, 131
Let's Draw Animals, book, 454, ref. 462
LeWinn, E., 167, ref. 197
Lind Climber, 251, 252, ref. 158, 271
Lippincott, 281
Listening exercises, 391
Living with Children, 440, ref. 463
Locomotor movements, 202
Martin, P. L., 426, 428, ref. 463

M

Massey, J., ref. 95
Math techniques, 363
  class games, 361–362
  computations, 345
  counting methods, 342–344
  counting money, 361
  math packets, 350
  place value, 353–359
  sequence, 366
  teaching equals, 344
  use of number rods, 364–365
  word problems, 347
Math tests, 83, 339
Maturational lag, 38, 46
McCaskill, 160, ref. 197
McCormick, M., ref. 413
McGuffy Readers, 276
Medication, 115–117
Memory for Sentences, 64, 378
Menninger, K., 62–63, ref. 95
Merrill Reading Series, 281, 297
Metropolitan Achievement Tests, 273, 274, 287, ref. 333
Midbrain function, 163
Midline problem, 163, 164, 165
Mifflin, H., 289
Millichap, J. G., 115
Mimetics, 261

Minimal Cerebral Dysfunction (MCD),
43–55, 91, 93, 103, 106, 110, 113, 383,
401
  causes, 50
  diagnosis, 44
  premature births, 51
  symptoms, 43, 46
Mirroring, 19, 161, 194
Monroe, M., 46
Montessori, 126, 311, 457, ref. 130
Mosston, M., 147, ref. 158, 271
Motivation Theory For Teachers, film,
464
Motor coordination, 17
  see Physical education, Chapter 8
Movement exploration, 202, 216, 261
  basic movements, 202
  combinations, 203
  film, 272
  methods, 217–237
  see Exercise equipment
Movigenic Curriculum, film, 198
Murtha, J., ref. 271
Myklebust, H., 372, 374, ref. 413

N

Name writing, 323
National Geographic Magazine, 455
Negative reinforcement, 430
Neonatal Intensive Care Unit, 51
Neurological
  handicap, 43
  impairment, 43
  impress, 299
Neurons, 107–108, 110, 152
New math, 335, 338
New York Childrens' Hospital, 151
New York Institute of Child Develop-
  ment, 117
Niacin, 110
Nixon, S. B., 440, ref. 463
Number of Words Test, 65, 66, 67
Number rods, 364
Number sequences, 405
Nurse referrals, 55, 89, 90

O

Objective space, 103
Obstacle courses, 250

Ocular Pursuit, 79
  lack of, 17
  test, 79
Old McDonald, song, 407
Olfactory discrimination, 100
On-floor routines, 263–271
Open rope, exercises, 231
Organic method, reading, 287
Oral Language a Breakthrough to Read-
  ing, film, 413
Orton, S. T., 46, 281
Osborn, J., 380–388, ref. 413
Osmond, H., 117, ref. 130
Our Working World, book, 454
Outdoor games, 252–258
  action games, 252–256
  ball games, 256–258
  races, 258
  singing games or dances, 258
Outridge, 376, ref. 413
Owett, B., 190, ref. 197

P

Parent conferences, 90–93
Parent Effectiveness, 461, ref. 262
Partner activities, 222
Pattern cards, 317
Patterson, G. R., 440, ref. 463
Pauling, L., 117, ref. 130
Payne, R., 27, 45, 50, 53, ref. 32, 60
Peabody Picture Vocabulary Test, 64,
  378, ref. 413
Peer relationships, 445
Pencil techniques, 324
Pencil Use Test, 65, 66, 67
Perception and Communication, film,
  198, 413
Perceptual constancy, 21
  exercises, 190–192, 194
  symptoms, 21
Perceptual Development, I and II, film,
  198
Perceptual Forms Test, 67, 70, 75, 76,
  78, 164, 176, 275, 288
  Bizarre figures, 74
  figures, 71
  immature figures, 73
Perceptual-motor match, 155–158

Perceptual Motor Training and Developing Visual-Motor, film, 198
Peripheral vision, 18
see Chalkboard routines
Perseveration, 30
Petitclerc, G. M., 123, ref. 130
Phleger, F., 394
Phona-Visual, 280
Phonetic Keys, 280, 281
Physical disabilities, 16
Physical education program, 200
  balance, 234–239
  ball skills, 223–230
  calisthenics, 208-216
  inclement weather activities, 258–263
  jump rope skills, 231–234
  keeping score, 207–208
  lawn activities, 219
  movement exploration, 202–204, 216–223
  on-floor routines, 263–271
  organizing the program, 204–207
  other equipment, 239–252
  outdoor games, 252–258
  partner activities, 222
  see Chapter 8
Piaget, J., 98, 102, 103, 139, ref. 131
  empirical space, 103
  objective space, 103
  practical space, 102
Pither, M. S., ref. 60
Place value, 353, 354
  cards, 354
Playground behavior, 446–452
Portrait of a Disadvantaged Child, film, 61
Positive reinforcement, 424–425
  see Reinforcement
Posture Pencil Grips, 325, ref. 333
Practical space, 102
Predictive Index, test, 10, 65–75, 278, 378
  adapting index, 66–75
  study, 65
  see deHirsch
Preventing Failure in the Primary Grades, book, 338
Preventing failure program, 337, 338, 339

Primary emotional problems, 57
Pritchard, S., 454
Programmed math instruction, 337
  see Distar Math
Program structure, math, 340
Public School Programs For Learning Disabilities, film, 61
Punishment, 425–430
Pupil profile, 86–87
Purdue Perceptual-Rating Survey, test, 164
Puzzling Children, film, 61
Pyridoxine, 110, 116

R

Races, games, 258, 341
Racetracks, chalkboard routines, 314
Radler, D. H., 7, 10, 93, 168, 315, 316, ref. 15, 95, 197, 333
Rainbow tracing, 320
Random motor movements, 99, 103
Rasmussen, D., ref. 333
Reading, 273–310
  Engelmann-Bruner techniques, 290–291, 293–295
  errors, 274–275
  instruction, 299
  language approaches, 288
  leisure, 300, 333
  organic method, 287
  programs, 281
  Slingerland techniques, 289
  teachers, 283
  tests, 67, 69, 84, 304
  texts, 280–281, 297
  total school program, 292
  workbooks, 331
  visual memory training, 306–310
Reality Therapy, 418–420, ref. 462
Rebellion
  with aggression, 55
  with withdrawal, 56
Reception
  of language, 372
  problems, 368
Rees, E. L., 110, 111, 117, ref. 131
Reinforcement Theory for Teachers, 452

Reinforcement
　based on motivational levels, 435–438
　negative, 430
　schedules of, 430–435
　short goals as, 438
　social, 442
　therapy, 423–438
Relaxation, teaching, 122, 123
Remedial reading, 298
Report cards, 94
　see Parent conferences
Reticular system, 105, 106, 115, 370
Revised Illinois Test of Psycholinguistic
　Abilities, film, 413
Rhythm, 16, 147–148, 258, 261–262
Rimland, B., 110, 116, 370, 371, ref. 131,
　413
Roach, E. G., 95
Roberts, C., 190, ref. 197
Rosenthal, R., 283, 441, ref. 333, 463

S

Santa Monica Project, film, 464
Scat Scoota, 240
Schaefer, H. H., 426, 428, ref. 463
Schlein, M., 190, ref. 197
Schopler, E., 422, ref. 463
School Readiness Survey, 65
Schools Without Failure, ref. 452
Scoop throw and catch, 226
Scooter board, 243
Scott, L. B., 289, ref. 333
Seatwork
　math packets, 350–353
　reading workbooks, 331
　templates, 186-189
　writing stories, 329–331
　see Writing
Secondary emotional problems, 57
Senesh, L., 454, ref. 463
Sense integration, 100
　see Perceptual motor match
Sensorimotor, 18
　development, 99–107, 173–175
　tests, 79
Sensoritonic Readiness Program, film,
　198

Sensory perception, 41, 99
　see Auditory; visual; tactile and kin-
　esthetic
Sequencing
　behavior sequences, 406
　items, 406
　language, 401–412
　math sequences, 366
　number sequences, 405
　story and song sequences, 405–410
　teaching before and after, 402–404
　teaching days of week, 401
　teaching months of year, 404
　teaching seasons, 404
　temporal sequence, 402–405
　test, 82
　visual sequential memory, 410
　see Auditory and visual sequencial
　memory
Showers, P., 139, ref. 158
Sighting eye, 165
Singing games or dances, 258
Skinner, B. F., 418, 450, ref. 463
Slausen test, 34
Slingerland, B., 280, ref. 333
　large-lined paper, 327
　techniques in reading, 289-290
　tracing letters, 320–323
Slow learner, 5, 37–39
Social-emotional behavior, 26
　see Chapter 12
Social skills, lack of, 32
Sound discrimination, 391–393
　see Auditory discrimination
Spatial concepts, 41, 318, 320
　behind, 172
　horizontal, 160
　in writing, 317–320
　vertical, 159
Spatial relations, 20, 169, 194
　exercises, 192–197
　symptoms, 20
　test, 80
Speech articulation, 50
Spencer, E. M., ref. 95
Splinter skill, 16, 149, 236
Spraings, V., 57, ref. 60
　Multiple Choice Bender Gestalt, 34

S.R.A. Linguistic Series, 281, 292, 297, 332

Static balance, 162, 170, 177, 234

Stanford Achievement Test, Primary I Reading Tests, 290, 291, 304, ref. 333

Stanford-Binet Test, 33, 34, 63, ref. 95

Stegel, 251, ref. 158, 271

Stein, Jess, ref. 95

Stein, Joe, ref. 271

Stepping stones, 248

Stern, C., ref. 333

Stilts, 242

Story sequence, 405

Strauss, A. A., 46, 72, 98, ref. 60, 131

Structure in classroom, 118–121, 452–455

Suchman, J. R., 418, ref. 463

Sullivan, 190, ref. 197
    programmed readers, 281

Supersensitive, 47
    see Tactile defensiveness

Sutfin, F. E., ref. 95

Symbols, math, 340

Synapses, 106, 108

T

Taba, H., 418, ref. 463
    techniques, 302

Tactile
    apraxia, 134–135
    defensiveness, 133
    discrimination, 100
    sense, 132–136
    training, 136

Take-homes, math worksheets, 339

Tanner, J. M., 39, ref. 60

Teaching aids references
    A. Daigger & Co., 197
    A.C.L.D., 59
    Child Guidance Toys, 198
    Creative Playthings, 198
    Cuisenaire Co. of America, 198
    Developmental Learning Materials, 158, 198
    Eye Gate House, Inc., 198
    Hap Palmer Record Library, 271
    I.D.A. Perception Blocks, 198
    Lakeshore Equipment Co., 198

Lind Climber, 158, 271
    Teaching Resources, 198
    Warren's Educational Supplies, 198
    Winter Haven Lions Publication Committee, 96

Teaching Resources, ref. 198

Teacher, the positive, 283–285, 440–442

Teaching Disadvantaged Children in the Preschool, 386, ref. 412

Team teaching, 445–458

Techniques of Non-Verbal Psychological Testing, film, 413

Template training, 186–189

Temporal sequence, 25, 402

Tests, informal classroom
    classroom tests, 78–84, 339
    conceptual development tests, 82–84
    expressive language, 82
    fine and visual motor, 78
    gross motor, 78
    math concepts, 83
    ocular pursuit, 79
    reading, 84
    sensorimotor, 79–82
    visual sequence, 82

Tests, standardized
    A Psychoeducational Survey of Basic Learning Abilities, 64, 67, 95, 378
    A Visual Motor Gestalt and Its Clinical Use, 75, 95
    see Bender Visual-Motor
    Basic Concept Inventory Test, 95, 378
    Beery's Developmental Test of Visual-Motor Integration, 64, 95, 176, 275
    Cooperative Primary, 291, ref. 332
    Digit Span, 64, 95, 378
    Frostig Developmental Test of Visual Perception, 64, 95
    Gates Advanced Primary Test, 65
    Goodenough Draw-a-Man Test, 67, 76, 78, 79, 95, 141
    Gray Oral Reading, 65
    Horst Reversals, 66, 67
    I.T.P.A., 34, 64, 376, 377, 378, 382, 412
    Kuhlmann-Anderson Test, 7, 30, 35, 287, 288, 333
    Memory For Sentences, 95, 378

Metropolitan Achievement Tests in Reading, 273, 274, 287, 333
Peabody Picture Vocabulary Test, 64, 378, 413
Pencil Use, 65, 66, 67
Perceptual Forms Test, 75, 164, 176, 275, 288
Predictive Index Test, 10, 65–75, 278, 378
Purdue Perceptual-Rating Survey, 95, 164
School Readiness Survey, 65, 95
Slausen, 34
Spraing's Multiple Choice Bender Gestalt, 34
Stanford Achievement Test, Primary I Reading Tests, 290, 291, 304, 333
Stanford-Binet Test, 34, 63, 95
W.I.S.C., 34, 63, 95, 378
W.R.A.T., 34, 64, 95, 304
Wepman Auditory Discrimination Test, 34, 64, 65, 67, 275, 378
There Was A Little Ford, song, 409
There Was An Old Woman, song, 408
Thinking, Moving, Learning, film, 272
Thompson, A., 450, ref. 60, 463
Throwing, 224
  against a wall, 228
  bean bags, 224
  scoop throw and catch, 226
  throw and catch, 229
Thursday's Children, film, 61
Tomkins, C., 375, ref. 413
Tonic labrinthian reflex, 153
Transactional Analysis, 420–423, ref. 463
Tumbling activities, 220–222
Tunnel vision, 18, 173
Twister, 243

U

U. Film, 306–308, ref. 333
Under Spreading Chestnut Tree, song, 407
Up and Over—Exploring on the Stegel, film, 272

V

Valett, R., 46, 64, 378, ref. 60, 95
Vertical space, 159

Vestibular sense, 152, 162, 243
Verbal Expression, 398–401
Visual decoding, 25, 397–398
Visual discrimination, 100
  see Figure-ground & Visual perception
Visual form perception, 179
  training, 186–197
Visual memory, 25
  training, 306–310
Visual-motor, 66
  association, 397
  control, 311–317
  test, 79
Visual Perception and Failure to Learn, film, 198
Visual Perception Research, film, 198
Visual Perception Training in the Regular Classroom, film, 198
Visual perception, 48, 66
  tests, 80–81
  see Figure ground; laterality; directionality; perceptual constancy; perceptual motor match; visual-motor control; and visual form perception
Visual reception, 371, 397–398
Visual sequence test, 82
Visual Sequential Memory, 410–411
Visual-vocal association, 398
Vitamin therapy, 110, 116–117
Vocal encoding, 24, 373
  see Language, expression
Von Hilsheimer, G., 54, 117, 129, ref. 60, 131
Vygotsky, L. S., 375, ref. 413

W

Walking beam activities, 237–239
Walking on cans, 241
Warner, S. A., 287, ref. 333
Warren's Educational Supplies, 198
We Hold These Truths, film, 199
  see Doman-Delacato
Wechsler, D., 63, ref. 95
  W.I.S.C., test, 34, 63, 378
Weidenbacker, R., 134, ref. 158
Wellman, B. L., 160, ref. 197
Wepman, J. M., 34, ref. 96, 413
  Auditory Discrimination Test, 34, 64, 65, 67, 275, 378

Why Billy Couldn't Learn, film, 61
Williams, R., 117
Winter Haven Lions Publication Committee, 96
Winter Haven Perceptual Forms Test, 67, 70, 71, 75, 76, 78, 164, 176, 275, 288
Wolff, J., 190, ref. 197
Wide-Range Achievement Test, W.R.A.T., 34, 64, 95, 304
Word Recognition I and II, test, 66
Word Reproduction, test, 66
Words in a Story, test, 65, 66, 67
Words in Color, 280
Word Problems, 347

World Outside, film, 370, ref. 413
World We Perceive, film, 199
Writing, 317–331
  box writing, 325
  large-lined paper, 327
  name writing, 323
  numerals, 358, 359
  pencil techniques, 324
  rainbow tracing, 320
  spatial concepts in, 318
  stories, 329

Z

Zedler, E. Y., 378, ref. 413